Global Applications of Pervasive and Ubiquitous Computing

Tao Gao
Electronic Information Products Supervision and Inspection Institute of Hebei Province & Industry and Information Technology Department of Hebei Province, China

Information Science REFERENCE

Managing Director:	Lindsay Johnston
Editorial Director:	Joel Gamon
Book Production Manager:	Jennifer Yoder
Publishing Systems Analyst:	Adrienne Freeland
Assistant Acquisitions Editor:	Kayla Wolfe
Typesetter:	Nicole Sparano
Cover Design:	Nick Newcomer

Published in the United States of America by
Information Science Reference (an imprint of IGI Global)
701 E. Chocolate Avenue
Hershey PA 17033
Tel: 717-533-8845
Fax: 717-533-8661
E-mail: cust@igi-global.com
Web site: http://www.igi-global.com

Library of Congress Cataloging-in-Publication Data

Global applications of pervasive and ubiquitous computing / Tao Gao, editor.
       pages cm
   Summary: "This book provides the global perspective and efforts in building and applying pervasive and ubiquitous computer technology"-- Provided by publisher.
   Includes bibliographical references and index.
   ISBN 978-1-4666-2645-4 (hardcover) -- ISBN 978-1-4666-2676-8 (ebook) -- ISBN 978-1-4666-2707-9 (print & perpetual access) 1. Ubiquitous computing. I. Gao, Tao, 1981- editor of compilation.
   QA76.5915.G56 2013
   004--dc23
                              2012029133

British Cataloguing in Publication Data
A Cataloguing in Publication record for this book is available from the British Library.

The views expressed in this book are those of the authors, but not necessarily of the publisher.

.

Associate Editors

List of Reviewers

Table of Contents

  Kashif Nisar, CAS—Universiti Utara Malaysia, Malaysia
  Angela Amphawan, University of Oxford, UK, and Universiti Utara Malaysia, Malaysia
  Suhaidi B. Hassan, Universiti Utara Malaysia, Malaysia

Detailed Table of Contents

Chapter 1

Feng Guo, Jiangsu Automation Research Institution, China

Zhenxing Yin, Jiangsu Automation Research Institution, China

Liang Wu, Jiangsu Automation Research Institution, China

Hao Shen, Jiangsu Automation Research Institution, China

Due to the development of embed computer, improvement the bandwidth of computer is required, in order to break the choke point of the bus' development. The text brings a hardware design method of computer based on CompactPCI Express bus, introduces the architecture of system and principle, goes into descriptions abouth the design of Swithboard, bridgeboard and rapid serial single PCB etc. The use of CompactPCI Express bus improves the bandwidth of computer system, reduces power, improves the performance of system, adapt the requirement of development.

Chapter 2

Yulong Tian, China University of Geosciences Great Wall College, China

*Tao Gao, Electronic Information Products Supervision and Inspection Institute of Hebei Province
    & Industry and Information Technology Department of Hebei Province, China*

Weifang Zhai, China University of Geosciences Great Wall College, China

Yaying Hu, Hebei University Computer Center, China

Xinfeng Li, China University of Geosciences Great Wall College, China

In this paper, a genetic algorithm with sexual reproduction and niche selection technology is proposed. Simple genetic algorithm has been successfully applied to many evolutionary optimization problems. But there is a problem of premature convergence for complex multimodal functions. To solve it, the frame and realization of niche genetic algorithm based on sexual reproduction are presented. Age and sexual structures are given to the individuals referring the sexual reproduction and "niche" phenomena, importing the niche selection technology. During age and sexual operators, different evolutionary parameters are given to the individuals with different age and sexual structures. As a result, this genetic algorithm can combat premature convergence and keep the diversity of population. The testing for Rastrigin function and Shubert function proves that the niche genetic algorithm based on sexual reproduction is effective.

Chapter 3

Guo Li, Beijing Institute of Technology, China
Xiang Zhang, Beijing Institute of Technology, China
Zhaohua Wang, Beijing Institute of Technology, China
Tao Gao, Hebei Electronic Information Products Supervision and Inspection Institute
& Industry and Information Technology Department of Hebei Province, China

In JIT assembly system, any supplier's postponement of delivery or incorrect delivery quantity will result in the manufacturer's incapability of assembling on schedule, which will not only damage the interests of other suppliers but also jeopardize the interests of enterprises and reduce the competitiveness of the supply chain. In this article, coordination of the upstream supply logistics from internal and external aspects is taken as the research object. In external supply system, three aspects of cost, quality and time are used to evaluate the coordination of supply logistics in JIT environment. From the internal aspect, reliability, flexibility, responsiveness, customer service and system suitability are selected for the performance evaluation. The eight indexes construct an index system and each performance index is described and analyzed. Finally, Analytic Hierarchy Process is used to evaluate the coordinated performance of supply logistics in JIT environment. An example is provided, which illustrate the method used in this paper is feasible and meaningful.

Chapter 4

Junjun Xu, Beijing University of Posts and Telecommunications, China
Haiyong Luo, Institute of Computing Technology Chinese Academy of Sciences, China
Fang Zhao, Beijing University of Posts and Telecommunications, China
Rui Tao, Beijing University of Posts and Telecommunications, China
Yiming Lin, Institute of Computing Technology Chinese Academy of Sciences, China
Hui Li, Institute of Computing Technology Chinese Academy of Sciences, China

As positioning technology is an important foundation of the Internet of Things, a dynamic indoor WLAN localization system is proposed in this paper. This paper mainly concentrates on the design and implementation of the WiMap-a dynamic indoor WLAN localization system, which employs grid-based localization method using RSS (received signal strength). To achieve high localization accuracy and low computational complexity, Gaussian mixture model is applied to approximate the signal distribution and a ROI (region of interest) is defined to limit the search region. The authors also discuss other techniques like AP selection and threshold control, which affects the localization accuracy. The experimental results indicate that an accuracy of 3m with 73.8% probability can be obtained in WiMap. Moreover, the running time is reduced greatly with limited ROI method.

Boning Zhang, Institute of Computing Technology, Chinese Academy of Sciences and Graduate
    University of Chinese Academy of Sciences, China

Xiangdong Wang, Institute of Computing Technology, Chinese Academy of Sciences, China

Yueliang Qian, Institute of Computing Technology, Chinese Academy of Sciences, China

Shouxun Lin, Institute of Computing Technology, Chinese Academy of Sciences, China

This paper presents a novel design using a mouse sensor to construct a system for motion detection in normal vision environment. A mouse sensor is packed under an optical mouse for detecting the motion of mouse on desktop and sending out the data and parameters to a controller or a computer directly. This paper introduces this kind of sensor to vision motion detection field by designing and building a circuit system. The feasibility of the design is demonstrated and degree of reliability is measured by experiments performed on the designed system. Additionally the authors point out the advantages of this design in comparison with other traditional methods or devices in brief.

Fang Yuan, Shenzhen Institute of Information Technology, China

Mingliang Li, Shenzhen Institute of Information Technology, China

Jing Li, Huawei Technologies Corporation, China

The identification of disease genes from candidated regions is one of the most important tasks in bioinformatics research. Most approaches based on function annotations cannot be used to identify genes for diseases without any known pathogenic genes or related function annotations. The authors have built a new web tool, DGHunter, to predict genes associated with these diseases which lack detailed function annotations. Its performance was tested with a set of 1506 genes involved in 1147 disease phenotypes derived from the morbid map table in the OMIM database. The results show that, on average, the target gene was in the top 13.60% of the ranked lists of candidates, and the target gene was in the top 5% with a 40.70% chance. DGHunter can identify disease genes effectively for those diseases lacking sufficient function annotations.

Qihua Chen, Institute of Computing Technology, Chinese Academy of Sciences, China

Xiangdong Wang, Institute of Computing Technology, Chinese Academy of Sciences, China

Yueliang Qian, Institute of Computing Technology, Chinese Academy of Sciences, China

For cell phone users and blind people using non-visual browsers, browsing Web by common browsers is quite inefficient due to the problem of information overload. This paper presents the TB-WPRO (Title-Block based Web Page Re-Organization) method, which hierarchically segments web pages into blocks using visual and layout information reflecting the web designers' intent. TB-WPRO segments the web pages with a clear goal to extract self-described title blocks. To reorganize web pages, the segmentation result is transformed to a serial of small web pages that could be easily accessed. Compared to current methods, the proposed approach obtains a promising segmentation result where blocks are visually and semantically consistent with original web pages.

In the JIT assembly system, if any supplier does not deliver the raw materials or components on time, or in the right quantity, the core manufacturers will not assemble on the schedule, which will bring great loss to the whole supply chain and greatly reduce the competitiveness and collaboration of the entire supply chain. Based on a survey on supply chain collaboration and operation model, supply logistics in JIT environment are analyzed from both the inside and outside system with the research goal of coordinating the upstream supply logistics. In order to help manufacturers implement the JIT production, the VMI-Hub operation mode is proposed from the aspect of inside system, and from outside system, cross-docking dispatch operation mode is considered to coordinate the supply logistics in assembly system.

Biological pharmaceutical industry not only has the continuous pulling action to region economy, also makes a positive contribution on the human productivity and quality of life. Biological pharmaceutical industry will become the leading industry of the century in quite a long time in the future. Taking Shijiazhuang as an example, according to the regional biopharmaceutical industry planning needs, building the industry competitiveness evaluation system, this paper analyzes the comparative advantage of Shijiazhuang in developing bio-pharmaceutical industry from 4 level evaluation index, including: the industry environment and policy, R & D capability, competitiveness of economic scale and industry support system. Provide a reference for local governments and business.

In the process of promoting the national intellectual property strategy, domestic enterprises should seize the opportunity to develop their own intellectual property system according to their actual situations. The communication industry as an example of statistical data and specific analysis of patent applications in emerging technology field in recent years are supplied in the article.

Chapter 11

The tomographic imaging of process parameters for oil-gas-water three-phase flow can be obtained through different sensing modalities, such as electrical resistance tomography (ERT) and electrical capacitance tomography (ECT), both of which are sensitive to specific properties of the objects to be imaged. However, it is hard to discriminate oil, gas and water phases merely from reconstructed images of ERT or ECT. In this paper, the feasibility of image fusion based on ERT and ECT reconstructed images was investigated for oil-gas-water three-phase flow. Two cases were discussed and pixel-based image fusion method was presented. Simulation results showed that the cross-sectional reconstruction images of oil-gas-water three-phase flow can be obtained using the presented methods.

Questionnaire on teachers periodically based on traditional and passive equipment management mode is put forward in order for better equipment maintenance, for the teaching demand and for maximize utilize of educational media. Questionnaire content is composed of educational media technique training, equipment faults, utilize and demand of electrified education resource and job evaluation. Practice has shown that questionnaire that was favorably reviewed in school has made manager have an insight into the operation of equipment and teaching demand, improved educational service level.

The smart grid is an important application field of the Internet of things. This paper presents a method of user electricity consumption pattern analysis for smart grid applications based on the audio feature EEUPC. A novel similarity function based on EEUPC is adapted to support clustering analysis of residential load patterns. The EEUPC similarity exploits features of peaks and valleys on curves instead of directly comparing values and obtains better performance for clustering analysis. Moreover, the proposed approach performs load pattern clustering, extracts a typical pattern for each cluster, and gives suggestions toward better power consumption for each typical pattern. Experimental results demonstrate that the EEUPC similarity is more consistent with human judgment than the Euclidean distance and higher clustering performance can be achieved for residential electric load data.

Chapter 14

This paper investigates briefly the integrated portable reinforcement machine structure design and introduces its design and train of thought. The authors also discuss design methods in engineering applications, as well as how to achieve good heat dissipation effect and enhance the electromagnetic compatibility. The whole machine, with its small volume, good adaptability to environment, and electromagnetic compatibility, can be used as a reference for similar engineering design.

Yao Wan-Ye, North China Electric Power University, China

Yin Shi, North China Electric Power University, China

In the wind farms, fans are widely distribution with large amount and they arc away from the monitoring center, working environment is poor. In order to ensure the safe and stable operation of the wind farms, the wind power operation requirements need to be satisfied, own better function performance and stability of remote monitoring system to improve the management efficiency. In view of this, the power group increasing highly requirements on wind farm group management,but at present, the single SCADA system which the fan manufacturers offered has failed to meet the requirements. On the basis, this article designs the wind farm supervisory information system (SIS), and realizes wind farm cluster control, data analysis, performance optimization and fault warning.

Chunyan Wang, State Intellectual Property Office, China

As one of the techniques beyond 3G, because of the effective performance of high spectrum utilization and anti-fading for frequency selecting and adopted multi-carrier modulation technique that meets the requirement of the explosive traffic capacity, Orthogonal Frequency Division Multiplexing (OFDM) has carried great weight in wireless communications. This paper expounds OFDM technical characteristics and performs computer simulation on the OFDM system based on Inverse Fast Fourier Transform (IFFT) by means MATLAB. During the course of simulation, comparison between OFDM and traditional single-carrier technology is performed. The simulation results have great significance for research and applications in the field.

Yan Jiang, State Intellectual Property Office, China

Mobile communication plays an important role in the future of communication systems. To meet personalized and intelligent requirements, mobile communication has evolved from single wireless cellular network to heterogeneous mobile communication network, including wireless cellular network, wireless local network, and wireless personal network. In the heterogeneous communication system, to entirely fulfill the spectrum resource complementary advantages of such a heterogeneous wireless network, the spectrum resource trade algorithm has attracted tremendous research efforts. In this paper, the advantages and disadvantages of dynamic spectrum allocation and load balancing are discussed and spectrum auction takes the place of spectrum allocation to maximize the operation revenue. The authors design a joint spectrum auction and load balancing algorithm (SALB) based on heterogeneous network environment to develop a more flexible and efficient spectrum management. The simulation result shows that SALB increases the operation profit significantly.

Chapter 18

Ping Jiang, University of Jinan, China

Tao Gao, Electronic Information Products Supervision and Inspection Institute of Hebei Province, China

In this paper, an improved paper defects detection method based on visual attention mechanism computation model is presented. First, multi-scale feature maps are extracted by linear filtering. Second, the comparative maps are obtained by carrying out center-surround difference operator. Third, the saliency map is obtained by combining conspicuity maps, which is gained by combining the multi-scale comparative maps. Last, the seed point of watershed segmentation is determined by competition among salient points in the saliency map and the defect regions are segmented from the background. Experimental results show the efficiency of the approach for paper defects detection.

Chapter 19

Liu Chong, Heibei Finance University, China

Wang Mei, Heibei University, China

An Wen Guang, Heibei Finance University, China

To update school websites, incorporating personality and ease of maintenance and management, the authors propose the use of a Content Management System (CMS). A CMS is a self-publishing Website platform for university information resources. The system has many features, such as self-service, fast station, self-service custom modules, dynamic replacement site style template, flexible adjustment of dynamic website contents and structures, search engine optimization (SEO) measures, and so forth. Each institution can customize according to their own information platform needs. A CMS greatly shortens the development cycle of the site and promotes the development of information tec hnology on campus.

Chapter 20

Shuying Wang, Southwest Jiaotong University, China

Jizi Li, Wuhan Textile University, China

Shihua Ma, Huazhong University of Science & Technology, China

In this paper, by analyzing the characteristics of data exchange process of SaaS-based collaboration supporting platform for industrial chain, a dynamic and secure business data exchange model for the platform is established. On this basis, methods for business data automatic obtain and format conversion, client authentication based on encryption lock and SOAP extension, business data encryption based on public key of the platform, and instant key created by client is discussed. The implementation of these methods is studied based on a .NET environment. Furthermore, the dynamic and secure business data exchange model is used in the SaaS platform of the automotive industry chain and SaaS platform of the injection industry chain, as it meets the multi-source and heterogeneous information exchange requirements.

Stereo video object segmentation is a critical technology of the new generation of video coding, video retrieval and other emerging interactive multimedia fields. Determinations of distinctive depth of a frame features have become more popular in everyday life for automation industries like machine vision and computer vision technologies. This paper examines the evaluation of depth cues through dense of two frame stereo correspondence method. Experimental results show that the method can segment the stationary and moving objects with better accuracy and robustness. The contributions have higher accuracy in matching and reducing time of convergence.

This paper proposes new approaches for designing a bipolar DS acquisition system to reduce the harm of external factors on equipment, as well as fulfill system requirements at the veracity and reliability of the equipment to quickly connect. The design method chosen is ACPL-224 for chip of the interface about data acquisition on the FPGA device, including system principle, interface circuit logic, the method of data processing, and so forth. Now that this method has been applied, it has achieved good results, including extending the system's adaptive range of external signal and enhancing the efficiency of the interface to quickly connect.

The operating status of an enterprise is disclosed periodically in a financial statement. Financial distress prediction is important for business bankruptcy prevention, and various quantitative prediction methods based on financial ratios have been proposed. This paper presents a financial distress prediction model based on wavelet neural networks (WNNs). The transfer functions of the neurons in WNNs are wavelet base functions which are determined by dilation and translation factors. Back propagation algorithm was used to train the WNNs. Principal component analysis (PCA) method was used to reduce the dimension of the inputs of the WNNs. Multiple discriminate analysis (MDA), Logit, Probit, and WNNs were employed to a dataset selected from Chinese-listed companies. The results demonstrate that the proposed WNNs-based model performs well in comparison with the other three models.

Background images are identified by analyzing the changes in texture of the image sequences. According to the characteristics of highway traffic scenes, in this paper, the author presents a new algorithm for identifying background image based on the gradient projection statistics of the binary image. First, the images are blocked by road lane, and the background is identified by projection statistics and projection gradient statistics of the sub-images. Second, the background is reconstructed according to the results of each sub-image. Experimental results show that the proposed method exhibits high accuracy for background identification and modeling. In addition, the proposed method has a good anti-interference to the low intensity vehicles, and the processing time is less as well. The speed and accuracy of the proposed algorithm meets the needs of video surveillance system requirements for highway traffic scenes.

Chapter 25

Zhengrong Tao, Jiangsu Automation Research Institute, China
Zhenxing Yin, Jiangsu Automation Research Institute, China

In this paper, the authors present a method of measuring the switching time of a dual redundant NIC. The accuracy of the authors' method of measuring switching time can reach milliseconds. The authors' method uses Internet Control Message Protocol (ICMP) packets to test, is easy to operate, has high precision, and can be applied to all types of dual redundant device switching time measurement.

Chapter 26

Chunling Liu, Wuhan Textile University, China
Jizi Li, Wuhan Textile University, China
Guo Li, Beijing Institute of Technology, China
Xiaogang Cao, Wuhan Textile University, China

The huge market and perfect production system in China are attracting more multi-national companies' interest to invest in China in the form of Foreign Direct Investment (FDI). Therefore, multi-national companies are willing to integrate and optimize global supply chain networks of their own, which enable them to reduce cost and improve market response. As a result, multi-national companies usually embed into local industrial clusters through financial and technological comparative merits to sharpen their competitive edge. This paper considers the across-chain network equilibrium problem involving process of competition and melting between this new global chain and an already existing local chain. The authors model the optimizing behavior of these two chains, derive the equilibrium conditions, and establish the variational inequality formulation, and solve it by using the modified algorithm. Finally, the authors illustrate the model through numerical example and discuss relationships among the price, quantity, technological progress, and satisfaction among two dynamic phases.

Chapter 27

Kashif Nisar, CAS—Universiti Utara Malaysia, Malaysia
Angela Amphawan, University of Oxford, UK, and Universiti Utara Malaysia, Malaysia
Suhaidi B. Hassan, Universiti Utara Malaysia, Malaysia

Voice over Internet Protocol (VoIP) has grown quickly in the world of telecommunication. Wireless Local Area Networks (WLANs) are the most performance assuring technology for wireless networks, and WLANs have facilitated high-rate voice services at low cost and good flexibility. In a voice conversation, each client works as a sender or a receiver depending on the direction of traffic flow over the network. A VoIP application requires high throughput, low packet loss, and a high fairness index over the network. The packets of VoIP streaming may experience drops because of the competition among the different kinds of traffic flow over the network. A VoIP application is also sensitive to delay and requires the voice packets to arrive on time from the sender to the receiver side without any delay over WLAN. The scheduling system model for VoIP traffic is an unresolved problem. The objectives of this paper are to identify scheduler issues. This comprehensive structure of Novel Voice Priority Queue (VPQ) scheduling system model for VoIP over WLAN discusses the essential background of the VPQ schedulers and algorithms. This paper also identifies the importance of the scheduling techniques over WLANs.

Preface

Modern communication is entering an exciting and challenging new era in which ubiquitous computing concepts, the "Internet of things," wireless communications, and real-time information processing are integrated into the everyday lives of the average consumer. This book is a comprehensive representation of the third volume of the *International Journal of Advanced Pervasive and Ubiquitous Computing* (IJAPUC). The following chapters will provide a foundation for discussion on various ubiquitous computing and communication concepts, including intelligent systems, smart devices, Internet security, manufacturing, and more.

The book begins with "Design and Implementation of the Embed Computer Based on CompactPCI Express Bus" by Feng Guo *et al.* Due to the development of embed computer, improvement of the bandwidth of computer is required, in order to break the choke point of the bus' development. This chapter brings a hardware design method of computer based on CompactPCI Express bus, introduces the architecture of system and principle, goes into descriptions about the design of Swithboard, bridgeboard, and rapid serial single PCB, et cetera. The use of CompactPCI Express bus improves the bandwidth of computer system, reduces power, improves the performance of system, and adapts the requirement of development.

In the next chapter, "Niche Genetic Algorithm Based on Sexual Reproduction and Multimodal Function Optimization Problem" by Yulong Tian *et al.*, a genetic algorithm with sexual reproduction and niche selection technology is proposed. Simple genetic algorithm has been successfully applied to many evolutionary optimization problems. However, there is a problem of premature convergence for complex multimodal functions. To solve it, the frame and realization of niche genetic algorithm based on sexual reproduction are presented. Age and sexual structures are given to the individuals referring the sexual reproduction and "niche" phenomena, importing the niche selection technology. During age and sexual operators, different evolutionary parameters are given to the individuals with different age and sexual structures. As a result, this genetic algorithm can combat premature convergence and keep the diversity of population. The testing for Rastrigin function and Shubert function proves that the niche genetic algorithm based on sexual reproduction is effective.

Chapter 3

In JIT assembly system, any supplier's postponement of delivery or incorrect delivery quantity will result in the manufacturer's incapability of assembling on schedule, which will not only damage the interests of other suppliers but also jeopardize the interests of enterprises and reduce the competitiveness of the supply chain. In "Coordination Performance Evaluation of Supply Logistics in JIT Environment" by Guo Li *et al.*, coordination of the upstream supply logistics from internal and external aspects is taken as the research object. In external supply system, three aspects of cost, quality, and time are used to evaluate the coordination of supply logistics in JIT environment. From the internal aspect, reliability, flexibility, responsiveness, customer service, and system suitability are selected for the performance evaluation. The eight indexes construct an index system and each performance index is described and analyzed. Finally, Analytic Hierarchy Process is used to evaluate the coordinated performance of supply logistics in JIT environment. An example is provided, which illustrate the method used in this chapter is feasible and meaningful.

As positioning technology is an important foundation of the Internet of Things, a dynamic indoor WLAN localization system is proposed in chapter 4, "The WiMap: A Dynamic Indoor WLAN Localization System" by Junjun Xu *et al.* This chapter mainly concentrates on the design and implementation of the WiMap-a dynamic indoor WLAN localization system, which employs grid-based localization method using RSS (received signal strength). To achieve high localization accuracy and low computational complexity, Gaussian mixture model is applied to approximate the signal distribution and a ROI (region of interest) is defined to limit the search region. The authors also discuss other techniques like AP selection and threshold control, which affects the localization accuracy. The experimental results indicate that an accuracy of 3m with 73.8% probability can be obtained in WiMap. Moreover, the running time is reduced greatly with limited ROI method.

The following chapter, "A Novel Design of Motion Detector Using Mouse Sensor" by Boning Zhang, presents a novel design using a mouse sensor to construct a system for motion detection in normal vision environment. A mouse sensor is packed under an optical mouse for detecting the motion of mouse on desktop and sending out the data and parameters to a controller or a computer directly. This chapter introduces this kind of sensor to vision motion detection field by designing and building a circuit system. The feasibility of the design is demonstrated and degree of reliability is measured by experiments performed on the designed system. Additionally, the authors point out the advantages of this design in comparison with other traditional methods or devices in brief.

In "Identifying Disease Genes Based on Functional Annotation and Text Mining," Fang Yuan *et al.* define the identification of disease genes from candidated regions as one of the most important tasks in bioinformatics research. Most approaches based on function annotations cannot be used to identify genes for diseases without any known pathogenic genes or related function annotations. The authors have built a new web tool, DGHunter, to predict genes associated with these diseases which lack detailed function annotations. Its performance was tested with a set of 1506 genes involved in 1147 disease phenotypes derived from the morbid map table in the OMIM database. The results show that, on average, the target gene was in the top 13.60% of the ranked lists of candidates, and the target gene was in the top 5% with a 40.70% chance. DGHunter can identify disease genes effectively for those diseases lacking sufficient function annotations.

Chapter 7

For cell phone users and blind people using non-visual browsers, browsing Web by common browsers is quite inefficient due to the problem of information overload. Qihua Chen *et al.*, in "TB-WPRO: Title-Block Based Web Page Reorganization," present the TB-WPRO (Title-Block based Web Page Re-Organization) method, which hierarchically segments web pages into blocks using visual and layout information reflecting the web designers' intent. TB-WPRO segments the web pages with a clear goal to extract self-described title blocks. To reorganize web pages, the segmentation result is transformed to a serial of small web pages that could be easily accessed. Compared to current methods, the proposed approach obtains a promising segmentation result where blocks are visually and semantically consistent with original web pages.

"Constructing the Collaborative Supply Logistics Operation Mode in Assembly System under JIT Environment" by Guo Li *et al.* explores how, in the JIT assembly system, if any supplier does not deliver the raw materials or components on time, or in the right quantity, the core manufacturers will not assemble on the schedule, which will bring great loss to the whole supply chain and greatly reduce the competitiveness and collaboration of the entire supply chain. Based on a survey on supply chain collaboration and operation model, supply logistics in JIT environment are analyzed from both the inside and outside system with the research goal of coordinating the upstream supply logistics. In order to help manufacturers implement the JIT production, the VMI-Hub operation mode is proposed from the aspect of inside system, and from outside system, cross-docking dispatch operation mode is considered to coordinate the supply logistics in assembly system.

The following chapter, "Construction Competitiveness Evaluation System of Regional BioPharma Industry and Case Study: Taking Shijiazhuang as an Example" by Bing Zhao *et al.*, investigates the biological pharmaceutical industry, which not only has the continuous pulling action to region economy, but also makes a positive contribution on the human productivity and quality of life. Biological pharmaceutical industry will become the leading industry of the century in quite a long time in the future. Taking Shijiazhuang as an example, according to the regional biopharmaceutical industry planning needs, building the industry competitiveness evaluation system, this chapter analyzes the comparative advantage of Shijiazhuang in developing bio-pharmaceutical industry from 4 level evaluation index, including: the industry environment and policy, R & D capability, competitiveness of economic scale, and industry support system. It provides a reference for local governments and business.

In the process of promoting the national intellectual property strategy, domestic enterprises should seize the opportunity to develop their own intellectual property system according to their actual situations. The communication industry as an example of statistical data and specific analysis of patent applications in emerging technology field in recent years are supplied in Chapter 10: "Development of Intellectual Property of Communications Enterprise and Analysis of Current Situation of Patents in Emerging Technology Field" by Wenjia Ding.

Lifeng Zhang, in "Image Fusion of ECT/ERT for Oil-Gas-Water Three-Phase Flow" explains how the tomographic imaging of process parameters for oil-gas-water three-phase flow can be obtained through different sensing modalities, such as electrical resistance tomography (ERT) and electrical capacitance tomography (ECT), both of which are sensitive to specific properties of the objects to be imaged. However, it is hard to discriminate oil, gas, and water phases merely from reconstructed images of ERT or ECT. In this chapter, the feasibility of image fusion based on ERT and ECT reconstructed images was investigated for oil-gas- water three-phase flow. Two cases were discussed, and pixel-based image fusion method was presented. Simulation results showed that the cross-sectional reconstruction images of oil-gas-water three-phase flow can be obtained using the presented methods.

Next, Hou Jie explores "Modern Educational Technique Center Educational Media Management Based on Design and Practice of Questionnaire." A questionnaire on teachers periodically based on traditional and passive equipment management mode is put forward in order for better equipment maintenance, for the teaching demand, and for maximized utility of educational media. Questionnaire content is composed of educational media technique training, equipment faults, utility, and demand of electrified education resource and job evaluation. Practice has shown that questionnaire that was favorably reviewed in school has made manager have an insight into the operation of equipment and teaching demand, improved educational service level.

The smart grid is an important application field of the Internet of things. "Residential Load Pattern Analysis for Smart Grid Applications Based on Audio Feature EEUPC," by Yunzhi Wang *et al.*, presents a method of user electricity consumption pattern analysis for smart grid applications based on the audio feature EEUPC. A novel similarity function based on EEUPC is adapted to support clustering analysis of residential load patterns. The EEUPC similarity exploits features of peaks and valleys on curves instead of directly comparing values and obtains better performance for clustering analysis. Moreover, the proposed approach performs load pattern clustering, extracts a typical pattern for each cluster, and gives suggestions toward better power consumption for each typical pattern. Experimental results demonstrate that the EEUPC similarity is more consistent with human judgment than the Euclidean distance and higher clustering performance can be achieved for residential electric load data.

Chapter 14, "The Design of Portable Integration Strengthening Machine" by Li Yuan et al., investigates briefly the integrated portable reinforcement machine structure design and introduces its design and train of thought. The authors also discuss design methods in engineering applications, as well as how to achieve good heat dissipation effect and enhance the electromagnetic compatibility. The whole machine, with its small volume, good adaptability to environment, and electromagnetic compatibility, can be used as a reference for similar engineering design.

The next chapter, "The Information Construction of Wind Farm Based on SIS System" by Yao Wan-Ye and Yin Shi, focuses on wind farms, where fans are widely distribution with large amount and they are away from the monitoring center, working environment is poor. In order to ensure the safe and stable operation of the wind farms, the wind power operation requirements need to be satisfied, own better function performance and stability of remote monitoring system to improve the management efficiency. In view of this, the power group is highly increasing requirements on wind farm group management, but at present, the single SCADA system which the fan manufacturers offered has failed to meet the requirements. On the basis, this chapter designs the wind farm supervisory information system (SIS), and realizes wind farm cluster control, data analysis, performance optimization, and fault warning.

As one of the techniques beyond 3G, because of the effective performance of high spectrum utilization and antifading for frequency selecting and adopted multi-carrier modulation technique that meets the requirement of the explosive traffic capacity, Orthogonal Frequency Division Multiplexing (OFDM) has carried great weight in wireless communications. In chapter 16, "Beyond 3G Techniques of Orthogonal Frequency Division Multiplexing and Performance Analysis via Simulation," Chunyan Wang expounds OFDM technical characteristics and performs computer simulation on the OFDM system based on Inverse Fast Fourier Transform (IFFT) by means MATLAB. During the course of simulation, comparison between OFDM and traditional single-carrier technology is performed. The simulation results have great significance for research and applications in the field.

Yan Jiang writes in "Dynamic Spectrum Auction and Load Balancing Algorithm in Heterogeneous Network" how mobile communication plays an important role in the future of communication systems. To meet personalized and intelligent requirements, mobile communication has evolved from single wireless cellular network to heterogeneous mobile communication network, including wireless cellular network, wireless local network, and wireless personal network. In the heterogeneous communication system, to entirely fulfill the spectrum resource complementary advantages of such a heterogeneous wireless network, the spectrum resource trade algorithm has attracted tremendous research efforts. In this chapter, the advantages and disadvantages of dynamic spectrum allocation and load balancing are discussed, and spectrum auction takes the place of spectrum allocation to maximize the operation revenue. The authors design a joint spectrum auction and load balancing algorithm (SALB) based on heterogeneous network environment to develop a more flexible and efficient spectrum management. The simulation result shows that SALB increases the operation profit significantly.

In "A Novel Detection Method of Paper Defects Based on Visual Attention Mechanism" by Ping Jiang and Tao Gao, an improved paper defects detection method based on visual attention mechanism computation model is presented. First, multi-scale feature maps are extracted by linear filtering. Second, the comparative maps are obtained by carrying out center-surround difference operator. Third, the saliency map is obtained by combining conspicuity maps, which is gained by combining the multi-scale comparative maps. Last, the seed point of watershed segmentation is determined by competition among salient points in the saliency map and the defect regions are segmented from the background. Experimental results show the efficiency of the approach for paper defects detection.

To update school websites, incorporating personality and ease of maintenance and management, Liu Chong *et al.* propose the use of a Content Management System (CMS) in "Research and Implementation of Self-Publishing Website Platforms for Universities Based on CMS." A CMS is a self-publishing website platform for university information resources. The system has many features, such as self-service, fast station, self-service custom modules, dynamic replacement site style template, flexible adjustment of dynamic website contents and structures, search engine optimization (SEO) measures, and so forth. Each institution can customize according to its own information platform needs. A CMS greatly shortens the development cycle of the site and promotes the development of information technology on campus.

In "Dynamic and Secure Business Data Exchange Model for SaaS-Based Collaboration Supporting Platform of Industrial Chain" by Shuying Wang *et al.*, by analyzing the characteristics of data exchange process of SaaS-based collaboration supporting platform for industrial chain, a dynamic and secure business data exchange model for the platform is established. On this basis, methods for business data automatic obtain and format conversion, client authentication based on encryption lock and SOAP extension, business data encryption based on public key of the platform, and instant key created by client, are discussed. The implementation of these methods is studied based on a .NET environment. Furthermore, the dynamic and secure business data exchange model is used in the SaaS platform of the automotive industry chain and SaaS platform of the injection industry chain, as it meets the multi-source and heterogeneous information exchange requirements.

Tao Gao returns in "3-D Video Based Disparity Estimation and Object Segmentation" to investigate stereo video object segmentation, a critical technology of the new generation of video coding, video retrieval and other emerging interactive multimedia fields. Determinations of distinctive depth of a frame features have become more popular in everyday life for automation industries like machine vision and computer vision technologies. This chapter examines the evaluation of depth cues through dense of two frame stereo correspondence method. Experimental results show that the method can segment the stationary and moving objects with better accuracy and robustness. The contributions have higher accuracy in matching and reducing time of convergence.

Chapter 22, "Design and Implementation of Bipolar Digital Signal Acquisition and Processing System Based on FPGA and ACPL-224" by Guangfu Lin *et al.*, proposes new approaches for designing a bipolar DS acquisition system to reduce the harm of external factors on equipment, as well as to fulfill system requirements at the veracity and reliability of the equipment to quickly connect. The design method chosen is ACPL-224 for chip of the interface about data acquisition on the FPGA device, including system principle, interface circuit logic, the method of data processing, and so forth. Now that this method has been applied, it has achieved good results, including extending the system's adaptive range of external signal and enhancing the efficiency of the interface to quickly connect.

The operating status of an enterprise is disclosed periodically in a financial statement. Financial distress prediction is important for business bankruptcy prevention, and various quantitative prediction methods based on financial ratios have been proposed. "Financial Distress Prediction of Chinese-Listed Companies Based on PCA and WNNs" by Xiu Xin and Xiaoyi Xiong presents a financial distress prediction model based on wavelet neural networks (WNNs). The transfer functions of the neurons in WNNs are wavelet base functions which are determined by dilation and translation factors. Back propagation algorithm was used to train the WNNs. Principal Component Analysis (PCA) method was used to reduce the dimension of the inputs of the WNNs. Multiple Discriminate Analysis (MDA), Logit, Probit, and WNNs were employed to a dataset selected from Chinese-listed companies. The results demonstrate that the proposed WNNs-based model performs well in comparison with the other three models.

In "Highway Background Identification and Background Modeling Based on Projection Statistics" by Jun Zhang, background images are identified by analyzing the changes in texture of the image sequences. According to the characteristics of highway traffic scenes, in this chapter, the author presents a new algorithm for identifying background image based on the gradient projection statistics of the binary image. First, the images are blocked by road lane, and the background is identified by projection statistics and projection gradient statistics of the sub-images. Second, the background is reconstructed according to the results of each sub-image. Experimental results show that the proposed method exhibits high accuracy for background identification and modeling. In addition, the proposed method has a good anti-interference to the low intensity vehicles, and the processing time is less as well. The speed and accuracy of the proposed algorithm meets the needs of video surveillance system requirements for highway traffic scenes.

Next, in "Method of Measuring the Switching Time of Dual Redundant NIC," Zhengrong Tao and Zhenxing Yin present a method of measuring the switching time of a dual redundant NIC. The accuracy of the authors' method of measuring switching time can reach milliseconds. The authors' method uses Internet Control Message Protocol (ICMP) packets to test, is easy to operate, has high precision, and can be applied to all types of dual redundant device switching time measurement.

Chapter 26, "Modeling of Across-Chain Network Dynamic Competition for MNC in Industrial Cluster" by Chunling Liu *et al.*, describes how the huge market and perfect production system in China are attracting more multi-national companies' interest to invest in China in the form of Foreign Direct Investment (FDI). Therefore, multi-national companies are willing to integrate and optimize global supply chain networks of their own, which enables them to reduce cost and improve market response. As a result, multi-national companies usually embed into local industrial clusters through financial and technological comparative merits to sharpen their competitive edge. This chapter considers the across-chain network equilibrium problem involving process of competition and melting between this new global chain and an already existing local chain. The authors model the optimizing behavior of these two chains, derive the equilibrium conditions, and establish the variational inequality formulation, and solve it by using the modified algorithm. Finally, the authors illustrate the model through numerical example and discuss relationships among the price, quantity, technological progress, and satisfaction among two dynamic phases.

Finally, "Comprehensive Structure of Novel Voice Priority Queue Scheduling System Model for VoIP Over WLANs" by Kashif Nisar, deals with Voice over Internet Protocol (VoIP), which has grown quickly in the world of telecommunication. Wireless Local Area Networks (WLANs) are the most performance assuring technology for wireless networks, and WLANs have facilitated high-rate voice services at low cost and good flexibility. In a voice conversation, each client works as a sender or a receiver depending on the direction of traffic flow over the network. A VoIP application requires high throughput, low packet loss, and a high fairness index over the network. The packets of VoIP streaming may experience drops because of the competition among the different kinds of traffic flow over the network. A VoIP application is also sensitive to delay and requires the voice packets to arrive on time from the sender to the receiver side without any delay over WLAN. The scheduling system model for VoIP traffic is an unresolved problem. The objectives of this chapter are to identify scheduler issues. This comprehensive structure of Novel Voice Priority Queue (VPQ) scheduling system model for VoIP over WLAN discusses the essential background of the VPQ schedulers and algorithms. This chapter also identifies the importance of the scheduling techniques over WLANs.

Chapter 1
Design and Implementation of the Embed Computer Based on CompactPCI Express Bus

Feng Guo
Jiangsu Automation Research Institution, China

Zhenxing Yin
Jiangsu Automation Research Institution, China

Liang Wu
Jiangsu Automation Research Institution, China

Hao Shen
Jiangsu Automation Research Institution, China

ABSTRACT

Due to the development of embed computer, improvement the bandwidth of computer is required, in order to break the choke point of the bus' development. The text brings a hardware design method of computer based on CompactPCI Express bus, introduces the architecture of system and principle, goes into descriptions abouth the design of Swithboard, bridgeboard and rapid serial single PCB etc. The use of CompactPCI Express bus improves the bandwidth of computer system, reduces power, improves the performance of system, adapt the requirement of development.

INTRODUCTION

Along with the development of information equipment, as the core of the system, the embedded computerneed to handle larger, more sources, higher precision, faster speed of information flow, thereby the data bus bandwidth has been puted forward higher requirements. At present the popular CompactPCI bus in the new application requirements in the industrial control and other special areas, have become relatively backward, it is difficult to adapt to the computer system for high bandwidth, low power consumption and other aspects of the development, development space is very limited. CompactPCI Express bus emerge as the times require, it is a kind of brand-new buses,

DOI: 10.4018/978-1-4666-2645-4.ch001

has obvious advantages, its high transmission performance, makes Gigabit Network and serial ATA completely satisfy the requirement of high speed access and enter the practical state of load.

CompactPCI Express bus is the current hot research, has a very broad application prospects.

COMPACTPCI EXPRESS BUS

CompactPCI Express bus is a third generation high performance IO bus, the bus structure to take the fundamental changes, mainly manifested in two aspects: one is from the parallel bus to serial bus (first and second generation IO bus is a parallel bus), two is a point-to-point interconnect. In 2005 July CompactPCI Express PICMG EXP.0 R1.0 published draft, the draft based on the third generation bus PCI Express electrical characteristics based on the combination of CompactPCI bus mechanical structure form, which in the implementation of PCI-E bus architecture, break through the bandwidth at the same time, for the computer to provide a highly reliable, modular and fast dynamic reorganization of solution.

CompactPCI Express evolved from PCI Express bus and CompactPCI bus, it inherited not only the traditional advantage of its own family's products, and fully absorb the advantages of other bus standard, has a distinct technical advantage, can fully solve the CompactPCI bus technology problems. First of all, it is difficult with that, the PCI and CompactPCI all devices sharing the same bus of different resources, CompactPCI Express bus using peer-to-peer technology, can assign a exclusive channel bandwidth for each device, without the need for sharing resources between such equipment, fully ensure the device's bandwidth resource, improving the data transmission rate. Secondly, CompactPCI Express bus uses a unique dual transfer mode, greatly improving the speed of data transmission. The physical layer is provided on the 1 ~ 32 speed optional channel bandwidth characteristics make it can

easily achieve almost " unlimited" expanding the transmission capacity.CompactPCI Express bus system, link (Link) is a physical connection between two devices, each link use point-to-point method to interconnect two equipment. A link is equivalent to a bus which just hang only one device. A link includ a plurality of channels, can choose the channel number X1, X2, X4, X8, X16 or X32. The X1 model peak bandwidth can reach i 0.5 Gbps, has greatly exceeded the peak bandwidth, X16 model can achieve 8Gbps. Flexibility and extensibility.CompactPCI Express bus can extend into the system outside, using special cable to connect a variety of peripherals directly with the CompactPCI Express bus within system. Secondly, compared with the CompactPCI bus, CompactPCI Express bus signal line number reduced by almost 75%, data will accelerate and the data does not require synchronization. At the same time as the printed board line less, so that by increasing the number of the line to upgrade bus width method is easier to realize, at the same time, the line between the interval can be more broadly, reducing mutual crosstalk. Finally, the software layer remains compatible with CompactPCI. Cross platform compatible is a very important characteristic of CompactPCI Express bus, and it provides a smooth upgrade platform for the majority of users.

In view of so many advantages, the CompactPCI Express technology becomes a current hot research topic at home and abroad.

SYSTEM PRINCIPLE

CompactPCI Express bus embedded computer uses the modular design; the module can be replaced conveniently. By CPU plate, bottom plate, plate, mixed bus interchange bridge plate, CompactPCI Express bus, CompactPCI bus peripheral plate outer panel and a power supply. System principle block diagram as shown in Figure 1.

Figure 1. System principle block

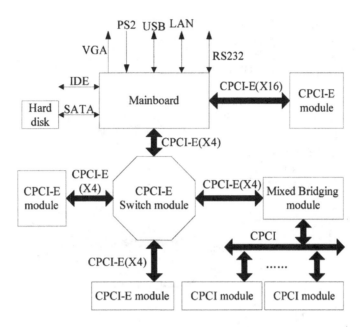

CompactPCI Express bus computer system provide to CompactPCI Express Express X4 and X16 bus by the CPU board, while providing basic interface such as a display, keyboard, mouse, Ethernet, serial port, USB, IDE, SATA. Link stands for CompactPCI Express port, the system Link connection using a two Link mixed mode (this mode has the direct mode and pure exchange model, design of moderate difficulty), one group of Link is CompactPCI Express X16 bus, directly provided to the outer panel. Another group of Link is CompactPCI Express X4 bus, as a switching module uplink bus, through the switching module to expand the number of Link (downlink bus) for the system to provide multiple sets of CompactPCI Express X4 bus. Considering the current CompactPCI module has very strong application foundation, the existing CompactPCI peripheral plate type and quantity are many. Therefore, by extending out of the 1 CompactPCI Express X4 bus through bridging modules extend out of a group of CompactPCI bus, allowing the system to be compatible with the use of CompactPCI bus peripheral coaming.

EXCHANGE BOARD DESIGN

Due to the resource constraints provided by chip set, the number of Link provided by CPU plate directly is very limited, and in some cases cannot meet the requirements of the system, such as in the case that the CompactPCI Express contains slot more, we need to expand the number of Link. Therefore, need to use the CompactPCI Express bus switching technology.

The exchange of resources among all ports between the average allocation, signal input, output to the switching chip as the core. Switching device selection depends mainly on the computer system for port and channel resource needs, design exchange board of the port number is 8, channel 32. Exchange principle diagram as shown in Figure 2.

Select the PEX8532 device as the core design exchange board, 1 CompactPCI Express X4 by bus connector is provided to the PEX8532 as an uplink port, the PEX8532 extensions for down the road 7 port. It is the original can only connect a CompactPCI Express device port after PEX8532 can be articulated 7 equipment. The host can be

Figure 2. Switch board of schematic diagram

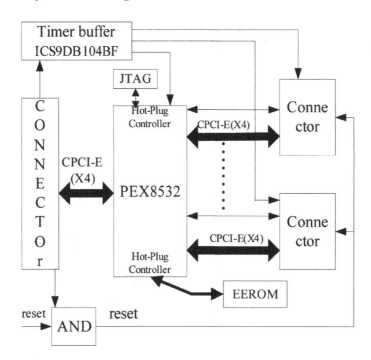

initiated through uplink port to PEX8532 as well as articulated in PEX8532 downlink port on the equipment configuration and read, write operation.

There is two ways of Device access to the clock input, that is the use of the board and the use of an external input clock, this design using an external clock. Since the clock precision requirement is high, the design uses a spread spectrum clocking (Spread Spectrum Clocking, SSC) function, SSC is a method for slow modulation clock frequency technology, in order to reduce EMI radiation noise at the center frequency of the clock. With SSC radiation energy is 2.5GHZ does not produce noise spikes, because the radiation energy is dispersed into 2.5GHZ around small frequency range. In this design the path of the input clock signal by clock buffer (buffer) is divided into multiple synchronous clock signal using.

MIXED BRIDGING PLATE DESIGN

In order to make the system can be compatible with CompactPCI bus module, the specific implementation method is adding CompactPCI CompactPCI Express hybrid bridge circuit board in the system.

Hybrid bridge board schematic diagram as shown in Figure 3, bridging initialization is the CompactPCI Express X4 bus. In addition to providing normal CompactPCI bus address / data signal, bridge chip also provides CompactPCI bus arbitration signal, clock signal is provided to different CompactPCI interface through the clock buffer.

Bridging chip selection mainly considers the ends of the chip bus interface parameters. From the CompactPCI Express bus to CompactPCI bus bridge is needed to ensure that data transmission bandwidth of the CompactPCI Express end is greater than the bandwidth of the CompactPCI bus terminal, it is equivalent to the rapid bus hanging slow peripherals. So the CompactPCI

Figure 3. Hybrid bridge plate of schematic diagram

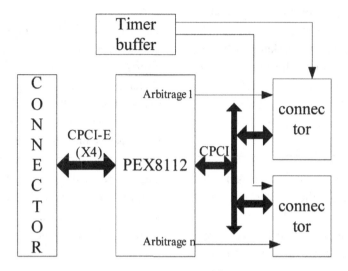

Express bus interface main consider the number of contained channels, channel number contained in general need to guarantee no bandwidth bottleneck when communicate with CompactPCI interface. The CompactPCI bus data transmission rate is 266M Byte/S, so CompactPCI Express bus port width choice X4 can completely satisfy the system requirements. Selection of PLX hybrid bridge chip PEX8112 is used.

HIGH SPEED SERIAL BUS CIRCUIT DESIGN

CompactPCI Express bus belongs to high speed signal, is close to universal printed board process can reach. In the design of transmission in the PCB on the high speed signal quality has very high demand, high speed signal simulation is the key and core of design. Due to the high speed PCB design needs to consider many factors, such as media, plane segmentation, signal equal, and so on, the traditional design criterion is no longer accurate, so need to rely on a simulation tool to provide design basis.

Printed board high speed signal needs strict control characteristic impedance of the printed line. Printed circuit board transmission line is divided in to the stripline and microstrip line. Microstrip line is Located near the top of the line, and it is in between two media such as air and the printed circuit board. Stripline is located on a printed circuit board inner layer, and it is in a homogeneous medium package.

Strip line characteristic impedance calculation formula:

$$Z_0 = \frac{87\Omega}{\sqrt{1.41 + \varepsilon_r}} In\left(\frac{5.98h}{0.8 + t}\right)$$

Microstrip line characteristic impedance calculation formula:

$$Z_0 = \frac{60\Omega}{\sqrt{\varepsilon_r}} In\left(\frac{2b + t}{0.8w + t}\right)$$

Z_0 represents characteristic impedance, unit is Ω; h represents medium thickness between the signal line and plane, the unit mil; w represents the line width, the unit mil; b represents the plane spacing, the unit mil; h represents signal lines metal layer thickness, the unit mil; ε_r represents the material dielectric constant.

If you ignore the signal line thickness t affects, these two kinds of structure of the characteristic impedance only relevant with the ratio of dielectric thickness and width. By adjusting the medium thickness and width of the line to get the required characteristic impedance.

In order to reduce design risk, it is verified at the beginning of the circuit design using the simulation tool according to the simulation results, and constantly adjusts our own design. After the PCB is complete, observe signal through high speed oscilloscope or logic analyzer, through the instrument measured results verify our own simulation effect, in order to provide the basis for the simulation. In this design the simulation tool is Mentor Hyperlynx GHz. the simulation results as shown in Figure 4. The amplitude of the signal meet the requirements, in the scope that receiver can identify

SYSTEM DEBUGGING

The embedded computer system is running the Windows XP operating system through the SATA interface hanging disk, and install the operating system, driver and test software. Use of test tool BurnInTest to CPU plate performance for validation, to its interface test. Through the CompactPCI Express bus and CompactPCI bus outer panel and panel testing, validation system bus, switch board and mixed bridging plate work. After commissioning, the embedded computer system is running normally, the function and the performance indicators have reached the design requirements.

CONCLUSION

The embedded computer system based on CompactPCI Express bus is a high performance computer, its design solves the embedded computer system bus bandwidth, single board power consumption and other aspects of the problem, it provides a platform for the high performance peripheral function board (such as graphics, Gigabit Ethernet and other applications), at the same time

Figure 4. The receiving end of PCB simulation results

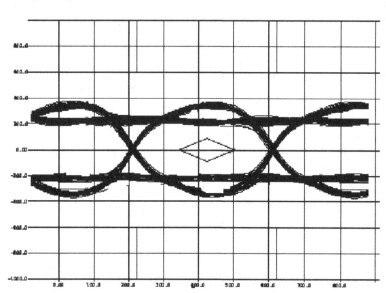

that the embedded computer system development to a new level. In addition, the system can be compatible with the use of CompactPCI bus peripheral plate, which can rest us assured that the use of the new CompactPCI Express bus in order to improve the performance of the whole system and the simple transplantation past the peripheral card, and protect our substantial investment of time and money for former CompactPCI.

REFERENCES

Li, X. (2005). *Study of signal integrity, power integrity and electromagnetic compatibility in high-speed PCB*. Unpublished doctoral dissertation, Sichuan University, Chengdu, Sichuan, China.

Ma, M., Zhu, J., & He, H. & Du, W. (2007). *PCI, PCI-X and PCI express principle and system structure*. Beijing, China: Tsinghua University Press.

PICMG. (1999). *PICMG 20 R30 @CompactPCI Specification*.Retrieved from http://www.picmg.org/v2internal/specifications.htm

PICMG. (2005). *CompactPCI Express PICMG EXP.0 R1.0 Specification*.Retrieved from http://www.picmg.org/v2internal/specifications.htm

Wang, Q. (2010). *PCI express architecture guide*. Beijing, China: Machinery Industry Press.

Wang, X., Zhu, Y., & Liu, B. (2010). Design and implementation of compact express communication interface module based on FPGA. *Application of Electronic Technology*.

Zhang, T., & Zhang, S. (2009). *Analysis of CPCI-E comparing with VPX bus technology*. Industrial Control Computer.

This work was previously published in the International Journal of Advanced Pervasive and Ubiquitous Computing, Volume 3, Issue 1, edited by Tao Gao, pp. 1-6, copyright 2011 by IGI Publishing (an imprint of IGI Global).

Chapter 2
Niche Genetic Algorithm Based on Sexual Reproduction and Multimodal Function Optimization Problem

Yulong Tian
China University of Geosciences Great Wall College, China

Weifang Zhai
China University of Geosciences Great Wall College, China

Tao Gao
Electronic Information Products Supervision and Inspection Institute of Hebei Province & Industry and Information Technology Department of Hebei Province, China

Yaying Hu
Hebei University Computer Center, China

Xinfeng Li
China University of Geosciences Great Wall College, China

ABSTRACT

In this paper, a genetic algorithm with sexual reproduction and niche selection technology is proposed. Simple genetic algorithm has been successfully applied to many evolutionary optimization problems. But there is a problem of premature convergence for complex multimodal functions. To solve it, the frame and realization of niche genetic algorithm based on sexual reproduction are presented. Age and sexual structures are given to the individuals referring the sexual reproduction and "niche" phenomena, importing the niche selection technology. During age and sexual operators, different evolutionary parameters are given to the individuals with different age and sexual structures. As a result, this genetic algorithm can combat premature convergence and keep the diversity of population. The testing for Rastrigin function and Shubert function proves that the niche genetic algorithm based on sexual reproduction is effective.

DOI: 10.4018/978-1-4666-2645-4.ch002

INTRODUCTION

Genetic algorithm is a probability search algorithm, enlightened by Darwin's evolution theory and Mendel's genetics, simulates the creature's genetic and evolutionary process. It has been drawn wide attention since Michigan University's professor John Holland proposed the conception of Simple Genetic Algorithm (SGA) in 1970s. According to the struggle for existence principles, produced new generations and evolved to the optimal solution through a series of genetic manipulation such as selection, crossover and mutation by leveraging colony searching technology. Compared with other optimizing methods, genetic algorithm described the researching problem in the form of string, simply used fitness function for optimization, without the need of derivative or other auxiliary information, especially for dealing with complex and nonlinear problems, which traditional search methods were difficult to solve, can be widely used in combinatorial optimization, machine learning, adaptive control and image processing and other fields.

Although genetic algorithm has been successfully applied to many fields, but a lot of practice and research show that the simple genetic algorithm has poor search ability and premature convergence defects, especially in dealing with multimodal function, this problem has become more prominent. It can only find a few optimal solutions, and sometimes gets a local optimal solution, but we often want to optimize the algorithm to identify the optimal solution for all. The same problem solving many times may help us to find multiple solutions, but the solution results are random, we cannot guarantee to find all global optimal values. Some theoretical studies have proved that traditional simple genetic algorithm did not converge to the global optimum (Rudolph, 1994). To overcome this problem, many researchers improved the genetic algorithm from the encoding, genetic operators, population patterns,

the producing way of next generations and other aspects (Schraudolph & Belew, 1992; Chen & Wang, 2009; Lis & Eiben, 1997; Kuo & Hwang, 1996; Zhang, Wang, Luo, & Cong, 2010; Song, Qu, & Han, 2003). Although the global convergence rate and optimizing efficiency has been improved in some degrees, it needs further research and development. Simple genetic algorithm simulates the genetic evolution process relatively simple, less considering the individual characteristics of age, gender, reproduction. Niche Genetic Algorithm (NGA) (Huang & Chen, 2004; Xie, 2005) has good performance when be used in solving the premature convergence defects. Therefore, this article drew lessons from the sexual reproduction, introduced niche technology in the genetic algorithm, proposed the Niche Genetic Algorithm Based on Sexual Reproduction (NGABAR).

NICHE GENETIC ALGORITHM BASED ON SEXUAL REPRODUCTION

Algorithm Structure

Niche refers to a specific living environment in biology (Lei et al., 2005). Generally, the same species always live together to produce offspring in the biological evolution process, "feather flock together, people in groups" is a niche phenomenon. They are also survived in particular geographic areas, such as tropical fish cannot survive in colder areas and polar bears cannot survive in the tropics. This offers the possibility of new species formation and maintains infinite diversity of the biosphere. Draw lessons from sexual reproduction, niche and the individual fertility changes with age, we construct the new genetic algorithm. Genetic individuals were divided into males and females, males have strong optimizing and exploring abilities in the larger space, females quickly in a small area for local optimization. Male and female individuals have been given the age parameters. According to the law of higher organisms experienced growth period, mature period and decline phase, the male and female individuals run crossing operation for heterosexual cross-breeding. This algorithm is not easy to fall into local convergence, has a strong ability to jump out of local minima, and converged quickly. The local research and global research abilities are all strong.

The algorithm structure was described as follows:

First, randomly generated initial population and initialized, set the initial age of each individual;

```
while (algorithm terminal conditions
not satisfied) do
{
if (reach the age of childbearing)
Male and female individuals run
crossing operation for heterosexual
cross-breeding;
else
Male and female individuals run
cross-
matching operation for asexual repro-
duction in their respective groups.
Male and female individuals run ge-
netic manipulation according to dif-
ferent age
Individual fitness evaluation;
Male and female individuals run se-
lecting operation based on the niche
technology;
The age of Male and female individu-
als adds one respectively.
}
```

For special problems, the genetic algorithm can also accelerate the convergence speed by changing the individual's gender, transgender males to females or females to males.

Coding

In biology, diploid chromosome are individuals which contain two homologous diploid genomes, each of the chromosome contains same features of genetic information. Experiments have confirmed that the genes in the diploid are divided into dominant and recessive genes, two types of genes determined individual characteristics by the following rules: In each locus, when one of two homologous chromosomes is dominant, the corresponding traits is dominant. Only when two homologous chromosomes are all recessive, the corresponding traits are expressed as recessive.

Figure 1(1) shows a diploid dominant binary encoding rules, which dominant operation using "and" operator; Figure 1(2) shows a diploid dominant float encoding rules, which dominant operator is similar to float coding cross-operation. The dominant operation in Figure 1(2) as follows:

$$\alpha \times 5.4 + (1 - \alpha) \times 4.6 = 5.0,$$

$$\alpha \times 3.6 + (1 - \alpha) \times 5.8 = 4.7,$$

(control parameters $\alpha = 0.5$).

Diploid provides a mechanism that can memorize the previous useful genes and protect the memorized genes combination against harmful selecting operation. When we define the individual's gender, for the binary encoding, the individual last position performance is "0" indicates that the individual as a male; otherwise, indicates that the individual as a female; Figure 1(1) shows the individual last position performance is "1", so the individual is a female. For float encoding, when the individual last position performance is "0.0", then the individual as a male, such as the individual last position is "1.0", so the individual is a male. Otherwise, it's a female.

Figure 1. Diploid dominant rules

(1) Diploid dominant binary encoding rules (2) Diploid dominant float encoding rules

Matching Method

In this article, the matching method was described as follows:

1. Judge whether the individual's age reached the initialized child-bearing age.
2. If not reach the age, the males and females run asexual genetic manipulation respectively.
3. If reached, the males and females queued with fitness function values respectively, and then were matched one by one.

In nature, individuals have good reproduction ability in mature period, so they can produce excellent descendants. Generally, good males always try to select the best females to be matched. It is proved that this matching method is relatively stable, so we can design the matching mode of sexual reproduction according to the nature phenomenon, order the males and females according to the individual merits, and then match them one by one, which can help us as soon as possible to find the global optimum. Simple genetic algorithm completely random matched the individuals in a wide range, but this matching method relatively limited the speed to find the global optimal solution. We can use the features to pair males and females, which males work well in global optimization and females well in local optimization, making the algorithm has a stronger global convergence and local fast convergence capability (Li, Xiong, & Ma, 2003; Zhu & Li, 2006).

Crossover

Binary encoding cross operation uses single-point crossover (Zhou & Sun, 1999). If the relationship between adjacent loci can provide better individual traits and higher individual fitness, then this single-point crossover operation could reduces damage to the individual character and fitness.

Float encoding cross operation is as follows:
Let two parent individuals are:

$$\begin{cases} X_A^t = (x_1^{(1)}, x_2^{(1)}, ..., x_m^{(1)}) \\ X_B^t = (x_1^{(2)}, x_2^{(2)}, ..., x_m^{(2)}) \end{cases} \qquad (1)$$

Assume $\alpha_i \in (0,1), i = 1, 2, ..., m$, two new individuals after the crossover operation are:

$$\begin{cases} X_A^{t+1} = (y_1^{(1)}, y_2^{(1)}, ..., y_m^{(1)}) \\ X_B^{t+1} = (y_1^{(2)}, y_2^{(2)}, ..., y_m^{(2)}) \end{cases} \qquad (2)$$

In Formula 2,

$$\begin{cases} y_i^{(1)} = \alpha_i x_i^{(1)} + (1 - \alpha_i) x_i^{(2)} \\ y_i^{(2)} = \alpha_i x_i^{(2)} + (1 - \alpha_i) x_i^{(1)} \end{cases} \qquad (3)$$

In Formula 3, α is a parameter, it can also be a determined by the evolution of algebraic variable.

Through such a crossover method, we can get a variety of possible results. Not only between two individuals can be fully realized "information exchange", but also it is very beneficial to finding the global extreme value, and the results will lead to improve the performance and convergence rate of genetic algorithms.

In this algorithm, the male and female individuals respectively run cross-operation within their groups in the growth period or over the mature period. Only the different sex individuals can do cross-matching operation in the mature period, which only males can be cross-matched with females, and between individuals of similar gender cannot be cross-matched.

Mutation

Binary encoding using the basic bit mutation, which is to every individual loci, according to the mutation probability p_m was designated as mutation points, the value of their genes is inversion operation value or instead by other alleles gene value, then producing a new individual.

Float encoding using a non-uniform mutation, the specific operation is as follows:

Assume $X = (x_1, x_2, ..., x_k, ..., x_m)$ is a parent individual, after performing mutation operation, the next generation individual is $X^{'} = (x_1, x_2, ..., x_k^{'}, ..., x_m)$. If the mutation point x_k $(1 \leq k \leq m)$ gene value range is $[U_{min}^k, U_{max}^k]$, the new gene value $x_k^{'}$ is determined by the following formula:

$$x_k^{'} = \begin{cases} x_k + \Delta(t, U_{max}^k - x_k), & if \\ x_k - \Delta(t, x_k - U_{min}^k), & if \end{cases}$$
$$random(0,1) = 0$$
$$random(0,1) = 1 \qquad (4)$$

where, $\Delta(t, y)$ (y is $U_{max}^k - x_k$ and $x_k - U_{min}^k$) represents a random number which is accord with non-uniform distribution within the range $[0, y]$, requires $\Delta(t, y)$ close to zero probability increased with the evolution times t increasing. For example, $\Delta(t, y)$ can be defined as follows:

$$\Delta(t, y) = y \cdot (1 - r^{(1-t/T)b}) \qquad (5)$$

where, r is a random number which is accord with uniform distribution within the range $[0, 1]$. T is maximum evolution times, b is a system parameter, it determines the random disturbance dependency on the evolution times t.

From Formula 4 and 5, we can know that, Non-uniform variation can make the genetic algorithm run uniform random search in the initial phase (when t is small), which makes the search point more freely in the search space. So it can increase the diversity of population; In the late phase (when t is closer to T), it runs local search. Its gene value is closer to the original value than any other genetic variation method. Therefore, with the genetic algorithm run, non-uniform variation makes the search process of optimal solution more concentrated focus in a desired area.

In this genetic algorithm, the mutation rate for males was made larger than females, the purpose is to make males stronger in global optimization, females stronger in local optimization, and it can increase the diversity of population.

Selection Method

We use two generations competition sorting method to select the new individuals, that is reordered the parent and offspring individuals respectively, and then choose the optimal preservation strategy. Introduced niche technology to increase the probability of searching for other extreme points (Zhu & Zhang, 2006). The basic idea is calculated the relative distance (the algorithm uses the "Hamming distance") between each generation produced individuals and the best preservation individuals, if the relative distance is less than a specified distance L (L can be an integer multiple Hamming distance between two individuals designated), then eliminate it. Hamming distance is calculated as follows:

$$\| X_i - X_j \| = \sqrt{\sum_{k=1}^{P} (X_{ik} - X_{jk})^2} \qquad (6)$$

X_i and X_j are two individuals in the population, P is the number of independent variables.

The Experiment to Solve Multimodal Function

In order to test the optimization ability and convergence speed of the genetic algorithm based on sexual reproduction, we selected two typical multimodal functions as test functions, using the above described algorithm to solve these two functions, find the global optimal solution.

Test Function

1. Rastrigin function:

$$f_1 = 20 + x_1^2 + x_2^2 - 10(\cos 2\pi x_1 + \cos 2\pi x_2)$$
$$-5 \le x_i \le 5, i = 1,2$$

This function has many local minimum, however, has only one global minimum, in the point [0,0], the function value is 0. Any point different from [0,0] of the local minimum, Rastrigin function values are greater than 0. Local minimum at the farther away from the origin, the value of Rastrigin function is greater. Rastrigin function graph is shown in Figure 2

Shubert function:

$$f_2 = \sum_{i=1}^{5} i \cos[(i+1)x_1 + i] \bullet \sum_{i=1}^{5} i \cos[(i+1)x_2 + i]$$
$$-10 \le x_i \le 10, (i = 1,2)$$

This function is also a multimodal function, has 760 local minimum points within its definition, including 18 global minimum. Global minimum is $f = -186.731$. Shubert function graph is shown in Figure 3.

Figure 2. Rastrigin function graph

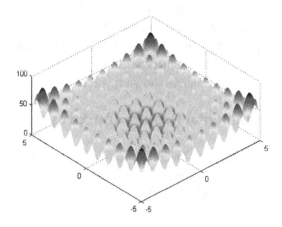

Figure 3. Shubert function graph

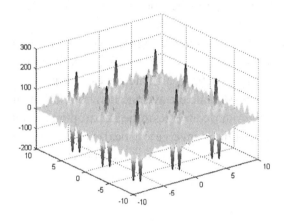

Operating Parameters

The simple genetic algorithm and the niche genetic algorithm based on sexual reproduction are both used float encoding.

For the niche genetic algorithm based on sexual reproduction, the maximum evolution generation times (denoted as T) is used as the maximum individual lifespan. In the range between $0 \sim 0.2T$ and $0.7T \sim T$, male and female individuals run cross-matching operation for asexual reproduction in their respective groups. In the range $0.2T \sim 0.7T$, male and female individuals run crossing operation for heterosexual cross-breeding. The male and female individuals are determined according to a diploid dominant float encoding rules, where the control parameter α is a uniformly distributed random number at range (0,1). when the individual last position performance is "0.0", then the individual as a male. Otherwise, it's a female.

Other parameters shown in Table 1.

Experimental Results and Analysis

For multimodal function optimization problem, the algorithm requires not only the convergence speed is quickly, but also it can find the global optimum and avoid falling into local extreme points. To evaluate the algorithm performance proposed in the paper, we compared its running results with the simple genetic algorithm. As the initial groups of genetic algorithm are random selected, the results cannot explain the problem only by a few times, we respectively run the two genetic algorithms 50 times for optimizing the Rastrigin function, calculate the results arithmetic average, statistic the average iteration times that the algorithm converges to the global optimum and the algorithm converge to a local extreme point in 50 times (If the algorithm still cannot converge to

the optimal point after enough iterations, we can think that the algorithm falling into local extreme points). The statistics, the optimization results are shown in Table 2.

According to Table 2, the two genetic algorithms both can converge to Rastrigin function extremum, but the niche genetic algorithm based on sexual reproduction converges much faster and the results accuracy has also been improved.

The two algorithms results distribution of Shubert function is shown in Figure 4. According to Figure 4, we can see that the niche genetic algorithm based on sexual reproduction found the 18 global optimal solutions, while simple genetic algorithm only found some of the local optimal solutions.

In order to compare the niche genetic algorithm based on sexual reproduction and the niche genetic algorithm proposed in [14]. We mapped the local and global optimal solutions into the X-Y plane, the results distribution shown in Figure 5. It is very obvious that the niche genetic algorithm based on sexual reproduction is superior to the niche genetic algorithm.

Table 1. Test function operating parameters

function	initial population	cross rate	mutation rate(asexual)	mutation rate(sexual)
f_1	80	0.8	0.1	male: 0.7;female: 0.1
f_2	80	0.8	0.1	male: 0.7;female:0.1

Table 2. Rastrigin function optimization results

SGA				NGABSR			
Extremum	x_1	x_2	Average iterations	Extremum	x_1	x_2	Average iterations
0.00049	0.00007	0.00019	97.96	0.00016	0.00005	0.00012	32.74

Figure 4. NGABSR and SGA local optimal solution distribution

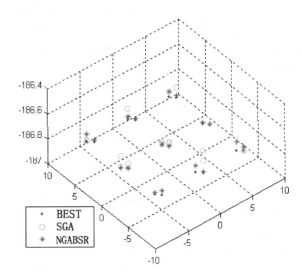

Figure 5. NGABSR and NGA local optimal solution mapping distribution

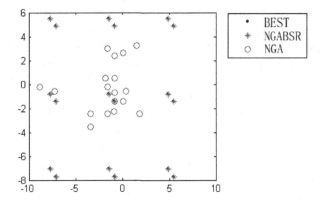

CONCLUSION

Genetic algorithm provides us a new way to solve high-dimensional, multimodal, non-linear function, but the simple genetic algorithm is not efficient to the complex and multimodal function, it's prone to premature and slow convergence. In order to overcome the premature convergence phenomenon, we draw lesson from the sexual reproduction and "niche" phenomenon, combined with gender, age and diploid encoding method, importing the niche selecting techniques, propose the niche genetic algorithm based on sexual reproduction. This method used male and female individuals in the reproductive period to produce good offspring by cross-matching, give full play to the male individual strong global capabilities and female strong local optimization ability. As a result, this genetic algorithm can combat premature convergence and keep the diversity of population. The testing for Rastrigin function and Shubert function proves that the niche genetic algorithm based on sexual reproduction is effective.

ACKNOWLEDGMENT

The authors thank the anonymous referees for their comments and suggestions. This work was supported by the National Science Foundation of China (No.71102174, 70972005, 71072035), and the Science Foundations of Tianjin under Grant No. 10ZCKFSF01100.

REFERENCES

Chen, X., & Wang, X. (2009). An improved multi-population genetic algorithm. *Journal of Liaoning University of Technology*, *32*(2), 160–163.

Huang, C., & Chen, X. (2004). Improvements on niche genetic algorithm. *Journal of Beijing Institute of Technology*, *24*(8), 675–678.

Kuo, T., & Hwang, S. Y. (1996). A genetic algorithm with disruptive selection. *IEEE Transactions on Systems, Man, and Cybernetics*, *26*(2), 299–306. doi:10.1109/3477.485880

Lei, Y., Zhang, S., & Li, X. (2005). *MATLAB genetic algorithm toolbox and application*. Xi'an, China: Xidian University Press.

Li, M., Xiong, X., & Ma, C. (2003). A genetic algorithms with sexual reproduction. *Journal of Image and Graphics*, *8*(5), 509–515.

Lis, J., & Eiben, A. E. (1997). A multi-sexual genetic algorithm for multiobjective optimization. *IEEE Transactions on Evolutionary Computation*, *1*(2), 59–64.

Rudolph, G. (1994). Convergence properties of canonical genetic algorithms. *IEEE Transactions on Neural Networks*, *5*(1), 96–101. doi:10.1109/72.265964

Schraudolph, N. N., & Belew, R. K. (1992). Dynamic parameter encoding for genetic algorithms. *Machine Learning*, (n.d.), 1–8.

Song, W., Qu, J., & Han, S. (2003). An improved hybrid genetic algorithm for optimizing muitiapices function. *Journal of Tianjin Normal University*, *23*(2), 47–54.

Xie, K. (2005). *Crowding niche genetic algorithms and application*. Unpublished doctoral dissertation, Anhui Institute of Technology.

Zhang, J., Wang, Z., Luo, W., & Cong, H. (2010). Research and application of population diversity in genetic algorithms. *Automation Technology and Application*, *29*(10), 1–3.

Zhou, M., & Sun, S. (1999). *Principle and Application of genetic algorithms*. Beijing, China: National Defence Industry Press.

Zhu, X., & Zhang, X. (2006). Niche genetic algorithm to solve multi-modal function global optimization problem. *Journal of Nanjing University of Technology*, *28*(3), 39–43.

Zhu, Y., & Li, M. (2006). A genetic algorithm with sexual reproduction in image recovering. *Computer Simulation*, *23*(11), 168–172.

This work was previously published in the International Journal of Advanced Pervasive and Ubiquitous Computing, Volume 3, Issue 1, edited by Tao Gao, pp. 7-15, copyright 2011 by IGI Publishing (an imprint of IGI Global).

Chapter 3
Coordination Performance Evaluation of Supply Logistics in JIT Environment

Guo Li
Beijing Institute of Technology, China

Xiang Zhang
Beijing Institute of Technology, China

Zhaohua Wang
Beijing Institute of Technology, China

Tao Gao
Hebei Electronic Information Products Supervision and Inspection Institute & Industry and Information Technology Department of Hebei Province, China

ABSTRACT

In JIT assembly system, any supplier's postponement of delivery or incorrect delivery quantity will result in the manufacturer's incapability of assembling on schedule, which will not only damage the interests of other suppliers but also jeopardize the interests of enterprises and reduce the competitiveness of the supply chain. In this article, coordination of the upstream supply logistics from internal and external aspects is taken as the research object. In external supply system, three aspects of cost, quality and time are used to evaluate the coordination of supply logistics in JIT environment. From the internal aspect, reliability, flexibility, responsiveness, customer service and system suitability are selected for the performance evaluation. The eight indexes construct an index system and each performance index is described and analyzed. Finally, Analytic Hierarchy Process is used to evaluate the coordinated performance of supply logistics in JIT environment. An example is provided, which illustrate the method used in this paper is feasible and meaningful.

DOI: 10.4018/978-1-4666-2645-4.ch003

1. INTRODUCTION

Coordination of supply chain management is a new mode, although its proposed time is not long. It has received a wide range of attention from academic circles and enterprise circles since proposed. For example, in 1995 the international well-known retailer Wal-Mart and others proposed the effective strategies oriented to coordination of supply chain management----Collaborative Planning, Forecasting and Replenishment (CPFR) (Bin & Zhang, 2000). In 1999, IBM developed its supply chain solutions, and constructed its collaborative supply chain (IBM, n. d.). In 2002, the American consulting firm ARC proposed Collaborative Manufacturing Management (CMM) strategy based on collaborative value network and established the CMM model (ARC Advisory Group, 2002). Turkay, Oruc, Fujita, and Asakura (2004) constructed the model and made quantitative analysis between chemical industry enterprises. Akkermans, Bogerd, and van Doremalen (2004) established a theoretical model of supply chain collaboration, focusing on non-technical factors which affected the realization of coordination.

Currently, studies on coordination of supply chain management mainly involve three aspects: the strategic level, tactics level and technical level. Tactics level coordination is the main problem in coordination of supply chain management. The related details are as follows: demand collaborative tactics with a direct supply and demand relationship between the upstream and downstream business, product design collaboration tactics, collaborative inventory tactics, collaborative production tactics, collaborative logistics tactics, collaborative procurement tactics etc. Most scholars attach great importance to the coordination in tactics level, because supply chain coordination in tactics level is the core problem of the supply chain coordination (Ren, 20050.

Customer demand affects the supply chain coordination. Chen et al. (2000) analyzed that centralized demand information can reduce the "bullwhip effect", but can't completely eliminated it. Helo (2000) applied system dynamic simulation method to study amplified effect of the demand in supply chain, the role of capacity fluctuations and ability compromise. The results show that fewer orders for all levels of synchronization and capacity analysis can be used as the method for effective supply chain responsiveness.

Inventory problem has always been a typical problem in coordination of supply chain management. Therefore, it is also the core problem of supply chain coordination in tactics level. Fu and Piplani (2004) established the coordination model evaluated supply side based on inventory. Through modeling the traditional supply chain and collaborative supply chain respectively, the distributor's performance before and after the collaboration is simulated. The results show that supply-side coordination can enhance the entire supply chain performance. Teruaki and Salleh (2000) modeled and analyzed the two echelon coordinated inventory control with random demand.

The research on production planning and cooperative control has achieved some results. Schneeweiss and Zimmer (2004) studied the coordination / integration plan of production and sales with emphasis on contribution of corporate earnings. Yang, Ma, and Li (2004) used two layer planning as the response time modeling method of collaborative planning in supply chain, and described in detail planning process that each node enterprise interior allocates production time and the logistics. Zhou and Wang (2001) studied supply chain production plan with Multi-location Plants and multiple distributors, and attempted to obtain the optimal production plan by system engineering, but this goal in the actual application is not reached. As for logistics coordination, Ellinger (2000) studied relationship between the internal supply chain marketing and logistics cross-functional coordination by analyzing the incentive mechanism, cross-functional collaboration, effective integration and service performance of marketing and logistics department.

There is so much literature about supply chain coordination, but these articles focus on the supply chain. As for the upstream assembly system, few scholars has studied. Now how to build a scientific supply logistics coordination evaluation system and objective measure logistics operation processes in the academic circle is still unsolved. From the actual situation of our manufacturing industry, due to the lack of readily available statistical index system, analysis of supply logistics statistics is very difficult. In the JIT environment, Supply coordination plays a vital role in the core manufacturing enterprises to ensure the normal production. Therefore, this article will establish index system for coordination of the supply logistics system in the JIT environment, and put forward a better evaluating method to improve coordination of supply logistics system, which can provide a powerful reference for decision making.

2. LITERATURE REVIEW

2.1. JIT and its Development

JIT, which is Just in Time, means the required material should be delivered to the right place within the right time and the required products should be produced according to the desired quantity. As a general management mode, JIT can not only be applied to each process in production and operation management, but also widely used in supply chain management and warehousing management in commercial circulation. JIT is a management philosophy which is built based on the elimination of all waste and continuously improves productivity (McIvor, Humphreys, & McCurry, 2003).

Chen and Chen (1998) had done a special investigation about Chinese automotive industry procurement and supply in JIT environment from nine aspects such as JIT purchasing, long-term contracts, supplier evaluation standard, the quality of suppliers, reliable delivery, small batch, data exchange, operating plans etc. The result reveals

relationship status between manufacturers and suppliers in the Chinese automotive industry, which provides a reasonable proposal for implementing JIT procurement in China. Liu (2001) studied the tactics of purchasing management in supply chain. According to the importance of material itself and supply market complexity, the purchased material can be divided into strategic materials, important materials, general materials, bottleneck materials, and then different procurement and inventory strategies can be taken. Dong et al. (2006) analyzed the supply chain procurement mode based on JIT theory, pointed out that JIT procurement is a new type of procurement in supply chain environment, which needs to be supported by electronic business and other modern information technology. However, as to JIT implementation, there remain the following problems:

1. Constraints of supply chain make transfer of information can't adapt to the JIT requirements. Among the members in supply chain, information sharing is very little and information transmission may be certain defects. Due to quick change of market demand, the enterprise must make quick response according to the needs of market, so for the enterprise arranging the production time is not so much. Many enterprises' inventory is really zero or reduced but the orders are often delayed after implementation of JIT production system. The reason for the phenomenon is that suppliers do not deliver raw materials on time, resulting in delays of the manufacturers' production.

2. The deliver quantity of raw material is uncertain or the quality of components can't meet the JIT requirements. The material purchased in assembly production is based on required demand. Therefore, the excessive delivery or insufficient delivery of raw material, or any quality defects will bring forth the manufacturers' postponement.

As can be seen, in the supply logistics system, when delivery can't meet the JIT requirements, manufacturing enterprises are unable to assemble on schedule, which affect the overall coordination of supply chain, and bring losses to the whole supply chain. This paper will mainly aim at this problem, and build a reasonable index system to evaluate the coordination of logistics systems.

2.2. Review on Evaluation of Supply Chain Coordination

As to evaluation of supply chain coordination, Mason-Jones and Towill (1999) analyzed importance of lead time in the agile supply chain. To enhance coordination of the entire supply chain, it is necessary to implement the supply chain information sharing, and shorten the lead time of supply chain, and improve responsiveness of supply chain (Mason-Jones & Towill, 1999).

Thomas and Griffin (1996) took thorough analysis on the supply chain procurement, production and distribution, and in the face of fierce market competition environment proposed coordination and information sharing in three aspects, thereby to improve supply chain operations and competitiveness.

Chandra and Fisher (1994) studied suppliers' coordinated inventory decision in the two echelon supply chain between suppliers and distributors, established supplier collaborative model, evaluated from the view of distributors. The distributors' inventory decision will consider supplier inventory decision and potential inventory information.

Chen (2004) divided the performance of supply chain coordination into four major categories with single index based on the logistics coordination, workflow coordination, capital flow and information flow coordination, gave the quantitative formula of these indexes, and analyzed coordination problem between supply and demand from satisfaction, trust and value-added, but didn't give no specific applications (Chen, 2004).

Tang and Huang (2005) analyzed performance evaluation of supply chain from the aspect of synergetic, and pointed out that the evaluation indexes of supply chain coordination system are the response time (Time), operating costs (Cost), robustness (Robustness) and adaptability (Scope of Change). They established a coordinated performance evaluation model and introduced the performance evaluation methods based on fuzzy algorithm, but did not give a specific application and empirical research (Tang & Huang, 2005).

Dudek and Stadtler (2005) established a virtual electronic chain to achieve supply chain coordination. Through the study of supply chain coordination framework in the virtual environment, they classified the role of cooperated partner, distinguished the key ability forming collaborative relationships, and assessed its coordination.

Huo et al. (2004) studied the performance evaluation system of supply chain with the improved gray correlation method. They first distinguished different subjects, and built a performance evaluation index system of supply chain based on the process. As to evaluation with multiple indicators and multiple objects, this method requires only the calculation of correlation, and can determine the weight of each index in the system and the comprehensive performance of various objects, which greatly reduced the workload of evaluation (Huo et al., 2004).

Luo et al. (2007) constructed the performance evaluation index system in the supply chain life cycle. They first analyzed performance evaluation aspects and key points of supply chain in different life stage.

Jiang et al. (2007) tried to construct the integrated supply chain performance evaluation index system from the three angles such as the internal, the external and the overall supply chain. The framework included the three first level indexes such as the customer value, the supply chain value, development ability and potential. Customer value included four indexes such as flexibility, reliability, price, quality. The supply chain value consisted of three indexes which are input, output, and finance. The development capacity and potential included information sharing, and innovation and learning (Jiang et al., 2007).

In summary, there is much literature about evaluation of supply chain coordination, but the most are focused on the whole supply chain. The evaluation of supply logistics coordination in upstream supply chain is rare. As the supply logistics system is part of the supply chain, the evaluation index system of the whole supply chain coordination can't be fully applicable to the supply logistics system. This paper will innovatively and comprehensively analyze the coordination of supply logistics system based on existing evaluation index of supply chain coordination.

3. EVALUATION INDEX SYSTEM FOR SUPPLY LOGISTICS SYSTEM IN JIT ENVIRONMENT

In supply logistics system, there exist internal and external system environment which is complex. For internal system environment, the integrated system is combined with plan, organization, coordination and control of human, financial and material resources. On the contrast, the external system environment is a competitive business and the complex and ever-changing customer demand. With the rapid development of information technology, internal and external environment of the supply logistics system are changed. These changes force enterprises in the supply system to have to pay attention to internal and external coordination, and improve internal and external operation efficiency.

The internal supply logistics system is mainly evaluated from the aspects of cost, time, and quality. For external supply logistics system, the aspects of reliability, flexibility, responsiveness, customer service and the adaptability of the system are considered. The evaluation indexes

are mainly applicable to manufacturing supply logistics system, and manufacturing enterprises operating characteristics are mainly considered to establish the indexes.

3.1. Evaluation Indexes for Internal System Environment

1. **Cost:** As for the internal system, cost is a very important index. The input of cost largely determines the coordination ability of supply logistics system. The total cost of purchasing cost consists of cost of procurement in hardware and software, the total cost of personnel and management process in supply logistics system (Wang, Chen, Ji, & Zhang, 2005).
2. **Time:** Time is also an important index, especially in the supply logistics system based on JIT environment. In order to make supply logistics system achieve JIT, firstly we must meet the timing of these requirements.
    a. Procurement cycle refers to the period from orders issued by the procurement department to goods delivered to the designated location. This is a main index that measure supply cycle of each supplier.
    b. The average transportation time of raw material.
3. **Quality:** Quality is particularly important in the supply system. If the raw materials provided by suppliers are unqualified, the production process of the manufacturer may stop, which affects the response speed of supply chain.
    a. **Qualified Ratio of Delivery:** Proportion of the qualified number when the materials are delivered.
    b. **The Qualified Rate of Incoming Materials:** The qualified rate of incoming materials:= qualified batches sampled/sampling batches.

The qualified rate of incoming materials is not only an index of evaluating purchase department working efficiency, but also an index of reflecting delivery quality of supplier (Shi & Zhan, 2002).

c. **Ratio of the Purchase Order with High Quality:** Ratio of the purchase order with high quality is proportion delivered without error. A perfect purchase order should be delivered on time and without loss. Each link must have a document, accurate article content, accurate quantity in order to meet the requirement of each production line.

3.2. Evaluation Indexes for External System Environment

1. Reliability
    a. **Delivery On-Time Rate:** Ratio of orders completed which is on time or ahead of time.
    b. **Fill Rate:** The percentage of received orders shipped immediately.
2. **Flexibility:** Procurement response time: response time of the supply logistics system to the change of procurement plans.
3. Response Ability
    a. **The Lead Time of Completing Order:** The percentage of the actual completion ahead of time.
    b. **The Order Completing Cycle:** The average cycle time of completing orders. Each order cycle starts from supplier's accepting orders, and terminates at its order delivery acceptance of customers (Tomlin, 2009).
4. Customer Service
    a. **The Order Fulfillment Rate:** The ratio of completing the order number in the supply logistics system. The higher the ratio is, the better degree coordination in supply logistics system can achieved.

b. **Order Response Speed:** The time from manufacturers' accepting orders to delivering order in supply logistics system.
5. The system adaptability: the three aspects of the evaluation index system are used to reflect the overall level of coordination, which can be calculated through expert scoring method. These three aspects are goal congruence, system cooperation ability, trust level (Tomlin & Wang, 2005).

The different indexes are associated with each other, and we can obtain Figure 1.

According to several design principles of coordinated performance evaluation in supply logistics system, the coordinated performance can be evaluated from external and internal environment, and the index system can be constructed based on basic steps of collaborative evaluation system. Evaluation index system of supply logistics system provides the basis for evaluating the supply logistics system, which is our main contribution.

4. THE COORDINATE EVALUATION AND APPLIED RESEARCH OF SUPPLY LOGISTICS SYSTEM IN JIT ENVIRONMENT

Analytic Hierarchy Process (AHP) is a kind of level of weight decision analysis method, which is put forward by Professor Satty in the early 1970s. AHP regards a complex multi-objectives decision problem as a system, which is decomposed into many goals or standards, Thereby these goals are decompose into different level with multiple indexes (or standards, constraints). AHP calculate each hierarchy weight and the whole system by fuzzy quantizing qualitative indexes. Based on

Figure 1. Hierarchical structure of coordinated performance assessment model for supply logistics system in JIT environment

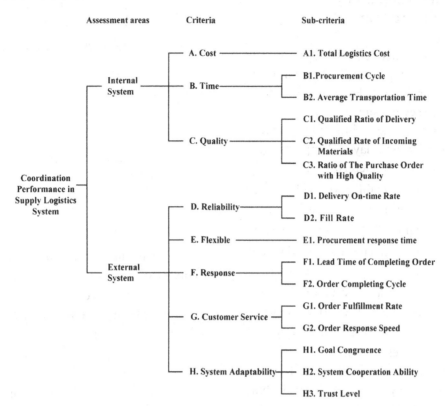

the analysis of the complicated decision problem essence, influencing factors and internal relations, the characteristics of AHP make the thinking process of the decision mathematical, and thus provides easy decision method for multi-goal, multi-standard or complex decision which have no structure characteristics. AHP is especially suitable for the decision occasions results of which are difficult to be directly counted accurately.

4.1. Basic Procedure of Coordination Evaluation Based on the AHP in JIT Environment

1. **Build Hierarchical Analysis Structure Model:** Practical problems should be analyzed completely, and the relevant factors should be stratified from top layer to upper layer (goals-standards or index-plan

or object). All factors in each layer should be relatively independent (Van Mieghem, 2003).

2. **Construct Pair wise Comparison Matrix:** The Pair wise Comparison Matrix should be constructed in each layer with 1-9 scales, which is corresponding to the factors in upper layer.

3. **Calculate vector weight and does consistency check of combination:** The biggest characteristic root and for each pair matrix should be calculated, and consistency inspection should be made. The feature vector is the weight vector if passed.

4. **Calculate the combination of weight vector and does consistency check:** Combination of weight vectors can be used as the quantitative evidence of the decision.

4.2. The Main Steps of Coordination Assessment Based on the AHP in JIT Environment

Step 1: Construct the hierarchical analysis model. The model for top layer is the target layer, middle layers are rule layer, and the layers bellows are several sub criteria.

Step 2: Weight of elements in this layer corresponding to the upper layer. Compare in pair the importance of elements A_i and A_j $(i, j = 1, 2, \cdots, n)$ in this layer with its corresponding upper layer C_k $(k = 1, 2, \cdots, m)$, then the judgment matrix $(a_{ij})_{n \times n}$ can be obtained. The a_{ij} can be determined with 9 levels.

Step 3: Try to get the feature vector of judgment matrix $(w_1, w_2, \cdots, w_n)^T$, and vector $A_1, A_2, \cdots, A_n$ should be sorted according to importance corresponding to the elements in the upper layer. Generally, feature vector can be obtained by methods of linear algebra, such as sum calculation.

For judgment matrix, the sum of each column is $\sum_{j=1}^{n} a_{ij}$, let $b_{ij} = a_{ij} / \sum_{j=1}^{n} a_{ij}$, and then

$$w_i = \sum_{j=1}^{n} b_{ij} / n \qquad (1)$$

Step 4: calculate the maximum feature value $\lambda_{\max}$ and do consistency examination for judgment matrix. If comparative matrix A satisfies this property, then A is consistency matrix. The judgment matrix can be written as follows.

$$A = (a_{ij})_{n \times n} = \begin{bmatrix} w_1 / w_1 & w_1 / w_2 & \cdots & w_1 / w_n \\ w_2 / w_1 & w_2 / w_2 & \cdots & w_2 / w_n \\ \vdots & \vdots & & \vdots \\ w_n / w_1 & w_n / w_2 & \cdots & w_n / w_n \end{bmatrix}$$

$$(2)$$

$$A W = A \begin{bmatrix} w_1 \\ w_2 \\ \vdots \\ w_n \end{bmatrix} = n \begin{bmatrix} w_1 \\ w_2 \\ \vdots \\ w_n \end{bmatrix} = n W \qquad (3)$$

where n is feature value. If the judgment matrix is completely consistent, then $\lambda_{\max} = n$. If the judgment matrix have consistency errors, then $\lambda_{\max} > n$. The more errors are, the larger the value $\lambda_{\max} - n$ is, and

$$\lambda_{\max} = \frac{1}{n} \sum_{i=1}^{n} \left[\frac{\sum_{j=1}^{n} a_{ij} w_j}{w_j} \right] = \frac{1}{n} \sum_{i=1}^{n} \left[\frac{A W}{w_j} \right].$$

$$(4)$$

Consistency index(CI) is used as an index to check the consistency of judgment matrix, where

$$CI = \frac{\lambda_{\max} - n}{n - 1}. \qquad (5)$$

As matrix order number n is increasing, the consistency of judgment matrix becomes poor. In order to eliminate effect of consistency inspection influenced by matrix order number, corrected coefficient random index (RI) can be introduced, and the value of consistency ratio (CR) can be determined to check whether the judgment matrix can pass the consistency inspection, where

$$CR = \frac{CI}{RI} \qquad (6)$$

When the value CR calculated is less than 0.1, that judgment matrix is considered to be consistent.

4.3. Case Analysis

We provide an example to illustrate how to evaluate the coordination performance in supply logistics system of three different enterprises named A, B and C.

4.3.1. Index Weight Determined by AHP Method

The 9 scales are used to construct the judgment matrix with pair comparison based on expert opinion, see Table 1.

Calculate product of elements in each row, which can be drawn:

$$m_1 = 1 \times 1/5 \times 1/4 \times 1/4 \times 3 \times 2 \times 1/2 \times 2 = 0.113$$

$$m_2 = 5 \times 1 \times 2 \times 6 \times 2 \times 5 \times 3 \times 5 = 9000$$

$$m_3 = = 4 \times 1/2 \times 1 \times 1 \times 3 \times 4 \times 2 \times 3 = 114$$

$$m_4 = 4 \times 1/2 \times 1 \times 1 \times 3 \times 4 \times 2 \times 3 = 114$$

$$m_5 = 1/3 \times 1/6 \times 1/4 \times 1/4 \times 1 \times 1/3 \times 1/2 \times 1/2$$
$$= 1/3456$$

$$m_6 = 1/2 \times 1/5 \times 1/3 \times 1/3 \times 2 \times 1 \times 1/3 \times 1$$
$$= 0.0007$$

$$m_7 = 2 \times 1/3 \times 1/2 \times 1/2 \times 3 \times 3 \times 1 \times 2 = 3$$

$$m_8 = 1/2 \times 1/5 \times 1/3 \times 1/3 \times 2 \times 1 \times 1/3 \times 1$$
$$= 0.0007$$

Then
$$w_1 = 0.761, w_2 = 3.121, w_3 = 1.861, w_4 = 1.861$$
$$w_5 = 0.361, w_6 = 0.542, w_7 = 1.147, w_8 = 0.542,$$
Standardize the $W = (w_1, w_2, \cdots, w_8)$ and

$$w_1 = 0.761 / (0.761 + 3.121 + 1.861 + 1.861 + 0.361$$
$$+ 0.542 + 1.147 + 0.542) = 0.075$$

Similarly, $w_2 = 0.306$, $w_3 = 0.183$, $w_4 = 0.183$, $w_5 = 0.035$, $w_6 = 0.053$, $w_7 = 0.113$, $w_8 = 0.053$.

Table 1. Judgment matrix

Index	U1	U2	U3	U4	U5	U6	U7	U8
U1	1	1/5	1/4	1/4	3	2	1/2	2
U2	5	1	2	2	6	5	3	5
U3	4	1/2	1	1	4	3	2	3
U4	4	1/2	1	1	4	3	2	3
U5	1/3	1/6	1/4	1/4	1	1/2	1/3	1/2
U6	1/2	1/5	1/3	1/3	2	1	1/3	1
U7	2	1/3	1/2	1/2	3	3	1	2
U8	1/2	1/5	1/3	1/3	2	1	1/2	1

Then calculate maximum feature value $\lambda_{\max}$ as follows.

$(\mathrm{AW})_1 = 0.655, (\mathrm{AW})_2 = 2.491,$
$(\mathrm{AW})_3 = 1.502, (\mathrm{AW})_4 = 1.502,$
$(\mathrm{AW})_5 = 0.293, (\mathrm{AW})_6 = 0.435,$
$(\mathrm{AW})_7 = 0.918, (\mathrm{AW})_8 = 0.441$

$\lambda_{\max} = 1/8 * (0.655/0.075 + 2.491/0.306 + 1.502/$
$0.183 + 1.502/0.183 + 0.293/0.035 + 0.435/$
$0.053 + 0.918/0.113 + 0.441/0.053) = 8.288$

$\mathrm{CI} = (\lambda_{\max} - n)/(n-1) = 0.288/7 = 0.041$

$\mathrm{CR} = \mathrm{CI}/\mathrm{RI} = 0.041/1.41 = 0.029 < 0.1,$

which satisfy the consistency requirements.

4.3.2. Weight Calculation of Sub-criteria

$W(B1, B2) = (0.875, 0.125),$

$W(C1, C2, C3) = (0.310, 0.110, 0.580),$

$W(D1, D2) = (0.833, 0.167),$

$W(F1, F2) = (0.750, 0.250),$

$W(G1, G2) = (0.750, 0.250),$

$W(H1, H2) = (0.454, 0.454, 0.092).$

Calculate comprehensive weights of sub-criteria indexes corresponding to the goal evaluation, and Table 2 is the result.

4.3.3. Range Transformation

Each index data is generally divided into four types such as benefit index, cost index, fixed index and interval index.

For the benefit index, using the formula:

$$y_{ij} = (x_{ij} - \min x_{ij})/(\max x_{ij} - \min x_{ij});$$

For the cost index, using the formula:

$$y_{ij} = (\min x_{ij} - x_{ij})/(\max x_{ij} - \min x_{ij});$$

For a fixed index, firstly use the formula $\left| fix\ value - x_{ij} \right|$ to transform data into standard type, then use the cost index formula;

Table 2. Comprehensive weights of sub-criteria indexes

Index	Weights	Index	Weights
Total Logistics Cost	0.075	Procurement response time	0.035
Procurement Cycle	0.268	Lead Time of Completing Order	0.040
Average Transportation Time	0.038	Order Completing Cycle	0.013
Qualified Ratio of Delivery	0.057	Order Fulfillment Rate	0.085
Qualified Rate of Incoming Materials	0.020	Order Response Speed	0.028
Ratio of The Purchase Order with High Quality	0.106	Goal Congruence	0.024
Delivery On-time Rate	0.152	System Cooperation Ability	0.024
Fill Rate	0.031	Trust Level	0.005

For the interval index, firstly use the formula: upper limit value – date which exceeds the upper limit value or interval lower limit – date which exceeds the lower limit value, transform data into standard type, then reuse the cost formula.

4.3.4. Final Evaluation Value

According to the score vectors and weight vector of index system, final evaluation value H of supply logistics system can be obtained.

$$H = \sum_{i=1}^{n} w_i M_i \qquad (7)$$

According to value H the coordination performance of manufacturing enterprise in supply logistics system can be determined. The larger the value H is, the better coordination ability the enterprises have.

4.3.5. Original Indexes Data and Range Change

Original indexes data and each index weights for three enterprises such as A, B, C are shown in Table 3.

Through calculation, H_A=0.3229, H_B=0.575, H_c=0.50025

From the data, we can see $H_B > H_C > H_A$. Coordination performance of enterprise B in supply logistics system is best, and coordination performance of enterprise A is the worst. And from the above table, enterprise A is inefficient in several aspects such as the interior of the time, external reliability, flexibility, customer service, and enterprise B are inadequate mainly in aspects of the inner cost, quality and the external system adaptability, and enterprise C is deficiency mainly in several aspects such as the interior of the time, external flexibility and responsiveness.

Table 3. Original indexes data and final index weights

Index	Original data			Results after range transformation			weights
	A	B	C	A	B	C	
Total Logistics Cost	**56million**	**65 million**	**62 million**	**1**	**0**	**0.333**	**0.075**
Procurement Cycle	16days	12 days	14 days	0	1	0.5	0.268
Average Transportation Time	5 days	4 days	6 days	0.5	1	0	0.038
Qualified Ratio of Delivery	99.1%	99.5%	99.0%	0.2	1	0	0.057
Qualified Rate of Incoming Materials	98%	96%	96.5%	1	0	0.25	0.020
Ratio of The Purchase Order with High Quality	85%	84%	88%	0.25	0	1	0.106
Delivery On-time Rate	97%	96%	98%	0.5	0	1	0.152
Fill Rate	84%	90%	87%	0	1	0.5	0.031
Procurement response time	3 days	2 days	3 days	0	1	0	0.035
Lead Time of Completing Order	93%	91%	88%	1	0.6	0	0.040
Order Completing Cycle	10 days	9 days	11 days	0.5	1	0	0.013
Order Fulfillment Rate	99.5%	99.8%	99.3%	0.4	1	0	0.085
Order Response Speed	2 days	2 days	1 days	0	0	1	0.028
Goal Congruence	87cents	92 cents	88 cents	0	1	0.25	0.024
System Cooperation Ability	84 cents	81 cents	87 cents	0.5	0	1	0.024
Trust Level	90 cents	88 cents	92 cents	0.5	0	1	0.005

5. CONCLUSION

The future competition is no longer individual competition between the enterprises, but between the different supply chain. At present, the supply chain has been widely acknowledged and developed. Supply logistics system is connected with the external resources as one of the most important part in manufacturing enterprises, which embodies the thought of supply chain management, emphasizes the upstream supply chain cooperation and coordination between enterprises, and thus improves the competitiveness of the entire supply chain.

The paper conducted a preliminary study based on supply logistics system. In JIT environment, characteristic in supply logistics system was analyzed, and the hierarchy structure of coordination performance model was given as follows.

1. For a longtime, the research on this field has not been penetrated into by the academe, so that there are lots of blank even mistaken opinions. There is not a very good and systemic evaluation index system for the supply logistics. The main innovation of the paper is aimed at this one. From two respects of the supply logistics system such as internal and external system, a coordination index system of supply logistics system was created. In the internal system, the paper established index system from the cost, time and quality, and in the external system, index system from the aspects of the reliability, flexibility, responsiveness customer service and the adaptability were established. Finally the paper made a detailed description for each index.

2. The paper pointed out key issues of the supply logistics system in coordination evaluation and calculation process. The analytic hierarchy process was used effectively to solve several issues such as integration of the calculation model and the index system, standarlization of index value and so on.

ACKNOWLEDGMENT

The authors thank the anonymous referees for their comments and suggestions. This work was supported by the National Science Foundation of China (No.71102174, 70972005, 71072035), Program for New Century Excellent Talents in University, China (No. NCET-10-0043, NCET-10-0048), Beijing Natural Science Foundation, China(No.9102016), Excellent Young Teacher in Beijing institute of Technology, China(No.2010YC1307), and Basic Research in Beijing institute of Technology, China (No.20102142013).

REFERENCE

Akkermans, H., Bogerd, P., & van Doremalen, J. (2004). Travail, transparency and trust: A case study of computer-supported collaborative supply chain planning in high-tech electronics. *European Journal of Operational Research, 153*(2), 445–456. doi:10.1016/S0377-2217(03)00164-4

ARC Advisory Group. (2002). *Collaborative manufacturing management strategies*. Retrieved from http://www.slideshare.net/AChatha/collaborative-manufacturing-management-strategies

Bin, D., & Zhang, X. (2000). Supply chain oriented collaborative planning, forecasting and replenishment. *3*(1), 36-38.

Chandra, P., & Fisher, M. L. (1994). Coordination of production and distribution planning. *European Journal of Operational Research, 72*(3), 503–517. doi:10.1016/0377-2217(94)90419-7

Chen, F., Drezner, Z., Ryan, J. K., & Simchi-Levi, D. (2000). Quantifying the bullwhip effect in a simple supply chain: The impact of forecasting, lead times, and information. *Management Science, 46*(3), 436–443. doi:10.1287/mnsc.46.3.436.12069

Chen, S., & Chen, R. (1998). Manufacturer-supplier relationship in JIT environment: JIT purchasing and supply in Chinese automobile industry. *Journal of Industrial Engineering/Engineering Management, 12*(3), 46-52.

Chen, Z. (2004). Performance measures system for supply and demand coordination based on agile supply chain. *Computer Integrated Manufacturing Systems, 10*(1), 99–105.

Dong, G., Zhang, C., & Ma, L. (2006). Purchasing mode of supply chain based on JIT theory. *Modern Management Science*, (2), 93-94.

Dudek, G., & Stadtler, H. (2005). Negotiation-based collaborative planning between supply chains partners. *European Journal of Operational Research, 163*(3), 668–687. doi:10.1016/j.ejor.2004.01.014

Ellinger, A. E. (2000). Improving marketing/logistics cross-functional collaboration in the supply chain. *Industrial Marketing Management, 29*, 85–96. doi:10.1016/S0019-8501(99)00114-5

Fu, Y., & Piplani, R. (2004). Supply-side collaboration and its value in supply chains. *European Journal of Operational Research, 152*, 281–288. doi:10.1016/S0377-2217(02)00670-7

Helo, P. T. (2000). Dynamic modeling of surge effect and capacity limitation in supply chains. *International Journal of Production Research, 38*(17), 4521–4533. doi:10.1080/00207540050205271

Huo, J., Sui, M., & Liu, Z. (2002). Construction of integrated supply chain performance measurement system. *Journal of Tongji University, 30*(4), 495–499.

IBM. (n. d.). *Collaborative supply chain management solution from IBM.* Retrieved from http://www-03.ibm.com/industries/ca/en/retail/col_sup_mgmt_bus.html

Jiang, F., Zhu, C., & Xu, L. (2007). The construction of the evaluation index system of integration supply chain. *Journal of Jingling Institute of Technology, 21*(3), 46–51.

Liu, L. (2001). Material purchasing strategy in supply chain management. *Chinese Journal of Management Science, 9*(3), 49–54.

Luo, M., Ma, W., & Zhou, Y. (2007). Study on SC performance evaluation index system under the life cycle. *Logistics Technology, 26*(10), 81–84.

Mason-Jones, R., & Towill, D. R. (1999). Total cycle time compression and the agile supply chain. *International Journal of Production Economics, 62*(1-2), 61–73. doi:10.1016/S0925-5273(98)00221-7

McIvor, R., Humphreys, P., & McCurry, L. (2003). Electronic commerce: supporting collaboration in the supply chain. *Journal of Materials Processing Technology, 139*(1-3), 147–152. doi:10.1016/S0924-0136(03)00196-1

Ren, J. (2005). *Research on two-echelon supply chain collaboration based on just-in-time purchase.* Unpublished master's thesis, Northeastern University, Boston, MA.

Schneeweiss, C., & Zimmer, K. (2004). Hierarchical coordination mechanisms within the supply chain. *European Journal of Operational Research, 153*, 687–703. doi:10.1016/S0377-2217(02)00801-9

Shi, L., & Zhan, C. (2002). Research on outside effects evaluation system of supply chain management enterprise. *Journal of Harbin University of Commerce*, (4), 49-50.

Tang, X., & Huang, Y. (2005). Application of synergetics in supply chain coordination. *Journal of Information*, (8), 23-25.

Teruaki, I., & Salleh, M. R. (2000). A blackboard-based negotiation for collaborative supply chain system. *Journal of Materials Processing Technology, 107*(1-3), 398–403. doi:10.1016/S0924-0136(00)00730-5

Thomas, D. J., & Griffin, P. M. (1996). Coordinated supply chain management. *European Journal of Operational Research, 96*, 1–15. doi:10.1016/0377-2217(96)00098-7

Tomlin, B. (2009). Impact of supply learning when suppliers are unreliable. *Manufacturing & Service Operations Management, 11*(2), 192–209. doi:10.1287/msom.1070.0206

Tomlin, B., & Wang, Y. (2005). On the value of mix flexibility and dual sourcing in unreliable newsvendor networks. *Manufacturing & Service Operations Management, 7*(1), 37–57. doi:10.1287/msom.1040.0063

Turkay, M., Oruc, C., Fujita, K., & Asakura, T. (2004). Computer-assisted supply chain configuration based on supply chain operations reference (SCOR) model. *Computers & Chemical Engineering, 28*, 985–992.

Van Mieghem, J. A. (2003). Capacity management, investment, and hedging: Review and recent developments. *Manufacturing & Service Operations Management, 5*(4), 269–302. doi:10.1287/msom.5.4.269.24882

Wang, P., Chen, R., Ji, X., & Zhang, J. (2005). Strategies of JIT purchasing in automobile industry. *Journal of WUT (Information & Management Engineering), 27*(4), 259-271.

Yang, W., Ma, S., & Li, L. (2004). Coordinated planning model based on response time of supply chain. *Forecasting, 23*(5), 52–56.

Zhou, J., & Wang, D. (2001). Production planning model for supply chain for multi-location plants and distributors. *Information and Control, 30*(2), 169–172.

This work was previously published in the International Journal of Advanced Pervasive and Ubiquitous Computing, Volume 3, Issue 1, edited by Tao Gao, pp. 16-28, copyright 2011 by IGI Publishing (an imprint of IGI Global).

Chapter 4
The WiMap:
A Dynamic Indoor WLAN Localization System

Junjun Xu
Beijing University of Posts and Telecommunications, China

Rui Tao
Beijing University of Posts and Telecommunications, China

Haiyong Luo
Institute of Computing Technology Chinese Academy of Sciences, China

Yiming Lin
Institute of Computing Technology Chinese Academy of Sciences, China

Fang Zhao
Beijing University of Posts and Telecommunications, China

Hui Li
Institute of Computing Technology Chinese Academy of Sciences, China

ABSTRACT

As positioning technology is an important foundation of the Internet of Things, a dynamic indoor WLAN localization system is proposed in this paper. This paper mainly concentrates on the design and implementation of the WiMap-a dynamic indoor WLAN localization system, which employs grid-based localization method using RSS (received signal strength). To achieve high localization accuracy and low computational complexity, Gaussian mixture model is applied to approximate the signal distribution and a ROI (region of interest) is defined to limit the search region. The authors also discuss other techniques like AP selection and threshold control, which affects the localization accuracy. The experimental results indicate that an accuracy of 3m with 73.8% probability can be obtained in WiMap. Moreover, the running time is reduced greatly with limited ROI method.

DOI: 10.4018/978-1-4666-2645-4.ch004

1. INTRODUCTION

From the Internet of Things architecture it can be seen that people utilize RFID and sensors to access to a wide variety of information from the physical world; the information has spread through the network to the end user or server, providing users with a variety of services. Meanwhile, all collected information must be associated with the specific location information of sensors; otherwise the information will not make any sense. So it can be said that the positioning technology is an important foundation of the Internet of Things.

The WiMap system is implemented in the context of 802.11 wireless LANs (IEEE Computer Society, 2009) and devoted to achieve high accuracy indoor localization with light computational complexity. Nowadays most commonly used methods to calculate the unknown position of a target includes Proximity Sensing, Lateration, Angulation and Dead Reckoning; and many of these methods when used alone give levels of accuracy which are insufficient for most users (Curran, Furey, Lunney, Santos, & Woods, 2009). WiMap uses RSS (Received Signal Strength) to locate the mobile target.

Like most researches -21] on localization systems (Bahl & Padmanabhan, 2000; Bahl, Padmanabhan, & Balachandran, 2000; Youssef & Agrawala, 2005; Kushi, Plataniotis, & Venetsanopoulos, 2010; Ngyuen, Jordan, & Sinopoli, 2005; Addesso, Bruno, & Restaino, 2010; Ji, Biaz, Pandey, & Agrawal, 2006; Chiou, Wang, Yeh, & Su, 2009), WiMap works in two phases: offline training phase and online positioning phase. During the offline phase, a radio map associating RSS with the selected known grid locations is established. During the online phase, WiMap tries to find the grid location in the radio map with the most "similar" signal characteristics.

The WiMap system locates the target by calculating the probability under the Bayesian framework. During the process of building the radio map, we assume the signal characteristic

satisfies the GMM (Gaussian mixture model), instead of single Gaussian model. And the EM (expectation-maximization) algorithm is used to calculate the parameters of GMM. And the state estimation of the mobile target is assumed to satisfy the Markov model. To lower the computational complexity, a ROI (region of interest) center with the last estimated grid location is outlined as the target searching area for the next localization. Moreover, AP selection is implemented to achieve both higher accuracy and less computational complexity by discriminating grid locations better and reducing the likelihood probability calculation range as a subset of all APs. However, these methods work well only in the premise that the last estimated results are reliable enough. Otherwise it just returns worse estimated results. So to solve this problem, we propose the threshold control technique that let the system carry out a global search in a larger ROI than the former one when the biggest posterior probability is less than some threshold value, which can be inferred from the experimental statistics. In this paper, we present the details of localization techniques and show how they work together to achieve its goal.

The rest of the paper is organized as follows: Section 2 provides an overview of the WLAN localization and related researches in the area. In Section 3 we present an overview of the WiMap system and introduce the models and the techniques used to achieve the goal. Section 4 shows the experimental results of our system and compares its accuracy to the accuracy without these techniques. Finally, Section 5 concludes the main findings of the paper and gives the future work to improve the WiMap system.

2. RELATED WORK

WLAN localization, based on whether using the trained dataset, can mainly be categorized into parameter-estimation-based technique or pattern-mapping technique. Parameter-estimation-based technique usually considers severe multipath and shadowing conditions and nonline-of-sight propagation caused by the presence of walls, humans and other objects in indoors (Kushi, Plataniotis, & Venetsanopoulos, 2010), trying to give the estimation through geometrically or statistically calculating distance, angle and connection information between unknown nodes and anchor points (nodes with known location). One such model is Goldsmith (2005):

$$P_r(dB) = P_t(dB) + 10 \log_{10} K - 10\gamma \log_{10}(d / d_0) - \psi(dB) \tag{1}$$

In this model, log-normal shadowing $\left(\psi(dB)\right)$ and path loss (γ) are considered.

Parameter-estimation-based technique usually has a higher efficiency, but due to the signals noises and environment factors, the unique solution to polynomial equation is hard to obtain. So the pattern-mapping technique is necessary.

Pattern-mapping also becomes complicated in indoor environment and it's hard to find a good mapping between RSS and location, vector of RSS in any location still reflects a discriminative characteristic of the location. The most typical pattern-mapping technique is fingerprinting. Fingerprinting uses a radio map to implicitly characterize the relationship between RSS and location through training the RSS values at anchor points whose locations are known. Traditionally, radio map is constructed in the training phase or so called offline phase, which is prior to the operation of the localization phase, or online phase.

In the offline phase, RSS values from different APs at different locations are collected to build up a radio map, which reflects the direct mapping between RSS and location and can avoid the localization error caused by the inaccurate mapping between RSS and distance. During building up the radio map, the location space can be discrete space represented by grids or continuous space represented by coordinates.

In the online phase, the real-time received RSS by the mobile target is used to "search" in the radio map for location. This "search" method can be deterministic or probabilistic. The former represents the signal strength received from an AP at a location by a scalar value such as the mean value and uses deterministic approaches like nearest neighborhood technique, which is proposed in the Radar system (Bahl & Padmanabhan, 2000; Bahl, Padmanabhan, & Balachandran, 2000) to infer the target location. The latter, however, would use probability distribution such as Gaussian distribution to calculate the statistic characteristic of each location beforehand, and employs probabilistic techniques such as the Bayesian Network approach, employed by the Nibble system (Castro, Chiu, Kremenek, & Muntz, 2001; Castro & Muntz, 2000) to estimate the target location. Roos, Myllymaki, Tirri, Misikangas, and Sievanen (2002) and Kontkanen, Myllymaki, Roos, Tirri, Valtonen, and Wettig (2004) compare deterministic approaches with probabilistic ones and proves theoretically that the probabilistic ones can achieve higher accuracy.

In this paper, we introduce the RSS-grid based WiMap system, under Bayesian estimation framework, using Gaussian mixture model to capture the RSS-location relationship. The prior probability is provided by the pedestrian motion model based on Markov model. The likelihood probability is calculated from the Gaussian mixture distribution. So the posterior probability is obtained and the grid location with the largest posterior value is returned. Moreover, if one estimated result goes too far from the true location, it may corrupt the following estimation process. So a threshold control is employed to solve this problem. The further the estimation is from the true location, the more different the observed RSS characteristic is from the grid of interest, with the result of relatively small likelihood probability, so is the posterior probability. And once the largest posterior probability is less than some threshold, WiMap would search the grid again, in a global range, instead of in the region of interest.

3. THE WIMAP SYSTEM

In the section, we present the overview and main modules of WiMap.

A. Overview

WiMap is RSS-grid based localization system containing four main modules: sampling module, training module, positioning module and threshold control module. Figure 1 shows the workflow of these modules. Sampling module stores RSS and grid information in the database. Training module uses Gaussian mixture model to describe the signal distribution of each grid and obtains the parameter through Expectation-Maximization algorithm. Positioning module estimates the target location based on the observed RSS, and re-estimates the location in a larger ROI if the threshold control module "regards" it's necessary. As we can see in Figure 2, positioning module estimates the location through the upper three steps in normal situation. If the control returns to positioning module from the threshold control module, the positioning module would go through the lower two steps in Figure 2 to re-estimate the location in a larger ROI, as "Global Search" in the figure. Threshold control module examines the largest posterior probability calculated by the positioning module and determines if it's necessary to do a global search.

The following explains each module in details.

B. Sampling Module

Sampling module records RSS values received from APs and the corresponding grid locations. Let $MR_i = \{(m_1, r_1) \ldots (m_k, r_k)\}$ be one-time sample data sampled in grid G_i. r_i is the RSS value received from the AP with mac address m_i. Due to the temporal and spatial features of signal, more than one sample are necessary for each grid. The sampling frequency is related to the number of APs, room size and other factors. Here we take 30 samples for each grid.

C. Training Module

Based on the samples and grids the sampling module stored in the database, we can construct a radio map $R = \{(G_i, F_{Gi})\}_{i=1}^{N}$, where G_i is the grid number, $F_{Gi} = \{mr_i(1) \ldots mr_i(k)\}$, $mr_i(j)$ is a vector of RSS values received from the jth AP.

Due to the complex indoors factors such as temperature changes, humidity changes, multi-path and shadowing effect, the wireless signals of AP can significantly vary under different temporal and spatial conditions (as shown in Figure 3). And single Gaussian model is obviously not qualified to fit the signal strength data. So we employ Gaussian Mixture Model (GMM) to train the RSS. The M-dimension mixture model is represented as:

Figure 1. WiMap workflow

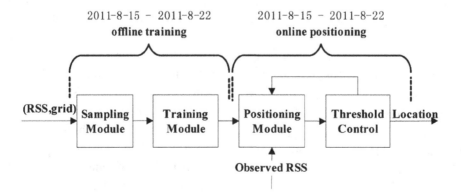

Figure 2. Positioning module workflow

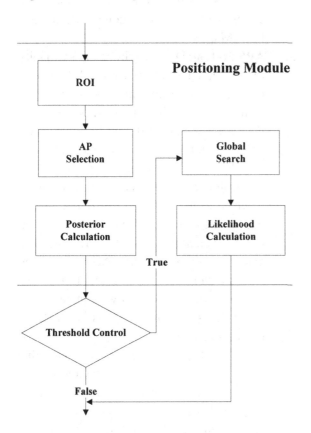

$$p(x \mid \Theta) = \sum_{i=1}^{M} \alpha_i p_i(x \mid \theta_i) \qquad (2)$$

$$\Theta = (\alpha_1, \ldots, \alpha_M, \ \theta_1, \ldots, \theta_M), \ \sum_{i=1}^{M} \alpha_i = 1. \ p \text{ is}$$

the probability of location x under GMM with parameter Θ. α_i denotes the weight value of the one single Gaussian $p_i(x \mid \theta_i)$. θ_i is the mean and variance (μ_i, Σ_i) for the ith Gaussian.

We employ Expectation-Maximization algorithm to obtain Θ, the key parameters of GMM. Given the initial guess parameter Θ^g, what we need do is maximize

$$Q(\Theta, \Theta^g) = \sum_{i=1}^{M} \sum_{j=1}^{N} \log(\alpha_i) p(i \mid x_j, \Theta^g)$$
$$+ \sum_{i=1}^{M} \sum_{j=1}^{N} \log[p_i(x_j \mid \theta_i)] p(i \mid x_j, \Theta^g)$$
$$(3)$$

According to Dempster, Laird, and Rubin (1977), Redner and Walker (1984), and Xu and Jordan (1996) (μ_i, Σ_i) can be calculated through the iteration of the following recurrence relations.

Figure 3. Signal strength of two randomly selected APs

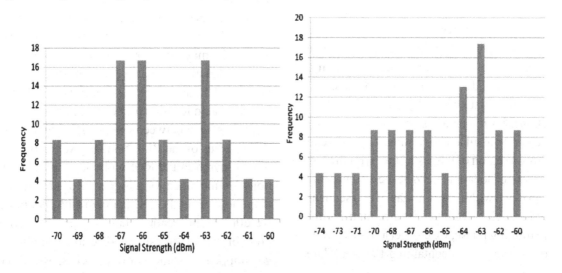

$$\alpha_i^{new} = \frac{1}{N}\sum_{j=1}^{N} p(i \mid x_j, \Theta^g) \qquad (4)$$

$$\mu_i^{new} = \sum_{j=1}^{N} x_j p(i \mid x_j, \Theta^g) \bigg/ \sum_{j=1}^{N} p(i \mid x_j, \Theta^g) \qquad (5)$$

$$\Sigma_i^{new} =$$
$$\sum_{j=1}^{N} p(i \mid x_j, \Theta^g)(x_j - \mu_i^{new})(x_j - \mu_i^{new})^T \bigg/ \sum_{j=1}^{N} p(i \mid x_j, \Theta^g) \qquad (6)$$

a. Positioning Module

Positioning module finds the location x that maximizes the probability $P(x/s)$, given a signal strength vector $r = (r_1 \dots r_k)$. i.e., argMax$[P(x/s)]$. According to Bayesian theory, this is equivalent to argMax$[P(x/s)]$ = argMax$[P(s/x)]$ (Moon & Stirling, 2000) And $P(s/x)$ can be calculated using radio map as:

$$P(s/x) = \prod_{i=1}^{n} P(s_i/x) \qquad (7)$$

This is the basic estimator formula for positioning. To get the posterior probability, we need to get the prior probability and likelihood probability.

1. **Region of Interest:** Consider the motion dynamics, people with the mobile node cannot reach a too long distance within a limited period of time, frequency of the signal (Kushki, Plataniotis, & Venetsanopoulos, 2006). So it's unnecessary to calculate the posterior in all anchor points. Thus, we can draw a region of interest center with the last estimated location. Let d be the distance one can reach within the time gap of two sequential signals, given the distance matrix built in training phase, we can get a subset (ROI) of anchor points containing the candidate locations. Through this way, computation complexity can also be reduced efficiently. In WiMap, $d = 3$m.

2. **AP Selection:** Due to environment's variability and signal instability, some APs maybe lost during the sampling process, when it comes to calculating $P(s/x)$, APs of current RSS values can be different from the set of APs in training phase. It's meaningless to calculate $P(s/x)$ if these two sets of APs are different. And normally signals can be received from more than a dozen of APs in one grid, so we compare current APs with APs from anchor points selected before, and generate a common set APs. At last, we select K APs with largest signal strength from the common set, with which we can calculate $P(s/x)$. This step can benefit us from at least two aspects:

   a. K APs selected can discriminate the characteristics across anchor points very well, resulting more accurate likelihood.

   b. Compared with calculating likelihood in all APs, the computation complexity caused by selecting APs is lowered.

b. Threshold Control

These modules mentioned can work very well in the premise that the last estimated location is close or the same with the true location. Otherwise, the results may get worse and worse. A reasonable explanation is that the prior outweighs the likelihood. Imagine such a scenario: Let G_i be the last estimated location and G_j be the true one we want. Distance between G_i and G_j is bigger than d, the radius of the ROI. So the next positioning would search in the ROI without G_j in it. Locations around G_i enjoy a bigger prior probability than those around G_j. This may result that those we-don't-want locations have a bigger posterior probability. So the estimated results can always get trapped in some confined areas, while the real location always runs out of the ROI. In order to solve this problem and catch up with the real location, we define a threshold T which is concluded from the statistical results, to make sure the result can get out of the confined areas. If the largest posterior probability is less than T, then a global positioning on a larger ROI is performed. By manually examining the posterior probability values and the mapping between the estimated locations with the real locations we logged, we can conclude a range for T and a value of D for the larger ROI. Through this global positioning the estimation can get out of the confined areas in time and give a more accurate result. The complete localization algorithm is shown in Figure 4.

4. EXPERIMENTS AND RESULTS

In this section, experiments are performed to verify the WiMap system and find the appropriate values for some parameters used in it. For comparison convenience, we change one single factor with other factors remaining the same.

D. Experiment Design

Experiments are performed in a real workplace, which is on the 7th floor of Institute of Computing Technology, China Academy of Sciences. The dimensions of this site are 16 m * 24 m, consisting of 196 grids. A total number of 60 APs, scattered in the experimental area, are all detectable throughout this floor, but none of them can cover this whole area. 30 samples are collected for each grid. The WiMap system is running under the Windows XP professional operating system.

E. Localization Accuracy

We show the performance of the modules and techniques employed in WiMap in the following sections.

Figure 4. Complete localization algorithm

Inputs:
  Observed RSS at time t: $r(t)$.
  Distance matrix of all grids: $M(G)$
  Posterior probability calculating function: $FP(R, M(G), r, g)$, R is the radio map mentioned before, r is observed RSS and g is grid number
  Likelihood probability calculating function: $FL(R, r, g)$
  Estimated grid location at time $t-1$: x_{t-1}
  ROI obtaining function: $FR(M(G), d, x)$, d is the ROI radius and x is the last estimated grid location
  Threshold value T
Outputs:
  Estimated grid location x_t at time t that maximizes $P(x/s)$
1: Max = 0
2: $ROI = FR(M(G), d, x_{t-1})$
3: **for** g **in** ROI
4:     $P = FP(R, M(G), r, g)$
5:     **if** $P >$ Max **then**
6:         $x = g$
7:         Max = P
8:     **end if**
9: **end for**
10: **if** Max $< T$ **then**
11:     $d = 3d$
12:     Max = 0
13:     $ROI = FR(M(G), d, x_{t-1})$
14:     **for** g **in** ROI
15:         $P = FL(R, r, g)$
16:         **if** $P >$ Max **then**
17:             $x = g$
18:             Max = P
19:         **end if**
20:     **end for**
21: **end if**

a. Training Module (GMM)

In Figure 5, we compare the effects brought by three different training techniques: Gaussian mixture model, single Gaussian model and Variance adjust technique (Youssef & Agrawala, 2005). Here we use three Gaussian distributions to make up a Gaussian mixture distribution. We can learn that the accuracy at the error distance of 3.0 m is increased from 40% to 64.2% by using Gaussian mixture model instead of single Gaussian model. It's also 12% higher than the Variance adjustment technique. That shows GMM can better depict the characteristic of signals.

b. AP Selection

Figure 6 plots the statistical results of accuracy at different error distance with different apNum in AP selection phase as mentioned. In this test of number of APs to select, make a comparison among 3 strongest APs to 8 strongest APs. It's impractical to cover a grid location with too many APs, so we select 8 as the largest number of APs.

At the error distance of 3.0 m, the accuracy can reach 73.8% with 3 APs selected at best. Like the intention of AP selection, less AP better characterize the grid and give a better result.

c. Threshold Control

Figure 7 depicts the results with different max-posterior thresholds values. From the statistical max-posteriors we logged we can learn that the max-posterior ranges from 0.0019 to 0.0044 and most of the values concentrate on the range from 0.0028 to 0.0040. Threshold T=0.0028~0.0030 gives the best result that the accuracy can reach 70.9% at the error distance of 3.0 m.

F. Complexity Analysis

a. ROI (Anchor Points Selection)

As for computation complexity, adding anchor points (ROI) and AP selection may bring some extra time complexity $O(N)$, the big O notation is used to provide an upper bound on the complexity and N is the number of grid locations. But the overall time complexity is $O(N) + K*O(R^2)$, K is the number of selected anchor points and R is the number of RSS values in one sample data. ($K<R<N$) Smaller than $O(N)*O(R)$, which is the computation complexity of the simple Bayesian model. The time cost without ROI is 1.612 seconds for one localization process, 0.272 seconds more than that one with ROI, which costs 1.34 seconds.

5. CONCLUSION

In this paper we present each module and localization techniques employed in the RSS-grid based WiMap indoor localization system. Due to the signal instability and environment variability, it's hard, even impossible, to get a model that can cover this problem completely precisely. So what we can do is to focus more on details and make some changes, such as handling the probability distribution with GMM, dealing with AP selection and defining a threshold to step out for global positioning. And our experimental results demonstrate that based on these techniques, the WiMap can achieve its goal: high accuracy and low computational complexity. However, WiMap fails to take the time-varying factor of signal into consideration and builds a static radio map, which requires lots of labor to update the RSS-grid dataset. In the future, we plan to improve the construction of radio map to a dynamic one, with reference points settled beforehand.

ACKNOWLEDGMENT

This work is supported in part by the National Natural Science Foundation of China under Grant No.60873244, No.60973110, No.61003307, the Natural Science Foundation of Beijing City of China under Grant No.4102059 and the Major Projects of Ministry of Industry and Information Technology under Grant No.2010ZX03006-002-03.

Figure 5. Accuracy at error distance with different techniques adopted in training phase

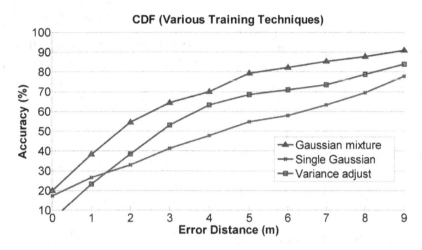

Figure 6. Accuracy at error distance with different numbers of APs selected

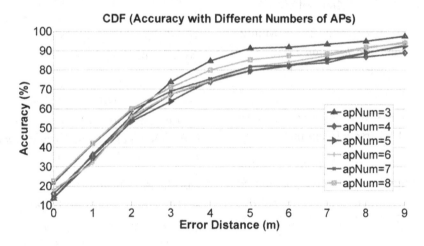

Figure 7. Accuracy at error distance with different threshold values

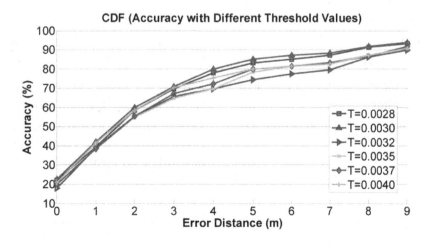

REFERENCES

Addesso, P., Bruno, L., & Restaino, R. (2010). Adaptive localization techniques in WiFi environments. In *Proceedings of the 5th International Symposium on Wireless Pervasive Computing* (pp. 289-294).

Bahl, P., & Padmanabhan, V. N. (2000). RADAR: An in-building RF-based user location and tracking system. In. *Proceedings of the IEEE International Conference on Computer Communications, 2,* 775–784.

Bahl, P., Padmanabhan, V. N., & Balachandran, A. (2000). *Enhancements to the RADAR user location and tracking system* (Tech. Rep. No. MSR-TR-00-12). Cambridge, UK: Microsoft Research.

Castro, P., Chiu, P., Kremenek, T., & Muntz, R. (2001). *A probabilistic location service for wireless network environments.* Ubiquitous Computing.

Castro, P., & Muntz, R. (2000). *Managing context for smart spaces.* IEEE Personal Communications.

Chiou, S.-Y. S., Wang, C.-L., Yeh, S.-C., & Su, M.-Y. (2009). Design of an adaptive positioning system based on wifi radio signals. *Computer Communications, 32*(7-10). doi:10.1016/j.comcom.2009.04.003

Curran, K., Furey, E., Lunney, T., Santos, J., & Woods, D. (2009). *An evaluation of indoor location determination technologies.* Northern Ireland, UK: University of Ulster.

Dempster, A. P., Laird, N. M., & Rubin, D. B. (1977). Maximum-likelihood from incomplete data via the em algorithm. *Journal of the Royal Statistical Society. Series B. Methodological, 39.*

Goldsmith, A. (2005). *Wireless communications.* Cambridge, UK: Cambridge University Press.

IEEE. Computer Society. (2009). *IEEE Standard 802.11 - Wireless LAN medium access control (MAC) and physical layer (PHY) specifications.* Washington, DC: IEEE Computer Society.

Ji, Y., Biaz, S., Pandey, S., & Agrawal, P. (2006). ARIADNE: A dynamic indoor signal map construction and localization system. In *Proceedings of the IEEE International Conference on Mobile System, Applications, and Services* (pp. 151-164).

Kontkanen, P., Myllymaki, P., Roos, T., Tirri, H., Valtonen, K., & Wettig, H. (2004). Topics in probabilistic location estimation in wireless networks. In *Proceedings of the 15th IEEE International Symposium on Personal, Indoor and Mobile Radio Communications,* Barcelona, Spain (Vol. 2, pp. 1052-1056).

Kushi, A., Plataniotis, K. N., & Venetsanopoulos, A. N. (2010). Intelligent dynamics radio tracking in indoor wireless local area networks. *IEEE Transactions on Mobile Computing, 9*(3), 405–419. doi:10.1109/TMC.2009.141

Kushki, A., Plataniotis, K., & Venetsanopoulos, A. N. (2006). Location tracking in wireless local area networks with adaptive radio maps. In. *Proceedings of the IEEE International Conference on Acoustics, Speech, and Signal Processing, 5,* 741–744.

Moon, T. K., & Stirling, W. C. (2000). *Mathematical methods and algorithms for signal processing.* Upper Saddle River, NJ: Prentice Hall.

Ngyuen, X., Jordan, M., & Sinopoli, B. (2005). A kernel-based learning approach to ad hoc sensor network localization. *ACM Transactions on Sensor Networks, 1*(1), 134–152. doi:10.1145/1077391.1077397

Redner, R., & Walker, H. (1984). Mixture densities, maximum likelihood and the em algorithm. *SIAM Review*, *26*(2). doi:10.1137/1026034

Roos, T., Myllymaki, P., Tirri, H., Misikangas, P., & Sievanen, J. (2002). A probabilistic approach to WLAN user location estimation. *International Journal of Wireless Information Networks*, *9*(3), 155–164. doi:10.1023/A:1016003126882

Xu, L., & Jordan, M. I. (1996). On convergence properties of the em algorithm for Gaussian mixtures. *Neural Computation*, *8*, 129–151. doi:10.1162/neco.1996.8.1.129

Youssef, M., & Agrawala, A. (2005). The Horus WLAN location determination system. In *Proceedings of the Third International Conference on Mobile Systems, Applications, and Services* (pp. 205-218).

This work was previously published in the International Journal of Advanced Pervasive and Ubiquitous Computing, Volume 3, Issue 1, edited by Tao Gao, pp. 29-38, copyright 2011 by IGI Publishing (an imprint of IGI Global).

Chapter 5
A Novel Design of Motion Detector Using Mouse Sensor

Boning Zhang
Institute of Computing Technology, Chinese Academy of Sciences and Graduate University of Chinese Academy of Sciences, China

Xiangdong Wang
Institute of Computing Technology, Chinese Academy of Sciences, China

Yueliang Qian
Institute of Computing Technology, Chinese Academy of Sciences, China

Shouxun Lin
Institute of Computing Technology, Chinese Academy of Sciences, China

ABSTRACT

This paper presents a novel design using a mouse sensor to construct a system for motion detection in normal vision environment. A mouse sensor is packed under an optical mouse for detecting the motion of mouse on desktop and sending out the data and parameters to a controller or a computer directly. This paper introduces this kind of sensor to vision motion detection field by designing and building a circuit system. The feasibility of the design is demonstrated and degree of reliability is measured by experiments performed on the designed system. Additionally the authors point out the advantages of this design in comparison with other traditional methods or devices in brief.

1. INTRODUCTION

Due to various demands and applications, motion detection has become an important field of digital and semiconductor technologies, which is attracting more and more attention. In traditional vision motion detection, CCD and CMOS sensors are widely used, mostly with a complex servo in background such as a server of a DSP (Digital Signal Processor) with a customized algorithm. Therefore, a new conception which is cheaper to build, easier to develop, more portable, and more reliable to use is desired by engineers and users.

DOI: 10.4018/978-1-4666-2645-4.ch005

A number of de-interlacing algorithms are widely and commonly adopted in the motion detection field (Han, Shin, Choi, & Park, 1999; Lee, Chang, & Jen, 1991; Shahinfard, Sid-Ahmed, & Ahmadi, 2008) which are based on TV signal. However, the improved fabrication technology and architecture bring forward some other applications based on CMOS Image Sensors (CIS) directly (Ma & Chen, 1999; Sohn, Kim, Lee, Lee, & Kim, 2003). Lately, SOC replaced the foregoing techniques and became the dominate technology in motion detection area for its low power consuming and compatibility. But sometimes SOC costs a long development cycle because of the developer must grasp the overall situation of hardware and software.

During the past several years, the progress of the optical navigation area has leaded us to a new period of time that solid-state optical mouse has inevitability become a new standard. Inspired by the mouse devices and considering the situation of motion diction, we attempted to use the mouse CMOS sensor which is in low resolution ratio for motion detection. An experimental system was built tentatively to validate this idea. The feasibility of the design is demonstrated and degree of reliability is measured by experiments performed on the designed system.

In this paper, Section 2 will introduce what is mouse CMOS sensor, and explain the elements of it. Section 3 is the design of it that prototype is showed. In Section 4, we designed a series of experiments to test the system in resolution, color, texture, and luminance. Then advice is given for the application that needs the function with this module.

MOUSE CMOS SENSOR

The heart of an optical mouse is a mini camera in low-resolution. Just as Figure 1 showed that the navigation LED in the mouse illuminates a surface, and the light reflects off the surface to the lens. When the mouse is moved, the mini camera of the

Figure 1. Mouse structure

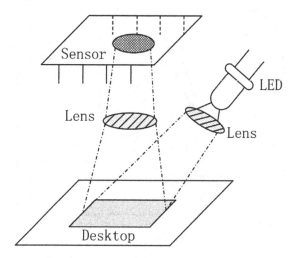

mouse (the sensor) takes continuous snapshots of the surface. The built-in digital signal processor (DSP) would process the data and determine the distance and direction of the movement. Then the micro-controller will send the result to the PC via the USB wire or other communication channel.

Figure 2 displays the algorithm of motion detection in the mouse DSP. When the mouse is moved, image A and B are captured by the CMOS sensor continuously. Ref is the same sub-image on both A and B, so that it can be a reference of image for A and B. In other words, it must be made sure that there is something on the image which is captured by the CMOS sensor. Then the DSP will figure out the vector of the movement based on the reference.

Because the resolution of CMOS of mouse senor is very low (about 200 pixel in our prototype), and the DSP is making use of the algorithm for simple figure and point, the cost of the processor is low. So this is the reason of low power and high speed.

2. DESIGN

In this section, we presents a novel design taking full advantage of the mouse sensor introduced above to achieve motion detection with lower cost and faster response.

Figure 2. Sketch map for motion detection algorithm

Figure 3 shows how we change the typical usage of mouse sensor to a novel one, where we abandon the desktop and put the chip upside and replace the single lens with an optical camera lens. Therefore, an optical path is generated and the image will appear on the CMOS. Then the motion of object which we are concerning about can be detected by the sensor.

The high level design of the system is illustrated by Figure 4, which is simple to implement. A controller is used for sequential process control. In our work, an AVR MCU is chosen for this role. For this prototype, we choose the mouse sensor model: ADNS5030. This IC provide an I^2C (Inter Integrated Circuit) communication port to transmit data. Since I^2C bus has a lot of advantages such as small footprint, low cost, long distance,

high speed transmit etc., this bus is quite suitable for this project. Then we put an output modular here not only to display the result of our testing, but also for future expanding.

Figure 5 is the prototype of this design. The circuit is divided to two parts: control board and sensor camera. The MCU is on the control board, which has done most of the job: initializing the sensor, reading the sensor state, transmitting the data to the USB port IC, and displaying result by the LED on the board. On the right is the mouse sensor which is packed in a small plastic box as a light tight box. The wire not only provides a communication way but also the power supply. The power for this system is provided via the USB port because only less than 100mA current is required.

3. EXPERIMENTAL RESULTS

We have made a prototype to show off the feasibility of the system. In order to measure the reliability of the system, a series of testing in which statistic analysis is widely used are conducted for the mouse sensor.

Analysis shows out the most important characters and parameters of the mouse sensor: resolution, color, material, luminance, sampling rate. A targeted test method is brought forward here.

Figure 3. Novel application

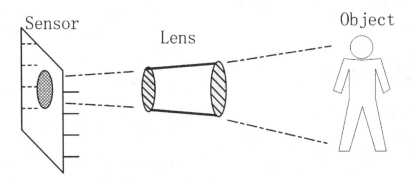

Figure 4. High level structure for prototype

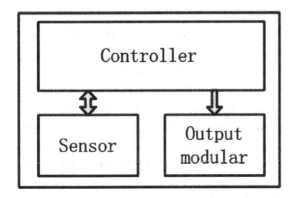

Figure 5. Proto picture

Resolution Testing

For resolution testing we design a method shown in Figure 6. Paper with a point of different size on each page is used for this testing. During the testing, each page is moved before the camera lens in a constant speed. Then the result feedback is read by the interface of the circuit. Accuracy is the statistical data for 20 times experiment. The exact size of the CMOS on ANDS5030 is not provided on the datasheet, therefore we cannot figure out the proportion of the scale of the point's image.

For each size of point, Table 1 gives the result of the testing. The result is interesting that A B C are incremental changing but D. The reason of the increment the resolution of the sensor is so low that if the point is too small the point maybe cannot occupy just a whole pixel on the CMOS.

Along with the size increment the point will take over the part of CMOS more to better result. But when situation point D, it is too big to only be a part on CMOS but the whole.

Color Testing

Since generally mouse only uses red LED, the effect of other colors is kept unknown and is necessary to be investigated. The same method is suitable for this one, except that we replace the black points with colored blocks.

It is inferred that the CMOS sensor of mouse is with achromatopsia from the data of Table 2. It is the most unexpected that the red is not the worst but the yellow and orange. We think the reason of Yellow getting zero is that the contrast between yellow and the background white is very low, and the sensor cannot tell it out.

Figure 6. Point for testing

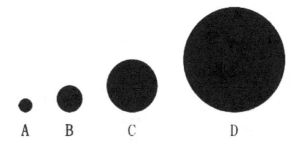

Table 1. Result of resolution testing

Point Name	A	B	C	D
Size of Point(mm)	5	10	20	30
Accuracy Rating	35%	80%	90%	80%
Image Distance		100mm		
Parameters of Camera Lens		1.9mm1/3 M12 F2.5		
Luminance of Environment		93Lux		

Table 2. Result of color testing

Color	Red	Orange	Yellow	Green	Blue
Accuracy Rating	45%	20%	0%	75%	90%
Background Color		White			
Size of Color Block		10mm x 10 mm			
Image Distance		100mm			
Parameters of Camera Lens		1.9mm1/3 M12 F2.5			
Luminance of Environment		93Lux			

Table 3. Texture testing

Pic Name	A	B	C	D	E
Accuracy Rating	100%	90%	95%	100%	90%
Image Distance		150mm			
Parameters of Camera Lens		1.9mm1/3 M12 F2.5			
Luminance of Environment		93Lux			

Table 4. Luminance testing

Luminance(Lux)	30	60	90	120	150
Accuracy Rating	5%	60%	90%	100%	100%
Image Distance		150mm			
Parameters of Camera Lens		1.9mm1/3 M12 F2.5			

Material Testing

Mouse is designed for the desktop application, so the material of the desktop will affect the mouse function. Optical mouse cannot be used on a smooth surface because the picture captured by the CMOS sensor is blank. The five different textures shown in Figure 7 are used for testing, using the same testing method.

The performance of the sensor in this testing is pretty good. All results are equal to or above 90%. It can be seen that the texture with high contract and the points in large scale gets the best 100% (Table 3).

Luminance Testing

The last testing is for luminance (Table 4). Being an optical sensor, the luminance sensitivity is an important target. We measure the luminance of the environment and calculate the accuracy rate. Experimental result shows that when the luminance gets to about 90Lux, we can get ideal result.

All in all, we can infer from the results before that this kind of motion detection modules can be used in the environment which satisfies some condition that adequate lighting is provided and a proper camera lens is equipped.

Figure 7. Texture for testing

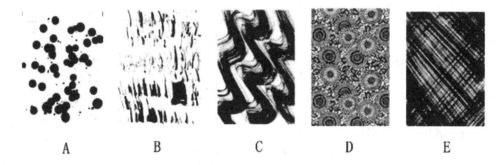

A   B   C   D   E

4. CONCLUSION

This paper describes a novel design for motion detection, and a prototype device is made for testing. Performance and parameters are good as expected. This kind of devices has a lot of advantage like small volume, low power, low price. So it would play an important role in the security, auto control field etc.

REFERENCES

Han, D., Shin, C.-Y., Choi, S.-J., & Park, J.-S. (1999). A motion adaptive 3-D de-interlacing algorithm based on the brightness profile pattern difference. *IEEE Transactions on Consumer Electronics, 45*(3), 690–697. doi:10.1109/30.793572

Lee, C. L., Chang, S., & Jen, C. W. (1991, June). Motion detection and motion adaptive pro-scan conversion. In. *Proceedings of the IEEE International Symposium on Circuits and Systems, 1*, 666–669.

Ma, S.-Y., & Chen, L.-G. (1999). A single-chip CMOS APS camera with direct frame difference output. *IEEE Journal of Solid-state Circuits, 34*, 1415–1418. doi:10.1109/4.792618

Shahinfard, E., Sid-Ahmed, M. A., & Ahmadi, M. (2008, October). A motion adaptive deinterlacing method with hierarchical motion detection algorithm. In *Proceedings of the 15th IEEE International Conference on Image Processing* (pp. 889-892).

Sohn, S.-M., Kim, S.-H., Lee, S.-H., Lee, K.-J., & Kim, S. (2003). A CMOS image sensor (CIS) architecture with low power motion detection for portable security camera applications. *IEEE Transactions on Consumer Electronics, 49*(4), 1227–1233. doi:10.1109/TCE.2003.1261221

This work was previously published in the International Journal of Advanced Pervasive and Ubiquitous Computing, Volume 3, Issue 1, edited by Tao Gao, pp. 39-44, copyright 2011 by IGI Publishing (an imprint of IGI Global).

Chapter 6
Identifying Disease Genes Based on Functional Annotation and Text Mining

Fang Yuan
Shenzhen Institute of Information Technology, China

Mingliang Li
Shenzhen Institute of Information Technology, China

Jing Li
Huawei Technologies Corporation, China

ABSTRACT

The identification of disease genes from candidated regions is one of the most important tasks in bioinformatics research. Most approaches based on function annotations cannot be used to identify genes for diseases without any known pathogenic genes or related function annotations. The authors have built a new web tool, DGHunter, to predict genes associated with these diseases which lack detailed function annotations. Its performance was tested with a set of 1506 genes involved in 1147 disease phenotypes derived from the morbid map table in the OMIM database. The results show that, on average, the target gene was in the top 13.60% of the ranked lists of candidates, and the target gene was in the top 5% with a 40.70% chance. DGHunter can identify disease genes effectively for those diseases lacking sufficient function annotations.

1. INTRODUCTION

The identification of genes involved in inherited human diseases plays an important role in elucidating pathogenesis and developing diagnosis and prevention measures. Through complex-trait linkage studies, many disease genes are located within one or more specific chromosomal regions (McCarthy, Smedley, & Hide, 2003). It is time-consuming and labor-intensive to perform random mutation analysis for the hundreds of genes in the regions of interest. Clearly, predicting the best candidate genes by computational approaches is necessary to facilitate the identification of disease-related genes for further study.

DOI: 10.4018/978-1-4666-2645-4.ch006

Disease phenotypes provide a window into the gene function. Franke et al. (2006) observed that GO annotation is the most effective data resource, and the accuracy based on GO was slightly improved by adding other types of data. Several approaches to identify disease related genes based on function annotations have been presented in recent years (Perez-Iratxeta, Bork, & Andrade, 2002; Perez-Iratxeta, Wjst, Bork, & Andrade, 2005; Perez-Iratxeta, Bork, & Andrade-Navarro, 2007; Turner, Clutterbuck, & Semple, 2003). However,these tools often suffer from annotation bias as they cannot deal with diseases lacking known causative genes. Neither can these tools handle known genes lacking sufficiently detailed function annotations. The phenotype method of G2D developed by Perez-Iratxeta et al. can be used to make prediction for those diseases (Perez-Iratxeta, Bork, & Andrade, 2002; Perez-Iratxeta, Wjst, Bork, & Andrade, 2005). It firstly mines the disease-related GO terms from the MEDLINE/PubMed database, then associates the RefSeq sequence with the disease according to their function annotations, finally prioritizes the candidate genes by sequence similarity searches. The assumptions of this method are that similar sequences are paralogs, and that paralogs have the same or similar function. However, function similarity does not always require sequence similarity. For example, both P53 (Vogelstein & Kinzler, 1992) and BRCA1 (Thompson, Jensen, Obermiller, Page, & Holt, 1995) function as tumor suppressor genes. Similar to BRCA1, mutations in P53 have also been found in breast cancer patients (Davidoff, Humphrey, Iglehart, & Marks, 1991). However, the two genes share no sequence homology. As a result, sequence similarity may not be able to reveal functional similarity. Therefore, the assumptions could easily produce false-positive and false-negative results.

To avoid this problem, we have developed a computational web tool, DGHunter. It allows users to predict candidated causative genes for a genetic disease lacking known causative genes. Starting with the assumption that genes involved in phenotypically similar diseases share similarity in their functional annotation (Jimenez-Sanchez, Barton, & David, 2001) DGHunter makes prediction by using a combination of text mining and gene-function similarity analysis. The process of the text mining of DGHunter adopts similar approach as that of G2D, and the function-similarity analysis uses a novel algorithm based on the GO directed acyclic graphs (DAG). More details can be found in the following sections.

2. METHODS

2.1. The Flowchart of DGHunter

Given a phenotypical definition of a disease, and a chromosomal region where to search for causative genes associated with the disease of interest, the flowchart of DGHunter for prioritizing candidate genes is shown in Figure 1. It includes the following two phases:

1. Mining a set of GO terms related to the given disease from MEDLINE and protein function annotation database GOA provided by the GO Project, and weighting them. The text mining and weighting procedures are described in detail in Section 2.2.

2. Prioritizing the candidate genes in the chromosomal region of interest by function similarity analysis. Firstly, we retrieve the GO terms of the candidate genes in the given chromosomal region. Secondly, based on the GO DAG, the function similarities between the GO terms of candidate genes and the set of GO terms mined from biomedical literatures are analyzed, and the possible relations of candidate genes to the disease are computed. Finally, we prioritize the candidates according to the scores of the relation degrees of the candidates to the disease of interest. The algorithm for function similarity analysis is presented in detail in Section 2.3.

Figure 1. The flowchart of DGHunter for prioritizing candidate disease genes in the region of interest

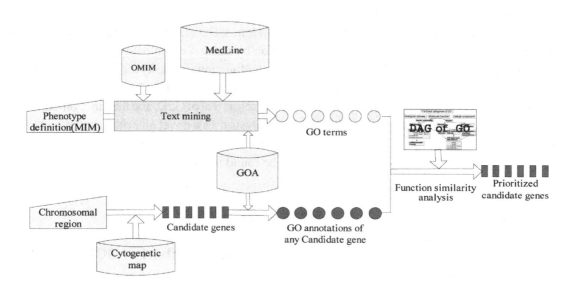

2.2. Mining Disease-Related GO Terms from the Biomedical Literature Database

The OMIM IDs are taken from OMIM-morbid map lists as the phenotypical definition of a disease. For a given OMIM ID, there are some MEDLINE references, given as PubMed IDs annotations in OMIM database. And most of the references in MEDLINE are annotated with a controlled set of MeSH C ('Disease Category', describing the phenotype of the disease) terms. So we can collect a set of MeSH C terms from MEDLINE.

However, there is often not enough literature in MEDLINE to directly relate disease phenotypes, represented by MeSH C terms, to gene product functions, represented by GO terms. While genes can be related to diseases symptoms through chemical features of molecules, they are represented by MeSH D terms ('Chemicals & Drugs'). Mesh D terms are used as an alternative way to annotate the biomedical literature in MEDLINE, similar to MeSH C terms. In these cases, we take MeSH D terms as the intermediate to increase the relation between MeSH C terms and GO terms.

The GO annotation database by the GO projects provides comprehensive, non-redundant functional annotations of gene products, i.e., proteins. And every annotation submitted to GO in the database must be attributed to a source, which is a kind of evidence to support the association between the gene product and the GO term. The evidence is often a PubMed ID linked to a biomedical reference in MEDLINE. Therefore, we can use the biomedical literature to associate MeSH D terms with GO terms.

Obviously, according to the transitive relations of MeSH C to OMIM, MeSH D to MeSH C, and MeSH D to GO terms, we can retrieve a set of GO terms associated with the given disease phenotype (shown in Figure 2), and weight them by the following algorithms.

The Evaluation of the Association between MeSH C and OMIM

Given a disease phenotype as o, and the set of MeSH C terms associated with o as MC:$\{$ mc_1, mc_2, ..., mc_m $\}$, the relation degree of any MeSH C term mc_i in MC to o is scored by:

Figure 2. Mining GO terms associated with disease phenotypes

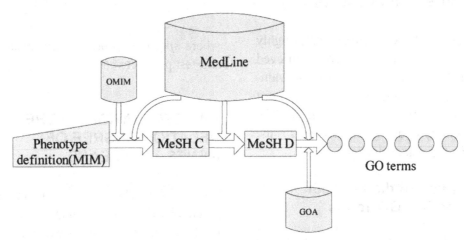

$$mc2o\,(o,\,mc_i) = \frac{|mc_i|}{|o|} \qquad (1)$$

where $|o|$ represents the number of the MEDLINE references linked by o, and $|mc_i|$ represents the number of the ones annotated by mc_i.

The Evaluation of the Association between MeSH D and MeSH C

To obtain the association between MeSH C (mc) and MeSH D (md), the co-occurrence frequency of mc and md is considered. We assume that these two terms are highly related if they frequently appear together. Here the strength of the association between mc and md is evaluated by counting the co-occurrences of both terms.

$$md2mc(mc,\,md) = \frac{|mc \cap md|}{|mc \cup md|} \qquad (2)$$

where $|mc \cap md|$ denotes the number of the MEDLINE references annotated by both mc and md, and $|mc \cup md|$ denotes the number of the MEDLINE references annotated by either mc or md.

The Evaluation of the Association between GO Term and MeSH D

Given a MeSH D term as md, and a GO term as go, the association between md and go is assigned a score by the following formula: Where $|go|$ represents the number of the MEDLINE references which have been found to be the evidences of go in the GOA database, and $|md|$ represents the number of the ones annotated by md among the $|go|$ references.

The Evaluation of the Association between GO Term and OMIM

According to the transitive relations of MeSH C to OMIM, MeSH D to MeSH C, and MeSH D to GO term, We weight the contribution of a GO term, go, to the disease phenotype, o, by:

$$go2o(o,\,go) = mc2o(o,\,mc) \times md2mc(mc,\,md)$$

$$\times go2md(md,\,go) \qquad (4)$$

here, the higher scored GO terms are considered to contribute more to the disease phenotype.

2.3. Prioritizing the Candidate Genes by Function Similarity Analysis

Based on the set of the weighted GO terms highly contributive to a given disease which are retrieved from MEDLINE by text mining, we can evaluate the possibility for a gene to be the cause of the disease by function similarity analysis. The function similarity of any given two terms is the basis to make the risk evaluation.

The Evaluation of the Function Similarity of Two GO Terms

Recent years, the GO consortium has established a set of structured, controlled vocabularies to describe gene functions. The GO ontologies are structured as directed acyclic graphs (DAG), which are similar to hierarchies but differ in that a child (more specialized) GO term has more than one parent (less specialized) GO terms.

In most previous methods, only the genes with shared (identical) GO terms can be retrieved. DG-Hunter, however, can also identify the candidate genes with similar (not necessarily the same) GO terms, using a new functional similarity algorithm, which is based on the GO directed acyclic graphs (DAG).

Every GO term in DAG must obey the true path rule: if the child term describes the gene product, all its parent terms must also apply to that gene product. This means that two GO terms will be considered to have similar functions, if they have one or more same ancestors. Obviously, through their co-ancestry nodes, the two terms can be connected by one or more, short or long paths. Here, we define that the unit distance between two adjacent GO terms is 1, and of course the distance of a GO term to itself is 0. under the definition, the functional similarity degree of two terms, go_i and go_j, is calculated according to the shortest distance between them, as shown in the following equation.

$$go2go(go_i, go_j) = \frac{1}{sp(go_i, go_j) + 1} \tag{5}$$

where $sp(go_i, go_j)$ denotes the distance of the shortest path between go_i and go_j.

THE EVALUATION OF THE RELATION DEGREE OF GENES TO DISEASE

The possible relation of a candidate gene to a given disease can be computed by analyzing the functional similarity between the GO terms annotating the candidate gene and the set of GO terms related to the disease phenotype mined from MEDLINE. Here, given the set of GO terms mined as S_G: { go_1, go_2,..., go_m}, and the set of GO terms related to a candidate gene g in the target region as S_C: { go_1, go_2,..., go_n}, obviously, if the more similar GO terms in S_C and those in S_G are, the more closely associated the candidate and the disease are.

Before defining the relation between a candidate gene and the disease, we need to evaluate the association of a single GO term of the candidate to the disease phenotype. Here, we define the correlation degree between a single GO term go_k of the candidate and the disease phenotype given as o, as the following formula.

$$cgo2o(o, go_k) = go2o(o, go_h)* \max\{go2go(go_i, go_k)| go_i \in S_G\} \tag{6}$$

where go_h is the one in S_G most similar to go_k and makes $go2go(go_h, go_k)$ the max value.

Finally, the relation of the candidate gene *g* to the disease phenotype is assigned a score by the following equation.

$$g2o(o, g) = \frac{1}{m} \sum_{i=1}^{n} cgo2o(o, go_i) \tag{7}$$

The score is associated with each single GO terms of the candidate, and equals the value of the sum of the correlation degrees between all GO terms and the respective disease phenotype divided by the number of disease related GO terms. The scores are used to rank all the candidates in the region of interest in the descending order. The top ones with high scores of the prioritized list are considered as the candidate genes related to the given disease with high risk.

3. TEST AND DISCUSSION

3.1. Test and Result

To evaluate the performance of DGHunter, a test set consisting of 1506 genes involved in 1147 OMIM phenotypes is derived from Morbid Map table in the OMIM database. To assure the validity of the test, the diseases in the test set must be assumed to have no known related genes, and must contain at least one related GO terms by mining MEDLINE.

To test the methods, we picked a fixed target gene for each disease, and we took a region of 30 Mb around this gene as the target region, in which all genes are candidates to be ranked. To evaluate the performance of our approach, we calculated sensitivity (*Sn*) and specificity (*Sp*) (Aerts et al., 2006).

For the test dataset, DGHunter reached a high performance, as the solid curve shown in Figure 3. The result shows that 40.70% target genes were ranked among the top 5% of the prioritized list, the correct disease genes was in the top 10% with a 55.18% chance, and on average the target gene was within the top 13.60% of the ranked lists of candidates. The AUC score was as high as up to 0.8640, indicating that DGHunter could identify correct disease gene with high effectiveness.

Figure 3. The ROC graphs of the DGHunter and the DGHunter with only shared GO terms considered

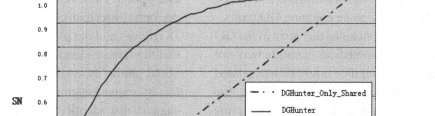

3.2. Discussion

Improvement of the Performance bBy Functional Similarity Analysis Based on DAG

The important while different feature of the algorithm of DGHunter is that we can retrieve not only genes with shared GO terms but also genes with similar GO terms by analyzing the functional similarity between GO terms based on GO DAG. To evaluate the effects on the performance when both similar and shared GO terms are taken into account, we carried out another test only considering the same GO terms. In this test, we used the same test dataset as mentioned above. Especially, the target gene ranked randomly if it could not be retrieved for some reason. The ROC of the test is shown as the dotted curve in Figure 3. The calculated AUC was only 0.5823, which is much lower than that of the DGHunter. Tests using more specific data indicate that the correct disease genes could be among the very top ones if they were extracted; however, there were still about 85% target genes which could not be identified by sharing some common GO terms.

It can be easily concluded that most of the GO terms mined from biomedical literature may not be the exact ones, and they might be just related to the disease in some extent. Therefore, the functional similarity analysis between GO terms is of particular importance to effectively retrieve candidate genes for those diseases lacking detailed GO annotations in our method.

COMPARISON WITH OTHER METHODS

Most existing tools that identify disease genes based on GO annotation were developed mainly for the diseases which have known causative genes with detailed GO annotations. However, there are still quite a number of diseases which do not have known related genes or have known

genes but lack GO annotations. These cases cannot be handled by such tools. Therefore, they are ignored. Our tool, DGHunter, is developed to identify genes for those diseases. DGHunter is also based on GO terms, which are extracted from biomedical literature through text mining as previously discussed.

Similarly, the Phenotype method of G2D can also make predictions for such diseases lacking detailed GO terms. G2D identifies disease genes through sequence similarity analysis based on the assumption that sequence homology indicates common functions.

To compare DGHunter to the phenotype method of G2D, the same test dataset, derived from the website of G2D (http://www.ogic.ca/projects/g2d_2/table_benchmark_complex.html), has been used to evaluate the performance of our method. The corresponding ROC values of DGHunter and G2D were plotted as the solid curve and the dotted curve, respectively (Figure 4). the AUC for DGHunter is 0.885, higher than that for G2D (0.740). Besides, the ROC of DGHunter was also completely higher than that of the later method at every point. These results suggest that DGHunter performs better than G2D. The difference between DGHunter and the phenotype method of G2D is that the former identifies disease genes by functional similarity analysis, while the later does this by sequence similarity analysis. Our results suggest that identifying disease genes through functional similarity analysis is likely more reliable than through sequence similarity analysis.

Although DGHunter performs better than the Phenotype method of G2D, it cannot reach the performance by most methods based on the GO terms with known diseases genes. This is due to the fact that the GO terms mined from MEDLINE are not usually as accurate as the direct GO annotations for disease genes. Therefore, our method is not suitable to make predictions for diseases with sufficient GO annotations. Instead, it aims at hunting for candidate genes for diseases which lack detailed GO terms and are usually neglected by previous methods.

Figure 4. The ROC graphs of the DGHunter and the Phenotype method of G2D

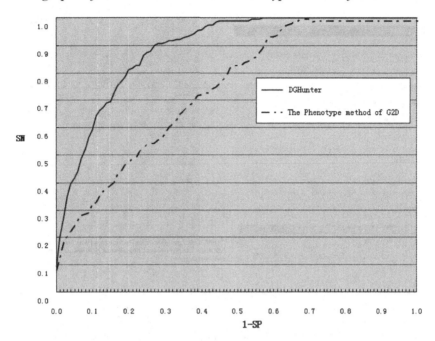

4. IMPLEMENTATION

We have developed a web tool, DGHunter, to search causative genes for human diseases. Basically, the algorithm needs two inputs to work with. One is a phenotypical definition of a disease, given as an OMIM identifier, the other is the definition of a chromosomal region where users look for mutations. The definition of a chromosomal region consists of a chromosome number and a positional interval of interest. The interval can be defined in three ways: two base positions (e.g., 35000000 45000000), two cytogenetic markers (e.g., D9S201 D9S298), or cytogenetic bands (e.g., p. 13).

To illustrate how DGHunter searches for the candidate gene from a chromosomal region, we will be using a genetic disease Saethre-Chotzen syndrome as an example to demonstrate the analysis procedures. The corresponding OMIM identifier for Saethre-Chotzen syndrome is 101400, and we define the interval between 102043098bp and 132043098bp of chromosome 10 as the target region, which contains 308 genes. In this particular

case, you would enter 101400 in the DISEASE PHENOTYPE box and 102043098 132043098 in the POSITION box, and also select the chromosome, 10 and 'Positions' in the POSITION box (Figure 5(a)).

DGHunter retrieved 31 references from MEDLINE according to OMIM:101400. Among these, 6 references are with MeSH C annotations, whose corresponding PubMed IDs are 862213, 2002481, 4073118, 4145271, 4393456 and 7450776, respectively. And the 6 MeSH C terms involved are Mental Retardation, Hypospadias, Sensorineural Hearing Loss, Growth Disorders, Microcephaly, Congenital Hand Deformities. According to the frequencies of occurrence in the 6 references above, the relation degrees of the MeSH C terms to OMIM:101400 were scored as 0.096770, 0.064510, 0.032250, 0.032250, 0.032250, 0.032250, respectively. Furthermore, according to the co-occurrence of MeSH C and MeSH D terms in MEDLINE, 3 MeSH D terms were found, which are Human Growth Hormone, Insulin-Like Growth Factor I, Connexins. Based on the co-occurrence frequencies of MeSH C and MeSH D

Figure 5. Example of analysis of DGHunter

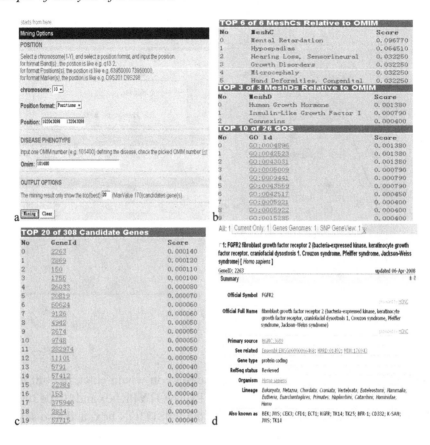

terms, and the scores of MeSH C terms to OMIM:101400, we weighted the relation degree of the 3 MeSH D terms to OMIM:101400 as 0.001380, 0.000790, 0.000400. Likewise, 26 GO terms were extracted based on the co-occurrence of MeSH D and GO terms, and were weighted according to the co-occurrence frequencies of GO and MeSH D terms, and the scores of MeSH D terms to OMIM:101400. Of the 26 GO terms, only the top scored 10 ones were selected as the Saethre-Chotzen syndrome related GO terms for analysis, including 0004869, 0042523, 0043031, 0005009, 0009441, et al. (Figure 5(b)).

We analyzed the function similarities between the 10 GO terms mined from MEDLINE and the GO annotations of the 308 candidates in the region of interest, and then weighted and prioritized the candidates according to their similarity degrees. The top 20 were picked out as the candidate

genes related to Saethre-Chotzen syndrome with high risk (Figure 5(c)). The candidate genes were linked to their corresponding webpage of on NCBI, through which more details about the ones of interest could be obtained (Figure 5(d)). As expected, the best scored gene, locId:2263, was confirmed to be the causative gene for Saethre-Chotzen syndrome.

5. CONCLUSION AND PROSPECT

We have presented a novel web tool, DGHunter, to predict candidate disease genes by a combination of text mining and function similarity analysis. DGHunter makes predictions mainly for diseases lacking known causative genes and/or diseases with known genes but lacking sufficient function annotations.

However, the GO terms mined from biomedical literatures may not be accurately related to a disease and this may result in predictions with poor precision. And, there are many diseases have no known genes or no related GO terms mined, which cases are beyond the range of DGHunter. For those cases, it might be a better idea to integrate some other information, like sequence features, expression information, and so on, to improving the coverage and accuracy.

ACKNOWLEDGMENT

This work was supported by the Doctor Innovative Project of SZIIT (Grant No. BC2009011).

REFERENCES

Aerts, S., Lambrechts, D., Maity, S., Van Loo, P., Coessens, B., & De Smet, F. (2006). Gene prioritization through genomic data fusion. *Nature Biotechnology, 24,* 537–544. doi:10.1038/nbt1203

Davidoff, A. M., Humphrey, P. A., Iglehart, J. D., & Marks, J. R. (1991). Genetic basis for p. 53 overexpression in human breast cancer. *Proceedings of the National Academy of Sciences of the United States of America, 88,* 5006–5010. doi:10.1073/pnas.88.11.5006

Franke, L., Bakel, H., Fokkens, L., de Jong, E. D., Egmont-Petersen, M., & Wijmenga, C. (2006). Reconstruction of a functional human gene network, with an application for prioritizing positional candidate genes. *American Journal of Human Genetics, 78,* 1011–1025. doi:10.1086/504300

Jimenez-Sanchez, G., Barton, C., & David, V. (2001). Human disease genes. *Nature, 409,* 853–855. doi:10.1038/35057050

McCarthy, M. I., Smedley, D., & Hide, W. (2003). New methods for finding disease-susceptibility genes: impact and potential. *Genome Biology, 4,* 119. doi:10.1186/gb-2003-4-10-119

Perez-Iratxeta, C., Bork, P., & Andrade, M. A. (2002). Association of genes to genetically inherited diseases using data mining. *Nature Genetics, 31,* 316–319.

Perez-Iratxeta, C., Bork, P., & Andrade-Navarro, M. A. (2007). Update of the G2D tool for prioritization of gene candidates to inherited diseases. *Nucleic Acids Research, 35,* 212–216. doi:10.1093/nar/gkm223

Perez-Iratxeta, C., Wjst, M., Bork, P., & Andrade, M. A. (2005). G2D: a tool for mining genes associated with disease. *BMC Genetics, 6,* 45. doi:10.1186/1471-2156-6-45

Thompson, M. E., Jensen, R. A., Obermiller, P. S., Page, D. L., & Holt, J. T. (1995). Decreased expression of BRCA1 accelerates growth and is often present during sporadic breast cancer progression. *Nature Genetics, 9,* 444–450. doi:10.1038/ng0495-444

Turner, F. S., Clutterbuck, D. R., & Semple, C. A. (2003). POCUS: mining genomic sequence annotation to predict disease genes. *Genome Biology, 4,* 75. doi:10.1186/gb-2003-4-11-r75

Vogelstein, B., & Kinzler, K. W. (1992). P. 53 function and dysfunction. *Cell, 70*(4), 523–5265. doi:10.1016/0092-8674(92)90421-8

This work was previously published in the International Journal of Advanced Pervasive and Ubiquitous Computing, Volume 3, Issue 1, edited by Tao Gao, pp. 45-54, copyright 2011 by IGI Publishing (an imprint of IGI Global).

Chapter 7
TB–WPRO:
Title–Block Based Web Page Reorganization

Qihua Chen
Institute of Computing Technology, Chinese Academy of Sciences, China

Xiangdong Wang
Institute of Computing Technology, Chinese Academy of Sciences, China

Yueliang Qian
Institute of Computing Technology, Chinese Academy of Sciences, China

ABSTRACT

For cell phone users and blind people using non-visual browsers, browsing Web by common browsers is quite inefficient due to the problem of information overload. This paper presents the TB-WPRO (Title-Block based Web Page Re-Organization) method, which hierarchically segments web pages into blocks using visual and layout information reflecting the web designers' intent. TB-WPRO segments the web pages with a clear goal to extract self-described title blocks. To reorganize web pages, the segmentation result is transformed to a serial of small web pages that could be easily accessed. Compared to current methods, the proposed approach obtains a promising segmentation result where blocks are visually and semantically consistent with original web pages.

1. INTRODUCTION

The last two decades have seen an explosion of the World Wide Web (WWW). The major way of accessing the WWW is viewing Web pages offered by the website designer using a PC Web browser. However, nowadays, more and more people are using small screen devices such as cell phones to access the WWW. Obviously, it is difficult for users to view whole web pages on a small screen using common browsers. Furthermore, for non-visual browsers which are used by people with visual disability, current web pages also face the challenge of information overload, which makes the browsing very inefficiency. Therefore, for these applications, analysis and reorganization of the web page become inevitable.

DOI: 10.4018/978-1-4666-2645-4.ch007

For web pages containing a main text (e. g., a news story), the problem is relatively easy, since the main story can be segmented and extracted according to text percentage and area. However, for web pages without main text and serving as "index pages" or "hub pages" (e. g., home page of most websites), analysis and reorganization of such web pages remains a major challenge. Earlier methods merely extract all texts from web pages and reorganized the texts and display them on small screens or transform them into speech for non-visual browsing. Obviously, these methods do not solve the problem of information overload and make browsing inefficient. Nowadays, much research effort has been paid on segmenting a web page into small blocks and transforming the web page into a sequence of blocks. However, for both methods using text information or visual information, current segmentation performance remains dissatisfactory: Blocks obtained by current methods are often not visually and semantically consistent with the original web pages. Furthermore, current methods just segment web pages into blocks and allow users to skip between blocks, which are still inefficient in browsing.

In this paper, the TB-WPRO (title-block based web page reorganization) method is proposed. The method segments web pages from the designer's perspective using both visual information and page layout. The method is mainly used for segmentation of "index pages" or "hub pages" as introduced above. The main idea is to extract *title blocks* from web pages and reorganize them in a hierarchical way. A title block is a block with a title which describes the category of the block and a main content within the category. Compared to current methods, the proposed approach can obtain a promising segmentation result where blocks are visually and semantically consistent with original web pages. Furthermore, the proposed method can filter less important contents such as navigation bars and some advertisements by only considering title blocks, which helps in dealing with the challenge of information extraction.

The rest of this paper is organized as follows: Section 2 provides a brief review of related work. Section 3 and Section 4 presents the page segmentation method and content reorganization methods in TB-WPRO, respectively. Experimental results are given and analyzed in Section 5. Finally, conclusions are drawn in Section 6.

2. RELATED WORK

A variety of methods have been proposed to segment web pages into small blocks. The early way is considering the tag information in the DOM tree such as <P> (paragraph), <TABLE> (table), <UL> (list). <H1>-<H6> (heading), etc. Lin and Ho (2002) partition a page into several content blocks according to HTML tag <TABLE> and then use entropy to distinguish redundant block from the information block. Hattori et al. (2007) propose a hybrid method using content-distances and layout information to segment the webpage. However, the HTML tags do not contain any semantic information and could be misused. A FOM model is proposed by Chen et al. (2001). It treats each object in the webpage as either a basic or composite FOM which describe the object functionality. But the model does not describe the concrete segmentation method. The VIPS algorithm is proposed by Cai et al. (2003) which analyzes the webpage using the vision separator to segment the content into different areas. However, a parameter PDoC (Permitted Degree of Coherence) must be given by the user to get segmentation result. The paper does not tell how to determine proper PDoC to get blocks visually and semantically consistent with the original web page. Baluja (2006) uses a learning method to divide a webpage into 9 parts which the user could select to zoom. Chakrabarti et al. (2004) puts the nodes in DOM tree into a weighted graph, and formulates an appropriate optimization problem on it. The optimization problem is solved by a learning framework. But such machine learning method need a training process and is difficult to implement.

3. WEB PAGE SEGMENTATION

3.1. Overview

In most of the web pages, a block is often organized with a title on the top to indicate the category of the content below. Figure 1(b) shows an example: the line contains "REAL ESTATE" informs us that the content below tells stories of "real estate". This pattern is generally adopted by the designers of web pages when they designed the body of the page excluding the navigation bar on the top of the page, the contact information at the bottom of the page, and some advertisements. In this paper, such a block is referred to as a *title block*. Obviously, title blocks are self-explaining by its title and could be easily extracted as an independent unit without missing any useful information when it is detached from the original web page. So we

design an algorithm aiming at extracting title blocks from a web page accurately. The algorithm includes two parts, the first part is to mine *single title blocks* from the web page. The second part is to analyze a series of node to find *combined title blocks*.

3.2. Single Title Block

A Single title block is the simplest representation of a title block in DOM tree. It corresponds to a node in the DOM tree which has two or three child nodes and one of its children constitutes a large principal part. We call this principal part the body of the title block. When rendered by a browser, the body will occupy large percentage of the total area of the parent node on the screen. Figure 1(b) show an example of a single title node. It can be seen from Figure 1(a) and Figure 1(b) that a single title block has a block title, a block content, and some addition information which is optional. Figure 1(c) is the corresponding DOM tree node of Figure 1(b). It has three children which map the three parts in Figure 1(a) one by one.

A single title block is a self-explaining and semantic-coherence block. So the first step of our algorithm is identifying this kind of block. This is achieved by mining the relationships between the areas occupied by child nodes of the block

Figure 1. (a) The layout of the page (b) An instance of the layout (c) The corresponding DOM tree

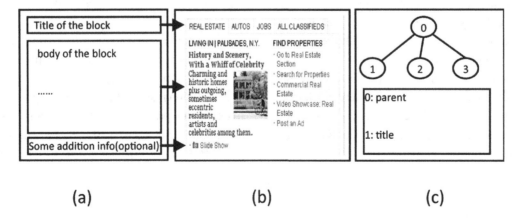

node. The relationship could be described as: (1) A small height rectangle on top which represent the title of the block. (2) A larger height rectangle in the middle which occupy main area of the whole node. (3) Some small-height additional info at the bottom area. This rule is truly simple, but it uses the layout of the node properly and captures the designer's design pattern. So it could sufficiently mine the title node from the DOM tree semantically.

However, because of the diversity of web pages and the designers' preferences, there are no general rules to determine whether the height is small or large. To avoid subjective judgment of the height, another feature called *line number* is used to enhance this method. The line number of a node is the number of lines a DOM node contains. To get the line number we develop the algorithm LineNum, it traverses a DOM node to find all the leaf descendant of the node, put the area rectangles these leaf node occupy in a set, then remove all rectangles that are horizontal overlapped with another. The line number is approximately the line number seen on the screen except cases when a line is very long and is wrapped automatically. For these cases, the algorithm will still treat it as one line.

With the help of the algorithm LineNum, according to the rule for single title block described, an algorithm called IsSingleTitleBlock is developed as follows.

```
Algorithm IsSingleTitleBlock
Input: a DOM tree node N
Output: true of false
1 childnode = GetAllChild(N);
2 if(2 <= childnode.size <= 3 &&
LineNum(firstchild)== 1)
3 for each childnode child_i
4 if (area (child_i) > 0.6* area (N))
5 return true;
6 end if
7 end for
8 end if
9 return false
```

This algorithm first makes sure if the first child of the node *N* is a one-line node. Then it uses the area information to find the body of the node. If the body is found, the node *N* is considered to be a single title block.

Figure 2. (a) DOM tree style 1 (b) The view of the content (c) DOM tree style 2 (d) DOM tree style3: flat style

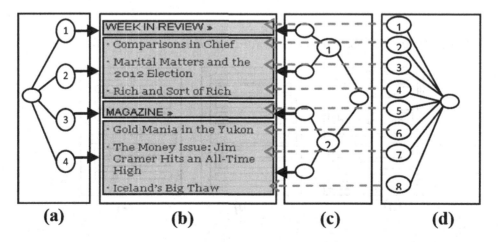

(a) (b) (c) (d)

3.3. Combined Title Block

There are many well designed DOM nodes (e. g., the node shown in Figure 1(c)) which has the layout pattern of Figure 1(a). However, not all the layouts like Figure 1(a) have the structure of Figure 1(c). Therefore, in some cases, the algorithm in 3.2 suffers a problem referred to as the *flattening problem*. An illustration is given in Figure 2.

In Figure 2, Figure 2(c) is the structure we discussed above, in which each block has a corresponding DOM node (node 1 and 2). Figure 2(a) shows a kind of flattening. Compared to Figure 2(c), it node 1 and 2 in Figure 2 (c) are missing, and the level of the block is reduced from three to two. Figure 2(d) show an extreme case whose DOM structure is totally flat.

The visual structure is displayed accordingly in Figure 3. Figure 3 (a) is perfect vision which we will use to find single title block. Figure 3 (b) is a satisfactory vision by which we will find combined title block. Figure3(c) is a degraded vision (user vision) which only has lines and need more work.

Flat structure misses some information that non-flat structure has. Therefore, structure thrown by flattening (e. g., node 1 and 2 in the Figure 2(c) for Figure 2(a)) should be recovered by analyzing both visual and layout information of DOM nodes. In Figure 2(a), it can be seen that a title is always followed by a content body. So our method traverses all the child nodes and finds the pattern of combination of a title and a block. The node found is called a combined title node. The algorithm is shown as follows.

```
Algorithm: FindCombinedTitleNode
Input: A DOM node N
Output: Set of CombinedTitleNode
1 s = sequence of the childnode of N
2 Find all title and body combination
"ab" in s
3 Replace "ab" with new combination
node
4 if(all node in s is combination
node) return s
5 if(all node in s is not combination
node) return s
6 for each non-combination node_i
7 if(IsTitle(node_i) == 1)
8 InsertTitle(node_i);
9 else
10 Append (node_i)
11 end if
12 end for
13 return s
```

The algorithm puts a title and a body (content) together to form a combination node. The main difference between the single title block and combined title block is single title block is just a DOM node and the combined title block contains two or more nodes. But this does not affect the

Figure 3. (a) Perfect vision (b) Satisfactory vision(c) Degraded vision(user vision)

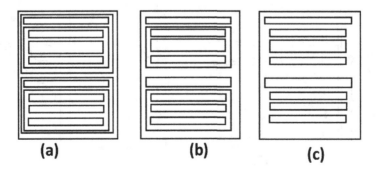

(a) **(b)** **(c)**

essence that they both represent a semantic block. Line 2 and 3 in the algorithm find the combination node and replace it with a new node. If all nodes in the block are put into a combination node then the algorithm return all the combination blocks in Line4, if there is no combination node, the result will also be returned. When there is some other nodes not put in a combination node, the relation between the nodes and the previous and next combination nodes are analyzed. Line 7 judges whether node_i is a title node. From the vision of node N and next node *next(N)*, if it holds that *N*.font.wight = bold or *N*.font.size > *next(N)*.font. size or *N*.font.color != black or *N*.tag = "hd", then *n* is considered as a title. The DOM node's tag could also be useful because <hd> is widely used and have a good indication.

If node *i* in line 7 is a title node, then it will be inserted into the next combination as a title in Line 8. Otherwise, it will be appended to the previous combination node in Line 10. In Figure 4, node 2 and 3 will be first combined, and node 1 will be left. When node 1 is found as a title node, it will be inserted into the combination of node2 and node3 as a title. Node 4 is not a title so it is appended to previous combination node of node 2 and node 3. At last, the correct block is obtained from the algorithm.

Figure 2(d) is a totally flat structure with minimum hierarchical information. Since we have an algorithm to handle the case in (a), so what we need to do is to transform the case in Figure 2(d) to that of Figure 2(a). Obviously, we need to merge node 2, 3, 4 in Figure 2(d) into a node 2 in Figure 2(a). Node 2, 3, 4 in Figure 2(d) is parallel and certainly has same vision. So for two neighbor node N_1 and N_2, if N_1.font.size = N_2.font.size and N_1.font.weight= N_2.font.weight and N_1.font.color = N_2.font.color and N_1.alignment = N_2.alignment, these nodes are merged to form a new hierarchy. This mergeing process is called unflattening. When the process finished, algorithm FindCombinedTitleNode can be used to further process the unflattened nodes.

3.4. The Whole Segmentation Procedure

The whole algorithm traverses the DOM tree and finds title blocks and non-title blocks. They are distinguished in the result.

```
Algorithm Segmentation
Input: Dom node N
Output: a tree represent the hierar-
chical block outTree
1 if(IsSingleTitleBlock (N))
2 outTree.add_title_child (N)
3 segment all childnodes of N
4 return;
5 end if
6 Unflattening(N) ;
7 combinedblocks =
FindCombinedTitleNode(N);
8 if(!combinedblocks.empty)
9 outTree.add_title_
childs(combinedblocks);
10 segment all childnodes of N;
11 else
12 outTree.add_nontitle_child(N);
13 end if
```

Figure 4. Complex node

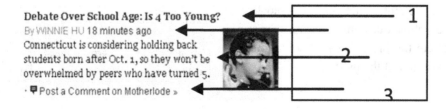

In the algorithm, Line 2 find the title and body combination "*ab*" by layout just as IsSingle-TitleBlock does. When "*a*" is one line node and $0.6*area(b) > area(a)$, "*ab*" is considered as a combination node. Line 1-4 judge and handle the case of SingleTitleBlock., Line 6 unflattens the structure in Figure 2(d), then FindCombinedTitle-Node in line 7 will further process the nodes. If no combined blocks are found, the node will be added as a non title node. The whole algorithm aims at finding a title block by mining the visual information from the designer except when the designer's vision degrade to the user's vision in Figure 2(d). The algorithm first handles the easiest case of (c), then do some extra work to handle the (a), (d) to recollect the missing information in (a), (d).

4. WEB PAGE TRANSFORMATION

The hierarchical segmentation result with title block is a natural form of the web page. We transform the segmentation result to small pages to enable small screen browsing and non-visual browsing. The transformation process is as follows: Each block is transformed to a link which is the title of the block, and the block content is transform to a page which is pointed to by the title link. The entrance page is all the title links from the first level block of the hierarchical segmentation result. The non-title blocks are discarded.

To make the result more informative, we re-order the blocks by the observation that many ads and less-important content appear on the marginal areas of web pages. So if a block has a small width and is on the marginal areas of a web page, it is moved to the end of the block sequence. This is because when a page comes to the reader, they usually focus on the center and large-width blocks. This is also the webpage designers' design pattern. We do not delete the block because sometimes ads could be the aim of the user.

5. EXPERIMENTAL RESULTS

To evaluate the performance of TB-WPRO, we randomly select 77 Chinese pages and 23 English web pages from the internet which include different categories about news, technology, travel, books, finance and so on. We asked five volunteers to mark the title blocks in the web pages The TB-WPRO algorithm is run on all the pages and then the volunteers are asked to count the number of the title blocks correctly found and false alarmed by the algorithm. The result is shown in Table 1.

Therefore, it can be calculated that the recall rate is $1395/1642 = 85\%$ and the precision is $1395/(1395+220) = 86\%$. We also find that for the English page the performance of TB-WPRO decreases. This is because we adjust our algorithm on Chinese pages and the design pattern changes a little due to cultural difference.

We also compared our method with the VIPS algorithm in Cai, Yu, Wen, and Ma (2003). Figure 5 is the best VIPS segmentation result with pDoc= 9. Figure 6 ① is our result. In Figure 5, there is three huge blocks with a large height on the left, but on the right there are many single line blocks. Adjusting pDoc cannot fix both problems. However, in Figure 6 ①, our algorithm catch semantic information of blocks well. At the top of Figure 5, the title is separate from the blocks below. Although VIPS is hierarchical, finding different pDoc to reflect different semantic levels is truly hard. Our algorithm is born for semantic level analysis and can perceive the level easily.

Figure 6 also gives a demonstration of our transformation result. First we can see the top part and the bottom part of the page are excluded from the transformation result because they are not regarded as title blocks. Then we can see the hi-

Table 1. Experiment result

All title blocks	Correctly found	False alarm
1642	1395	220

Figure 5. VIPS result

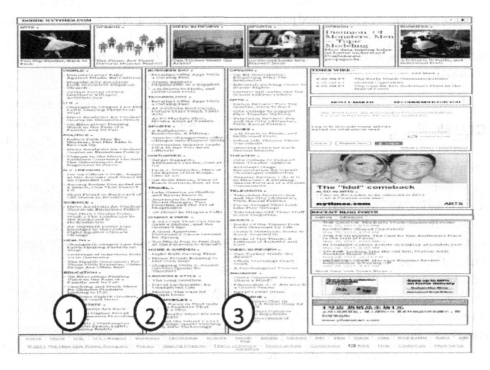

Figure 6. Transformation result

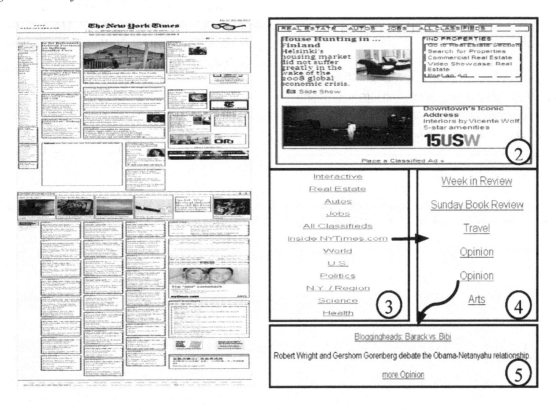

erarchy, the content in red line are sub blocks of the block in blue line, for more complicated page, it could has more levels. The transform result is partly show in ③④⑤, the arrow show the relationship of ③④⑤.

6. CONCLUSION

In this paper, we propose a method that hierarchically segments web pages into blocks using visual and layout information which reflecting the web designers' intent. It segments the web pages with a clear goal to extract self-described title blocks. It distinguishes title and non-title blocks in the process of the segmentation. Then the segmentation result is transformed to a serial of small web pages that could be easily accessed. Compared to current methods, the proposed approach can obtain a promising segmentation result where blocks are visually and semantically consistent with original web pages.

REFERENCES

Baluja, S. (2006). Browsing on small screens: Recasting web-page segmentation into an efficient machine learning framework. In *Proceedings of the 15ᵗʰ International Conference on World Wide Web* (pp. 33-42).

Cai, D., Yu, S., Wen, J.-R., & Ma, W.-Y. (2003). *VIPS: A vision-based page segmentation algorithm* (Tech. Rep. No. MSR-TR-2003-79). Cambridge, MA: Microsoft Research.

Chakrabarti, D., Kumar, R., & Punera, K. (2004). A graph-theoretic approach to extract storylines from search results. In *Proceedings of the 17th International Conference on World Wide Web* (pp. 216-225).

Chen, J., Zhou, B., & Zhang, H. (2001). Function-based object model towards website adaptation. In *Proceedings of the 10th International World Wide Web Conference* (pp. 587-596).

Hattori, G., Hoashi, K., Matsumoto, K., & Sugaya, F. (2007). Robust web page segmentation for mobile terminal using content-distances and page layout information. In *Proceedings of the 16th International Conference on World Wide Web* (pp. 361-370).

Lin, S.-H., & Ho, J.-M. (2002). Discovering informative content blocks from Web documents. In *Proceedings of the Eighth ACM SIGKDD International Conference on Knowledge Discovery and Data Mining* (pp. 588-593).

This work was previously published in the International Journal of Advanced Pervasive and Ubiquitous Computing, Volume 3, Issue 1, edited by Tao Gao, pp. 55-62, copyright 2011 by IGI Publishing (an imprint of IGI Global).

Chapter 8
Constructing the Collaborative Supply Logistics Operation Mode in Assembly System under JIT Environment

Guo Li
Beijing Institute of Technology, China

Tao Gao
Hebei Electronic Information Products Supervision and Inspection Institute and Industry, China

Lun Ran
Beijing Institute of Technology, China

ABSTRACT

In the JIT assembly system, if any supplier does not deliver the raw materials or components on time, or in the right quantity, the core manufacturers will not assemble on the schedule, which will bring great loss to the whole supply chain and greatly reduce the competitiveness and collaboration of the entire supply chain. Based on a survey on supply chain collaboration and operation model, supply logistics in JIT environment are analyzed from both the inside and outside system with the research goal of coordinating the upstream supply logistics. In order to help manufacturers implement the JIT production, the VMI-Hub operation mode is proposed from the aspect of inside system, and from outside system, cross-docking dispatch operation mode is considered to coordinate the supply logistics in assembly system.

1. INTRODUCTION

Generally speaking, enterprise logistics can be divided into in-bound logistics, in-plant logistics, out-bound logistics, returned logistics and waste material logistics. For an assembly enterprise, in-bound logistics is the most complicate and important part. Especially when enterprises emphasize core-competitiveness and outsource the most non-core business, supply logistics cost accounts for more and more of the sales. In order to reduce the storage and relevant cost, assembly enterprises require their suppliers to deliver raw materials or components in small amount, high

DOI: 10.4018/978-1-4666-2645-4.ch008

frequency and right time to support the their JIT production. Many component suppliers have to invest building factories or warehouse around the assembly plants, or rent warehouses to store the components, so that they can become partners of big assembly enterprises, but the above policies are not beneficial for economy of scale and increase the cost of inventory and transportation. Apparently, assembly enterprises will benefit, but the substantial reduction of the inventory cost is always counteracted by shifting component price raised by suppliers, which is harmful to the whole supply chain.

In order to solve these problems caused by JIT production, some new management ideas and operating models have been proposed and practiced. Some assembly enterprises start to fetch raw materials or components from suppliers in the "Milk run" to reduce the over-high transportation cost caused by suppliers who provide raw materials or components in high frequency and small amount, rather than require suppliers to deliver raw materials or components to the door. Some assembly enterprises start to use the "Supply-hub" operation mode between assembly factories and suppliers, which means that the cooperated 3PL(the third-party provider of logistics service) or assembly enterprises rent unified warehouses, then the suppliers deliver raw materials or components to the warehouses according to orders placed by assembly enterprises, and finally the 3PL deliver raw materials or components to the work station of assembly enterprises according to the production schedule, just so as to reduce excess components inventory and over-high management cost in traditional decentralized VMI model.

These new operating models are based on the collaboration of assembly enterprises with the supply logistics(in-bound logistics). Although they have been used in the management practice and achieved some good results, there are still many problems needed to be solved in both theory and strategy, such as how to control and manage the storage rate of "Supply-hub", how to balance

the order quantities of different components and choose the right transport way, and how to deal with orders during the operation process and share information among partners who consider the matching attribute among components and the difference in loading capacities of single batch of components. Based on some research results the above problems, the authors try to conduct deep study and discussion on collaborative supply logistics operation mode in assembly system under the JIT environment, try to explore the reasons of the problem, and finally propose new ideas and new ways of coordinating supply logistics in assembly system.

2. LITERATURE REVIEW

Generally speaking, collaboration between enterprises or partners in the supply chain can be divided into strategy level collaboration, tactics level collaboration and technical level collaboration. However, the strategy level collaboration is the highest level, but the technical collaboration can realize the synchronous operation between partners in the supply chain and the information sharing supported by collaboration technology. The collaboration can also be divided into demand forecasting collaboration, product design collaboration, plan collaboration, purchase collaboration and inventory collaboration from the aspect of collaboration content.

Strategy level collaboration is based on conceptual model and collaborative management idea, which is mainly focused on in-depth discussion and analysis of key elements of supply chain collaboration management, expected value gains of collaboration, collaboration mechanism and collaboration nature. Xu and Beamon (2006) proposed the four-step strategy for enterprises about how to choose the right collaboration mechanism based on the four aspects, such as resource structure, decision type, control level and risk / revenue sharing between enterprises and their partners in the supply chain. Manthou et al. (2004) established the virtual e-chain of the supply chain collaboration, constructed the framework of supply chain collaboration in virtual environment, classified the relationship between collaborative partners, and distinguished the key abilities that constitute collaborative relationships, which achieved the expected collaboration. Petrson and Lora (2001) in Grartner company constructed a supply chain collaboration matrix, and pointed out the key elements of supply chain collaboration. Akkermans and Paul (2004) established the theory model of supply chain collaboration, and proved that the Joint effort of each node enterprises of supply chain, trust and transparency were the key elements of supply chain collaboration realization by case study of high-tech electronics supply chain. Sabri and Beamon (2000) studied model of several independent phases in supply chain such as suppliers, factories, distributors and customers, and optimized supply chain nodes and logistics resources. Ito and Salleh (2000) proposed the negotiation model of supply chain based on the electronic blackboard. Rosenzweig (2009) studied the performance influenced by manufacturer's collaboration with suppliers based on internet. Zimmer (2002) studied the supply chain collaboration when there was uncertainty JIT delivery between manufacturers and suppliers, and realized flexible distribution of supply chain cost among collaborative enterprises by establishing the two coordination mechanisms with penalty and bonus.

Tactics level collaboration is the central issue of supply chain collaboration management. It mainly contains demand information sharing strategy, inventory collaboration strategy, production collaboration strategy, logistics collaboration strategy, purchase collaboration strategy and so forth among the upstream and downstream enterprises. The above strategies are related to the Manufacturers' supply logistics. In the realization of demand information sharing mechanisms, the most important practice is Wal-Mart's retail connecting program, and Wal-Mart sends the POS sale data of merchandise through the online system to its suppliers (Gill & Abend, 1997). How suppliers and their downstream manufacturers share demand information becomes the key factors of rapid response (Quick Response, QR) (Lee et al., 2000) and effective customer response (Efficient Consumer Response, ECR) (Cachon & Fisher, 1997). Information sharing becomes an important mechanism of supply chain management model such as Vender Managed Inventory (VMI) and Continuous Replenishment Programs (CRP), and succeeds through the practice of some companies (Chen, 2001). Other supply chain models related to information sharing include Collaborative Planning, Forecasting and Replenishment (CPFR) (Holmström et al., 2000), Centralized Inventory Management (CIM) (Lee, 1997) and so on. Disney and Towill (2003) established traditional supply chain model and VMI supply chain simulation model respectively, and verified by simulation that VMI could reduce the bullwhip effect effectively through information sharing.

Inventory collaboration is another important issue in the operation layer collaboration of supply chain (Zipperer, 2003). CPFR is another kind of Collaborative inventory management techniques. It uses a series of processing and technical models to conduct the information-interactive management and monitoring according to the execution efficiency of different clients and nodes in supply chain. Through improving the partnership between retailers and suppliers, managing Business processes together and sharing information, forecasting accuracy can be improved, and at last, the goals of improving supply chain efficiency, reducing inventory and enhancing consumer satisfaction can be achieved. In a word CPFR as an effective strategy for the supply chain reflects the idea of collaborative management of supply chain, and can realize broader and deeper coordination among the partners of supply chain (Akkermans, 2004). Fu and Piplani (2004) established inventory-based assessment model of supply-side collaboration from the supply point of view. Production collaboration means that manufacturers make the work shop layer collaborate effectively with external system, and the internal manufacturing processes and business processes collaborate with business process of external partners, and combine the production agility with the synchronized ability of business processes to respond to customers' demand flexibly and quickly. The Well-known American ARC consulting company focused on tactics of collaborative production planning, and proposed the workshop layer-based multi-dimensional collaboration (ARC, 2002). Dudekr and Stadtler (2005) proposed a negotiation-based collaborative planning model of supply chain. As to logistics collaboration, Ellinger (2000) studied cross-functional collaboration issue between internal marketing and logistics. Chen and Chen (2005) studied the supply chain collaboration problem in the case of joint replenishment and channel coordination, and established a corresponding optimization model of supply chain collaboration. Yao and Chiou (2004) established a replenishment coordination model between suppliers and multiple buyers. Garg et al. (2006) showed that quick delivery of the supply chain could be realized through the distribution of certain cumulated demand variance. Lee et al. (1999) proposed a kind of member Incentive mechanism, in which the behavior of members in the chain can achieve the best system performance. Lim (2000) put forward an incentive contract that made third-party logistics provider Truth-telling. Gupta and Weerawat (2000) studied three different incentives mechanism such as designating components inventory levels, providing part of the revenue for suppliers and two-part revenue sharing scheme. Fan et al. (2000) constructed the incentive structure in decentralized organizations under supply chain environment, and designed market-based coordination system combined with incentives.

Under JIT environment, as a new kind of supply logistics collaboration model, Supply-Hub has been used by some manufacturing enterprises in Europe and America for a long time, especially in

Electronics and automotive industry, while Asia followed quickly. Compaq is one of the earliest practitioner, and in 1998, it cooperated with CTI (Customized Transportation Inc.) to carry on the pre-position model. CTI set up Houston materials center, and designed JIT system, so that it could response to Compaq's production demand in time (Zuckerman, 2000). In addition, Bax Global as a Supply-Hub for Apple, Dell and IBM in Southeast Asia, can avoid problems such as High inventory costs and component obsolescence caused by Economic fluctuations. In China, the components provided by suppliers of Shanghai General Motors Dong Yue Co., Ltd are converged to Tonghui Logistics Optimization Center (LOC), where mixed line production is supported by pressing the light delivery, Scheduling delivery, or Kanban delivery, etc. 4000 kinds of spare parts in Dongfeng Peugeot Citroen Automobile Co., Ltd can be operated to realize synchronization distribution, Kanban delivery, direct delivery to work station and other JIT operation with the help of the Jie Fu Kai Logistics distribution center close to its production plant. At present the theory studies of supply-hub include supply-hub strategy level analysis and aspects of the operation layer such as inventory strategies and collaborative scheduling. Barnes et al. (2000) defined supply-hub as the places near the manufacturer factory used to store all or part of supply material, where they were paid after the items were used according to the agreement. They thought that Supply-hub was a kind of innovation strategy used in some industry (especially electronics) to reduce costs and improve responsiveness, and was a kind of reflection of delayed procurement. Lee (2002) considered that Supply-hub was a way of ensuring stable and reliable supply of components. Cheong et al. (2007) showed that when a 3PL provided supply-hub services for multiple suppliers and multiple manufacturers to support manufacturers of JIT production, the use of consolidation-hubs to integrate transportation could save shipping costs and resources, etc. Shah and Goh (2004) analyzed changes of the total cost of supplier under different min-max policies, and provided some reference for policy formulation of Supply-hub under the situation that Supply-hub used penalty costs to shortage and excessive storage.

In addition, some scholars made preliminary research on supply logistics collaboration in assembly enterprises. Glüer and Bilgic (2009) considered a decentralized assembly system under random supply and random demand, and established expected supply chain profit model with multiple suppliers. They proposed two contracts, and showed through compelling, supply chain members can be collaborated, and penalty payment was essential, especially for the worst performing supplier. Gurnani and Gerchak (2007) considered that in the context of decentralization, parts suppliers chose their production based on their own cost structure, and assembly enterprises made the order decision based on their own cost structure. When suppliers could control their input, but the output was random, the system collaboration became very complicated. In that case, incentive alignment control mechanisms were proposed so that the suppliers could choose the production under centralized decision. They also analyzed the condition to achieve system coordination under participation constraint, and proposed further the best components collaborative ordering policy, and then got the optimal collaborative punishment measures. Zou et al. (2008) considered a supply agreement mode of an assembly system under central or decentralized control. Centralized control model considered unique decision-makers and made a global optimal solution, while decentralized control mode considered that each participants of the agreement were decision-makers. The individual optimal solutions based on each participant's production and cost characteristics were proposed. Through parameter adjustment of some individual optimal solutions, supply chain collaboration could be realized. Boeck and Vandaelee (2008) considered to coordinate the supply logistics between two suppliers and one assembly enterprise by Synchronization warehouse, and the research showed that reliability of supply and order intervals had important great effects on supply chain performance.

To sum up, recent researches have the following characteristics:

1. Studies of supply chain collaboration on the strategic level concentrate on key elements and mechanisms to implement supply chain collaboration, but the literature about operation of supply chain collaboration and its mode are not thorough.

2. The researches on supply-hub are still in its infancy such as concepts, the operating model and etc. However, deep researches on decision-making mode and model of supply logistics in supply-hub are rarely made.

3. In terms of supply logistics coordination of assembly enterprises, part of the literatures focused on collaborative model between single manufacturer and multiple suppliers, but few papers related to the collaboration model among multiple suppliers matched with the assembly enterprise.

As a result, this paper will mainly study and build collaboration model of supply logistics in assembly system under JIT environment.

3. COLLABORATIVE MANAGEMENT MODES OF EXTERNAL SUPPLY LOGISTICS UNDER JIT ENVIRONMENT

3.1. Collaborative Management of Suppliers Based on JIT

Supplier collaboration is supply business collaboration based on the core enterprises and their suppliers in supply chain operation. Real-time information will be shared with suppliers, and supply and production cooperate closely to improve operating efficiency with suppliers. Partnerships can be built with suppliers and enterprises, and a competitive supply chain system for enterprises can be constructed according to production and market changes.

Logistics supply operation based on JIT procurement is strict with the timeliness and consistency control of Supplier delivery. Therefore, the implementation of supply chain management is closely related to suppliers' support and active cooperation. It requires that relationship between manufacturers and suppliers is a long-term mutually beneficial partnership under the JIT environment. Besides, mutual support and mutual trust among manufacturers and suppliers are also required to achieve double-win effect. Manufacturers should regard suppliers as an extension of JIT system. Evaluated suppliers should ensure JIT delivery to the manufacturer, which means they provide raw materials and components meeting the quality requirements according to the desired quantity, time and place.

Manufacturers' JIT procurement requires the suppliers to implement the JIT delivery. Suppliers' reliable delivery is very important for JIT system, because JIT system eliminates the buffer stock, and failure in any supplier's delivery will lead to the shutdown of production line. As a result, the successful implementation of JIT purchasing requires the manufacturers and suppliers to coordinate and work together to improve supply logistics system interoperability and achieve an overall optimization.

3.2. Collaborative Operation Mode of Procurement and Supply Based on JIT

JIT mode pursues zero inventories. Recently, in order to realize JIT production, the new supply chain management mode-Vendor Managed Inventory (VMI) is introduced, which is a great innovation for supply chain. VMI can bring great advantages to supply chain such as reducing inventory and lead time of supply chain, decreasing the adverse impact of bullwhip effect, and improving response ability to fluctuation of market demand. Consequently, the core enterprises have a strong competitive advantage in the industry.

In the traditional supply operation mode, decentralized VMI mode was used (Figure 1).

As the characteristics of manufacturer's production, the production scale is very large, and the production is stable, so daily demand for raw

Figure 1. Decentralized VMI operation mode

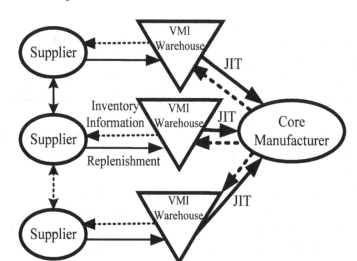

materials, spare parts has little change, which requires the suppliers provide goods in high frequency, especially under JIT environment, shortage is not allowed. In this mode there must be hundreds of suppliers providing raw materials and spare parts for the manufacturers, and warehouses near the manufacturer are built by each supplier in decentralized VMI operation mode, which causes the following problems:

First, each component supplier has to choose to invest building warehouses or rent third-party storage facilities to manage by itself or completely outsource to third-party logistics, which causes an additional expenditure.

Secondly, each of the M suppliers has a system implementing VMI operation. If each supplier provides components in small scale, maintaining its VMI system needs high running cost. As a result, the total cost of the M VMI systems in the whole supply link is very high.

Thirdly, as each supplier runs its own VMI storage independently and dispersedly, there is lack of information exchange among them. Inevitably distortion and delay of supply information and demand information occurs, which makes suppliers unable to meet the needs of manufacturers quickly, accurately, and simultaneously.

The core manufacturer needs to face N-suppliers. If the manufacturer requires a high frequency of supply, it may occur that multiple suppliers simultaneously deliver the parts, and then chaotic scene of discharge may appear because of lacking scheduling, which has bad influence on production and bring inconvenience to enterprise's normal running.

Therefore, we introduce a new collaborative operation mode, namely VMI-Hub. VMI- Hub, as a buffer role, can avoid the situation by professional delivery (Figure 2).

If there wasn't VMI-Hub, suppliers were independent from each other, and the parts delivered were separated from each other. After VM-Hub appeared, it provides picking services before shipping, and VMI-Hub configures the components in accordance with the ratio of the finished product first and then delivers to the manufacturer, which improves the production efficiency of the core manufacturer.

In a word, building a VMI-Hub near the manufacturer can well realize the JIT production, and all kinds of components can be delivered in time, which enables the manufacturer to produce successfully.

Figure 2. Collaborative operation modes of supply logistics based on VMI-Hub

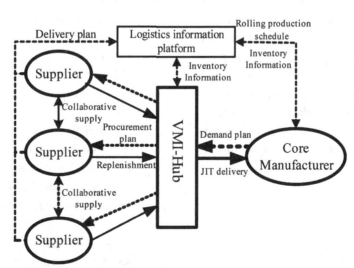

3.3. Collaborative Management Method of External Supply Logistics

Procurement is the core part of enterprise's supply chain management, and it's the key point for enterprises to reduce cost. We can introduce e-commerce in the procurement part, and it's not only the requirement to implement JIT supply logistics operation, but also the urgent requirement to meet the trend of global sourcing and internet procurement.

On-line procurement has many obvious advantages compared with traditional procurement flow. Using e-business models for online procurement can expand the range of suppliers, facilitate choosing the best suppliers and break through the limitations of traditional procurement. Additionally, Online-procurement can improve the logistics speed and the inventory turnover rate, and is helpful for supply logistics management to achieve the zero inventories and realize the JIT production. Online-procurement forms a fair price of market transaction between supply and demand sides which makes the two sides establish a long-term, mutually beneficial, and information sharing cooperative relationship on this base and achieve double-win situation.

This Internet-based IT systems of procurement must be able to provide efficient database engine technology to link the web, use visual development tools to connect the database end, and realize dynamic and interactive information management, which will make exchange of information more rapid and timely. The seamless connection technology of the database makes the enterprise's inside and outside form a united platform and realize information sharing and resource sharing, which is helpful to improve interoperability of supply logistics systems.

4. COLLABORATIVE MANAGEMENT MODES OF INTERNAL SUPPLY LOGISTICS BASED ON JIT

4.1. Total Logistics Cost Control Based on JIT

In supply logistics system, logistics cost occurs in many aspects. As a result, logistics cost control is a comprehensive system. In supply logistics system, we must manage the whole process of the entire supply logistics system include procurement, transportation, warehousing and so on, so that we can effectively control the total cost of logistics.

To establish and improve perfect logistics network control system is an important way of effective cost control based on JIT supply chain management. We must build a coordinated, convenient and full-featured network control system to implement system control to the total cost of logistics. According to the characteristics and requirements of system control of logistics cost, logistics network control system consists of subsystems such as organization assurance, process control, assessment accounts and information feedback.

By analyzing an enterprise's logistics cost, the basic ways to reduce logistics cost are as follows:

1. Reduce logistics cost by efficient distribution. Enterprises can realize efficient distribution, reduce transportation times, improve the loading rate, arrange reasonable automobile plan, and choose the best transportation way to reduce distribution cost.
2. Use logistics outsourcing to reduce logistics cost and investment cost. Enterprises can outsource logistics to specialized third-party logistics, which can shorten the transit time of goods and reduce the turnaround process cost and loss of goods. Qualified enterprises can use third-party logistics to supply on-line, so that they can achieve zero inventories and reduce cost.

3. Control and reduce logistics cost using modern information management system. In traditional manual management mode, the cost control of enterprises is affected by many factors, and it's not easy or possible to achieve optimal control of all aspects. The usage of information system by enterprises on the one hand allows a variety of logistics operations or business processes to run accurately and quickly. On the other hand, forecasting and analyzing with the data collection of Information system can control the occurrence of logistics cost.

4.2. Construction of Internal Collaborative Distribution System Based on JIT

There are many faults in the traditional supply system of warehousing and logistics, and it is now unable to satisfy the demand of efficient operation of supply logistics management based on JIT, which to a certain extent restricts the development of supply logistics and at the same time can't achieve the company's strategic objectives. For manufacturing industry, in order to reduce logistics cost and logistics cycle it is required to change the internal logistics model, improve logistics efficiency, and realize delivery with multi-variety, small-volume and multi-batch inside enterprises. So reform of supply management system and implementation of the internal logistics distribution have become the inevitable choice of implementation of JIT supply chain management.

The basic ideas for implementation of logistics distribution in the internal are as follows: Integrate and optimize logistics resources within the company so as to form the "Four in One" seamless operation model with Information network platform as the basis, the material as the main distribution, modern warehousing as the facility and a variety of means of transport as the way, as shown in Figure 3.

- Build the information and logistics hub systems of internal logistics distribution. The distribution center should have strong radiation, most advanced and complete logistics equipment and advanced management tools, which can deliver demand information quickly and accurately.
- Build transit warehouse with large coverage, a variety of delivery methods and high levels of logistics facilities and management methods.
- Build the transportation power which is able to meet the requirement of distribution operation and the low transport cost between distribution center and the transit warehouses.
- At last inside the enterprise realize the secondary distribution system in radial state covering the whole area with distribution center as the lead and the transit warehouses as the basic architecture.

4.3. Collaborative Mode of Internal Supply Logistics Based on JIT

Cross Docking means the goods flow from receipt process to delivery process directly crossing the storage, which can reduce inventory, eventually achieve zero inventory, and realize the advanced JIT logistics distribution. In cross docking system, the warehouses become the coordination point of

Figure 3. The "Four in One" seamless operation model

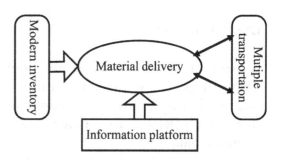

inventory rather than storage site. In typical cross docking system, the various goods from different suppliers reach the warehouse, and then they are delivered directly to truck loading area, and finally transported to different points of consumption in the shortest period of time. Therefore, the cross docking practice will greatly shorten the lead time, reduce the logistics cost of the goods, and improve the overall operational efficiency and competitiveness of supply logistics.

The operation process of cross docking is as follows:

- According to the demand plan, enterprise's information system aggregates the demand information, and then dispatch to the relevant authorities to review, and at last send purchase orders to suppliers.

- Suppliers prepare the parts needed by the manufacturer according to the orders. After supplier information center receives the demand orders of the demander, it first sends to the information center of the demander the Advanced Shipping Note (ASN), and then shipped the parts according to demand orders.

- After the information center receives the ASN, it notify the distribution center to make the necessary preparation do a serious of work such as sorting and assembling after parts arrive, and then distribute directly to the demand points. Usually it's required that the halting time on cross docking area should be less than one day.

5. CONCLUSION

According to the inside and outside analysis of supply logistics system, we can get the conclusion that successful and effective implementation of JIT-based supply chain management requires the following conditions:

1. Manufacturers should strengthen collaboration with suppliers, and build strategic partnership with suppliers, so as to make the suppliers fully support and understand the supply logistics system management based on JIT.

2. The various departments within the enterprise's supply chain need to strengthen exchange and cooperation, overcome sectionalism, try to eliminate the irrational parts among the nodes of the supply logistics systems, in order to achieve fast and efficient response to the demand thorough seamless operation of the process.

   a. In the supply logistics management based on JIT, enterprises should use advantage logistics managing technology, such as Hub, Cross-Docking, and at the same time, enterprises should have the logistics facilities and operational capabilities to implement these advanced technologies.

   b. The successful operation of supply logistics management based on JIT cannot do without the support of network, and so having a complete system information network is the key to success. Thus, enterprises should have an information system, which is able to meet the requirements of the operation of supply logistics system based on JIT, and realize the convenient exchange and sharing of information among all nodes in supply logistics system.

ACKNOWLEDGMENT

The authors thank the anonymous referees for their insightful comments and suggestions. This work was supported by the National Natural Science Foundation of China(No.71102174, 60979010), Program for New Century Excellent

Talents in University(NCET-10-0043), Beijing Natural Science Foundation(No.9102016), Excellent Young Teacher in Beijing institute of Technology (No.2010YC1307), the Key Project Cultivation Fund of the Scientific and Technical Innovation Program in Beijing Institute of technology(No.2011DX01001), and Basic Research in Beijing institute of Technology, China (No.20102142013).

REFERENCES

Akkermans, H., Bogerd, P., & van Doremalen, J. (2004). Travail, transparency and trust: A case study of computer-supported collaborative supply chain planning in high-tech electronics. *European Journal of Operational Research, 153*(2), 445–456. doi:10.1016/S0377-2217(03)00164-4

ARC Advisory Group. (2002). Collaborative manufacturing management strategies. *ARC Strategies*. Retrieved from http://www.arcweb.com

Barnes, E., Dai, J., & Deng, S. (2000). *On the strategy of supply hubs for cost reduction and responsiveness*. Singapore: National University of Singapore.

Boeck, D. L., & Vandaelee, N. (2008). Coordination and synchronization of material flows in supply chains: An analytical approach. *International Journal of Production Economics, 116*(2), 199–207. doi:10.1016/j.ijpe.2008.06.010

Cachon, G., & Fisher, M. (1997). Campbell soup's continuous replenishment program: evaluation and enhanced inventory decision rules. *Production and Operations Management, 6*(3), 266–276. doi:10.1111/j.1937-5956.1997.tb00430.x

Chen, F. (2001). *Information sharing and supply chain coordination*. New York, NY: Columbia University.

Chen, T.-H., & Chen, J.-M. (2005). Optimizing supply chain collaboration based on joint replenishment and channel coordination. *Transportation Research Part E, Logistics and Transportation Review, 41*(4), 261–285. doi:10.1016/j.tre.2004.06.003

Cheong, M. L. F., Bhatnagar, R., & Graves, S. C. (2007). Logistics network design with supplier consolidation hubs and multiple shipment options. *Journal of Industrial and Management Optimization, 3*(1), 51–69. doi:10.3934/jimo.2007.3.51

Disney, S. M., & Towill, D. R. (2003). The effect of vendor managed inventory (VMI) dynamics on the Bullwhip Effect in supply chains. *International Journal of Production Economics, 85*(2), 199–215. doi:10.1016/S0925-5273(03)00110-5

Dudek, G., & Stadtler, H. (2005). Negotiation-based collaborative planning between supply chains partners. *European Journal of Operational Research, 163*(3), 668–687. doi:10.1016/j.ejor.2004.01.014

Ellinger, A. E. (2000). Improving marketing/logistics cross-functional collaboration in the supply chain. *Industrial Marketing Management, 29*(1), 85–96. doi:10.1016/S0019-8501(99)00114-5

Fan, M., Stallaert, J., & Whinston, A. B. (2000). *Decentralized mechanism design for supply chain organizations using an auction market*. Seattle, WA: University of Washington.

Fu, Y., & Piplani, R. (2004). Supply-side collaboration and its value in supply chains. *European Journal of Operational Research, 152*(1), 281–288. doi:10.1016/S0377-2217(02)00670-7

Garg, D., Narahari, Y., & Viswanadham, N. (2006). Achieving sharp deliveries in supply chains through variance pool allocation. *European Journal of Operational Research, 171*(1), 227–254. doi:10.1016/j.ejor.2004.08.033

Gill, P. J., & Abend, J. (1997). Wal-Mart: the supply chain heavy-weight champ. *Supply Chain Management, 1*(1), 8–16.

Güler, M. G., & Bilgic, T. (2009). On coordinating an assembly system under random yield and random demand. *European Journal of Operational Research, 196*(1), 342–350. doi:10.1016/j.ejor.2008.03.002

Gupta, D., & Weerawat, W. (2000). *Incentive mechanisms and supply chain decision for quick response.* Minneapolis, MN: University of Minneapolis.

Gurnani, H., & Gerchak, Y. (2007). Coordination in decentralized assembly systems with uncertain component yields. *European Journal of Operational Research, 176*(3), 1559–1576. doi:10.1016/j.ejor.2005.09.036

Holmström, J., Framling, K., Kaipia, R., & Saranen, J. (2002). Collaborative planning forecasting and replenishment: new solutions needed for mass collaboration. *Supply Chain Management, 7*(3), 1359–8546.

Ito, T., & Salleh, M. R. (2000). A blackboard-based negotiation for collaborative supply chain system. *Journal of Materials Processing Technology, 107*(1-3), 398–403. doi:10.1016/S0924-0136(00)00730-5

Lee, H. L. (2002). Aligning supply chain strategies with product uncertainties. *California Management Review, 44*(3), 105–119.

Lee, H. L., Padmanabhan, P., & Whang, S. (1997). The bullwhip effect in supply chains. *Sloan Management Review, 38*, 93–102.

Lee, H. L., So, K. C., & Tang, C. S. (2000). The value of information sharing in a two-level supply chain. *Management Science, 46*, 626–643. doi:10.1287/mnsc.46.5.626.12047

Lee, H. L., & Whang, S. (1999). Decentralized multi-echelon supply chains: Incentives and Information. *Management Science, 45*(5), 633–640. doi:10.1287/mnsc.45.5.633

Lim, W. S. (2000). A lemons market? An incentive scheme to induce truth-telling in third party logistics providers. *European Journal of Operational Research, 125*(3), 519–525. doi:10.1016/S0377-2217(99)00210-6

Manthou, V., Vlachopoulou, M., & Folinas, D. (2004). Virtual e-Chain (VeC) model for supply chain collaboration. *International Journal of Production Economics, 87*(3), 241–250. doi:10.1016/S0925-5273(03)00218-4

Petrson, K., & Cecere, L. (2001). Supply collaboration is a reality-but proceed with caution. *Achieving Supply Chain Excellence through. Technology (Elmsford, N.Y.), 6*(3).

Rosenzweig, E. D. (2009). A contingent view of e-collaboration and performance in manufacturing. *Journal of Operations Management, 27*(6), 462–478. doi:10.1016/j.jom.2009.03.001

Sabri, E. H., & Beamon, B. M. (2000). A multi-objective approach to simultaneous strategic and operational planning in supply chain design. *International Journal of Management Science, 28*(6), 581–598.

Sahin, F., & Robinson, E. P. (2005). Information sharing and coordination in make-to-order supply chains. *Journal of Operations Management, 23*(6), 579–598. doi:10.1016/j.jom.2004.08.007

Shah, J., & Goh, M. (2006). Setting operating policies for supply hubs. *International Journal of Production Economics*, *100*(2), 239–252. doi:10.1016/j.ijpe.2004.11.008

Xu, L., & Beamon, B. M. (2006). Supply chain coordination and collaboration mechanisms: An attribute-based approach? *Journal of Supply Chain Management*, *42*(1), 4–12. doi:10.1111/j.1745-493X.2006.04201002.x

Yao, M.-J., & Chiou, C.-C. (2004). On a replenishment coordination model in an integrated supply chain with one vendor and multiple buyers. *European Journal of Operational Research*, *159*(2), 406–419. doi:10.1016/j.ejor.2003.08.024

Zimmer, K. (2002). Supply chain coordination with uncertain just-in-time delivery. *International Journal of Production Economics*, *77*(1), 1–15. doi:10.1016/S0925-5273(01)00207-9

Zipperer, J. (2003). *Accelerating inventory collaboration*. Retrieved from http://www.iw.com

Zou, X.-X., Pokharel, S., & Piplani, R. (2008). A two-period supply contract model for a decentralized assembly system. *European Journal of Operational Research*, *187*(1), 257–274. doi:10.1016/j.ejor.2007.03.011

Zuckerman, A. (2000). Compaq switches to preposition inventory model. *World Trade*, 72-74.

This work was previously published in the International Journal of Advanced Pervasive and Ubiquitous Computing, Volume 3, Issue 2, edited by Tao Gao, pp. 1-12, copyright 2011 by IGI Publishing (an imprint of IGI Global).

Chapter 9
Construction Competitiveness Evaluation System of Regional BioPharma Industry and Case Study:
Taking Shijiazhuang as an Example

Bing Zhao
Hebei University of Technology and Shijiazhuang University, China

Dong Sheng Zhang
Hebei University of Technology, China

Yong Zheng Zhao
CSPC Pharmaceutical Group Limited, China

ABSTRACT

Biological pharmaceutical industry not only has the continuous pulling action to region economy, also makes a positive contribution on the human productivity and quality of life. Biological pharmaceutical industry will become the leading industry of the century in quite a long time in the future. Taking Shijiazhuang as an example, according to the regional biopharmaceutical industry planning needs, building the industry competitiveness evaluation system, this paper analyzes the comparative advantage of Shijiazhuang in developing bio-pharmaceutical industry from 4 level evaluation index, including: the industry environment and policy, R & D capability, competitiveness of economic scale and industry support system. Provide a reference for local governments and business.

DOI: 10.4018/978-1-4666-2645-4.ch009

INTRODUCTION

Economic globalization changed the understanding for industrial geography and regional economy. New world division of labor will no longer follow state borders or political context, but the regional competitiveness. Industrial development not only depends on the country environment, but more importantly on the overall regional environment. Regional advantage will also form a community gathering effect and form the enterprise ecological system and network value chain within the community, thereby resulting in the regional industrial competitiveness with the competitive advantage. Biological pharmaceutical industry is a sunrise and knowledge-intensive industry, not only has the continuous pulling action to region economy, but also makes a positive contribution on the human productivity and quality of life. In recent years, China's various provinces and cities rank the biopharma industry as the key pillar industry of future development, but lack the study of the regional pharmaceutical industry field strengths and overall competitiveness, which cannot correctly guide the local development of pharmaceutical enterprises and medical community formation, resulting in repeat construction of medicine projects and technology and science Park in many areas with serious waste of funds and resources.

Domestic and foreign scholars made a lot of theory studies on competitiveness. In foreign general formed five different research perspectives such as: performance, structure, influence, etc.

Chen, Zhang, and Han (2004) domestic scholar, has been studied on the content of regional competitive power of science and technology, built a technological competitiveness evaluation system, and comparative analyzed the technological competitiveness in China's Yangtze river delta, pearl river delta and Bohai Economic Circle three big economic regions; Yang (2003) and Huang and Yang (2002) also described the content of the industrial technology competitiveness and built a evaluation index system. But, in the domestic, the evaluation of bio-pharmaceutical industry competitiveness still lack in-depth study. This paper conducted a further study and case analysis.

1. REGIONAL BIOPHARMACEUTICAL INDUSTRY COMPETITIVENESS EVALUATION SYSTEM

Biopharma industry is not only a particular pharmaceutical method, it is an integration for the biotechnology industry and medicine industry, covering six major components such as the relevant basic research systems, biological pharmaceutical enterprises, diagnostic techniques and products, biological medical equipment, testing services and wholesale marketing business. The characteristics are broad prospects, large investment, high risk, long industry chain etc. According to China's biopharmaceutical industry development situation and the related policy, focusing on the biological industry value chain, based on the previous study, Cai, Wu, and Wu (2004) set up a regional biopharmaceutical industry competitiveness evaluation system (Table 1), including 4 level evaluation index and 19 two evaluation index.

According to different characteristic in different areas, different levels of index can be adjusted. Assign value on index selection and weight of index by the Delphi method, and calculate the competitiveness through hierarchical analysis method. But the comparability between index should to consider when evaluating competition ability because of the regional differences of statistical indicators.

Table 1. Competitiveness evaluation system of regional pharmaceutical industry

level evaluation index	two evaluation index	The meaning of evaluation index
industry environment and policy	City location and resources	Refers to geographical location and natural conditions, reflecting whether it has the industrial base and resources
	Humanities and Public Relations	Refers to the population structure, living standards, consumption habits and human relations, mainly reflecting the demand and harmony of industrial.
	Industrial Structure	Refers to analysing proportion of GDP, industry structure, the growth rate, future projections and the composition of other industries in this region, which support the industry and have the symbiotic effect
	Industrial Policy	Refers to the special preferential policies to foster bio-pharmaceutical industry, given by Local government or Country
R & D capability	Number of R & D institutions	Reflecting the R & D capabilities in this region
	R & D investment	Reflecting the degree of attention paid for R & D
	New drugs in research projects	Reflecting R & D potential
	The amount of annual output of new drugs	Reflecting R & D output
	Number of patents	Reflecting the extent of own property and innovation capability
competitiveness of economic scale	City GDP	Reflecting the basis and space of industrial development
	Industry output	Reflecting the Bio-pharmaceutical industrial economies of scale and per capita creativity in this area, It can be subdivided into chemical medicine, Chinese medicine, bio-pharmaceuticals to statistics.
	Industrial added value	Reflecting the development capacity of industry
	The number of GMP enterprises	Reflecting the industrial activity and the industry attractiveness of capital.
	The number of foreign-funded enterprises	Reflecting the international degree and Enterprise cluster effect of industry
	The number of Scale western medicine products	A part of the competitive
	The number of Chinese protection products	One of the indicators, which evaluate the competitiveness of Chinese medicine industry
industry support system	The city infrastructure conditions	Refers to traffic, energy supply, communications facilities and a variety of business infrastructure, industry support platform, in this regional, reflecting the limits and supports for Biomedical Development Strategy.
	The number of GCP, GLP , GAP bases	One part of the national medical Standardization and modernization, the number of bases will become affecting factors for the regional industry.
	The number of CRO companies, Consulting companies, Intermediary institutions, etc.	One important component of the industry Service system, reflecting the industry hatching ability and maturity

2. COMPARATIVE ADVANTAGE OF SHIJIAZHUANG BIOPHARMA INDUSTRY BASED ON THE EVALUATION SYSTEM

Regional pharmaceutical industry competition ability is a comprehensive ability with comprehensive, dynamic and diverse characteristics. In Shijiazhuang this specific region as an example, the evaluation system around the biological industry value chain and regional pharmaceutical industry competitiveness objectively, accurately analyzes the comparative advantage of Shijiazhuang in developing bio-pharmaceutical industry. provide support and information of Shijiazhuang biolpharma industry and realizing the sustainable development of biopharma industry.

3. INDUSTRY ENVIRONMENT AND POLICY

3.1 City Location and Resources

Shijiazhuang is the capital of Hebei Province with integration of political, economic, cultural center. It is also an important city in the Beijing-Tianjin-Hebei Metropolitan Area triode and the dominant position is prominent. The geography condition of Shijiazhuang area is better with plains, mountain, grassland and rich species, providing support resources for the development of biomedicine and can use biology technology from these resources to screen valuable substances and provide many opportunities for drugs development. Shijiazhuang autumn weather conditions, temperature, humidity and are suitable for biological engineering: winter is not extremely cold and is conducive to microbial cultivation. The long time nearly 30 degrees average temperature and heat in summer can provide a good environment for microbial growth. In recent years, Shijiazhuang economy development is rapid, especially for new technology, new industry absorbing rate is very high. In

early 2005, with the pharmaceutical industry's size and strength Shijiazhuang become the first batch of national biological industry base and formed important business cards of the pharmaceutical industry development in Hebei. From a regional perspective, Shijiazhuang can be convenient to undertake the industrial transfer between Beijing and Tianjin rely on its comparative advantage of the land, water resource, labor costs and other factors. The biopharma industry development in Shijiazhuang is the breakthrough for the thought of development integration of Beijing, Tianjin and Hebei (Mahui, 2007).

3.2 City Humanities

Shijiazhuang has jurisdiction over 6 districts, 12 counties, 5 county-level cities and 1 state-level high-tech Development Zone with a total area of 15800 square kilometers. At the end of 2009, the resident population reaches 9774100 people, nearly 1 millions of people need to eat and take medicine. And the medical care consumption of Shijiazhuang residents presents growth trend year after year (Figure 1) and biological medicine industry has a huge market demand. According to the research, economic growth and the demand for drugs are positively related and drug consumption growth is generally higher than that of GDP growth. According to statistics, developed country, medium developed country and developing country average per capita annual drug consumption were $500, $100 and $30. With speeding up aging population, the improvement of people's living standard and the urban medical insurance reform in China, the medicine circulation system reform will effectively promote the growth of demand of medical health care products market.

3.3 Industrial Structure

Shijiazhuang city is a big city of traditional medicine and biological products, the pharmaceutical industry occupies a prominent position in the

Figure 1. Shijiazhuang resident medical care consumer price index figure

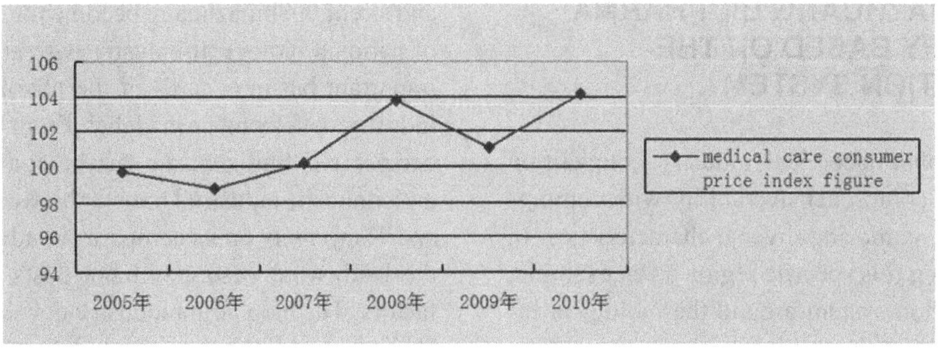

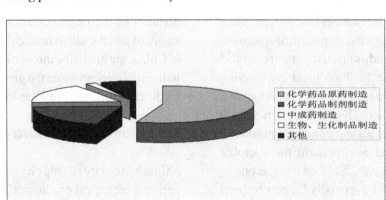

Data from Shijiazhuang Statistical Information Net

city's economic and social development. Currently, overall strength of Shijiazhuang biopharma industry has ranked No.1 in the country, accounting for 6% of total national pharmaceutical industry and accounting for 80% of Hebei pharmaceutical industry, in 2009 pharmaceutical manufacturing enterprises above Designated Size industrial added value of 7.9 billion yuan, accounting for 70% of Hebei medical industry added value. The manufacturing industry added value of chemicals manufacturing, chemical finished drug manufacturing industry, TCM manufacturing industry, biological and biochemical products respectively accounted for 54.7%, 20.1%, 16.9% and 1.9% (Figure 2) Yao and Yu (2008) of the city pharmaceutical industry added value. Shijiazhuang

has established a pharmaceutical industry system including pharmaceuticals, herbal medicine, veterinary medicine production, circulation service, education and scientific research, and already became the capital city with industry production characteristics throughout the country.

3.4 Industrial Policy

Shijiazhuang municipal Party committee and city hall attaches great importance to the development of Shijiazhuang biopharma industry, Formulate a series of policies and measures to promote bio-industry development, such as: "Shijiazhuang Construction Program of Action", "Shijiazhuang-Chinese Medicine Capital pharmaceutical industry

Figure 2. Shijiazhuang pharmaceutical industry structure

development Guidance Catalogue", "Biological (Medicine) Industry Restructuring and Revitalization of Opinions on the Implementation of such Policy Documents"," Hi-tech landing incentives "etc. Implement special preferential policies on the biological medicine industry, set up special organizations and institutions, establish special fund, accelerate construction of pharmaceutical industrial bases, spare no effort to build" Chinese medicine Capital". And adopt listing protection, administrative directory, financial services, finance and taxation support, innovation incentives and other measures to support the development of industry, committed to the development of Shijiazhuang into the state of major biological drug innovation base of industrialization of technology of biology pharmacy, national cleaner production demonstration zone, the State Pharmaceutical size and ability to mark area, Hebei Province biopharmaceutical industry development leading area, and domestic and foreign well-known enterprises in Hebei biopharmaceutical transfer to undertake the project area and investment destination.

4. R AND D CAPABILITY

Shijiazhuang City currently has 3 bio-industry academicians of the Chinese Academy of Sciences and Chinese Academy of Engineering, Dr. about 200 people, more than 6400 people above intermediate grade. Shijiazhuang has more than 20 universities and research institutions such as: Chinese Academy of Sciences, institute of genetics and developmental biology research center, institute of agricultural resources, Hebei Academy of Sciences, Hebei Academy of Medical Sciences, Hebei Academy of Agricultural Sciences, Hebei Province biological research institute, Hebei Provincial Institute of medicine, etc. Shijiazhuang gathers more than 95% pharmaceutical innovation platform of science and technology in Heibei province has 1 national engineering research centers, 2 national key laboratories, 2 industrial

technology innovation and strategic alliances lead unit, 4 state-level enterprise technical centers, 9 provincial-level enterprise technical centers, and a large number of provincial-level key laboratories and engineering Research Center (Shijiazhuang Daily, 2011). With science and technology as the lead, Shijiazhuang pays attention to the investment of funds and technology, focus on the development of high-end chemical pharmaceutical drugs, drugs, Chinese patent medicine, biotechnology and pharmaceutical technology innovation capacity building. According to Shijiazhuang FDA statistics, by the end of 2009, there are following biotechnology drugs having certain market and impact in the country: Jim Yan, Ji Saixin, Mai decoction, genetic engineering hepatitis B vaccine; Among the Hebei province key support 106 extending pharmaceutical industrial chains and new drug project in 2010, Shijiazhuang city projects amounted to 56. In the "Eleventh Five-Year" period, Shijiazhuang cumulative undertakes 22 national bio-pharmaceutical high-tech industrialization demonstration projects

Biopharmaceutical R & D require substantial capital investment, in some large pharmaceutical companies, R & D costs accounted for about 50% of its sales. The government of Shijiazhuang attaches great importance to the development of bio-pharmaceutical industry, constantly increasing financial investment and credit strength. In 2007, the National Development Bank branch in Hebei Province, Shijiazhuang development and investment limited liability company, North China Pharmaceutical Group New Drug Research and Development Company---the three parties signed the" Immunosuppressant Drug Industrialization Project Loan Contract". In 2009, Shijiazhuang city hall, Hebei province science and technology hall and the Provincial Department of Education decided in the next 3 years each year allots special funds respectively 20 million Yuan, 10 million Yuan and 5 million Yuan to establish "Provincial Industry-University-Institute Cooperation Fund", focusing on support the technology innovation project serving Shijiazhuang modern industry system establishment. Shijiazhuang city finance also plans to arrange 3 billion Yuan in three years of 2010-2012 to establish special funds for the development of modern industry.

5. COMPETITIVENESS OF ECONOMIC SCALE

In 2010, Shijiazhuang bio-pharmaceutical industry completed the main business income of 50.2 billion yuan, accounted for 14.8% of the city's GDP, industrial added value 15.1 billion yuan, profits and taxes 7.0 billion. In 2011,1-8, Shijiazhuang biomedical industry complete the main business income 42 billion yuan, industrial added value 12.0 billion, profits and taxes 60 billion, year-on-year respectively increased of 25%, 19% and 22%. Currently, Shijiazhuang has 136 above-scale bio-pharmaceutical enterprises, employing 6.5 million people, the biomedical industry output accounted for about 75% the proportion of Hebei province. Shijiazhuang has built a most important production base of vitamins and antibiotics in the world, the largest abamectin production base in Asia and an important modern medicine production base in China.

Shijiazhuang also has a large number of scale, unique, vitality and competitiveness of the pharmaceutical production, circulation and service enterprises. At present, the city has 5 enterprises were listed into the top 100 national pharmaceutical enterprises, 8 enterprises successfully listed (NCPC, CSPC, CSPG, Shijiazhuang Yiling Pharmaceutical Group, Shijiazhuang No.4 Pharmaceutical Co., Ltd., Hebei Veyong Bio-Chemical Co. Ltd, Hebei Changshan Biochemical Pharmaceutical Co. Ltd, Hebei AO XING group pharmaceutical co., ltd), Formed a large pharmaceutical enterprise group, represented by NCPC, CSPC; a modern enterprise group, represented by China Shineway Pharmaceutical Group and Shijiazhuang Yiling Pharmaceutical Group; a bio-pharmaceutical enterprise group, represented by NCPC GeneTech Biotechnology development Co., Ltd. and Hebei Changshan Biochemical Pharmaceutical Co. Ltd; a Biomedical engineering enterprise group, represented by Medical University Biotechnology Center, Shijiazhuang YiShengTang Medical Products Co., Ltd.; a Bio-agricultural enterprises group, represented by Hebei Veyong Bio-Chemical Co., Ltd., Hebei YuanZheng Pharmaceutical Co., Ltd and Hebei Ji Feng Seed Co., Ltd.; a Bio-manufacturing enterprise group, represented by HebeiHuaDan Complete Biodegradable Plastics Co., Ltd., Shijiazhuang Xinyu Sanyang Industry Co., Ltd. and Hebei xing cypress pharmaceutical group Co., Ltd.; a Pharmaceutical intermediates business group, represented by Shijiazhuang Baiqi Chemical Co., Ltd. and Lonzeal Pharmaceuticals Co., Ltd.

According to statistics, shijiazhuang focus on promoting 90 bio-pharmaceutical projects, which investment more than billion, the total investment about 73.6 billion yuan. Among them, the total investment 12 billion yuan new cephalosporin projects in a NCPC new industrial park have been completed, six production lines have passed the GMP certification, new projects are under construction;

FDA cephalosporin preparations and Oral preparation International projects have entered the test phase, with total investment of 10 billion yuan, in CSPC new industrial park; in Shijiazhuang Yiling Pharmaceutical Group, Projects of modern characteristic medicine and International agents industry are being implemented with total investment of 3.1 billion yuan, Phase extraction plant, pre-treatment plant has been capped; The first main projects of shenwei modern medicine industrial park have been completed With total investment of 40 billion (Shijiazhuang Daily, 2011). Construction and implementation of these projects will have a positive role in promoting the development of Shijiazhuang bio-pharmaceutical industry (Shijiazhuang Daily, 2011).

6. INDUSTRIAL SUPPORTING SYSTEM

If Shijiazhuang bio-pharmaceutical industry want to become a new bright spot to promote industrial structure optimization and upgrading, Shijiazhuang need to build a support system for bio-pharmaceutical industry in nine areas, including policy, talent and technological innovation, financial, capital, resources, environment, government, legal, services, information (Yan, Yan, & Ni, 2011). Along with leading pharmaceutical companies continue to grow and the growing strength of the overall research, the combined effect of Shijiazhuang bio-pharmaceutical industry has gradually emerged. Shijiazhuang has formed 5 parks with different characteristics, such as Hebei high-end pharmaceutical industrial park, The bio-industry core area of Economic and Technological Development Zone, Shenze biological industrial park, Luancheng biological industrial park and Zhaoxian County biological industrial park, their main business income accounts for about 60% of Shijiazhuang bio-pharmaceutical industry. In addition to introduces a number of biological and pharmaceutical related projects biological, Shijiazhuang is also actively cultivating biological energy, agriculture, chemical and other emerging biotechnology industry. For example, Huaying company and the Chinese Academy of Sciences, international giants use alcohol instead of gasoline to conduct technology biological energy development and industrialization. The development plan of Shijiazhuang biomedical industry not only consider the industrial, enterprises, but also take full account the presence of biomedical R & D, business logistics and agency, Pay attention to the accumulation of technology and talent, Support for biological research and training

7. CONCLUSION

To sum up, the development of Shijiazhuang bio-pharmaceutical industry has certain advantages but also exists a few problems restricting industry development, such as: low energy utilization, serious environmental pollution problems; rely on traditional medicine raw materials, industry technology innovation system is not perfect, the core competitiveness is low; raw material medicine production increase year by year, medical product structure imbalance; The number of GCP, GLP, GAP base is smaller; industrial supporting system is relatively weak. Shijiazhuang should actively solve the problems and exerts its advantage to develop the pharmaceutical industry bigger and stronger.

REFERENCES

Cai, G., Wu, S., & Wu, C. (2005). Competitiveness of the regional bio-pharmaceutical industry. *Journal of GuangDong College of Pharmacy*, *21*(5), 643–645.

Chen, G., Zhang, H., & Han, J. (2004). A comparative research on competitive power of science and technology on grey system theory. *Journal of Jinan University*, *25*(1), 19.

Huang, J., & Yang, G. (2002). Research of index system of evaluation and connotation about competitive power of industrial science and technology. *Science of Science and Management*, (11), 21.

Mahui. (2007, April 2). Integration new ideas of Beijing, Tianjin and Heibei: Shijiazhuang is a breakthrough. *21st Century Business Herald*.

Shijiazhuang Daily. (2011, September 13). Bio-pharmaceutical industry became the first leading industry of Shijiazhuang, 8 companies listed. *Shijiazhuang Daily*.

Yan, G., Yan, T., & Ni, B. (2011). On the Supporting Measures for the Leap-forward Development of Pharmaceutical Industry—A Case Study of the Biomedical Industry in Shijiazhuang. *Journal of JiShou University*, 32(2).

Yang, G. (2003). A Comparative Research on Competitive Power of Science and Technology in Regional Industries. *China Soft Science*, (3), 116.

Yao, W., & Yu, H. (2008). Research on the ability to Support Bases of Shijiazhuang Biopharmaceutical Industry. *China Science and Technology Information*, (2), 166-167.

This work was previously published in the International Journal of Advanced Pervasive and Ubiquitous Computing, Volume 3, Issue 2, edited by Tao Gao, pp. 13-20, copyright 2011 by IGI Publishing (an imprint of IGI Global).

Chapter 10
Development of Intellectual Property of Communications Enterprise and Analysis of Current Situation of Patents in Emerging Technology Field

Wenjia Ding
State Intellectual Property Office, China

ABSTRACT

In the process of promoting the national intellectual property strategy, domestic enterprises should seize the opportunity to develop their own intellectual property system according to their actual situations. The communication industry as an example of statistical data and specific analysis of patent applications in emerging technology field in recent years are supplied in the article.

INTRODUCTION OF NATIONAL INTELLECTUAL PROPERTY STRATEGY

The last decade, it is an important period for the rapid development of China's intellectual property. From central to local government, intellectual property is attracted unprecedented attention at all levels from corporate, with which the inputs associated are increasing continuously. Especially, intellectual property is first referred to the strategic level, as the National Intellectual Property Strategy is promulgated in 2008.

In early 2005, the State Council sets up the National Intellectual Property Strategy Formulation Leading Group, and launches the strategy development. The State Intellectual Property Office, State Administration for Industry & commerce, National Copyright Administration, Development and Reform Commission, Ministry of Science, Ministry of Commerce and other 33 units co-promote the strategy development.

April 9, 2008, the State Council executive meeting examined and approved in principle the "National Intellectual Property Strategy Outline."

DOI: 10.4018/978-1-4666-2645-4.ch010

"National Intellectual Property Strategy Outline" is a programmatic document of important national strategy for the use of the IP system for comprehensive development of economic and social, and guides the development of IP in China in a long period on the future, which made it clear that IP system is a basic system for development and use of knowledge resources, and will thereby promote transformation of economic development, ease constraints of resource and environment, and enhance the country's core competitiveness. Strategy Outline to establish and implement, will play inevitably an active role in the protection and promotion for long-term and healthy development of the national economy in the future.

THE CURRENT DEVELOPMENT STATUS OF INTELLECTUAL PROPERTY OF ENTERPRISES

The promulgation of intellectual property outline supplies an ambitious development plan and a bright future for intellectual property work. In the modern business world, intellectual property as a national important strategic resource and the company's core asset, its value can only be reflected through the commercial application. Therefore, the ultimate goal of intellectual property is in enterprise itself. This means enterprise must implement and improve its intellectual property strategy, convert innovation into tangible economic benefits, in order to truly reflect the value and significance of intellectual property.

As the saying goes "Rome was not built in a day." The current domestic enterprises, especially large and medium enterprises, as well as parts of the core backbone role in the field of private enterprise, the establishment of its own intellectual property system and use of intellectual property are basically in infancy.

Currently, the situations of intellectual property development in levels of business are broadly divided into the following categories.

The first category, intellectual property begun early, large investment, enterprise intellectual property system been initially established. The representatives are Huawei and ZTE as the leaders of domestic telecommunications industry.

Such enterprises pay more attention on building enterprises intellectual property strategy, because of their access to foreign markets early, and facing directly competition with the same types of world-class enterprises. Products are in direct competition with similar foreign products in the international market, and are often encountered intellectual property disputes, such as patent infringement disputes and litigation. High entrance fee at the initial stage is paid through the lessons, and then the enterprises increase the importance of intellectual property and investment. An early start, there is now a relatively robust enterprise intellectual property system, master of a considerable number of valid patents, and training a group of experienced intellectual property teams.

Up to now, Huawei has accumulatively patent applications in the global reached 40,148, of which China's total patent applications reached 31,869, 14,705 have been, 3,060 foreign applications have been authorized in total of 8,279, 85% of foreign patents are granted by developed countries in Europe and America.

In the 2009 Top list of invention patent applications of domestic enterprises announced by SIPO, ZTE and Huawei of two domestic companies are ranked first and second with 5,427 and 2,813 patent applications, and in the 2010 Top list of amount of invention patents Huawei is still on top depending on granted invention with 2,776.

The origination of intellectual property strategy in the enterprises of this type is for protecting the products and markets. Products where we go, also, the relevant patent are applied at there.

As accumulation in years, Huawei has set protection with the related patents and patent applications in all product lines. In a number of related disputes, there are in favor of litigation or settlement on overseas companies. In present, Intellectual Property Department not only provides a self-defense to develop markets for Huawei through a large number of active patents in hands, but also brings direct economic benefits for the company through patent licensing and other various means.

Although these enterprises have a solid step on the road of intellectual property, however, compared with similar foreign enterprises, the quantity and quality of patents are still lagging behind. In view of the level of overall intellectual property strategy, it is still in the "defensive back" stage.

The second category of enterprises, such as the National Grid in electric power industry, and various major telecom operators in telecommunication industry their overall strength is strong. Their intellectual property began a little late, but has made great progress.

And because the technology development in China went a different way compared with traditional power countries abroad. For example, UHV technology, because the problem of market demands in foreign countries, development is slowdown. Due to strong market support and technical R & D investment in china, this technology has been made a major breakthrough, and been at the leading in a certain direction (Intellectual property status of High-speed railway areas is similar with it, so that there are only two heights that Chinese enterprises pace with development of international scientific and technological level). Therefore, it is also a comparative advantage position for the patent application in the field, but considering the overall of enterprises, intellectual property is still in its infancy. The current main task is patent application. The management of granted patent,

systematic management of intellectual property, formulation and implementation about intellectual property strategy of enterprise, are in the beginning stages of construction or embryonic stage.

The third category of enterprises, such as in the electric power industry, for example, Dongfang Electric Corporation, Harbin Power Group, Western Power Group.

As for the traditional manufacturing enterprises, they are in the long-term technology and market dominance in the industry. And there are large-scale manufacturing, technology-intensive, capital-intensive, high barriers to market access, and little competitive pressure in intellectual property. Only in recent years, with "going out" strategy of water electricity, the necessity and urgency for building intellectual property strategy is surfaced during competition in foreign markets, including intellectual property competition. Therefore, these enterprises started late in intellectual property, coupled with the construction of talent that will take a long thing. Many of these enterprises do not have independent intellectual property expertise. Intellectual property and patent work are subordinated to the enterprises' technology department. It is just still in the stage of learning patent and intellectual property strategy.

The fourth category of enterprises, such as a considerable number of domestic small and medium enterprises, for example, a large number of small private enterprises in the communications industry.

Their product types are few, technical advantages are not obvious, and the market is uncertainty. As the difficulties of training talent of intellectual property and financial needs of strategy construction, the state is powerless. There are basically in a certain number of patent applications and granted patents. They cannot afford to build their expertise intellectual property management team and strategic planning.

THE CURRENT STATUS OF THE DISTRIBUTION OF DOMESTIC PATENT

Huge Amount, Uncertain Quality

In 2011, China will lead the world in patent activity. The annual patent application amount will be larger than Japan and the United States. In other words, China will become the world first in this field. The latest data of SIPO also shows that in the "Eleventh Five-Year" period, the number of patent application increases greatly in china. The growth rate of total patent applications is 22%, and growth rate of invention patent applications is as high as 24% in the average annual.

But, now there are about six million patents in all, and valid patents are fewer than the half, wherein, the ratio is one to two about invention and sum of utility model & design. With regard to Patent validity for 10 years or more, foreign applicants are accounted for 90%. The data of SIPO also shows that in nearly 10 years, growth rate of foreign patent applications in China is more than 20% in average annual, which is five times the global average.

Serious Imbalance in the Distribution of Patent

SIPO Commissioner Lipu Tian recently wrote an article in "Seeking Truth" magazine No.1 of 2011, it is said that, the accepted domestic applicant's patent applications have reached 5.852 million until the end of November 2010, the amount of granted patents of domestic applicants to 3.319 million, and the amount of patent applications of foreign applicants to 1.027 million, wherein 508,000 of granted amount.

However, such as invention patents in 2009, 45% of patent applications is foreign in China, and 55% is the domestic people' application. Moreover, patent application of which enterprises have fixed business places in domestic also regarded as domestic applications. That is, this 55% also includes a number of domestic applications of joint ventures.

In some areas, such as computer, communication, digital circuit, the number of foreign applications is much higher than domestic applications. Meanwhile, there are some areas of which China has an advantage, such as laser photo-typesetting, traditional medicine and other industries. Due to 20-year patent term is about to expire, technology will be free, and the relevant industries are facing an increased competition situation.

ANALYSIS OF EMERGING TECHNOLOGY PATENTS IN COMMUNICATION INDUSTRY

Due to characteristics of communication, its domestic patent applications and granted amount always are maintained a high growth rate in recent years. At initial stage of the construction and development intellectual property system in domestic industries and enterprises in general in current situation, the backbone of domestic telecommunication enterprises are undoubtedly in the forefront through using intellectual property system in response to global competition, improving their competitiveness and promoting a long-term development. Their own intellectual property strategies of Huawei, ZTE, Datang Telecom and other enterprises also are constantly adjusted and improved through years of market competition as the market changes, whenever it is necessary.

If Huawei and other enterprises in the patent arrangement or other aspects are still passive in response to foreign competitors before, seeking defense and negotiating capital, and patent applications of various of technologies tend to lag behind their foreign counterparts, and compared the number of core patents and granted time with Qualcomm and other enterprises of patent giant, there is a large gap. So, this year, the patent arrangement of in some areas of communication emerging technology, Huawei, ZTE and other domestic companies have planned ahead timely moved, to reduce and even eliminate gradually the gap between themselves and foreign enterprises, and occupied a favorable opportunity in intellectual property competition.

For example, LTE technology is well known. The domestic telecommunication enterprises have carried out proper planning and adequate preparation all in time and quantity of patent applications and technology distribution.

3GPP Long Term Evolution (LTE) technology is the largest technology R & D project started by 3GPP in recent years, OFDM / FDMA as the core technology, can be seen as "quasi-4G" technology. In fact, compared LTE with 4G, in addition to two indicators of the maximum bandwidth and uplink peak rate slightly lower than the 4G requirements, the other technical indicators have all reached the 4G standard.

The main performance objectives of 3GPP LTE project include: providing 100Mbps downlink, 50Mbps uplink peak rates in 20MHz spectrum bandwidth; improving the performance of cell edge users; enhancing cell capacity; reducing system latency; supporting 100Km radius of cell coverage; providing >100kbps access services for 350Km/h high-speed mobile users; supporting paired or unpaired spectrum, and configuring flexibly multiple bandwidth from 1.25 MHz up to 20MHz, etc.. Technical superiority of LTE is reflected in the rate, latency and spectral efficiency, and other fields, allowing operators to have more powerful service offerings in the limited spectrum bandwidth resources.

Currently, key technology and product R&D of LTE are rapidly advancing. Terminal chips, instruments and other sectors have formed a relatively complete industrial chain. Among them, in the system equipment, Huawei, Datang, ZTE, Ericsson, Samsung, Bell and other telecommunication equipment manufacturers in domestic and foreign all have launched commercial or pre-commercial products, and actively participated in system validation.

It is a pleasure, the patent applications on LTE technology from Chinese telecommunication enterprises are not as backward as the application on 2G and 3G which has the difference of 5-7 years from foreign patent applicants. The first time is in 2005 regarding domestic invention patent application of LTE; in this year, Huawei and ZTE Corporation submitted their relevant applications respectively. The relevant applications of domestic enterprises are amounted to 45, accounting the domestic invention patent applications LTE about 60% of the total. The next few years, LTE-related applications quantity of domestic enterprises is growing steadily year after year; up to the LTE applications reached a peak in 2008, the number of applications relevant to domestic enterprises closes to 1500, and still maintains domestic applications accounted for 60% of the high proportion of the total. It can clearly be seen, this time, domestic telecommunications enterprises not only catch up with pace of the world in independent intellectual property awareness, but also the ability to apply intellectual property strategy. Compared to the time of 10 years ago they have made a huge progress.

Figure 1 is a diagram that the proportion of patent related to LTE of the domestic enterprise to the total domestic application in 2005-2009. The figure shows, from 2005 to 2009, the percentage of LTE-related domestic invention patent to the domestic application gross has been remained above 60%, the number of applications far exceeding the amount of foreign applications. The disadvantages of domestic core technology patent application on time and number are reversed in the communication industry.

Meanwhile, in the division of specific technical field, the patent application arrangement also showed the rationality closely associated with technology application.

Figure 1. The proportion of patent related to LTE of the domestic enterprise to the total domestic application

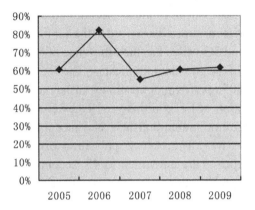

Base-band signal processing, network layer technology, multi-antenna technology and MBMS in LTE are more active areas of technology. The past five years, the percentage of above-mentioned application in all fields such as shown in Figure 2.

It can clearly be seen, base-band signal processing applications are accounted for the largest proportion, close to 40%, which is the most in-

Figure 2. The percentage of each technical field in the patent application related to LTE to the total application

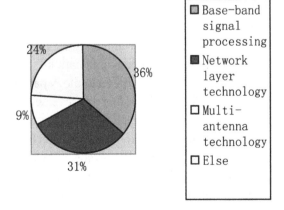

tensive technology in LTE patent applications. Meanwhile, the patentable segment technology covered by the base-band signal processing also is the most, including multiple accesses and spread spectrum communication, PAPR, link adaptation, frame structure and channel design, synchronization, random access, channel coding, interference suppression, cell search, up and down power control, equalization technology and other hundreds of patentable technology points.

To be able to account for the wave of commercial LTE opportunities, expand profits, the communication equipment manufacturers must combine with their technical superiority, product lines arrangement and the effective patent distribution of competitors, etc, and comprehensively plan and design their own technology in all segment point of the patent arrangement. These details must be fully considered in their own business development strategy-making process, each point may bring a profound implication on the competitiveness of enterprise's future product and market promotion.

Figure 3 shows the percentage of each patentable subdivision technology point to the total patent applications of baseband signal processing technology.

Referred to Figure 3, it shows the patent applications of frame structure and channel design are involved a large proportion. The reason is that OFDMA and MIMO are core technology in LTE, there is no extension of the GSM or 3GPP standard frame structure, but a new frame structure is designed. Technological change and innovation of related products have led to a high proportion in patent applications of frame structure aspect.

For example, the Hybrid Automatic Repeat Request (HARQ) technology as followed. A simple analysis is made of the situation of domestic related patent application.

HARQ is a key technology in LTE. Based on the different occurrence of repeat, HARQ can be divided into synchronous and asynchronous types.

Figure 3. The percentage of each patentable subdivision technology point to the total patent applications of baseband signal processing technology

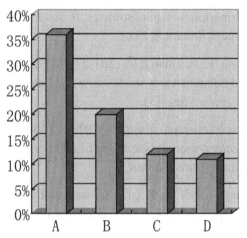

A: frame structure and channel design
B: link adaptation
C: interference suppression
D: channel coding

As the receiver in advance knows the occurrence of transmission in Synchronous HARQ, the process number of HARQ process can be obtained from the sub-frame; asynchronous HARQ process transmission can occur at any time, HARQ process number needs to be sent together with data.

As the HARQ can well compensate for signal transmission impacted by wireless mobile channel time varying and multiple path fading, it has become one of the key technologies in LTE. Related patent applications are also accounted a large proportion in area of base-band signal process.

ZTE and Huawei, two leading enterprises in domestic telecommunication industry, since 2005, began to actively arrange in various levels of patent in LTE technology. As the product line is closed, for taking the initiative in possible litigation and patent cross-license, there are a lot of cross application of several of segment technical points of them.

The HARQ technique, for example, Huawei applied data transmission method based on the HARQ in 2006. When the current data reaches the maximum number of HARQ repeat, sender HARQ entity deletes the data immediately has been sent to, as soon as possible to start next data transmission, to improve the overall HARQ transmission efficiency. After, receiver HARQ entity receives the data reached the maximum number of repeat, data status report is not returned in order to reduce the occupied signaling overhead for sending the data status report. Subsequently, a number of invention applications are submitted involving parameters configuration and detection in HARQ. Different HARQ parameters are configured according to different traffic configuration, in order to make up for deficiency, which in present technology, HARQ parameters of different service streams are configured without distinction, for seeking better quality of service QoS.

ZTE submits and a series of applications related to feedback channel division, the time spans from 2008 until 2011, involving the uplink HARQ feedback channel division method and uplink HARQ feedback channel realization method. Among them, the uplink HARQ feedback channel division method is used for wireless communication system uplink frame structure: uplink HARQ feedback region is constituted of multiple logical resource blocks, the block is divided into multiple segments, and each segment is divided into multiple sub-segment, all segments are divided into multiple transmission resource blocks of HARQ feedback channel, each transmission resource block of HARQ feedback channel contains at least one sub-segment, and each transmission resource block of HARQ feedback channel does not contain the same sub-segment among segments; for each sub-segment of each transmission resource block of HARQ feedback channel, all carries included in it are divided into data carrier and pilot carrier; they are multiplexed into the same transmission resource block of HARQ feedback channel in the way of code division multiplexing through multiple feedback channels, to improve the utilization ratio of uplink channel resource and ensure transmission performance of feedback information.

The interaction of patent technology in various segments field in two sides optimizes its own patent arrangement, can provide negotiating leverage for possible patent dispute, and maximizes benefits. From the enterprise's long-term development, there is no doubt its positive role.

CONCLUSION

In the patent arrangement of the communication emerging technology field, domestic enterprises have already begun making an overall planning, and made a proper arrangement and full preparation in the aspects of the patent application time, quantity, technical detail distribution, etc., thus winning the initiatives in the future intellectual property competition for themselves.

REFERENCES

Bao, D. (2008). LTE industry status and development trend. *Mobile Communication*, (16).

Cao, L. (2005). Research and analysis of patent information for patent strategy. *Technology Management Research*, (3).

Chang, F., & Huang, C. (2011). ETSI disclosure of LTE Patent Analysis. *Modern Telecommunication Technology*, (8).

State Intellectual Property Office. (2009). *Top 10 enterprises of patent application and grant*. Beijing, China: Author.

Zhang, T., & Lan, X. (n. d.). Patent analysis: One of corporate strategy and competitive analysis. *Information Science*.

Zheng, K., Wang, L., & Wang, W. (2007). *Hybrid automatic repeat request technique in LTE*. Folsom, CA: Communication World Network.

This work was previously published in the International Journal of Advanced Pervasive and Ubiquitous Computing, Volume 3, Issue 2, edited by Tao Gao, pp. 21-28, copyright 2011 by IGI Publishing (an imprint of IGI Global).

Chapter 11
Image Fusion of ECT/RT for Oil-Gas-Water Three-Phase Flow

Lifeng Zhang
North China Electric Power University, China

ABSTRACT

The tomographic imaging of process parameters for oil-gas-water three-phase flow can be obtained through different sensing modalities, such as electrical resistance tomography (ERT) and electrical capacitance tomography (ECT), both of which are sensitive to specific properties of the objects to be imaged. However, it is hard to discriminate oil, gas and water phases merely from reconstructed images of ERT or ECT. In this paper, the feasibility of image fusion based on ERT and ECT reconstructed images was investigated for oil-gas-water three-phase flow. Two cases were discussed and pixel-based image fusion method was presented. Simulation results showed that the cross-sectional reconstruction images of oil-gas-water three-phase flow can be obtained using the presented methods.

1. INTRODUCTION

The application of both electrical resistance tomography (ERT) and electrical capacitance tomography (ECT) techniques for the monitoring of industrial processes has been the subject of extensive research (Xie, Huang, & Hoyle, 1992; Dyakowski, 1996; Warsito & Fan, 2001; Jeanmeure, Dyakowski, Zimmerman, & Clark, 2002). Many of the contributions so far have been limited to image two-phase material distributions. Usually, ERT is used when the continuous

phase is conductive in multiphase flows, such as gas-water two-phase flow in vertical pipe. On the contrary, ECT is used when the continuous phase is nonconductive in multiphase flows, such as oil-gas two-phase flow. When it comes to oil-gas-water three-phase flow, it is hard for ERT or ECT to obtain good cross-sectional reconstructed images, from which oil, gas and water can be discerned clearly.

In order to obtain tomograms of oil-gas-water three-phase flow, an image fusion method was presented in this paper. The conductivity of oil, gas and water is different and that is the case for

DOI: 10.4018/978-1-4666-2645-4.ch011

the permittivity. Based on the fact that ERT is sensitive to the conductivity of objects and ECT is sensitive to the permittivity of objects, it is feasible to obtain the tomogram of oil-gas-water three-phase flow by image fusion based on the reconstructed images of ERT and ECT.

The following section describes the feasibility of the image fusion of ERT and ECT for oil-gas-water three-phase flow. After that, the reconstruction algorithms for image generation and the employed image fusion method are described briefly. Finally, simulation results were presented and discussed in detail.

2. ERT AND ECT SENSORS

2.1. The Structure of Sensors

The 16-electrode ERT and ECT sensors are depicted in Figures 1(a) and (b).

In ERT, the electrodes are mounted equally on the interior of pipe. The measured objects in pipe must be conductive and the electrodes must contact with them. While in ECT, the electrodes are mounted equally on the exterior of pipe. The measured objects in pipe must be nonconductive

or most of the mixture of the multi-phase material is nonconductive.

2.2. Image Reconstruction Algorithms

There are many different image reconstruction methods for ERT and ECT, which can be mainly classified into two categories, direct methods (linear back projection, Tikhonov regularization and truncated singular value decomposition) and iterative methods (Conjugate Gradient and Landweber) (Yang & Peng, 2003; Marashdeh, Warsito, Fan, & Teixeira, 2006; Wang, Tang, & Cao, 2007). In our study, Landweber iterative algorithm with optimal step length was adopted which is defined as (Liu, Fu, & Yang, 1999):

$$\mathbf{G}_{k+1} = \mathbf{G}_k + \eta_k \mathbf{S}^T (\lambda - \mathbf{S} \mathbf{G}_k) \qquad (1)$$

$$\mathbf{G}_0 = \mathbf{S}^T \lambda \qquad (2)$$

$$\eta_k = \left\| \mathbf{S}^T \mathbf{e}_k \right\|^2 \Big/ \left\| \mathbf{S} \mathbf{S}^T \mathbf{e}_k \right\|^2 \qquad (3)$$

Figure 1. The structure of sensor: (a) ERT sensor and (b) ECT sensor

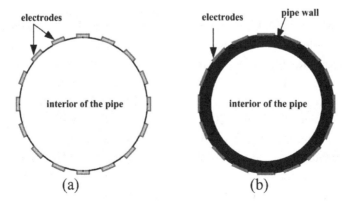

where $\mathbf{e}_k = \lambda - \mathbf{SG}_k$, λ is the measurements, η_k is the step length and $\mathbf{G}_k$ is the normalized image grey in the kth iteration, respectively.

3. IMAGE FUSION OF ERT AND ECT

For oil-gas-water three-phase flow, the conductivity (σ) and relative permittivity (ε_r) of oil, gas and water are given in Table 1 (Hjertaker, Tjugum, Hammer, & Johansen, 2005).

Two cases (named case I and case II) were investigated in this paper. The process of image fusion for the first case can be depicted in Figure 2. In this case, water is the continuous phase, while oil and gas are dispersed phases. Only bubbly flow with clearly discriminated oil and gas bubbles was considered.

It can be seen from the reconstructed image of ERT in Figure 2, conductive (water) and nonconductive (oil and gas) objects can be clearly separated. Oil and gas bubbles have the same area and are on the same radial locations. The reconstructed images of oil and gas bubbles after threshold filter are the same. The quality of the reconstruction image will not be affected by the permittivities of oil and gas. The result is that oil and gas bubbles cannot be discerned.

From the principle of ECT, objects with different permittivities can be reflected by the reconstructed images of ECT. It can be found from the reconstructed image of ECT in Figure 2 that the oil and gas bubbles can be discriminated by threshold filter. The area of gas bubble is larger than that of oil bubble on the reconstructed image. There is small difference between the permittivity

of gas and oil. The image filter threshold should be selected as large as possible, by which the difference between the area of oil and gas bubbles will be more obvious. From the ECT image after threshold filter, oil and gas bubbles can be clearly discriminated.

In this case, image fusion of ERT and ECT was carried out as follows: Firstly, the reconstructed images of ERT and ECT can be obtained. Secondly, from the reconstructed image of ECT after threshold filter, oil and gas can be discriminated. At last, combined the reconstruction image of ERT and the discriminated result from the image of ECT in the second step, image of oil, gas and water can be obtained with a grey threshold defined by user. The grey of oil, gas and water is defined as 1, 2 and 0, respectively.

The second case investigated can be depicted in Figure 3. Water is still the continuous phase. Gas bubbles are large, while several small oil bubbles surround gas bubbles. It can be seen from the reconstruction image of ERT that only gas bubble was reconstructed clearly. The reason for that is oil bubbles are small and wrapped by water. As a result, oil bubbles are taken as "water". Oil bubbles and gas bubble are close in Figure 3 and the difference of permittivity between oil and gas is small. Oil and gas bubbles are treated as one larger bubble. With a threshold filter, the reconstruction image of oil, gas and water can be obtained after image fusion.

In this case, the grey of oil, gas and water for image after fusion was obtained as follows:

1. Different thresholds were selected by user for reconstructed images of ERT and ECT in order to obtain the binary images.
2. For the reconstructed images of ERT and ECT, the grey value of each pixel was added and thus the image after fusion can be obtained.

Table 1. Parameters of three components

Component	σ (S m^{-1})	ε_r
Crude oil	10^{-6}	2.2
Gas		1
Process water	5	70

Figure 2. Image fusion of ERT and ECT for case I

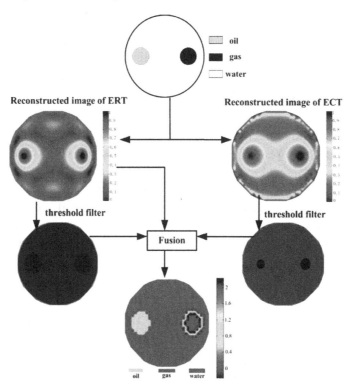

Figure 3. Image fusion of ERT and ECT for case II

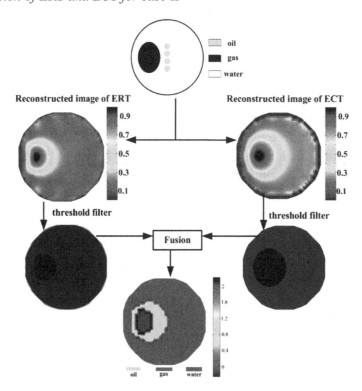

4. NUMERICAL SIMULATION

For the two cases discussed, simulation was carried out and the results were shown in Figure 4 and Figure 5, respectively.

It is can be seen from Figure 4 that the image of oil, gas and water with high quality can be obtained for the first case. Oil, gas and water can be discriminated clearly in this case.

However, the flow regime was complicated in Figure 5(a) and the reconstructed images of ERT and ECT cannot be satisfying, which will directly affect the image fusion effect. Gas bubbles can be discerned clearly from the reconstructed image after fusion (Figure 5(d)). Only a larger area including oil bubbles instead of accurate locations can be obtained.

5. CONCLUSION

To obtain reconstruction images of oil, gas and water for three-phase flow, image fusion of ERT and ECT were studied for two cases in this paper. Simulation results showed that oil, gas and water can be discerned clearly after fusion for the first case. For the second case, it is hard to obtain the accurate locations of oil bubbles. Further work will be focused on other image fusion methods to obtain more accurate image of oil bubbles and other cases will be investigated.

ACKNOWLEDGMENT

The author wishes to thank the Fundamental Research Funds for the Central Universities (11QG69).

Figure 4. Image fusion of ERT and ECT: (a) flow regime, (b) reconstruction image of ERT, (c) reconstruction image of ECT and (d) reconstruction image after fusion

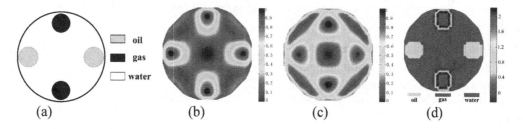

Figure 5. Image fusion of ERT and ECT: (a) flow regime, (b) reconstruction image of ERT, (c) reconstruction image of ECT and (d) reconstruction image after fusion

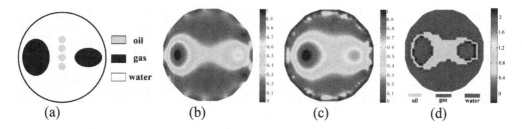

REFERENCES

Dyakowski, T. (1996). Process tomography applied to multi-phase flow measurement. *Measurement Science & Technology*, 7, 343–353. doi:10.1088/0957-0233/7/3/015

Hjertaker, B. T., Tjugum, S.-A., Hammer, E. A., & Johansen, G. A. (2005). Multimodality tomography for multiphase hydrocarbon flow measurements. *IEEE Sensors Journal*, 5(2), 153–160. doi:10.1109/JSEN.2005.843903

Jeanmeure, L. F. C., Dyakowski, T., Zimmerman, W. B. J., & Clark, W. (2002). Direct flow-pattern identification using electrical capacitance tomography. *Experimental Thermal and Fluid Science*, 26, 763–773. doi:10.1016/S0894-1777(02)00186-3

Liu, S., Fu, S., & Yang, W. Q. (1999). Optimization of an iterative image reconstruction algorithm for electrical capacitance tomography. *Measurement Science & Technology*, 10, 37–39. doi:10.1088/0957-0233/10/7/102

Marashdeh, Q., Warsito, W., Fan, L.-S., & Teixeira, F. L. (2006). A nonlinear image reconstruction technique for ECT using a combined neural network approach. *Measurement Science & Technology*, 17, 2097–2113. doi:10.1088/0957-0233/17/8/007

Wang, H. X., Tang, L., & Cao, Z. (2007). An image reconstruction algorithm based on total variation with adaptive mesh refinement for ECT. *Flow Measurement and Instrumentation*, 18, 262–267. doi:10.1016/j.flowmeasinst.2007.07.004

Warsito, W., & Fan, L.-S. (2001). Measurement of real-time flow structures in gas-liquid and gas-liquid-solid flow systems using electrical capacitance tomography (ECT). *Chemical Engineering Science*, 56, 6455–6462. doi:10.1016/S0009-2509(01)00234-2

Xie, C. G., Huang, S. M., & Hoyle, B. S. (1992). Electrical capacitance tomography for flow imaging: system model for development of image reconstruction algorithms and design of primary sensors. *IEEE Proceedings G: Circuits. Devices and Systems*, 139(1), 89–98. doi:10.1049/ip-g-2.1992.0015

Yang, W. Q., & Peng, L. H. (2003). Image reconstruction algorithms for electrical capacitance tomography. *Measurement Science & Technology*, 14, R1–R13. doi:10.1088/0957-0233/14/1/201

This work was previously published in the International Journal of Advanced Pervasive and Ubiquitous Computing, Volume 3, Issue 2, edited by Tao Gao, pp. 29-34, copyright 2011 by IGI Publishing (an imprint of IGI Global).

Chapter 12

Modern Educational Technique Center Educational Media Management based on Design and Practice of Questionnaire

Hou Jie
Tianjin Foreign Studies University, China

ABSTRACT

Questionnaire on teachers periodically based on traditional and passive equipment management mode is put forward in order for better equipment maintenance, for the teaching demand and for maximize utilize of educational media. Questionnaire content is composed of educational media technique training, equipment faults, utilize and demand of electrified education resource and job evaluation. Practice has shown that questionnaire that was favorably reviewed in school has made manager have an insight into the operation of equipment and teaching demand, improved educational service level.

INTRODUCTION

As manager and maintainer of educational media and equipment, modern educational technique center take on the work of media operation training, software and hardware maintenance, prompt elimination of errors in equipment and so on.

It is necessary for technical personnel to have technique of maintain of computer software and hardware, debugging multimedia system, modifying equipment. But as Lab manager, another important work is teaching service. It is more necessary for us to mastery the actual need of teaching, communication with equipment operator in order to better development of work. It is the important research project in our work.

DOI: 10.4018/978-1-4666-2645-4.ch012

In view of the above research project, In order to improve our way of work, it is proposed in this paper to design questionnaire to better understand equipment operation, the actual need of teaching.

This paper presents questionnaire contents, such as designs, statistical and question summarization. Investigation is concerned with the degree of knowledge possessed at equipment operation, educational multimedia training, equipment condition, the utilization and need of educational resource and evaluation of Lab manager's work.

1. MAIN CONTENT OF QUESTIONNAIRE AND QUESTION SUMMARIZATION

The scopes of questionnaire are teachers in the whole college, teaching-secretary and the external teachers.

1.1 Condition of Teacher Equipment Operation Knowledge and Technology Training (Table 1)

As to professional course teacher (such as language and computer) use professional Labs, Labs are classified into multimedia classroom, language classroom and computer room in order to observe teacher's knowledge about equipment from a certain professional Lab (Table 2).

From Table 2 we can see that there are more then half teachers attend training occasionally, ratio of never attend is 35%.It attribute to unstable way of teacher's working and partial external teachers. As to these teachers, we are planning to take training at the beginning of term and at odd moments. In order to meet the need of teacher, we will open up educational multimedia training resource database by using Campus Net to provide equipment guide of every kinds of Labs, software and hardware guides and elimination way of errors in equipment for easy to self-study.

Table 1. Educational multimedia training

Training	Every Term	Once in a while	Never
	11%	54%	35%
Suggested Training mode	Term Beginning	Dispersion	Combination
	39%	17%	44%

Table 2. Statistical of teacher's knowledge about equipment

Classroom Type	Equipment	Familiarity	Superficial Familiarity	Unfamiliarity
Multimedia Room	Computer Operation and Software Application	44%	54%	2%
	Projector Operation	25%	51%	24%
	DVD, Stereo	18%	55%	27%
Language Lab	Computer Operation and Software Application	15%	83%	2%
	Audio Teaching Platform	24%	65%	12%
	External equipment(DVD, Cassette)	10%	59%	31%
Computer Room	Computer Operation and Software Application	50%	38%	12%
	LanStar Teaching Platform	68%	23%	9%

In addition, from Table 2 we can see that equipments with that more than 20% teachers are unfamiliar are projector, DVD, Video Conference, Language Lab equipments (DVD, cassette and so on). The results show clearly that external teachers haven't got enough training. It is the main part of training content for us.

1.2 Condition of Errors in Equipment

Teachers that are long-term operators in the Lab can provide the first information of operation of equipment. As the fact of the condition and differences of equipments, Labs are classified by type and batches, the errors statistical of every type Labs are as follows (Table 3).

The statistic inference reflect the condition of equipment operation and errors type, it provides evidence for us to maintain equipment and our management work.

According to statistics of Table 3, we have made thorough examination for equipment with high failure rate and made an analysis of it. It is concluded that equipment with high failure such as headset and rate were attributed to high-usage patterns; equipment with high failure such as stereo, projection, teaching platform software were attributed to Unfamiliar with equipment and false operation; erratic operation of host computer were attributed to equipment part aging. So on the one hand we have to make regular checks and replace aging equipment, on the other more and better multimedia technique training should be done so as to decrease false operation.

1.3 Utilization and Need of Educational Resource

By statistics, 74% teachers considered that the existing equipment and teaching resource can meet the teaching need (Table 4). Besides, for resource need under concentrated reflection, like teaching software updates; Installation of multimedia system in professional Labs; network in multimedia classroom and so on. Through analysis

Table 3. The rate of equipment errors

Type	Equipment with more 20% errors	
Multimedia Room	Microphone, Stereo, Projector	
Language Lab	Lan Digital Audio System	Teaching Platform Software, Headset, Cassette
	NewClass Digital Audio System	Electric Switch, Headset, Computer Termination
	Panasonic Digital Audio System	Teaching Platform Software
Computer Room	Lenovo Commercial Computers	None
	实达 Commercial Computers	Hardware

and discussion about the above conditions accord to the facts, a series of implementation plans were drawn up. For example, <Application for Installing Teaching Software in Computer Room>was drawn up to increase work efficiency, network was up by effective network security technique in accordance with campus network.

1.4 Evaluation of Lab Manager's Work

From Table 5 we can see that our technical personnel were given credit for their technique and work attitude, which encouraged us to work hard so as to offer stronger guarantee for teaching.

Table 4. Teacher's satisfaction with teaching resource

Satisfaction	More Equipments and Resource
74%	16%

Table 5. Evaluation of Lab manager's work

Type	Good	Middle	Bad
Work Attitude	90%	10%	0%
Technique Level	93%	7%	0%

2. CONCLUSION

From the design of questionnaire to Implementation, data collection and analysis, our Lab management work was observed comprehensive inspection. In terms of the investigation to the teachers, we have got the whole knowledge of equipment operation, which provides basis for Lab management. By means of communication with teachers, we have found out teacher's equipment operation and teaching need, which provides basis for improvement of teaching quality. Evaluation of Lab manager's work has brought the active and prodding functions to our work.

Certainly, there also have some false in questionnaire content, data collection, which was the experience to our future work.

REFERENCES

Cai, S., & Huang, R. (2009). Service is the new need for digital campus. *Information Technology Education in School, 11*, 59–60.

Cao, Y., & Tao, Y. (2011). Exploring on educational technology training pattern for teachers in colleges. *Software Guide, 2*, 171–173.

Gong, C.-H., & Huang, R.-H. (2010). Seven key factors towards effective planning of teacher training. *Modern Educational Technology, 20*(12), 65–68.

Huang, R., Chen, G., Zhang, J., & Wang, Y. (2010). Research on informationization learning mode and its digital resource form. *Modern Distance Education Research, 6*, 68–73.

Liu, L.-L., & Xu, M. (2011). Research on the mode of digital educational resource sharing among colleges and universities. *Journal of Jiangsu Radio & Television University, 2*, 15–18.

Yan, H. (2011). Construction and management for laboratory in campus. *China Educational Technology & Equipments, 23*, 24–25.

Zhang, T. (2009). Managing strategies of college laboratories. *Journal of Nanjing Technical College of Special Education, 2*, 71–73.

This work was previously published in the International Journal of Advanced Pervasive and Ubiquitous Computing, Volume 3, Issue 2, edited by Tao Gao, pp. 35-38, copyright 2011 by IGI Publishing (an imprint of IGI Global).

Chapter 13
Residential Load Pattern Analysis for Smart Grid Applications Based on Audio Feature EEUPC

Yunzhi Wang
Institute of Computing Technology, Chinese Academy of Sciences and Graduate University of Chinese Academy of Sciences, China

Xiangdong Wang
Institute of Computing Technology, Chinese Academy of Sciences, China

Yueliang Qian
Institute of Computing Technology, Chinese Academy of Sciences, China

Haiyong Luo
Institute of Computing Technology, Chinese Academy of Sciences, China

Fujiang Ge
Fujitsu Research & Development Center Co., Ltd., China

Yuhang Yang
Fujitsu Research & Development Center Co., Ltd., China

Yingju Xia
Fujitsu Research & Development Center Co., Ltd., China

ABSTRACT

The smart grid is an important application field of the Internet of things. This paper presents a method of user electricity consumption pattern analysis for smart grid applications based on the audio feature EEUPC. A novel similarity function based on EEUPC is adapted to support clustering analysis of residential load patterns. The EEUPC similarity exploits features of peaks and valleys on curves instead of directly comparing values and obtains better performance for clustering analysis. Moreover, the proposed approach performs load pattern clustering, extracts a typical pattern for each cluster, and gives suggestions toward better power consumption for each typical pattern. Experimental results demonstrate that the EEUPC similarity is more consistent with human judgment than the Euclidean distance and higher clustering performance can be achieved for residential electric load data.

DOI: 10.4018/978-1-4666-2645-4.ch013

1. INTRODUCTION

The smart grid is an intelligent electrical power management system inherited from the conception of the Internet of Things. It is based on the physical electricity network, and benefits humanity by advanced technologies highly integrated, such as sensors, automation control and decision support. In the field of smart grid, electric load analysis has attracted considerable attention of researchers in recent years. According to the result of electric load analysis, electricity suppliers are able to improve power energy supply and distribution. What's more, electric load analysis is closely linked with consumers, helping them understand their own needs and make an arrangement of power energy consuming more wisely.

Current work on electric load analysis mainly includes two aspects. On one hand, many researchers analyze the impact of various factors on the electric load in order to facilitate load forecasting. Numerous methods have been proposed, such as Kalman filtering analysis, regression analysis, exponential smoothing forecasting, expert systems, fuzzy prediction, gray model, optimal combination forecasting, artificial neural networks, rough sets algorithm, fuzzy clustering, particle swarm optimization, and genetic algorithm. Based on these algorithms, researchers intend to figure out the relationships between the electric load and factors such as weather, economic growth and so on, and using the factors with high relevance, higher accuracy can be achieved in load forecasting.

On the other hand, there is also much research effort on user electric load pattern analysis, of which current research mainly focuses on clustering and classification of load patterns (daily or monthly load curves in practice). The purpose of load pattern clustering analysis is to group users' load patterns into several typical classes and thus help electricity suppliers get better knowledge of their customers and customize their supply strategies. For example, many researchers perform clustering analysis on load patterns of industrial

electricity customers such as companies and factories (Ding & Wang, 2008). They compare clustering results with economic type codes of customers, indicating that electric power load patterns can be effectively distinguished by patter modes and the results are approximately consistent with industry types. The limitation of this sort of research lies in three aspects: First, most current research work focuses on clustering of load data of industrial customers other than ordinary residential customers, and conclusions of this type of research cannot suit residential customers as consumption habits of industrial customers and residential customers are of considerable difference. However, clustering analysis of residential customers is of great significance, since the domestic load occupies a large part of total electricity consumption, and is usually not as stable as industrial consumption. Secondly, current methods only yield the result of clustering analysis and support of decision-making is not provided. To make decisions, users have to analyze the clusters of patterns manually to extract useful information. Thirdly, most current methods which deal with industrial load data use the Euclidean distance as the distance measurement of load patterns. However, for residential load data which are more unstable, similar patterns with consistent peaks and valleys may yield low similarity due to the difference in value, thus making results of clustering not satisfactory. Therefore, a different distance metric is needed, which measures the similarity in terms of the shape of the load curve (e.g., peaks and valleys on the curve) instead of simply comparing the values.

In this paper, an approach for residential electric load pattern analysis is proposed. The method focuses on analysis of residential electric load patterns and proposes a novel similarity function based on the audio feature EEUPC (which is named EEUPC similarity). The EEUPC distance exploits features of peaks and valleys on curves instead of directly comparing values as Euclidean distance does, and can obtain better performance for clustering analysis. Moreover, the approach proposed in this paper not only performs load pattern clustering, but also extracts a typical pattern for each cluster and gives suggestions of wiser consumptions with lower cost for each typical pattern.

The rest of this paper is organized as follows. In Section 2, related work on electric load analysis is presented. In Section 3, the electric load pattern clustering method based on the audio feature EEUPC is described in detail. And Section 4 presents the method for typical load pattern analysis after clustering. Experimental results are given in Section 5. And finally, conclusions are drawn in Section 6.

2. RELATED WORK

As mentioned above, there are mainly two kinds of research work on electric load analysis: relevance analysis of climatic and economic factors for load forecasting, and user load pattern analysis.

In recent years, there is a large amount of academic research on the analysis of factors associated with load forecasting (Li & Li, 2004; Hor, Watson, & Majithia, 2005; Mori & Kobyashi, 1996; Alfuhaid, 1997; Su & Song, 2010). Hor et al. (2005) analyzed the impact of weather variables on monthly electricity demand in England and Wales using a multiple regression model. Weather variables considered includes degree days, enthalpy latent days, and relative humidity. Mori and Kobyashi (1996) used the fuzzy inference system to forecast electricity load. They proposed a method for constructing an optimal structure of the simplified fuzzy inference that minimizes model errors and the number of the membership functions to grasp nonlinear behavior of power system short-term loads. Apart from these, ANN (artificial neural networks) is also widely used in multi-variable electricity load analysis and forecasting. In Alfuhaid (1997), an algorithm using

cascaded ANN together with historical load and weather data is proposed to forecast half-hourly power system load for the next 24 hours. The ANNs were trained and tested on the electric power system of Kuwait. Some other researchers analyzed electric load from the aspect of economy and society. For instance, Su and Song (2010) tried to make a comparative analysis of the weights of influencing factors of electrical energy consumption by weighted least squares (WLS) and quantile regression (QR).

For user load pattern analysis, current research work mainly focuses on clustering and classification of consumers' load data (Ding & Wang, 2008; Wang & Cao, 2007). The most common scheme is as presented in Wang and Cao (2007), in which load data clustering analysis is adopted to generate user load profiles for industrial consumers. Under the scheme, Euclidean distance is adopted as the distance measurement for clustering and various clustering algorithms may be used for clustering analysis. In Wang and Cao (2007), three algorithms, namely, K-means clustering, K-centers clustering and hierarchical clustering were compared to each other and experimental results showed that hierarchical clustering algorithm performed better than other algorithms. Also, for each cluster, a typical load pattern was extracted and compared with traditional economic industrial clusters. Other clustering algorithms such as fuzzy analogy were also used for clustering (Gao, Wang, & Song, 2008). There is also research work on analysis of electricity consumption patterns for making decisions in distribution management and price strategies. These researches mainly focus on analyzing peaks and valleys in the electricity consumption pattern to decide better price strategy (Hu et al., 2008; Tan, Yu, & Jiang, 2009). Those analyses are performed on consumption data of a city or county, and do not give information in terms of groups of users.

3. RESIDENTIAL ELECTRIC LOAD PATTERN CLUSTERING BASED ON THE AUDIO FEATURE EEUPC

The aim of clustering analysis is to classify data into categories where data in the same category are similar and data in different categories have a greater difference. Therefore, clustering analysis is on the basis of similarity measurement of data as it indicates differences between data while clustering.

There are many similarity and distance measurements to be taken into account for clustering analysis, such as the Euclidean distance, Minkowski distance and Mahalanobis distance, etc. As mentioned above, most current methods for electric load data clustering use the Euclidean distance which measures the difference between load values. However, for residential load data which are more unstable than industrial data, Euclidean distance cannot depict the similarity well as similar patterns with consistent peaks and valleys may yield low similarity due to the difference in value. In this paper, we propose a new similarity measurement function (the EEUPC similarity) based on EEUPC (Energy Envelop Unit Position and Confidence), which is an audio feature for efficient audio clip similarity measurement first used in audio retrieval (Zhao, Wang, Qian, Liu, & Lin, 2008; Wang, Li, Qian, Yang, & Lin, 2009). Unlike the Euclidean distance, the EEUPC similarity focuses on the shapes, especially peaks and valleys of curves and does not calculate similarity strictly according to the values on the curve. Since the electric load curve is different from audio data in terms of factors such as value range, degree of instability, etc., the calculation of EEUPC similarity used in this paper is a modified version of that for audio data (Wang et al., 2009). The definition and calculation of the similarity is detailed in the rest of this section.

3.1 The EEUPC Similarity

In the definition of EEUPC, the curve of energy is referred to as the energy envelope (Wang et al., 2009). In terms of shape of the curve, it can be observed that energy envelopes could be divided into units each contains one major peak and two low endpoints. Figure 1 shows an example of a residential consumer's power energy curve on all weekdays in a month. It can be seen that the curve can be divided into three units, in each of which exists a major peak of load value. Notice that in the first unit there are actually two peaks. However, the first peak is relatively short in time and not high enough to distinguish from the other peak, which implies that there may be noise or instability. Therefore, the two peaks are considered as one major peak to avoid influences of noise. In fact, this is the most important feature of EEUPC according to other unit segmentation methods.

To segment units of energy envelope, values of a *detection function* are calculated first. The detection function is defined as follows and is used to detect the maximum energy difference among J neighbor points after each point of the whole curve.

$$d_i = \max_{j=1,\dots,J}(E_{i+j} - E_i) \qquad (1)$$

where E_i denotes the electric load value of the ith point on the curve, and the value of J is to be decided by experiments. Notice that $E_{i+j} - E_j$ is used instead of E_{i+j} / E_j used in audio retrieval (Wang et al., 2009) due to the difference in the value range between load data and audio data.

According to the detection function, energy envelope units can be segmented. In order to improve accuracy, segmentation confidence is adopted instead of binary thresholding. The confidence is calculated as

Figure 1. An example of energy envelope units

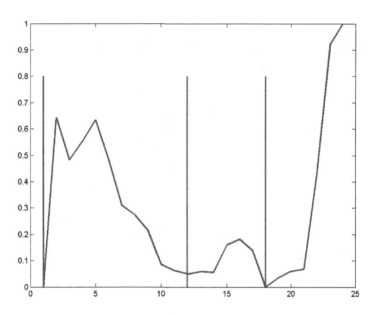

$$P(i) \begin{cases} 1, & d_i \geq T_2 \\ \dfrac{d_i - T_1}{T_2 - T_1}, & T_1 < d_i < T_2 \\ 0, & d_i \leq T_1 \end{cases} \qquad (2)$$

where d_i denotes the detection function value on the ith point on the curve, and T_1 and T_2 are pre-determined thresholds. After the segmentation confidence calculation, points with non-zero confidence are recorded as segmentation positions, and segments between these segment positions are recorded as segmentation units. The segmentation positions and confidence values are used together as the EEUPC (Energy Envelope Unit Positions and Confidence) representation of the electric load curve, which is denoted as $U = (u_1, p_1), (u_2, p_2), \ldots, (u_n, p_n)$, where U denotes a load curve, n is the number of energy envelope units, and u_i and p_i denote the position and confidence value of the ith unit, respectively. The procedure of energy envelope unit segmentation is illustrated in Figure 2. In the graph illustrating the

segmentation of energy envelope units, the position and height of each vertical line shows the position and the confidence value of each energy envelope unit.

Using the EEUPC representation of load curves, the EEUPC similarity can be calculated as follows. Suppose that there are two load curves, which can be represented by EEUPC as $U = \{(u_1, p_1), (u_2, p_2), \ldots, (u_m, p_m)\}$, and $V = \{(v_1, q_1), (v_2, q_2), \ldots, (v_n, q_n)\}$, where u_i, v_j and p_i, q_j ($i=1,2,\ldots,m$; $j=1,2,\ldots,n$) denote positions and confidences of unit segmentation, respectively. For each segmentation position u_i in U, if there exists v_j in V satisfying that $|u_i - v_j| < T$, where T is a pre-determined threshold, then u_i is said to be detected, and the detection confidence $p_i' = \min\{p_i, q_j\}$. Then, similarity based on EEUPC of the two curves U and V is calculated as

$$S(U,V) = \frac{2R(U,V)P(U,V)}{R(U,V) + P(U,V)} \qquad (3)$$

Figure 2. Procedure of energy envelope unit segmentation

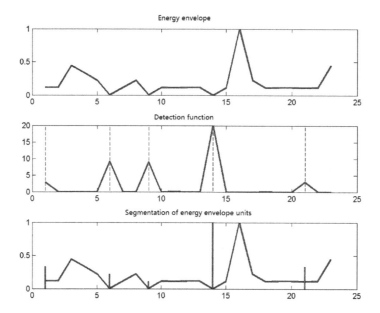

$$R(U,V) = \sum_k p_k' \Big/ \sum_{i=1}^m p_i , \quad P(U,V) = \sum_k p_k' \Big/ \sum_{i=1}^n q_i$$
(4)

It can be seen that $R(U,V)$ and $P(U,V)$ are similar to the widely used metrics of recall and precision, and $S(U,V)$ can be seen as the F1 value of R and P. Therefore, the EEUPC similarity actually calculates the consistence of unit segmentations between the two curves. Since the similarity depends on both the position and confidence (which essentially implies the magnitude of the peak), it considers both the position and height of the peak in a relatively approximate way instead of directly comparing values.

3.2 Residential Electric Load Pattern Clustering

Based on the EEUPC similarity, clustering of residential electric load patterns is performed. The aim of load pattern clustering is to cluster load patterns of different consumers into several classes

to better understand the consumers' behavior and support decision making. The load pattern of each residential consumer is represented by the load curve within a certain period. In our work, clustering is performed on daily load curves to explore the user load pattern within one day, where each point on the curve stands for the load of the hour, making totally 24 points on the curve.

Before clustering, some pre-processing is needed for the load data (Wang & Cao, 2007). First, for each consumer, a daily load curve should be obtained for clustering. Obviously, using the load curve of a certain day may incorporate random error into the results. Therefore, the ordinary method adopted is to average daily load curves within a period (e.g., a month or a year) to generate an average daily load curve. Furthermore, since the load on weekdays and weekends may differ considerably from each other, load curve clustering is performed separately for weekday curves and weekend curves and averaging is performed separately accordingly.

In order to emphasize the trend of a curve and to weaken the influence of absolute values, daily load data should be normalized before clustering. Suppose that load value of time t is denoted as E_t, the normalized value is calculated as

$$E_t^{'} = \frac{E_t - E_{min}}{E_{max} - E_{min}} \tag{5}$$

where E_{max} and E_{min} are the maximum and minimum load values on the curve.

For electric load pattern clustering, there are many commonly used clustering methods such as model-based methods, intensity-based methods and so on. Among them most widely used are K-means algorithm, K-center algorithm and hierarchical clustering. Which method to use depends on features of data. In our work, after tests on different methods, we choose hierarchical clustering as our final clustering method. In this algorithm, each load curve forms a cluster initially, and then in every step of the clustering procedure, the nearest two curves (which means that the two curves have the smallest distance or largest similarity) are found and emerged into one cluster. The procedure ends when the total number of clusters reduced to the cluster number pre-determined.

In the clustering process, distances between clusters can be calculated in different ways. Generally speaking, the most commonly used one is single-linkage, that is, when two clusters contain more than one curve, the distance between each point in cluster 1 and each point in cluster 2 are calculated and the minimum of all these distances is chosen as the distance between cluster 1 and cluster 2. Meanwhile, there are also other methods such as choosing the maximum of all distances (referred to as complete-linkage), and choosing the average distance (referred to as average-linkage). In our work, with comparison of all these methods, we finally used averaged-linkage as our distance calculating method. Suppose that there are two clusters P and Q. The average distance D_{PQ} is calculated as

$$D_{PQ}^2 = \frac{1}{n_P n_Q} \sum_{X_i \in P} \sum_{X_j \in Q} d_{ij}^{\,2} \tag{6}$$

where n_P is the number of all curves in cluster P, and n_Q is the number of all data points in cluster Q. X_i indicates the ith curve in cluster P, X_j indicates the jth curve belongs to cluster Q, and d_{ij} is the distance between X_i and X_j.

4. TYPICAL LOAD PATTERN ANALYSIS

After load pattern clustering, consumer load patterns are clustered into several classes, and further analysis is needed to explore the characteristics of each class. Some researchers end their work by presenting the classes to system users and leave the analysis and decision making to humans. Other research work extracts a typical pattern for each cluster, but does not perform automatic analysis on the typical pattern and thus cannot support the browse and retrieval of peaks and valleys of power consumption for each cluster of consumers.

In this paper, in addition to load pattern clustering, a method of typical load pattern analysis is proposed to extract useful information from each cluster and support browse, retrieval of those information. The main idea is to extract a typical pattern of each cluster, and extract information about peaks and valleys of power consumption. Extracted information can benefit decision making of power supplies and can also help consumers better understand their electric load patterns and better arrange their daily electricity consumptions.

4.1 Typical Load Pattern Extraction

Typical patterns can represent characteristics of the electric load pattern of a class of users. By analyzing typical patterns instead of performing separate analyses on each customer, influence of abnormal load patterns can be avoided and more robust conclusions can be achieved.

To extract the typical load patterns from each cluster, the method of averaging is used as in Wang and Cao (2007). For a cluster P, the typical load pattern p_t is calculated as

$$E_{tj} = \frac{1}{n} \sum_{p_i \in P} E_{ij}, \quad j = 1, 2, ..., N \quad (7)$$

where N denotes the dimension of the load pattern (for example, in our work, N=24 since daily load pattern with data of 24 hours are used.), n is the number of load patterns in cluster P, p_i is the ith load pattern in cluster P, and E_{ij} and E_{tj} are the jth load values of p_i and the typical pattern p_t, respectively.

Despite the fact that a typical pattern is not a real electric load curve, it reveals the characteristic of the electricity consuming habit of users in a cluster. Figure 3 shows an example of typical pattern extraction where all 190 daily load patterns in a cluster and the typical pattern (the bold curve in the figure) extracted by averaging are plotted. It can be seen that the typical pattern shows basic trends of most of the 190 patterns.

4.2 Analysis of the Typical Load Pattern

As mentioned above, typical patterns can be analyzed to indicate the features of clusters. In this paper, a method for analysis of the typical load pattern is proposed, which can provide two kinds of information for the typical load pattern of a cluster: First, the proportion that the consumers in the cluster take in all consumers is calculated to indicate the significance of the typical load pattern. Secondly, the typical load pattern curve is segmented into energy envelope units and the peaks of units are extracted and shown to system users for further decision making.

Figure 4 shows an example of typical load pattern analysis, where Figure 4(a) is a typical load pattern curve and Figure 4(b) shows the segmentation result of the typical pattern. It can be seen in Figure 4(b) that a peak of power consumption in the pattern may be extracted which appears at the hour between 17 o'clock and 23 o'clock. Therefore, the information extracted from the analysis will be presented to the system user in the following form.

Figure 3. An example for typical load pattern extraction

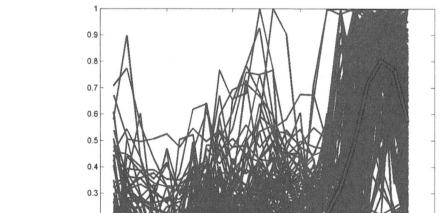

Figure 4. Example of typical pattern segmentation

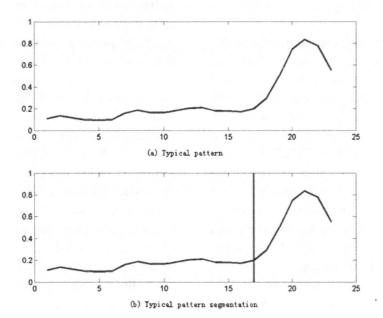

(a) Typical pattern

(b) Typical pattern segmentation

- This type of consumers takes a proportion of 38.0% in all consumers.
- There is one electric load peak in the typical load pattern.
- The load peak appears in 17:00 -23:00.
- The maximal load appears at 21:00.
- It might be encouraged that the customers consume electric power from 0:00 to 17:00.

With the aid of automatic analysis and suggestion, power suppliers are able to better understand their customers and make decision in power management and price strategies. Moreover, with the suggestions and impact of corresponding price strategies, electricity consumers are able to arrange power consuming plans wisely.

5. EXPERIMENTAL RESULTS ANALYSIS

To evaluate the method proposed in this paper, experiments are conducted using real electric load data recorded by smart meters. The data set includes daily load data of 500 household consumers of a community in Beijing within the year 2009. Each daily load datum is represented by a load curve with 24 points, which denotes the load in each hour within the day. As detailed in 3.2, for each consumer, all load curves in weekdays are averaged to generate the load pattern of the consumer, resulting in 500 load patterns. Clustering analysis are performed on the 500 load patterns. For most clustering algorithms, including the hierarchical clustering algorithm used in our work, the cluster number should be designated. In our work, after a number of experiments, the results showed that a cluster number of 7 to 10 seemed appropriate. In this paper, experimental results of cluster number 10 will be presented since results of other parameters are quite similar.

5.1 Euclidean Distance vs. EEUPC Similarity

To figure out the difference between Euclidean distance and the EEUPC similarity, both the Euclidean distance and the EEUPC similarity are calculated for each pair of the 500 consumers. We observed, compared and analyzed the top 100 pairs of each distance (similarity) measurement and came to the conclusion that the EEUPC similarity yields results more reasonable and consistent with human judgments. As mentioned above, this is because the EEUPC similarity emphasizes the shape of curves, especially the difference between peaks and valleys, and relatively weakens the impact of absolute values of the power loads.

As an example, Figure 5 shows a pair of daily load curves. For the pair of curves, the EEUPC similarity value $S_{EEUPC} = 0.3262$. To be compared with the Euclidean distance, we also calculate a *EEUPC distance* measurement, i.e., $d_{EEUPC} = 1 - S_{EEUPC} = 0.6738$. At the same time, the Euclidean distance between the two curves $d_{Euclidean} = 0.2907$. It can be seen from the results that the Euclidean distance is quite small and the EEUPC distance is quite large. The ranks of the two distance values among all distance values are consistent with these results, namely, the Euclidean distance ranks within the 100 smallest Euclidean distance values, while the EEUPC distance is larger than thousands of EEUPC distances.

The above example, along with many other similar cases we observed in observation and analysis, demonstrated the fact that the EEUPC similarity (distance) is more consistent with human comprehension in terms of similarity for load curves. As for the above example, from the view of humans, the two curves apparently, have different peaks within different periods: The peak of curve 1 occurs in the evening while the peak of curve 2 occurs in the middle of the day. In fact, the EEUPC similarity is calculated in a similar way to this human judgment by considering both the position and the confidence of peaks. On the contrary, the calculation of Euclidean distance uses directly the absolute value of each point, and yields a low distance value since the values on the two curves are close except for several special points, which are the peak values and should have been the focus when considering the differences between the two curves.

Figure 5. Two load curves for which the Euclidean distance is 0.2907 and the EEUPC distance is 0.6738

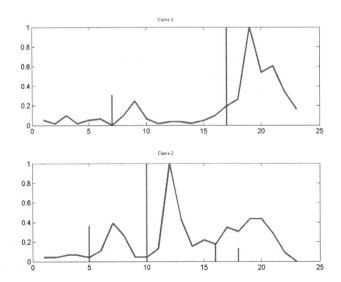

5.2 Experimental Results of Load Pattern Clustering

As mentioned above, all the 500 residential daily load patterns are clustered into 10 classes using the EEUPC similarity and hierarchical clustering algorithm as detailed in Section 3. For comparison, we also clustered all 500 data into 10 classes using the Euclidean distance with the same clustering method. The results are shown in Figures 6 and 7. In each graph thin lines show all load curves in the cluster and the bold line is the typical load pattern obtained by averaging all the curves.

From these experimental results it can be seen that compared to the Euclidean distance, the EEUPC-similarity-based method can divide data more evenly. On the contrary, when the Euclidean distance is used, there are some clusters that contain few curves, making these clusters 'abnormal' ones, and therefore lack of representativeness. The reason for this result is that the Euclidean distance use directly the values and the distance between some special patterns and other patterns will be quite large, whereas EEUPC mainly considers peaks and valleys and even special patterns may share several same peaks and valleys with other patterns. To reduce the impact of *"bad data"*, in our experiment, we tried to delete the curves one or two of which formed a single cluster and performed clustering for the rest of the data. However, the similar results occurred again with some clusters contain few curves, which indicated that the result was related to the using of the Euclidean distance instead of some bad data.

Moreover, it can be seen from Figure 6 that the patterns in each cluster have similar shapes, especially in terms of peaks and valleys, and the typical load pattern extracted can represent the patterns well. On the other hand, patterns in different clusters differ much in shape. For example, in Figure 6, the patterns in the first cluster have only 1 peak, and the patterns in the second cluster have 3 peaks. As for the Euclidean-distance-based method, clustering results reveal zigzagging

curves with more than 5 peaks a day, indicating that the Euclidean distance is too sensitive to instable data, as is mentioned in earlier part of this paper.

5.3 Experimental Results of Typical Pattern Analysis

As detailed in 4.2, in our experiment, typical pattern analysis was performed for each typical pattern extracted from each cluster. And descriptive information was also given by the system, addressing characteristics of the class of consumers and corresponding suggestions for electricity consumption. Figures 8 and 9 shows two clusters (cluster 2 and cluster 5 in Figure 6) as examples and the descriptions output by the system are as follows.

Description for Figure 8:

- This type of customers takes a proportion of 15.2% in all consumers.
- There are three electric load peaks in the typical load pattern.
- And they appear in 6:00-9:00, 12:00-13:00, and 19:00-23:00.
- The maximal load appears at 22:00, and the second highest peak appears at 8:00.
- It might be encouraged that the customers consume electric power from 0:00 to 5:00."

Description for Figure 9:

- This type of customers takes a proportion of 7.6% in all consumers.
- There are two electric load peaks in the typical load pattern.
- And they appear in 11:00-13:00, and 18:00-23:00.
- The maximal load appears at 21:00, and the second highest peak appears at 12:00.
- It might be encouraged that the customers consume electric power from 0:00 to 8:00."

Figure 6. Results of clustering based on EEUPC similarity

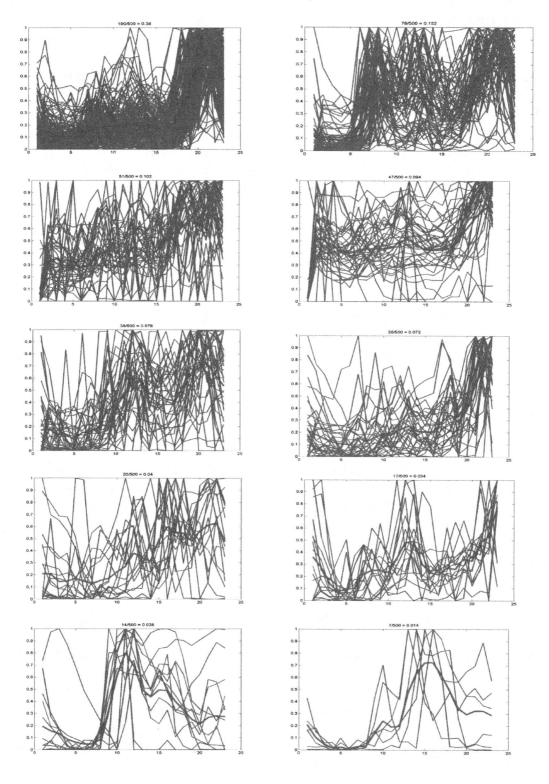

Figure 7. Result of clustering based on Euclidean distance

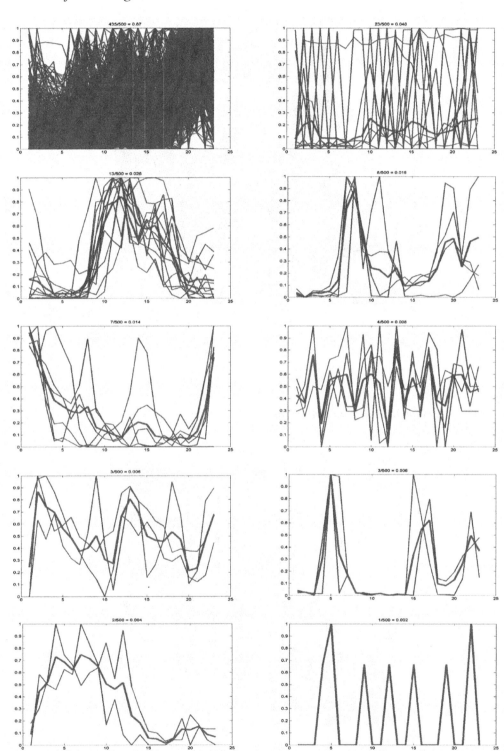

Figure 8. Two clusters for typical load pattern analysis

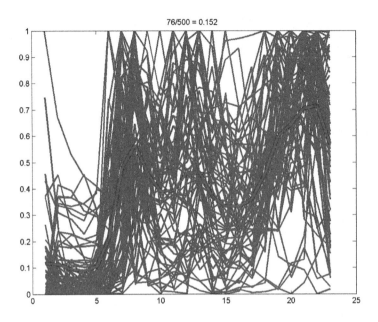

Figure 9. Two clusters for typical load pattern analysis

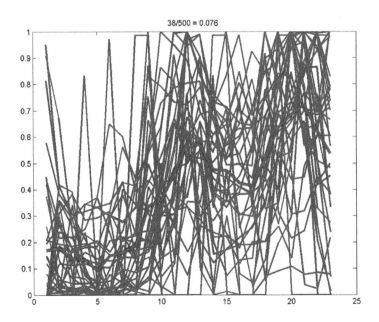

6. CONCLUSION

In this paper, an approach for residential electric load pattern analysis is presented. A novel similarity function based on the audio feature EEUPC (which is named EEUPC similarity) is proposed to better support clustering analysis. The EEUPC distance exploits features of peaks and valleys on curves instead of directly comparing values as the Euclidean distance does, and can obtain better performance for clustering analysis. Moreover, the approach proposed in this paper not only performs load pattern clustering, but also extracts the typical pattern for each cluster and gives suggestion of wiser consumptions with lower cost for each typical pattern. Experimental results demonstrate that the EEUPC similarity is more consistent with human judgment than Euclidean distance and better clustering performance can be achieved.

REFERENCES

Alfuhaid, A. S. (1997). Cascaded artificial neural network for short-term load forecasting. *IEEE Transactions on Power Systems, 12*, 1524–1529. doi:10.1109/59.627852

Ding, Q., & Wang, G.-Z. (2008). Application and cluster analysis of regional electric customer load modes. *Mechatronic Engineering, 25*(9), 31–33.

Gao, Z.-W., Wang, Y., & Song, W.-W. (2008). Daily Coherence Fuzzy Cluster Analysis Method of Power System Load Pattern. *Information Technology, 2008*(6), 36-38.

Hor, C.-L., Watson, S. J., & Majithia, S. (2005). Analyzing the impact of weather variables on monthly electricity demand. *IEEE Transactions on Power Systems, 20*(4), 2078–2085. doi:10.1109/TPWRS.2005.857397

Hu, J.-F., Lee, C.-J., et al. (2008). The relationship between price elasticity of demand and generation market equilibrium analysis based on game theory. In *Proceedings of the Chinese Society for Electrical Engineering* (pp. 89-94).

Li, R., & Li, Y-T. (2004). Design and Building of Data Warehouse for Relay Protection. *International Journal of Power and Energy Systems*, 71-75.

Mori, H., & Kobyashi, H. (1996). Optimal fuzzy inference for short-term load forecasting. *IEEE Transactions on Power Systems, 11*(1), 390–396. doi:10.1109/59.486123

Su, F.-L., & Song, B.-Y. (2010). Quantile Regression Study on Weights of Influencing Factors of China's Electrical Energy Consumption. *Journal of Hebei University of Science and Technology, 2010*(8), 380-384.

Tan, Z.-F., Yu, C., & Jiang, H.-Y. (2009). Analysis Model on the Impact of User TOU Electricity Price on Generation Coal-saving. *Systems Engineering. Theory into Practice*, (10): 94–101.

Wang, X., Li, X., Qian, Y., Yang, Y., & Lin, S. (2009). Break-segment detection and Recognition in Broadcasting Video/Audio based on C/S architecture. In *Studies in Computational Intelligence: Opportunities and Challenges for Next-Generation* []. Berling, Germany: Springer.]. *Applied Intelligence, 214*, 45–51.

Wang, Z.-Y., & Cao, Y.-J. (2007). Electric Power System Load Profiles Analysis. In *Proceedings of the CSU-EPSA 2007 Conference* (pp. 62-65).

Zhao, D., Wang, X., Qian, Y., Liu, Q., & Lin, S. (2008). Fast commercial detection based on audio retrieval. In *Proceedings of the International Conference on Multimedia and Expo*, Hannover, Germany (pp. 1185-1188).

This work was previously published in the International Journal of Advanced Pervasive and Ubiquitous Computing, Volume 3, Issue 2, edited by Tao Gao, pp. 39-53, copyright 2011 by IGI Publishing (an imprint of IGI Global).

Chapter 14
The Design of Portable Integration Strengthening Machine

Li Yuan
Jiangsu Automation Research Institute, China

Ximing Lu
Jiangsu Automation Research Institute, China

Ruifang Huang
Jiangsu Automation Research Institute, China

ABSTRACT

This paper investigates briefly the integrated portable reinforcement machine structure design and introduces its design and train of thought. The authors also discuss design methods in engineering applications, as well as how to achieve good heat dissipation effect and enhance the electromagnetic compatibility. The whole machine, with its small volume, good adaptability to environment, and electromagnetic compatibility, can be used as a reference for similar engineering design.

INTRODUCTION

Along with rapid development of the electronic chip technology, circuit competitive degree is taller and taller, equipment developed towards miniaturization, high performance. While the chassis as a basic factor of electronic equipment, and along with the electronic technology development its organization form is becoming more and more forward, towards miniaturization, the direction of

human development. While the wide application of electronic technology, and the constantly increasing demands to adapt to various environment, such as car, ship equipment onboard, medium, this also prompted the reinforcement of computer generated. The so-called reinforcement machine is adapted to a variety of harsh environment for a long time and reliable work, the design of computer on the various factors affect the performance of the computer (system structure, electrical proper-

DOI: 10.4018/978-1-4666-2645-4.ch014

ties, mechanical and physical structure), to take corresponding measures to ensure the computer. But in some special conditions, the installation position and space constraints, it is need integration design for small reinforcement machine. This paper mainly based on the experience of engaging in structure design of integration, from the portable reinforced computer chassis design, thermal design, electromagnetic shielding design, vibration resistance design and three designs was elaborated concisely and to the point.

1. CHASSIS DESIGN

Reinforcement machine uses the CPCI bus structure; on the CPCI bus structure advantage please see the introduction of related data. Case size: 214X360X280 (length X width X height), composed of a box body frame, the left panel, upper and lower cover plate and the liquid crystal panel. Chassis structure used a cavity type structure design idea, mainly considered improving and optimizing the electromagnetic compatibility performance of equipment, according to the main functions, it included digital, analog and panel cavity, Panel cavity is close to the front panel of the casing part, mainly comprises a liquid crystal display device and driving module, operation module, keyboard, power switch and an indicating lamp; digital cavity is mainly installed a series of computer digital simulation module; cavity is mainly installed a series of signal module, external signal input interface is located in the left panel reinforcement machine, using the series high performance electric connector, an external input analog signal may be nearby the input analog processing module, reduce interference. All modules are using cold plate for reinforcing heat dissipation, the cabinet side board mounting groove for mounting, the wedge locking device for locking and fixing.

2. THERMAL DESIGN

Here only for this case which involves thermal design from the material selection, structure design and the module design of three parts to be simplify elaborated.

2.1. Material Selection

In the material, antirust aluminum is selected for chassis frame, corrugated plate is selected for heat dissipation in ventilation, which is characterized by not only good solder ability, low prices, but the thermal conductivity and ductility is very good. Chassis panel, cover plate, ribbed all select duralumin, its features is the excellent heat-conducting property and light weight.

2.2. Structural Design

In the structure, integrated portable reinforced computer chassis frame used vacuum brazing, this not only reduces the thermal resistance between the parts, forming a seal channel, improve the external transfer and heat conduction effect, but also improve the chassis seal, electromagnetic compatibility and integrity. While the power module is placed on the chassis of the end, through the heat conducting plate and the chassis close to achieve the purpose of heat dissipation.

2.3. Module Design

All modules within the enclosure housing used aluminum alloy materials which have excellent thermal conductivity, and to be thin as far as possible on the premise of not affecting the strength, thick wall is made of ribs. This can reduce the weight and take heat exchange with air around, the shell takes anodic oxidation blackening treatment, to improve the heat radiation effect. High-power heat element of surface affixed the shell is fixed, and is added rubber pad with heat conduction to accelerate heat radiation.

3. ELECTROMAGNETIC SHIELDING DESIGN

Electromagnetic shielding effect is cut off the electromagnetic energy from the space propagation way, achieve the purpose of eliminating electromagnetic interference. The shielding plate shielding box of portable reinforced computer adopts high conductivity alloy aluminum or steel, and takes the conductive oxidation treatment, so that it can maintain long-term conductivity. While the contact surface the between chassis frame and the cover plate is smooth, and use screws as more as possible, thereby forming a reliable electrical connection. According to the different forms of electromagnetic leakage, we can take the following measures mainly about the structure the chassis from.

3.1. Power Supply Interference Control

In order to control the power supply interference, in addition to the power supply module layout in a separate space, the AC power at the entrance to increase power supply filter, also strictly grasp the power module design and power choice of filter and filter, but also to take the correct installation method. By this process, power line conduction immunity will be greatly raised, in order to achieve the design requirement.

3.2. Seam Shielding Enclosure

The chassis frame is made of aluminum alloy material integrally brazed and subjected to heat treatment, it and the upper and the lower cover plate and the left panel between the front panel seams as plagioclase joints, and the joints become equipment plagioclase electromagnetic leakage of the main channel, therefore, the box body frame and the cover plate, the contact surface machining concave panel seal groove, and then in the groove fixed conductive rubber, so the case frame and the cover plate, panel are arranged between the conductive rubber between the full contact, and the metal contact, thereby having good conductive effect and shielding function.

3.3. The Shielding Between Electrical Connector and the Contact Surface of Box

Because contact impedance between the electrical connector and the box body is relatively large, common mode conduction emission of the shielded cable becomes larger, in order to prevent the resulting radiation exceeding the standard, the solution is to the cable shielding layer and around the connector are electrically connected. The specific operation is arranging conductive pad between the connector and the panel and shielding body. The foot pad has good electrical contact performance, the overall EMI evaluation index can reach 1000dB; can effectively control electromagnetic leakage of the gap.

3.4. Display Window Shield

In order to reduce on equipment, the influence is electromagnetic leakage of the equipment internal interference source through the display window and external electromagnetic, the high performance EMC shielding glass is arranged between the display and the panel when design the chassis, the shielding glass used a low impedance of wire through a certain process, sandwiched between two layers of glass or plastic. It selected 100 mesh stainless steel wire mesh screen glass, light transmission rate can reach 81%. Metal mesh around the shielding glass is coated conductive adhesive when it is installed, and makes the panel bonding, and through a special aluminum alloy plate will shield glass and conductive layer panel fastening, to achieve reliable conductive continuous connection. Liquid crystal display and its driving module, an operation button, power indicator light and a power switch used steel shielding box design, installation figure as shown in Figure 1.

Figure 1. Display window shield design installation diagram

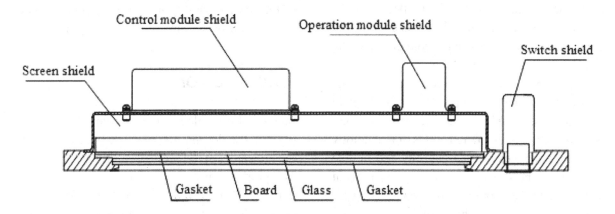

4. RESISTANCE TO VIBRATION AND SHOCK RESISTANT DESIGN

For printed board vibration and shock, in this design adopt wedge locking device, the structure such as shown in Figure 2.

翻译结果重试

抱歉, 系统响应超时, 请稍后再试

- 支持中文、英文免费在线翻译
- 支持网页翻译, 在输入框输入网页地址即可
- 提供一键清空、复制功能、支持双语对照查看, 使您体验更加流畅

The locking mechanism has a highly reliable locking function, small contact resistance and convenient flexible disassembly performance, it will be solid riveted in the opposite sides of the plate through rivets, and the side board of the box body is matched with the guide slot, can make the printed circuit board in a vertical direction to insert. apply retightening force to the locking structure of screw clockwise, or wedge block slides moves along the wedge surface, so as to the right and left direction and the lateral plate guide groove exposure, until the locking. The device not only greatly improve the installation condition, increase the resonant frequency, reduced

Figure 2. Schematic diagram of the wedge locking device

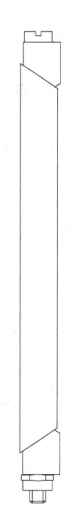

amplitude, thereby enhancing vibration resistance performance, and slide block and both sides of the groove plate pressing when it is cocked, the contact resistance between the cold plate and the chassis wall is greatly reduced.

Considering the tight connection between the chassis frame and the upper /lower cover plate and the panel, steel wire Lo sets of technology is used in the design. Wire Lo sets of technology not only enhances bearing capacity and fatigue strength of the thread connection, this prevent slippery phenomenon of wire tapping. And Lo sets of steel material are high quality steel, which is high toughness and corrosion resistance. And it will prevent rust and blocking, scratches and other undesirable phenomenon resulting from the thread connection, thereby further enhancing the overall shock resistant and impact resistance.

5. THE THREE-PROOFING DESIGN

Three proofings technology mainly refers to hot flashes, salt spray, mold three environmental factors influence on electronic products. Integrated portable reinforced computer chassis used whole sealing type aluminum alloy metal box, waterproof conductive sealing ring is used in close seams between the box body frame and the upper and lower cover plate, thereby ensuring that the whole complete sealing, greatly reducing corrosion damage on the surface of components of the impurities in air dust and water vapor. All bearing parts such as no falling screws, handle and the other mounting screws are made of stainless steel of 1CrI8Ni9Ti material; case frame, upper and lower plates, panels are Al / Ct.Ocd processing; chassis surface coated A04-60. II.H (orange peel paint); and a three-protection paint processing

spraying is used for printed circuit board. In order to improve the stability and reliability, but also it is easy to achieve the "three-proofing" requirements.

6. CONCLUSION

Integrated portable reinforced computer chassis through the design, manufacturing, testing, and the indicators of the products all meet standards. The product has been put into use, and with its portable, small, it is praised by customers. With the development of science and technology and materials science research is unceasingly thorough, the contents and requirements of electronic equipment cabinet will be more and more, as the structure design, we must uphold the scientific outlook on development spirit update the design concept, with new technology and new segment to carry out specific chassis design, to meet the needs of the electronic equipment development.

REFERENCES

Bai, X. (2002). Thermal design for a typical sealed electronic equipment cabinet. *Electro Mechanical Engineering, 18*(4).

Liu, J., & Li, H. (2011). EMC design for a certain case. *Ship Electronic Engineering, 26*(1).

Na, J., Li, S., & Yang, H. (2009). The structure design of a minitype incorporate inner-closure reinforcement machine. *Ship Science and Technology, 2009*(10).

Thermai, G. S. (2011). Design considerations for cabinet. *Mechanical Management and Development, 25*(5).

This work was previously published in the International Journal of Advanced Pervasive and Ubiquitous Computing, Volume 3, Issue 2, edited by Tao Gao, pp. 54-58, copyright 2011 by IGI Publishing (an imprint of IGI Global).

Chapter 15
The Information Construction of Wind Farm Based on SIS System

Yao Wan-Ye
North China Electric Power University, China

Yin Shi
North China Electric Power University, China

ABSTRACT

In the wind farms, fans are widely distribution with large amount and they are away from the monitoring center, working environment is poor. In order to ensure the safe and stable operation of the wind farms, the wind power operation requirements need to be satisfied, own better function performance and stability of remote monitoring system to improve the management efficiency. In view of this, the power group increasing highly requirements on wind farm group management, but at present, the single SCADA system which the fan manufacturers offered has failed to meet the requirements. On the basis, this article designs the wind farm supervisory information system (SIS), and realizes wind farm cluster control, data analysis, performance optimization and fault warning.

1. INTRODUCTION

Along with the global resources and environment worsening, the development and utilization of new energy has gotten more attention. While, comparing with traditional energy sources, wind energy is a clean renewable energy. In addition, the availability of wind energy is widely distributed around the globe. Because of these unique advantages, wind power has become an important part of sustainable development in many countries. Large-scale wind power operation will increase uncontrolled power output, which will generates a lot of pressure for electric power dispatching. The power grid dispatching can only pull restricted to reduce wind power influence on power grids, which gets a lot of wasting of energy. Therefore, establishing wind power generation enterprise information construction platform just like fan short-term power prediction, generator fault prediction and wind power remote monitoring can provide timely, complete and accurate information service, help enterprises to improve the wind power modern management level, and achieve data sharing.

DOI: 10.4018/978-1-4666-2645-4.ch015

2. THE PRESENT SITUATION OF THE WIND FARMS REMOTE MONITORING SYSTEM

Currently, the wind farm supervisory control and data acquisition (SCADA) system are provided completely by fan manufacturers, the main problems are shown as follows:

1. **Compatibility Issues:** There are more than 40 companies engaged in research and development wind generator, and more companies are developing proprietary fans components or complete machine. Large-scale wind farm are generally provided by multiple vendors, the manufacturers of SCADA systems are not compatible, different types of fans lack of effective monitoring and management studies, it is difficult to unified maintenance and management.

2. **Information Development Level:** At present, the problems of wind power still concentrate in the reliability of wind power generation, power prediction, and Security to the grid, etc. In the SCADA software, the application of information and centralized data collection is still the degree of showing. It is only available to supply operator real-time data and historical data without deeper level of information development, such as condition monitoring, fault diagnosis, operational guidance and so on.

3. THE OVERALL DESIGNING AND SOLUTION OF WIND FARM SIS SYSTEM

We are currently using remote monitoring system for wind farms, which refer to the experience of thermal power project. Using OPC technology, we have integrated the data that is from different fan manufacturers, and gathered real-time data of run fans and remote communication of booster station.

The Vestore is used as large real-time database storage platform, and this system can realize the remote monitoring, data analysis and processing, provides management with the power plant in the various operating statements, on the basis of this, we also realize equipment fault diagnosis and life management of funs, wind power prediction, and other functions.

Remote monitoring system for wind farm should include the following function modules: real-time data collection and monitoring, remote centralized control, performance statistics and analysis, fault early warning, life management, output statistics and forecasts, operation optimization. The functional design should include three levels. First, the underlying data collection and monitoring, namely: using OPC technology to achieve real-time collection for fans and booster station, which save in real time / history stored in the database. By the way, it is shown in web as configuration mode. The second is the upper fault warning analysis, life management function, which including: equipment failure records, fan performance comparison, statistics and fan life management. The third level is a fan of the forecasting and planning, which is on the basis of meteorological data and historical data. This module can get fan's model to predict short-term and even medium-term output forecast for the power grid to provide scheduling support.

The module used to implement specified data collection from existing SCADA systems and substation system. Base on the Web application technology and Browse/Server(B/S), when data uploaded to data center, users can access via IE overview of wind resources and wind farms, an operation status, substation operation, real-time wind data and other information, real-time operating status of individual fans, all kinds of alarm and fault information. this feature provide wind farm running status of monitoring real-time power and other information for leaders, and they can easily check the production of key information, including core businesses of production management, wind power generation, booster station operation and so on. All these things can acquire by IE browser. The framework of wind farms SIS system is shown in Figure 1.

4. THE DESIGN AND DEVELOPMENT OF SIS SOFTWARE

The main software interface (Figure 2), including the bottom interface, second layer database and top application software, the three layers of software system structure, is called bottom-up corresponding data layer, application layer and presentation layer.

The data level mainly focuses on collecting the operating parameters of wind fields and storing the data in real-time/historical database, with OPC as the collecting method. The application level deals with the applications of real-time database intensively, consisting of business com-

ponents like business processing service, system authentication service, data connection service, application management system, etc. Those business components can be deployed flexibly in accordance with the actual situation. We can either centralize them on one single computer or choose to deploy them discretely. The chief function of the presentation level, in which the system and users interact, lies in accomplishing man-machine interface works like monitoring, operating, system management, etc.

The system adopts the application system structure in which B/S and C/S combine with each other, which can be configured flexibly according to the actual situation of the scene and user's requirements. It adopts application service based on .NET, fulfils system applications using SVG and XML technology and possesses advantages like easy maintenance, high efficiency, easy to transplant, etc.

Figure 1. The framework of wind farms SIS system

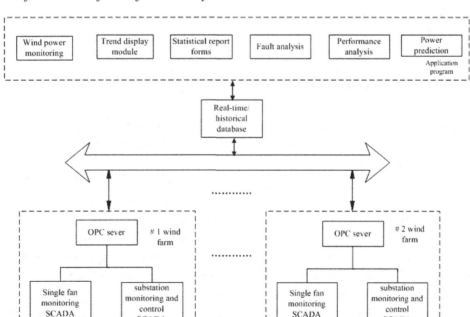

Figure 2. The framework of SIS software

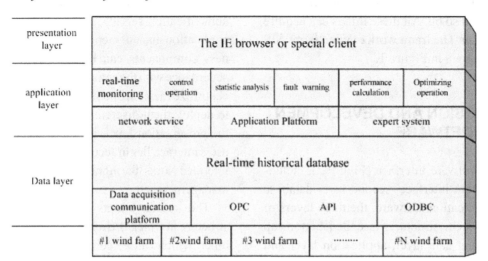

A. The Design of OPC Data Acquisition System

The OPC is an industry standard with a group of component object model and distributed component object model (COM/DCOM) technology. It is the definition of interface standard has nothing to do with the manufacturer. It is technology based on Microsoft's OLE (Active X), COM (component object model) and DCOM (distributed component object model), including the full set of interfaces, properties and methods of standard set that can be used to process control and manufacturing automation system. FactorySoft OPC Server DLL interface give users a set of OPC Sever for development interface with DLL form, as long as users follow the application programming interface API provide by this DLL, who can complete OPC Server development. StartFSServer is for start FSServer DLL function, StopFSServer is for to stop, RegisterServer is for the registration, UnregisterServer is the function for the unregistration, SetCallbackObject interface function for registration application callback function, FSServerInUse realizes evaluate whether OPC-Client connection, MatchPattern realizes matching item names and filter string, if match return true,

otherwise returns false. Category includes Ctag class, COPCCallback class, COPCBrowser class.

According to the present mainstream fan at home and abroad, research the third party communication protocol. Vestas and GE have OPC Sever; using OPC Client can complete data obtaining; Spain's Gamesa provide real-time database accessing with DLL's interface. Sinovel and DongQi provide Modbus server for accessing. Its principle is that sever communicate with the fan controller (PLC) real-time, and data results packages into Modbus message providing for a third party.

B. The Control Center Real-Time/History Database Platform

Data of Wind farms is the foundation of data analysis, data mining, control optimization and management optimization. There have to be thousands or even hundreds of thousands of data collecting units in one centralized control center which governs several wind farms. Due to the need for site monitoring and real-time analysis, the collected data is subjected to real-time changes. Such large-scale mass data is so difficult to be preserved for a long term in its prototype that the traditional relational database system is unable to accomplish this task at all. Therefore, real-time database comes into being. Real-time database is the combination of real-time data and database, the key point in the development of which is the compression and storage of mass data. In addition, problems like real-time data model establishment, transaction scheduling methods, resources allocation strategies, real-time data communication, etc. also need to be solved in real-time historical database.

VeStore widely used in power industry, the authorization point of which is 500,000 points. Database supports standard B/S (browser/server) structure, which can ensure all the real-time production process information of the electric field and calculation through effective compression methods. The recovery time of compressed data should not be more than 15 milliseconds and it should possess good expansibility and openness.

Real-time database should not only serve as the source of data needed in all the computing analysis programs, surveillance pictures, statistical forms and remote control and support standard linking approaches like application programming interface (API) and ODBC2.0, etc, but also provide the management information system (MIS) with required real-time data, calculation and analysis result. Its server and client hardware should be standard products from the third party, and the software module should fully support and be compatible with the Microsoft system structure and have good transparency and secondary development ability. VeStore real-time database should have backstage calculation engine, a tool that can convert raw data into powerful information. All kinds of complicated second operation can be done through using configuration.

The real-time database should have perfect data mirror function, through which it can mirror the data center of the subsidiary to that of the group company.

C. Wind Power Data Trend Analysis

By processing real-time/historical data, Report capabilities should generate automatically daily reports, monthly reports, availability, power generation losses, etc. which shall be used to assess the running effects of fans from suppliers. Tabular forms should be offered to all kinds of users acting as a basis for management and decisions.

Reports completed by the system are mainly real-time reports, including:

I. Real-Time Load Reports

Generate real-time load reports which display information on units, the installed capacity of Wind Farms, load and load rate through classification approaches such as branches, unit capacity, etc.

The average availability in any given cycle of each wind turbine of a wind farm should be calculated as follows:

Availability = TA / TCT * 100%

TA is the available time of a fan, namely the cumulated hours that fans operate or the time that fans possess operating conditions in any given cycle calculated by fan controller

TCT refers to all the calendar time calculated by hours within the computing cycles, for example, the TCT of the availability counted on an annual basis equals 8760 hours.

II. Reports on the Start-Stop Condition Of Units

Real-time unit start-stop report—employ flexible inquiry mode and display the present start-stop state of units according to query conditions like unit capacity, wind farm, etc.

Historical start-stop inquiry report—give a record of the start-stop conditions of units in wind farms, its history query time period can be selected arbitrarily.

III. Trend Analysis Reports

All the parameters can be displayed in multi-forms like trend chart, bar chart, related parameters groups, etc., displaying parameters value in real time and the maximum value, minimum value and average value in defined time period.

IV. Unit Real-Time Comparative Reports

The inquiry approaches designed in the system is flexible; it is inquired according to unit capacity and wind farms. You can choose any units or parameters that need to be compared from the units connected to the system to form real-time report of the comparison between parameters.

The real-time data and historical data query from 0 to 16 o'clock is shown in Figure 3.

D. The Wind Unit's State Detection and Early Fault Warning

Wind farm remote monitoring system will monitor and process the real time data condition of fans operating on-line and make a classification of fans under states such as running, fault, overhaul, reset, etc. It takes the structure of chain components, variable speed running condition and hostile using environment such as high or low temperature

into consideration. Through the use of reliable data collection system and international advanced fault diagnosis technology, it makes accurate judgment on the location where fault occurred and conducts remote and real-time monitoring of the running states of fan transmission chain (spindle, gear box and generator, etc.), the engine, vanes and tower drum, etc. It pre-warns diagnoses and analyzes the equipment faults. Abnormal states occurred in operation such as the malfunction of transmission device and generators caused by device state imbalance, rolling bearing damage, correcting error, etc. are detected out before fan fault happens. Thereby early fault diagnosis is achieved to determine the properties, types, location, degree, cause of faults. Then it points out the development trends and consequences, puts forward countermeasures to control its continued development and eliminate faults, and makes a classification of the fault types automatically. The faults include inverter reset overtime, generator speeding, temperature being exorbitant in high voltage transformer, temperature being too low in the cabin, etc. If failed to detect the fault, it will give rational proposals and instruct maintenance engineers to accomplish the overhaul of the fan. It also provides scientific basis for the preventive maintenance by users, thereby reducing fan maintenance cost significantly.

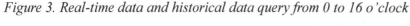

Figure 3. Real-time data and historical data query from 0 to 16 o'clock

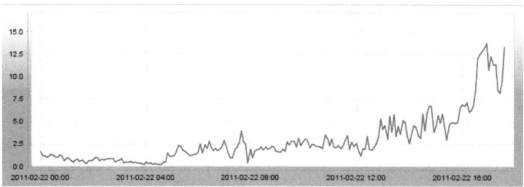

It monitors multi-groups of data simultaneously, including:rear bearing and fore beating rotation speed and vibration of Generator, rotate speed of high-speed shaft, cabin yaw state, gearbox low speed shaft, intermediate shaft., high-speed axis, input shaft, the gear ring vibration and oil temperature, vibration condition of Spindle fore bearing and spindle rear bearing, leaf temperature freezing, etc. Through the establishment of condition monitoring library of wind turbines of the same type, fans with big state variation are acquired automatically for fault forecast and analysis, thus completing fault pre-warning.

E. The Wind Power Prediction

The biggest difference which distinguishes wind power from other energies lies in the random variation and uncontrollability of its source power. Wind speed is not only influenced by large-scale atmospheric motion, but also affected by microscale atmospheric turbulence movement caused by many kinds of surface factors; therefore the wind speed presents strong random properties on instantaneous changes of time and space. Many key techniques in wind turbine control and wind farms grid-connected operation are developed to adapt to the randomness of wind variation.

With the increase of the proportion of wind generation in the power source structure of power grid, the randomness, intermittent and volatility of wind generation bring a series of problems to grid operation security. The dispatching departments can only roll blackouts to cope with those problems at the moment. Effective predictions on fan generating can help the dispatching departments in power system make various power dispatching plans so as to reduce wind power brownouts, thus reducing the economic loss that power brownouts bring to wind power owner and increasing the return of investment in wind power. The functional principle diagram is shown in Figure 4.

CONCLUSION

With the actual project of wind power remote monitoring and fault pre-warning as its background, this article introduces the overall system development process, SIS system development design.

Figure 4. The diagram of wind power prediction function principle

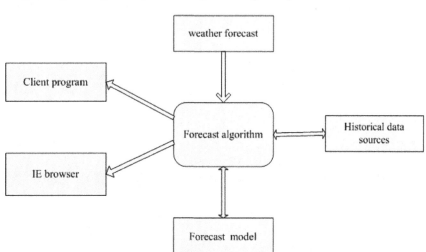

Though Wind power remote monitoring and fault pre-warning system is to accomplish the information platform of wind power enterprises and provide timely, complete and accurate information service, helping wind power enterprises improve their modern management level and realizing data share in all aspects. Wind firms production computerized management platform is built up according to the ideas of integration, platform initialization and componentization using the most advanced computer technology. Based on the most advanced enterprise production integrated management system, the system successfully carries out computerized managements according to the profession features of wind power companies on the operation of wind power companies, maintenance, statements, aided decision-making, prediction control, etc.

REFERENCES

Bai, X. (2009). *The research of wind power forecasting and AGC unit blend*. Beijing, China: Beijing Transportation University.

Bouter, S., Malti, R., & Fremont, H. (2008). Development of an HMI based on the OPC standard. In *Proceedings of the 19th Annual EAEEIE Conference* (pp. 163-167).

Wang, H. (2010). *The design of SCADA*. Beijing, China: Electronic Industry.

Wang, H., & Liu, H. (2006). Discuss of the integrated automation technology and information management in power plant monitoring. *Control Engineering, 5*.

Yi, L., Zhu, M., et al. (2010). Performance calculation method when wind power loading the northwest grid. *Power Grid Technology, 2*.

This work was previously published in the International Journal of Advanced Pervasive and Ubiquitous Computing, Volume 3, Issue 2, edited by Tao Gao, pp. 59-66, copyright 2011 by IGI Publishing (an imprint of IGI Global).

Chapter 16
Beyond 3G Techniques of Orthogonal Frequency Division Multiplexing and Performance Analysis via Simulation

Chunyan Wang
State Intellectual Property Office, China

ABSTRACT

As one of the techniques beyond 3G, because of the effective performance of high spectrum utilization and anti-fading for frequency selecting and adopted multi-carrier modulation technique that meets the requirement of the explosive traffic capacity, Orthogonal Frequency Division Multiplexing (OFDM) has carried great weight in wireless communications. This paper expounds OFDM technical characteristics and performs computer simulation on the OFDM system based on Inverse Fast Fourier Transform (IFFT) by means MATLAB. During the course of simulation, comparison between OFDM and traditional single-carrier technology is performed. The simulation results have great significance for research and applications in the field.

INTRODUCTION

OFDM is kind of both multi-carrier and multiplexing technique, which distributes a given channel into plurality of sub-channel. And each parallel transmitting sub-channel adopts single-carrier modulating. By this meaning, each sub-channel is flat relatively, and performs narrowband transmission. Signal bandwidth is less than related bandwidth, which eliminates interference between signal waveforms and improves frequency spectrum utilization because of signal orthogonality, frequency spectrum overlap (Ramasami, 2002).

DOI: 10.4018/978-1-4666-2645-4.ch016

OFDM discards the way using traditional band filter to distribute sub-carrier, and adopting frequency modulation meaning to select the signal waveforms that can keep orthogonality even while frequency spectrum aliasing. Therefore, OFDM is both modulating and multiplexing techniques.

For the traditional Frequency Division Multiplexing (FDM), guard band is used to avoid intercarrier interference (Figure 1), which induces frequency spectrum utilization. Whereas, OFDM system applies FFT technique into multi-carrier transmission system with orthogonal and aliasing frequency spectrum, so as to realize multiplex signal multiplexing and split conveniently. Here "orthogonal" indicates accurate mathematical relationship between carrier frequencies:

$$
\int_0^T \cos(2\pi m f_0 t) \cdot \cos(2\pi n f_0 t)dt = \begin{cases} \dfrac{T}{2}(m = n) \\ 0(m \neq n) \end{cases}
$$

$$
\int_0^T \sin(2\pi m f_0 t) \cdot \sin(2\pi n f_0 t)dt = \begin{cases} \dfrac{T}{2}(m = n) \\ 0(m \neq n) \end{cases} \tag{1}
$$

$$
\int_0^T \cos(2\pi m f_0 t) \cdot \sin(2\pi n f_0 t)dt = \begin{cases} \dfrac{T}{2}(m = n) \\ 0(m \neq n) \end{cases}
$$

and an important advantage of OFDM technique is that modulation and demodulation can be performed by adopting IFFT/FFT, so as to reduce complexity for realizing the system.

TECHNIQUE PRINCIPLE

The essential technical principle is to divides one high speed data flow into plurality of low speed data flows. And the low-speed data flows are modulated by orthogonal frequency and transmit data simultaneously, thus wide band becomes narrow bands, and consequently, the problem of selective fading can be solved. In addition, if adding a delayed protection to generated OFDM signal, intersymbol interference can be figured out (Gong & Jia, 2002; IEEE Computer Society, 1999). The modulation principle in OFDM system is seen in Figure 2.

After the modulating of MQAM, MPSK or DPSK, etc., taking advantage of sub-carrier orthogonality, the original signal is demodulated. The principle is seen in Figure 3.

One OFDM symbol includes signals which are combined by multiple modulated sub-carriers, and each sub-carrier can be modulated by PSK or QAM symbol. If N indicates the number of sub-channel, T indicates OFDM symbol density, d_i (i=0, 1, 2, ..., N-1) indicates data symbol distributed to each sub-channel, and f_c indicates the carrier frequency of the No. 0, rect(t)=1, |t|≤T/2, the original OFDM symbol can be indicated as following:

$$
s(t) = \mathrm{Re}\{\sum_{i=0}^{N-1} d_i rect(t - t_s - T/2)
$$
$$
\exp[j2\pi(f_c + i/T)(t - t_s)]\}, \tag{2}
$$

Figure 1. FDM frequency distribution

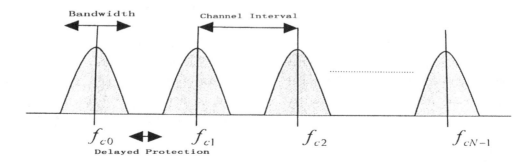

Figure 2. OFDM modulation principle

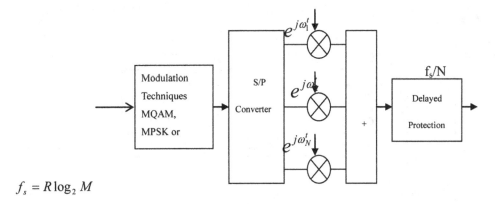

$$f_s = R \log_2 M$$

Figure 3. OFDM demodulation principle

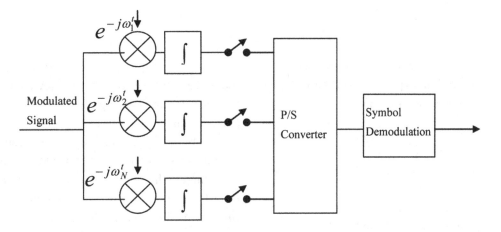

$$t_s \leq t \leq t + t_s$$

$$s(t) = 0, t < t_s \text{ or } t > t + t_s$$

OFDM output signal is described by equivalent baseband symbol:

$$s(t) = \text{Re}\{\sum_{i=0}^{N-1} d_i ret(t - t_s - T/2) \exp[j2\pi i / T(t - t_s)]\},$$
$$t_s \leq t \leq t_s + T$$
$$s(t) = 0, t < t_s ort > t + t_s$$

(3)

In the formula, the real pat and the imagination part is respectively corresponding to the phase component and the orthogonal component, and in the real, multiplies the cosine component and the sine component separately, so as to generate a final synthetic OFDM signal by sub-channel signals (Figure 4).

From the figure, it is known that respective N times modulating are not in the real calculation, and for the generator, that is similar to perform one IFFT, but for the receiver, modulating part is similar to performs one FFT.

Figure 5 describes an embodiment that one OFDM symbol includes three sub-carriers, in which all the sub-carriers have same amplitude and phase. Each sub-carrier includes integer multiple periods in one OFDM symbol period, and

Figure 4. OFDM system primary model diagram

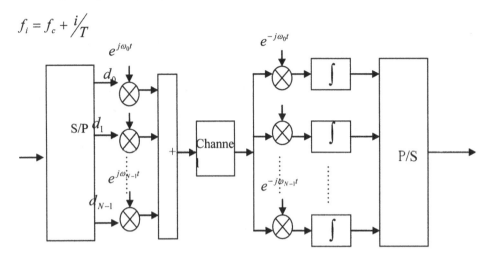

every two adjacent sub-carriers differs one period. This characteristic can explain the orthogonality between sub-carriers as following:

$$\frac{1}{T}\int_0^T \exp(j\omega_n t)dt = \left\{ \begin{matrix} 1, m = n \\ 0, m \neq n \end{matrix} \right\} \quad (4)$$

In the formulation, the carrier j is demodulated, and integrated within time length T;

$$d_j = \frac{1}{T}\int_{T_s}^{t+T_s} \exp[-j2\pi \frac{j}{T}(t-t_s)]\sum_{i=1}^{N-1} d_i x[j2\omega \frac{1}{T}(t-t_s)]dt$$

$$= \frac{1}{T}\sum_{i=0}^{N-1} d_i \int_{T_s}^{t_s+T} \exp[j2\pi \frac{i-j}{T}(t-t_s)dt = dj$$

$$(5)$$

Thus, carrier j is demodulated to restore the expected symbols. For other carriers, because that frequency difference is $\dfrac{(i-j)}{T}$ in one integral interval to generate integral multiple of periods, the integration result is zero (Guo & Li, n. d.; Tamaki & Tomohisa, 2002).

The orthogonality can be explained at the angle of frequency domain. According to the formulation (5), each OFDM symbol includes plurality of non-zero sub-carriers in period T. therefore, the spectrum can be viewed as a convolution for the rectangular pulse spectrum in period T and a group of δfunctions at each subcarrier frequency. The rectangular pulse spectrum amplitude is $\sin c[fT]$ function, and the zero is in the point at which the frequency is integral multiple 1/T (Figure 6). Aliasing sub-channels multiply each other on rectangular pulse to results in sine function spectrum. At the maximum of each sub-carrier, all other sub-carriers spectrum is exactly zero. Because during the course of modulating OFDM symbol, each sub-carrier frequency maximum, corresponding to the points, is calculated so as to extract every sub-channel symbol from multiple aliasing sub-channel symbols, thus avoiding interference from other sub-channels.

In accordance with Figure 6, OFDM symbol meets the Nyquist criterion, that is to say that the spectrum interference does not exist among the multiple sub-channels. Accordingly, in frequency domain, the spectrum maximum of a sub-channel corresponds to zero points of other sub-channels, which can avoid Inter-Carrier Interference (ICI).

Figure 5. OFDM symbol that includes three sub-carriers

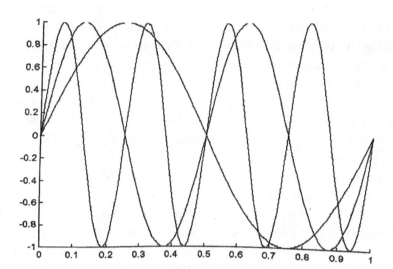

Figure 6. OFDM frequency spectrum

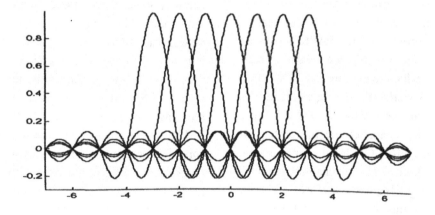

KEY TECHNIQUES

As a technique beyond 3G, OFDM has following key techniques.

1. **Synchronization of Time Domain and Frequency Domain:** OFDM system is sensitive to offset of timing and frequency, especially under the circumstance that FDMA, TDMA and CDMA etc. multiplexing in combination. Downlink synchronization is simple relatively, and easy to implement. In the uplink, signals from different mobile stations must arrive at the Base Station (BS), so that the inter-carrier orthogonality can be insured. That is important especially.

2. **Channel Estimation:** In OFDM system, there are two points in channel estimation: pilot information selection and channel estimator designation. Because the wireless channel is fading channel and channel tracking must be continuous, the pilot information

must be transmitted constantly. Channel estimator designation requires low-complexity and nice pilot tracking capability.

3. **Channel Encoding and Interleaving:** For improving digital communications system performance, channel encoding and interleaving are general technical meaning. Channel encoding avoids random errors in channels and channel interleaving avoids burst error in fading channel.

4. **Depressing Peak-to-Average Power Ratio (PAPR):** In OFDM signal time domain, orthogonal N sub-carrier signals overlay each other. When all the maximum of the N sub-carrier signals add together, the OFDM signal generates a peak, and the peak power is N times of the average power. Though the peak power value occurs seldom, however, for transmitting undistorted OFDM signal at high PAPR, the transmitter requires High Power Amplifier (HPA) with high linearity degree. Therefore, a high PAPR depresses OFDM system performance greatly, as well as the real allocation (Ramasami, 2002).

5. **Channel Equalization:** In general fading environment, because the OFDM technique has diversity characteristic of multi-path channel, therefore OFDM does not equalize. But in high scattering channel, channel memory length is great; therefore the Cyclic Prefix (CP) must be long enough so as to avoid the ICI, however, the CP length results in energy lost. Accordingly, adding equalization can be considered to reduce CP length. That means to improve frequency utility at the cost of increasing system complexity.

PERFORMANCE ANALYSIS VIA SIMULATION

In 1971, Weinstein and Ebert apply DFT to multi-carriers transmission system, which realizes multi-path signal multiplexing and decomposition of multi-path signal. Consequently, OFDM attracts great attention and is regarded as a beyond 3G hot technique in future mobile communications. In this part, in accordance with OFDM system model based on IFFT/FFT, numerical analysis software MATLAB is adopted to perform a mass of computer simulation. The simulation results embody OFDM system characteristic and performance intuitively (You, 2002; Gong & Jia, 2002).

Simulation Model

Figure 7 describes an OFDM system flow using MATLAB simulation. Wherein, the input data is binary data, and after baseband modulating (16QAM), mapping to be symbol data $(d_0 \sim d_{N-1})$, S/P converting, the parallel data is converted to be time domain sample point by IFFT/FFT.

Channel simulation describes some wireless channel generality characteristic, e.g., noise, multi-path. The noise is generated by adding random data to transmitting data. The multi-path is generated by copying the channeling with time-delay and fading. Definitively, the OFDM performed P/S converting is generated by aliasing plurality sub-channels, which results in great PAPR. When going through a nonlinear device, spread spectrum and band distortion emerges much. Accordingly, the peak clipping must be performed. After performing S/P converting to the serial data, the receiver executes FFT converting to the parallel data to acquire corresponding frequency domain data, and finally, after baseband demodulating (16QAM) and P/S converting, binary data is recovered.

During perform the simulation, there are the following hypothesis premises: ideal synchronization of the transmitting side and the receiving side, and ideal channel estimation; channel fading is flat, which means the channel is regarded as being constant in one OFDM symbol. Table 1 describes the simulation parameters.

Figure 7. Simulation diagram

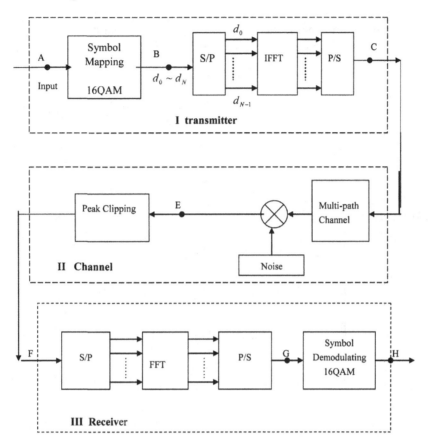

Table 1. Simulation parameters

Simulation parameter	Parameter value
FFT_size	128
Num_carrier	32 (fft_size/4)
Signal constellation	16QAM
Channel model	Two-path Gauss channel

SIMULATION RESULTS ANALYSIS

Figure 8 describes the simulation of binary data input/output and OFDM transmitting/receiving. The binary input data is performed 16QAM modulation as Figure 9, and the output data corresponds to the time domain signal waveform at B point in Figure 8.

Figure 8(c) and (d) is the waveform of OFDM signal going through two-path Gauss channel and recovered binary data separately. Sub-figure (c) corresponds to point F, (d) corresponds to point H. Comparing sub-figure (c) (d) with (b) (a) respectively, it is knowable that received OFDM signal waveform and recovered binary data all have weak distortion because that OFDM has great reflection of mitigating multi-path.

Figure 8. Binary data input/output, and OFDM signal transmitting/receiving

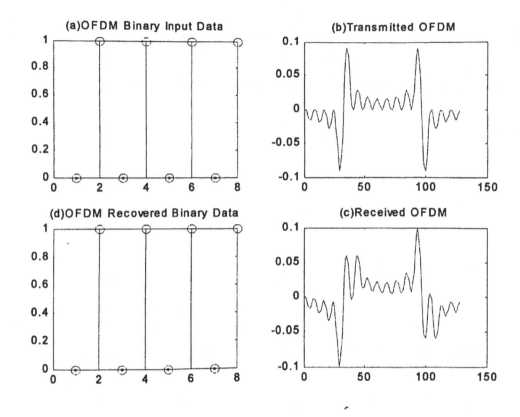

Figure 9. 16 QAM modulation principle

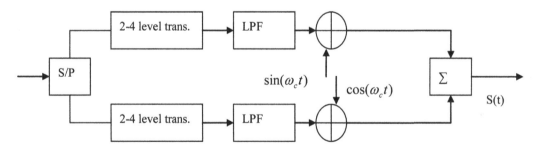

The S(t) may have two expression;

$$S(t) = a_n \cos(\omega_c t) - b_n \sin(\omega_c t) \quad (6\text{-}1)$$

$$S(t) = \mathrm{Re}\left[(a_n + jb_n)e^{j2\pi f_c t}\right] \quad (6\text{-}2)$$

The Equation 6-1 corresponds to the 16QAM output waveform in Figure 8. The Equation 6-2 is complex symbol data, $d_0, d_{1,\dots} d_{N-1}$, N is number of sub-carriers, generated after signal constellation mapping. After IFFT converting, the OFDM transmission wave-form (time-amplitude) described in Figure 8(b), namely, the wave-form at point C in Figure 7, is generated. The base-band signal at point C:

$$y(t) = \mathrm{Re}\left\{\sum_{n=0}^{N-1} d_n e^{j2\pi\frac{n}{T}t}\right\}, 0 \leq t \leq T$$

During the simulating, by adding random data complying with Gaussian to simulate channel noise and copying the transmitting signal consider fading and delay to simulate two-path channel, Figure 10 describes the simulation of two-path Gauss channel.

OFDM is kind of special multi-carrier, and for comparing with single-carrier modulating, modulation of 16QAM is adopted in the simulation. By simulating sub-carrier waveform receiving and binary data recovery, the comparison of OFDM system performance and single-carrier is reflected.

1. Selection of single-carrier modulation model

In OFDM system, sub-carrier modulating model may be MPSK, MQAM, or DQPSK. When source-rate, sub-carrier parameter and channel bandwidth are ensured to be invariable, in different SNR, the simulation of OFDM system of additive white Gaussian noise (AWGN) high speed voice-data compatible transmission is described in Figure 10. The modulation model and encoding rate are seen in Table 2.

From Figure 10, under the circumstance that EBR, sub-carrier and protection interval are same, for OFDM system, sub-carrier QAM modulation model is better than PSK modulation model.

Figure 10. SNR-BER graphs

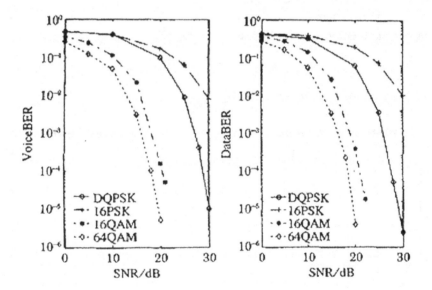

Table 2. Modulation model and encoding rate

Sub-carrier Modulation Model	Convolution Coding Efficiency
DQPSK	Uncoded
16PSK	1/2
16QAM	1/2
64QAM	1/3

2. Performance of single-carrier (16QAM) and OFDM

In Figure 11, as an example, 16 QAM single-carrier modulation system performs binary data recovery and QAM transmitting/receiving waveform are simulated. Comparing sub-figure (c), (d) in Figure 11 with (c), (d) in Figure 8, it is knowable that receiving waveform and data recovery distorts greatly. That embodies that, in OFDM system, the performance of anti-delay, anti-noise and anti-multipath interference is better than the single-carrier modulation system.

Figure 11 shows the simulation result of signal spectrum after FFT converting to OFDM, QAM signal. Comparing the sub-figure (a) with (b), it is knowable that the two has various greed of distortion after through two-path Gauss channel. Meanwhile, comparing Figure 12(c) with Figure 13(c), it is knowable that performance of anti-multipath effect of OFDM system is better than that of single carrier modulation system. Figure

12(a) and Figure 13(a) are spectrums of OFDM, QAM transmitting signal waveform after FFT converting. At the angle of spectrum utilization, OFDM sub-carrier spectrum has close distribution and concentrated energy.

During channel simulating, adding independent Gauss binary data with 0 mean and variance σ^2, channel noise is simulated. Figure 14 describes energy distributing for 16 QAM received signal constellations corresponding to different noise power, wherein, sub-figure (a), (b), (c) is respectively corresponding to received signal distribution when **σ** = 0.1, 0.3, 0.5.

The simulating results indicate; on low noise power (**σ** is small), the signal energy distributes centrally, and with the noise power level rising, the proportion of noise component increases and signal energy distribution tends to be decentralized, and BER affection to OFDM system is larger accordingly.

Figure 11. Sub-carrier recovers input binary data

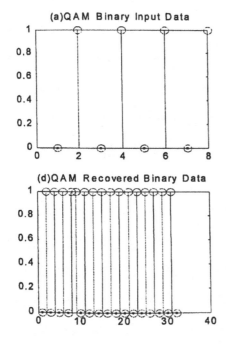

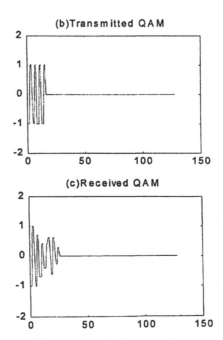

Figure 12. FFT of OFDM signal

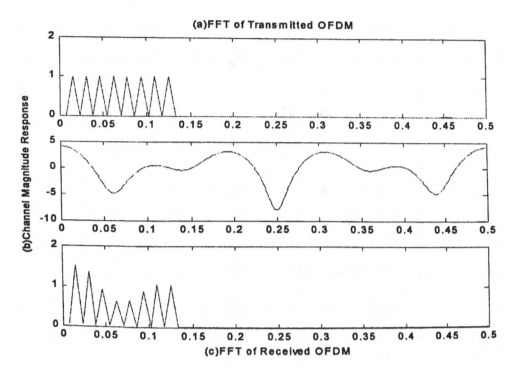

Figure 13. FFT of QAM signal

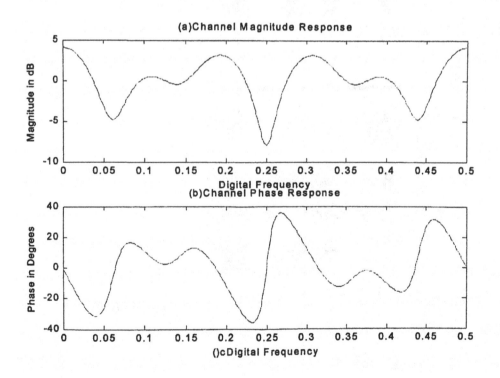

Figure 14. 16 QAM received signal constellation and decision boundary

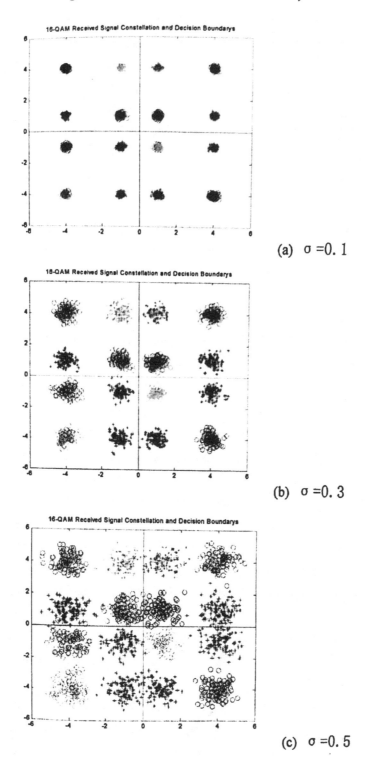

(a) σ =0. 1

(b) σ =0. 3

(c) σ =0. 5

CONCLUSION

The paper expounds OFDM technical characteristic, and performs computer simulating to OFDM system based on FFT/IFFT by means of MATLAB. During the course of simulation, comparison between OFDM and single-carrier technique (16QAM) is described in detail.

Generally speaking, because of the sub-carrier orthogonality, OFDM system reduces inter-carrier interference, and also increases spectrum utilizations. By adopting IFFT/FFT to modulate/demodulate signal, complexity of realizing the communications system is depressed. The low-speed data stream is modulated on orthogonal frequency and transmitted in the meantime, which changes the wide band to be narrow band, consequently, the problem of frequency selective fading is solved. By comparing with single-carrier system, it is embodied that OFDM has more advantage in fields of resisting multi-path interference and channel fading, and spectrum utilization.

Because that OFDM system has the advantages that sing-carrier communication system and traditional FDM system does not have, OFDM is considered as one of the most important techniques beyond 3G. In OFDM technical field, it is necessary to research further the techniques of time-frequency domain synchronization, channel encoding and interleaving, depressing PAPR and channel estimation, etc.

REFERENCES

Gong, J., & Jia, H. (2002). OFDM technique and simulation analysis thereof. *Railway Newspaper, 24*(3).

Guo, Y., & Li, J. (n. d.). *Mobile communications.* Sichuan, China. *Press of Xian Electronic Science & Technology University.*

IEEE. Computer Society. (1999). *IEEE 802.11a 1999. Part 11: Wireless LAN Medium Access Control (MAC) and Physical Layer (PHY) Specification.* Washington, DC: Author.

Ramasami, V. C. (2002). *Orthogonal frequency division multiplexing.* Retrieved from http://www.cetuc.puc-rio.br/~amanda.cunha/projeto/OFDM/Tutorial%20de%20Orthogonal%20Frequency%20Division%20Multiplexing.pdf

Saliga, S. V. (2000). An introduction to IEEE 802.11 Wireless LANs. In *Proceedings of the IEEE Radio Frequency Integrated Circuits Symposium* (pp. 11-14).

Tamaki, S., & Tomohisa, W. (2002). *Technical notes: Magna Design Net.* Retrieved from http://www.magnadesignnet.com/en/booth/technote/ofdm/

You, X. (2002). *Chinese mobile communication development in the future.*

This work was previously published in the International Journal of Advanced Pervasive and Ubiquitous Computing, Volume 3, Issue 3, edited by Tao Gao, pp. 1-13, copyright 2011 by IGI Publishing (an imprint of IGI Global).

Chapter 17
Dynamic Spectrum Auction and Load Balancing Algorithm in Heterogeneous Network

Yan Jiang
State Intellectual Property Office, China

ABSTRACT

Mobile communication plays an important role in the future of communication systems. To meet personalized and intelligent requirements, mobile communication has evolved from single wireless cellular network to heterogeneous mobile communication network, including wireless cellular network, wireless local network, and wireless personal network. In the heterogeneous communication system, to entirely fulfill the spectrum resource complementary advantages of such a heterogeneous wireless network, the spectrum resource trade algorithm has attracted tremendous research efforts. In this paper, the advantages and disadvantages of dynamic spectrum allocation and load balancing are discussed and spectrum auction takes the place of spectrum allocation to maximize the operation revenue. The authors design a joint spectrum auction and load balancing algorithm (SALB) based on heterogeneous network environment to develop a more flexible and efficient spectrum management. The simulation result shows that SALB increases the operation profit significantly.

INTRODUCTION

In the past few years, with the development of various radio communication systems such as UMTS, WLAN, DVB, LTE and so on and the rapid grows of the numbers of users, the spectrum resource became limited. The lack of spectrum resource leads to the decreases of the system performance and users' satisfaction (Leaves, Moessner, & Tafazolli, 2004).

The current method of assigning spectrum to different radio systems is fixed allocation, where the spectrum is divided into non-overlapping blocks and assigned to different radio communication systems (GSM, WLAN, DVD, LTE, etc.). However, fixed spectrum allocation does have disadvantages. For example, if the spectrum is allocated to cope with a certain maximum amount of traffic, called the "busy hour", this network utilizes its spectrum fully during this time, but it

DOI: 10.4018/978-1-4666-2645-4.ch017

is underused at all other times. If the spectrum is allocated based on the average amount of traffic, under the circumstance that different radio access networks cover certain areas, traffic various with time and some new radio access technologies approaches the market, some networks are lack of spectrum due to the increasing traffic requirement, and at the mean time, the spectrum of other networks is over enough because of the traffic decrease. With the rapid grows of all kinds of services, e.g., broadcasting, video call, downloading, fixed spectrum allocation scheme is not able to meet the demand for radio spectrum. This is the motivation for a more efficient technique, such as dynamic spectrum allocation (DSA), flexible spectrum management (FSM), spectrum action and spectrum trading.

Dynamic spectrum allocation scheme adjusts spectrum allocation according to different network traffic among some areas, thus the network requirements are met and the traffic QoS is improved.

SPECTRUM ALLOCATION

The spectrum allocation scheme allocates non-overlapping spectrum blocks to different radio access networks (RANs), wherein the widths of the spectrum blocks are fixed which are separated by fixed guard bands. It is called a fixed spectrum allocation (FSA) scheme that a wireless network operator with a license is able to utilize the spectrum blocks of its own. Interference between different wireless communication specifications is avoided and radio spectrum management is simplified when using FSA. But the disadvantages of FSA also exist: first, the demand for spectrum in wireless networks varies with time. For example, most of the wireless communication network allocates spectrum according to the maximum amount of traffic. The spectrum is allocated to cope with the traffic in the "busy hour". Since FSA is implemented, the spectrum

is fully used in the "busy hour" but underused in the other time. This situation often occurs in other services as well. For example, the requirement for the Video-On-Demand (VOD) service is higher after work, but lower during working hours; second, the demand for spectrum varies with locations. As services provided by different wireless access networks in different locations are different, demand for spectrum varies; third, with the development of various wireless communication systems and the growing number of users, spectrum shortages become more and more apparent. System performance and user satisfaction degrade due to the spectrum insufficient. In conclusion, FSA cannot adapt the rapid development of wireless communication environment. In the circumstance that traffic varies with time and locations, FSA cannot achieve high spectrum efficiency. In addition, with the growing demand for wireless mobile multimedia services and the increasing traffic demands, there is an urgent need for a more flexible spectrum allocation. The factors above drive researchers to work on a more flexible and efficient dynamic spectrum allocation (DSA) scheme. Recently, U.S. Department of Trade and Industry in a government white paper about cultural, education, media and sports state that: about to introduce new mechanism to enable communication companies to implement spectrum trading (UK Department of Trade and Industry, UK Department of Culture, Media and Sport, 2000).

IST (Information Society Technologies) DRiVE (Dynamic Radio for IP-services in Vehicular Environments) project funded by European commission aims to explore a method for improving spectrum efficiency and increasing spectrum capacity in a network environment with a variety of wireless communication standards co-exist, wherein the method includes new dynamic spectrum allocation scheme and flow control method (Tonjes, Xu, & Paila, 2000; Ghaheri-Niri, Leaves, Benko, Huschke, & Stahl, 2000).

Currently, several DSA schemes have been defined as follows (Leaves, Ghaheri-Niri, Tafazolli, & Huschke, 2002).

1. **Continuous DSA:** Continuous DSA can be regarded as an evolution scheme from FSA to DSA. It allocates continuous spectrum blocks separated by guard bands to each of the different radio access networks, which is similar to FSA. The difference is that the widths of the spectrum blocks allocated to RANs may increase or decrease according to the traffic demands. But adjustment is only made between adjacent spectrum blocks. In addition, continuous DSA also allows other RANs to using the free spectrum blocks.

2. **Fragment DSA:** All spectrum resources are treated as a spectrum pool in the fragment DSA. Any RAN can occupy exclusively spectrum fragments in any positions of the spectrum pool if needed. In this way, the spectrum resources acquired by RANs are no longer limited by the widths of the adjacent spectrum blocks. Thus, comparing with continuous DSA, a more flexible spectrum allocation scheme is provided. But the operation mechanism is more complex.

3. **Full-Dynamic DSA:** Full-dynamic DSA is a full-open distribution scheme, which allows each BS of the RANs to use any part of the spectrum resources. However, in order to prevent the malicious occupancy of the spectrum caused by the competition among RANs, restrictions will be made for spectrum occupancy (Peha, 2000).

However, there are two problems existing in the current DSA scheme:

1. The current DSA are executed periodically, about every half an hour, meaning that the spectrum re-allocations would be discrete along the time axis. During each executed period, the spectrum is allocated fixedly according to the load predication result ignoring the continuous variation of the load. The disadvantages of FSA also exist during each DSA period.

2. The current DSA does not consider the income of different RANs. DSA in the scenarios investigated in the previous studies is performed between different RANs which are totally cooperative and there is not confliction of interest. That is, the spectrum allocation is completely on-demand. Any network can get idle spectrum when needed and any network will release idle spectrum for other network when traffic declines. There is no conflict of interest among various networks. Under this assumption, the unique object of DSA is to improve the users' satisfaction ratios. But with the development of spectrum auction, DSA among different RANs which have their own interests separately are more and more common in the competitive communication market. The ultimate goal of each RAN is to maximize its income.

DYNAMIC LOAD BALANCING

In the past few decades, the amount of wireless network users and wireless networks increased dramatically. The emergence of multimedia services further exacerbates the data amount transmitted over networks. This requires the efficient use of network resources to meet spectrum bandwidth requirements of various services.

In the current wireless network, after a call is initiated by a user, if there is sufficient frequency band to support the call, this part of the spectrum band is assigned to this call, wherein the bandwidth depends on the service type. It is noteworthy that different services have different QoS requirements. For example, vides services require wider bandwidth than vice services. The call will be blocked off if the spectrum resource for this service is insufficient when the call is initiated. Dynamic load balancing scheme may improve the spectrum efficiency, reduce call blocking rate and drop call rate, thereby improve system performance. The improvement is much more obvious under the circumstance that hot cells and idle cells co-exist. Here, the hot cells refer to cells with higher traffic and higher drop call rate and the idle cells refer to cells with idle spectrum and may serve more users. At this time, the idle cells may bear the exceeded traffic of the hot cells (Yanmaz & Tonguz, 2004).

However, the current dynamic load balancing is carried out based on existing spectrum resources. During the process of dynamic load balancing, the spectrum amount is treated as a constant. Dynamic load balancing is implemented based on the spectrum occupancy and the traffic variation. Partial users are switched to other network when the spectrum occupancy rate is too high or traffic arrival rate is beyond a certain threshold. When the network overloads, the service will be blocked to access. Dynamic load balancing process is driven by events rather than implemented periodically. The dynamic load balancing process starts when the traffic amount is beyond the threshold. The traffic is re-assigned among networks. Therefore, the network resources are fully used in real-time under the premise of ensuring QoS. However, dynamic load balancing has its limitations when adjusting spectrum resource utilization: dynamic load balancing deals with the situation of network overload, which means that dynamic load balancing is implemented only in the case that existing spectrum resources are insufficient to meet the traffic requirements. Under the circumstance that traffic is low and idle spectrum exists, no proactive measure is taken resulting in a waste of spectrum resources.

Joint Dynamic Spectrum Allocation and Load Balancing

It can be seen that dynamic spectrum allocation and load balancing have their advantages and limitations respectively. In this paper, the dynamic spectrum allocation and load balancing are both taking into account and implemented at the same time. The ultimate goal is to maximize operation revenue.

1. The periodic adjustment of the dynamic spectrum allocation and the real-time load balancing are implemented jointly. To achieve the maximum operation revenue, the network spectrum is allocated periodically and the dynamic load balancing is carried out instantly when the traffic amount varies.

2. Dynamic spectrum allocation is implemented periodically to adjust network spectrum resources. The idle spectrum resources are sold to other networks to increase operation revenue.

3. The operation goal of profit-driven is set to meet the requirements of the increasingly competitive communication market and the actual needs of the operators. The ultimate goal is to maximize operation revenue rather than to improve the spectrum utilization or the customer satisfaction. Under this circumstance, dynamic spectrum allocation becomes spectrum auction (SA).

In this paper, a joint Spectrum Auction and Load Balancing scheme (SALB) is described.

Theoretical Tools

Traffic Prediction

DSA is based on the accurate prediction of network traffic. There are two main aspects to the prediction: (1) the history load, and (2) a time-series prediction algorithm. If unexpected traffic patterns occur, then the history load alone would not be able to adapt, leading to inappropriate dynamic spectrum allocations, so time series prediction is used to estimate these unexpected traffic loads.

Currently, three prediction methods are used, and in the equations for these, the following symbols are used:

$$\hat{y}_{l+1} = predicted\_load$$

$$y_l = current\_load$$

$$y_{l-n} = y - value\_n\_samples\_in\_the\_past$$

$$x_l = current\_time$$

$$x_{l-n} = x - value\_n\_samples\_in\_the\_past$$

Current Value Prediction

This is the most basic scheme, sometimes referred to as simple prediction. This takes the value of the last load measured as an estimate of the future load. The equation can be seen as follows:

$$\hat{y}_{l+1} = y_{l+1}$$

Linear Regression Prediction, n Samples Past

This takes the previous n samples, fits a straight line through the points, and uses this to estimate the value for the future sample. The equations can be seen as follows:

$$\hat{y}_{l+1} = a + b * x_{l+1}$$

$$\text{where: } a = \frac{\sum_{i=0}^{n-1} y_{l-i}}{n} - b * \frac{\sum_{i=0}^{n-1} x_{l-i}}{n}$$

$$b = \frac{n * \sum_{i=0}^{n-1}(y_{l-i})(x_{l-i}) - \left(\sum_{i=0}^{n-1} x_{l-i}\right)\left(\sum_{i=0}^{n-1} y_{l-i}\right)}{n * \sum_{i=0}^{n-1} x_{l-i}^2 - \left(\sum_{i=0}^{n-1} x_{l-i}\right)^2}$$

Exponential Regression Prediction, n Past Samples

This takes the previous n samples, fits an exponential curve through the points, and estimates the value for the next sample from this. The equations are seen as follows:

$$\hat{y}_{l+1} = p * q^{x_{l+1}}$$

where:

$$p = 10^a$$

$$q = 10^b$$

$$a = \frac{\sum_{i=0}^{n-1} \log(y_{l-i})}{n} - b * \frac{\sum_{i=0}^{n-1} x_{l-i}}{n}$$

$$b =$$

$$\frac{n * \sum_{l=0}^{n-1}(\log(y_{l-i}))(x_{l-i}) - \left(\sum_{i=0}^{n-1} x_{l-i}\right)\left(\sum_{i=0}^{n-1} \log(y_{l-i})\right)}{n * \sum_{i=0}^{n-1} x_{l-i}^2 - \left(\sum_{i=0}^{n-1} x_{l-1}\right)^2}$$

Combinations of the History Load and the Prediction Algorithms

Nine load prediction schemes for practical use are listed below using combinations of the history load and the prediction algorithms:

1. History combined with current value scheme;
2. History combined with linear regression scheme using 2 past samples;
3. History combined with linear regression scheme using 3 past samples;
4. History combined with exponential regression scheme using 3 past samples;
5. History only;
6. Current value scheme only;
7. Linear regression scheme using 2 past samples only;
8. Linear regression scheme using 3 past samples only;
9. Exponential regression scheme using 3 past samples only.

When the scheme applies a prediction method combined with history load, the history load is used for correcting the prediction results of the current value prediction, the linear regression prediction and the exponential regression prediction. If the prediction results of the current value prediction, the linear regression prediction and the exponential regression prediction are within a reasonable range (for example 1±5%) of the history, the history value is used as the final prediction, otherwise if the prediction results of the current value prediction, the linear regression prediction and the exponential regression prediction are outside a reasonable range (for example 1±5%) of the history, the prediction result is used as the final prediction.

The traffic variation scenarios in RANs can be divided into 4 categories:

1. Peak in traffic: most of the time, the network traffic is in line with historical statistics, but there are events, such as meetings or parades, during which traffic increases in a moment of sudden and significantly;
2. A general increase in traffic: the actual network traffic compared with the historical statistics increases;
3. A general decline in traffic: the actual network traffic compared with the historical statistics declines;
4. Equal to the history: the actual network traffic is equal to the historical statistics.

Analyses of the 9 load prediction schemes in the 4 traffic variation scenarios are made. It is known that the prediction result is more accurate by using the history load to correct the prediction result in the peak in traffic scenario. In addition, the history combined linear regression prediction with 2 (3) past samples and the history combined exponential regression prediction with 3 past samples both perform well in any traffic variation scenarios, therein there is no significant difference between the prediction results using the history combined linear regression prediction with 2 (3) past samples and the history combined exponential regression prediction with 3 past samples. In this paper, the history combined linear regression prediction with 2 past samples is used because of less calculation and accurate prediction.

Fitting a Curve

Usually in the curve fitting, the mathematical model is the "single-input single-out" (SISO), so its characteristics can be represented with a curve. To create a mathematical model with two inputs, then the feature can be represented as a surface, called surface fitting. The same concept can be extended to the mathematical models of "Multiple Input / Single Output" (MISO) or "Multiple Input / Multiple Output" (MIMO), such as artificial neural networks and so on. Both curve fitting or surface fitting (or other multi-input model fitting) are known as regression analysis or data fitting in data analysis. It involves mathematical theory and a wide range of analysis techniques. Regression analysis has a great relationship with the mathematical models used. If the model used is a linear model, it is called linear regression, on the other hand, if non-linear model is used, it is called nonlinear regression, wherein the linear regression is the most commonly used method, which has been established for a long time, the basic concept of which is to approximate a given set of data points with a parametric curve. If the parametric curve is a polynomial, this curve fitting is also known as polynomial fitting. In this paper, the polynomial fitting is used.

SALB ALGORITHM

In SALB algorithm, the traffic in the next DSA period is predict according to the history and the load samples in the past, the load curve is fitted, and the perfect spectrum purchase quantity is calculated based on the spectrum price the seller provided. The algorithm is divided into the following three steps:

Step 1: Traffic Prediction. The average load in the next period is predicted using the linear regression algorithm with 2 past samples and corrected with the history load. According to the statistics, the network traffic curves in days show similar trends, so the statistical average value of the nth loads in everyday past is the history load of the nth DSA period.

Step 2: Curve Fitting. The load curve during the next DSA period is fitted using the actual average load values of the two periods before and the prediction value in step 1.

Step 3: The Perfect Spectrum Quantity. The operation revenue is calculated with the spectrum trading quantity as a variable based on the load curve predicted in step 2, the spectrum price, the revenue for providing services and the current spectrum. The revenue is a func-

tion of the spectrum quantity. The spectrum quantity which maximizes the revenue is the perfect spectrum quantity for trading.

The SALB algorithm is as follows.

The traffic prediction in step 1 is divided into two sub-steps:

1. The predicted load of the nth period Pr_n' is predicted using the actual average loads R_{n-2}, R_{n-1} of the 2 SALB periods before;

2. Pr_n' is corrected using the history load P_n

$$\mathrm{Pr}_n = \begin{cases} P_n & (1+5\%)*P_n > \mathrm{Pr}_n' > (1-5\%)*P_n \\ \mathrm{Pr}_n' & (1-5\%)*P_n < \mathrm{Pr}_n' \ or \ \mathrm{Pr}_n' > (1+5\%)*P_n \end{cases}$$

The curve fitting of step 2 is performed in the nth DSA period using Quadratic Curve Fitting with (t_{n-2}, R_{n-2}), (t_{n-1}, R_{n-1}), (t_n, Pr_n) as inputs, wherein t_{n-2}, t_{n-1}, t_n are the middle time of the n-2th, n-1th, nth DSA periods, respectively. The equations are as follows:

$$a_0 + a_1 * t_{n-2} + a_2 * t_{n-2}^2 = R_{n-2}$$

$$a_0 + a_1 * t_{n-1} + a_2 * t_{n-1}^2 = R_{n-1}$$

$$a_0 + a_1 * t_n + a_2 * t_n^2 = \mathrm{Pr}_n$$

The matrix is as follows:

$$\begin{bmatrix} 1 & t_{n-2} & t_{n-2}^2 \\ 1 & t_{n-1} & t_{n-1}^2 \\ 1 & t_n & t_n^2 \end{bmatrix} \begin{bmatrix} a_0 \\ a_1 \\ a_2 \end{bmatrix} = \begin{bmatrix} R_{n-2} \\ R_{n-1} \\ \mathrm{Pr}_n \end{bmatrix}$$

The quadratic curve coefficients are calculated by the algorithm above and the equation of the fitting curve is determined as follows:

$$Tr(t) = f(t; a_0, a_1, a_2) = a_0 + a_1 * t + a_2 * t^2$$

The operation revenue is calculated with the spectrum trading quantity as a variable based on the load curve predicted in step 2, the spectrum price, the revenue for providing services and the current spectrum. The revenue is a function of the spectrum quantity. The spectrum quantity which maximizes the revenue is the perfect spectrum quantity for trading.

$F(n)$ is the current spectrum quantity and the spectrum quantity for trading is:

$$f(n) \begin{cases} > 0 \, spectrum \, buying \\ < 0 \, spectrum \, selling \end{cases}$$

Then the spectrum quantity after spectrum auction is:

$F(n) + f(n)$

Taking the spectrum auction and load balancing into consideration, the operation revenue during this SALB period is:

$I(n) = Pr(n) - Pa(n)$

Wherein $Pr(n)$ is the revenue for providing services, $Pa(n)$ is the price for selling or buying spectrum.

$Pr(n)$: When some spectrum is idle, the revenue is calculated using the load predicted.

$$Pr_1(n) = \int_{t \in T_1} Tr_k(t) * \alpha dt$$

where:

$$T_1 = \left\{ t \,\middle|\, (F(n) + f(n)) * k > Tr_n(t) \right\}$$

When the spectrum is not enough, the revenue is determined by the services provided.

$$Pr_2(n) = \int_{t \in T_2} (F(n) + f(n)) * k * \alpha dt$$

where:

$$T_2 = \left\{ t \,\middle|\, F(n) + f(n)) * k \leq Tr_n(t) \right\}$$

then,

$Pr(n) = Pr_1(n) + Pr_2(n)$

Wherein $Tr_n(t)$ is the curve fitted, α is the profit for providing services, k is service quantity supported by a unit.

$Pa(n)$: The revenue for spectrum trading is as follows:

$Pa(n) = f(n) * \beta$

Wherein β is the spectrum price per unit.

$I(n)$ is the total operation revenue in the SLAB period. The $f(n)$ value which maximizes $I(n)$ is the perfect spectrum quantity for trading:

$$f(n) = \arg \max I(n)$$

SALB SIMULATION

The traffic variation in 24 hours is divided into 12 DSA periods, 2 hours per period. The traffic is simulated by a double-Gaussian model which consists of two Gaussian functions, centered at two rush peaks. The model is as follows:

$$ap_{gauss}(t) = \begin{cases} p_1 * e^{-\frac{(t-h_1)^2}{2*d_1^2}}, t < h_l \\ p_2 * e^{-\frac{(t-h_2)^2}{2*d_2^2}}, t < h_l \end{cases}$$

where:

p_1 is the first Gaussian amplitude;

h_1 is the morning peak hour;

d_1 is the first Gaussian deviation;

h_l is the lunch hour;

p_2 is the second Gaussian amplitude;

h_2 is the afternoon peak hour;

d_2 is the second Gaussian deviation.

History Load

In SALB simulation, 30 load values of each DSA periods are produced as the history load by Poisson process according to the average value ($\lambda_1, \lambda_2, \lambda_3 \ldots \lambda_{12}$) of the double-Gaussian model:

$P_{1,1}, P_{1,2}, P_{1,3} \cdots P_{1,30}$;
$P_{2,1}, P_{2,2}, P_{2,3} \cdots P_{2,30}$;
$\vdots$
$P_{12,1}, P_{12,2}, P_{12,3} \cdots P_{12,30}$;

The average values ($P_1, P_2, P_3 \cdots P_{12}$) of the 30 load values in each SALB period are treated as the history load and used for correcting the predicted values.

Actual Load

The actual load is produced the same as the history load. 30 load values of each DSA periods are produced by Poisson process according to the average value ($\lambda_1, \lambda_2, \lambda_3 \ldots \lambda_{12}$) of the double-Gaussian model:

$R_{1,1}, R_{1,2}, R_{1,3} \cdots R_{1,30}$;
$R_{2,1}, R_{2,2}, R_{2,3} \cdots R_{2,30}$;
$\vdots$
$R_{12,1}, R_{12,2}, R_{12,3} \cdots R_{12,30}$;

The average values ($R_1, R_2, R_3 \cdots R_{12}$) of the 30 load values in each SALB period are treated as inputs of the load prediction algorithm and used for curve fitting with the predicted results.

Revenue Calculation

The actual operation revenue is calculated according to the spectrum trading quantity $f'(n)$.

$$I'(n) = Pr'(n) - Pa'(n)$$

where:

$$Pr_1'(n) = \int_{t \in T_1'} Tr_n'(t) * \alpha dt$$

$$T_1' = \left\{ t \middle| F(n) + f'(n)) * k > Tr_n'(t) \right\}$$

If the spectrum is enough, $Tr_n'(t)$ is the actual traffic load $R_{n,1}, R_{n,2}, R_{n,3} \cdots R_{n,30}$ produced by Poisson process,

$$Pr_2'(n) = \int_{t \in T_2'} (F(n) + f'(n)) * k * \alpha dt$$

$$T_2' = \left\{ t \middle| F(n) + f'(n)) * k \le Tr_n'(t) \right\}$$

If the spectrum is not enough, the traffic load supported is determined by the spectrum quantity.

$$Pr'(n) = Pr_1'(n) + Pr_2'(n)$$

The charge for spectrum trading is:

$$\wp a'(n) = f'(n) * \beta$$

Simulation Result

The network load model for SALB algorithm is as follows:

$$ap_{gauss}(t) = \begin{cases} p_1 * e^{-\frac{(t-h_1)^2}{2*d_1^2}}, t < h_l \\ p_2 * e^{-\frac{(t-h_2)^2}{2*d_2^2}}, t < h_l \end{cases}$$

In the model, the maximum load during a day is set to 100 and the other parameters are as follows.

The double-Gaussian model is simulated in Figure 1.

A DSA period is set to 2 hours and with 30 samples; the spectrum price per unit is set to 100; the revenue for serving per load is set to 1000.

Figure 1. Double-Gaussian model

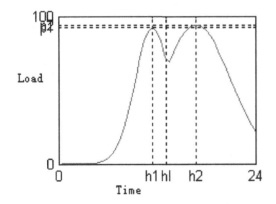

Figure 2. Simulation result

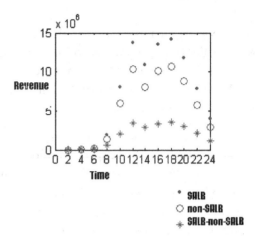

The operation revenues of using SALB and without SALB are calculated. The difference between SALB and non-SALB is shown in Figure 2.

The operation revenue rises by 34.9% according to the simulation result. As can be seen from the above simulation, the SALB algorithm which joints spectrum auction and load balancing can greatly improve the network operation revenue.

CONCLUSION

Based on the heterogeneous network environment, the advantages and shortages of dynamic spectrum allocation and load balancing are discussed. As the aim for network operators is to maximize revenue, the spectrum allocation is replaced by spectrum auction. A novel SALB algorithm is discussed in details to calculate the perfect spectrum trading quantity which may raise the operation revenue. The simulation result shows that SALB can greatly improve network operations revenue by as much as 34.9%.

REFERENCES

Ghaheri-Niri, S., Leaves, P., Benko, P., Huschke, J., & Stahl, W. (2000). *Traffic control and dynamic spectrum allocation in DRiVE*. Paper presented at the Workshop on Multiradio Multimedia Communications, Berlin, Germany.

Leaves, P., Ghaheri-Niri, S., Tafazolli, R., & Huschke, J. (2002). Dynamic spectrum allocation in hybrid networks with imperfect load prediction. In *Proceedings of the Third IEEE International Conference on 3G Mobile Communication Technologies*, London, UK (pp. 444-448).

Leaves, P., Moessner, K., & Tafazolli, R. (2004). Dynamic spectrum allocation in composite reconfigurable wireless networks. *Communications Magazine*, *42*(5), 72–81. doi:10.1109/MCOM.2004.1299346

Peha, J. M. (2000). Wireless communications and coexistence for smart environments. *IEEE Personal Communications*, *7*(51), 66–68. doi:10.1109/98.878543

Tonjes, R., Xu, L., & Paila, T. (2000, October 1-4). *Architecture for a future generation multi-access wireless system with dynamic spectrum allocation*. Paper presented at the IST Mobile Summit, Galway, Ireland.

UK Department of Trade and Industry, UK Department of Culture, Media and Sport. (2000). *A new future for communications*. London, UK: Author.

This work was previously published in the International Journal of Advanced Pervasive and Ubiquitous Computing, Volume 3, Issue 3, edited by Tao Gao, pp. 14-23, copyright 2011 by IGI Publishing (an imprint of IGI Global).

Chapter 18
A Novel Detection Method of Paper Defects based on Visual Attention Mechanism

Ping Jiang
University of Jinan, China

Tao Gao
Electronic Information Products Supervision and Inspection Institute of Hebei Province, China

ABSTRACT

In this paper, an improved paper defects detection method based on visual attention mechanism computation model is presented. First, multi-scale feature maps are extracted by linear filtering. Second, the comparative maps are obtained by carrying out center-surround difference operator. Third, the saliency map is obtained by combining conspicuity maps, which is gained by combining the multi-scale comparative maps. Last, the seed point of watershed segmentation is determined by competition among salient points in the saliency map and the defect regions are segmented from the background. Experimental results show the efficiency of the approach for paper defects detection.

1. INTRODUCTION

Inefficiencies in industrial process are costly in terms of time, money and consumer satisfaction. The global economic pressures have gradually led business to ask more of it in order to become more competitive. As a result, automated industrial inspection systems (Tanimoto, 1996; Gregor,

2001) based on hardware and/or software tools have been very successful in applications to on-line quality control applications by virtue of their ability to make repetitive measurements accurately, fast, and objectively. One of the industry fields where automated visual inspection systems are mostly needed is paper manufacturing. Typical characteristics of paper manufacturing are the

DOI: 10.4018/978-1-4666-2645-4.ch018

large values of web width and production speed. The web width of a modern paper machine makes about $3 \times 10^8 mm^2$ of paper each second, it is impossible to use human eyes to inspect the web. Thus, automated visual inspection systems play an important role in ensuring the quality of paper products. Inspection systems based on CCD technology adopt the CCD camera as the sensor unit, take a snapshot of running paper web, and transmit the images to computer. And then with advanced image processing technologies, inspection systems can locate the position of paper defect and classify the type of it.

The research on defect detection technique is now focused on the intelligent on-line measurement, whose purpose is to develop a machine vision system to realize exact detection and localization of defects with a fast and effective algorithm. Existing methods (Newman, 1995; Sezgin & Sankur, 2004; Iivarinen, Heikkinen, Rauhamaa, Vuorimaa, & Visa, 2000; Iivarinen, 2000; Brzakovic, Vujovic, & Liakopoulos, 1995) mainly fall into three types: thresholding method, morphological method and grey level statistics method. The threshold method sets up different thresholds to different paper defects. Morphological method defects the edge of paper defects with eroded and expanded edge detector. Grey level statistics method detects paper defects with the statistical characteristics of the image of paper defects. From the fewer reports of modern web inspection systems, one can concludes that thresholding method is the main algorithm in paper defect detection system.

Thresholding methods, which are mainly associated with uniform web materials, is to separate the defect regions from the uniform background by using the segmentation threshold. The segmentation threshold takes an important role in the process, which is usually selected on the basis of statistics to the background with the application domain. An important assumption in this process is that the statistics of defect-free regions are stationary, and these regions extend over a significant portion of inspection images. In real applications, the paper products usually have different texture structure (Tsai & Huang, 2003) such as uniform structure, random structure and patterned structure. Therefore, the segmentation threshold needs to be re-determined because of the difference of texture structures, which has great limitation to the defect detection system in real applications.

Usually, it is the defect regions (e.g., holes, stains) not the texture attracts the attention firstly when we observe it because the defect regions are more conspicuity or saliency than the background. Therefore, how to find these attractive regions and separate them from the defect-free background accurately and rapidly is the key problem for paper manufacturing, which can help to ensure the high quality of paper and improve the producing efficiency of the factories. In this paper, we presented a new segmentation method based on visual attention mechanism (Desimone & Duncan, 1995; Kastner & Ungerleider, 2000) to separate the defect regions from the background. The aim of the study presented in this paper is to achieve robust detection of paper defects by using visual attention mechanism. The emphasis of our work is to make the visual inspection system detect defects rapidly, accurately and robustly.

2. THE PROPOSED METHOD DESCRIPTION

Psychophysical and physiological evidence indicates that primates and humans have a remarkable ability to interpret complex scenes in real time, despite the limited speed of the neuronal hardware available for such tasks. A number studies concerning the detection, localization, and recognition of objects in the visual field have suggested a two-stage theory of human visual perception. The first stage is the "pre-attentive" mode, in which simple features are processed rapidly and in parallel over the entire visual field. In the second mode, "attentive" mode, a specialized processing focus, usually called FOA, is directed to particular locations in the visual field. This processing mechanism of human visual system is called visual attention mechanism (Desimone & Duncan, 1995; Kastner & Ungerleider, 2000). Inspired by the research results on the human visual system, Tsotsos, Culhane, Wai, Lai, Davis, and Nuflo (1995), Niebur and Koch (1998), Koch and Ullman (1995), and Itti, Koch, and Niebur (1998). etc., have proposed some calculation models by simulating the HVS, which are called bottom-up visual attention mechanism (BUVAM) computation model. The saliency regions can be computed using BUVAM computation model.

The paper defect detection method, proposed in this paper, is comprised of two steps. First, the saliency map is obtained by using BUVAM computation model. Second, watershed segmentation, in which the saliency value is used to be the seed point, and the saliency map are combined to separate the defect regions from the background.

A. BUVAM Model Description

BUVAM computation mode (Tsotsos, Culhane, Wai, Lai, Davis, & Nuflo, 1995; Niebur & Koch, 1998; Koch & Ullman, 1995; Itti, Koch, & Niebur, 1998) derives from feature integrate theory (Treisman & Gelade, 1980). The main idea is extracting different feature maps (e.g., intensity, color and orientation, etc.) in multi-scales of the input image, obtaining the comparative maps by using center-surround difference operation to the feature maps, combining the comparative maps to form conspicuity map of every feature respectively, and last combining all the conspicuity maps to form the saliency map. The whole computation process is as follows.

Step 1: Extracting feature maps in multi-scales: Five spatial scales $\sigma, \sigma \in [0, \cdots, 4]$ are created using Gaussian pyramid, which progressively low-pass filter and subsample the input image, yielding horizontal and vertical image-reduction factors ranging from 1:1 (scale zero) to 1:16 (scale four). Seven features are extracted in every scale using (1).

$$FM_I(\sigma) = \left(r(\sigma) + g(\sigma) + b(\sigma)\right) / 3$$
$$FM_C^{rg}(\sigma) = \left(r(\sigma) - g(\sigma)\right) / \max\left(r(\sigma), g(\sigma), b(\sigma)\right)$$
$$FM_C^{by}(\sigma) = \left(b(\sigma) - \min\left(r(\sigma), g(\sigma)\right)\right) / \max\left(r(\sigma), g(\sigma), b(\sigma)\right)$$
$$FM_O^{\theta}(\sigma) = \left\|F_I(\sigma) * G_0(\theta)\right\| + \left\|F_I(\sigma) * G_{\pi/2}(\theta)\right\|$$

$$(1)$$

Where $FM_I(\sigma)$ denotes the intensity feature maps, $FM_C^{rg}(\sigma)$ and $FM_C^{by}(\sigma)$ the color feature maps and $FM_O^{\theta}(\sigma)$ the orientation feature maps. $r(\sigma)$, $g(\sigma)$ and $b(\sigma)$ are the three channels information of red, green and blue of the input image. $G_\phi(\theta)$ is the Gabor function. $\phi \in \{0, \pi/2\}$, $\theta \in \{0°, 45°, 90°, 135°\}$ "$*$" means convolution operator.

In total, thirty-five multi-scale feature maps are computed: five for intensity, ten for color, and twenty for orientation.

Step 2: Obtaining comparative maps: Center-surround differences (defined "Θ") between a "center" fine scale c and a "surround" coarser scale s using (2), which derives from the retinal imaging theory of the human visual system.

$$CM_I(c, s) = \left|FM_I(c) \Theta FM_I(s)\right|$$
$$CM_C^{rg}(c, s) = \left|FM_C^{rg}(c) \Theta FM_C^{rg}(s)\right|$$
$$CM_C^{by}(c, s) = \left|FM_C^{by}(c) \Theta FM_C^{by}(s)\right|$$
$$CM_O^{\theta}(c, s) = \left|FM_O^{\theta}(c) \Theta FM_O^{\theta}(s)\right|$$

$$(2)$$

Where $CM_I(c,s)$ denotes the intensity comparative maps, $CM_C^{rg}(c,s)$ and $CM_C^{by}(c,s)$ the color comparative maps and $CM_O^{\theta}(c,s)$ the orientation comparative maps. $c \in \{0,1\}$ $s \in \{2,3,4\}$.

In total, forty-two comparative maps are computed: six for intensity, twelve for color, and twenty-four for orientation.

Step 3: Obtaining conspicuity maps: Combining the comparative maps in all scales for every feature, respectively. Salient objects, which appear conspicuity strongly in only a few maps, may be masked by noise or by less-salient if the comparative maps are combined directly. Thus, normalization operation (defined $"N(\times)"$) is carried out to every comparative map before combination. The process of $N(\cdot)$ is as follows:

1. Normalize the values in the map to a fixed range $[0 \cdots K]$.
2. Find the location with the global maximum K in the comparative map and compute the average $\bar{k}$ of all its other local maxima.
3. Globally multiply the map by $\left(K - \bar{k}\right)^2$.

Thus, three conspicuity maps can be obtained using Equation (3).

$$
\begin{aligned}
\overline{C}M_I &= \sum_{c \in \{0,1\}, s \in \{2,3,4\}} N\left(CM_I(c,s)\right) \\
\overline{C}M_C &= \sum_{c \in \{0,1\}, s \in \{2,3,4\}} N\left(CM_C^{rg}(c,s)\right) + \sum_{c \in \{0,1\}, s \in \{2,3,4\}} N\left(CM_C^{by}(c,s)\right) \\
\overline{C}M_O &= \sum_{c \in \{0,1\}, s \in \{2,3,4\}} N\left(CM_O(c,s)\right), \quad \theta \in \{0°, 45°, 90°, 135°\}
\end{aligned}
$$

(3)

Step 4: Obtaining the saliency map: Combining the conspicuity maps, which also need to be normalized using $N(\cdot)$ operation. The saliency map is obtained using Equation (4). The purpose of the saliency map is to represent the conspicuity or saliency at every location in the visual field to guide the selection of attended locations, based on the spatial distribution of saliency.

$$
SM = \frac{1}{3}\left(N\left(\overline{C}M_I\right) + N\left(\overline{C}M_C\right) + N\left(\overline{C}M_O\right)\right)
$$

(4)

At any given time, the maximum of the saliency map (SM) defines the most salient image location.

B. Defect Detection Method

Traditionally, segmentation threshold is determined by making statistics to the texture, which was assumed to be stationary. Thus, these thresholding methods have no adaptability for real applications. In order to overcome the problem a novel threshold determination method is presented by using BUVAM computation model. The saliency values are used as the seed of watershed and combined to the saliency map to separate the defect regions from the background. The whole defect detection architecture is shown in Figure 1.

3. EXPERIMENT RESULTS AND ANALYSIS

To verify the effectiveness of the proposed method, we carried out many tests on different paper with different defects, which appear in different background with texture structures. Figure 2 is the original images. Figure 3 shows the values distribution of Figure 2. Figure 4 is the relative saliency maps, which is obtained by using BUVAM computation model. Figure 5 is the segmentation results of defect regions, which is obtained by combining the saliency map and watershed segmentation method.

It can be found from Figure 3 that the pixel value distributions of the defect regions (except for Figure 3(c)) have no obvious difference capered to the background. Therefore, it is difficult to separate the defect regions from the background using traditional segmentation method. Large amount of images indicate that the defect regions are more conspicuity than the backgrounds for human eyes, that is, the defect regions can attract the observers' attention firstly. Figure 4 is the relative saliency maps of Figure 2. It can be found from Figure 4 that the saliency regions are just related to the defect regions, which indicates that the proposed method can find the defect regions accurately. Figure 5 shows the segmentation results. It can be found from Figure 5 that the defect regions can be separated from the background accurately by combing the visual attention mechanism and watershed segmentation method.

4. CONCLUSION

Human visual attention mechanism is used to obtain the saliency map and the winner saliency points are selected as the seed points of watershed segmentation. Experiments results show that the proposed method can separate the defect regions from the background accurately. Meanwhile, it indicates that the method is robust to paper defects detection with different texture structures.

Figure 1. Direction of a random geometry

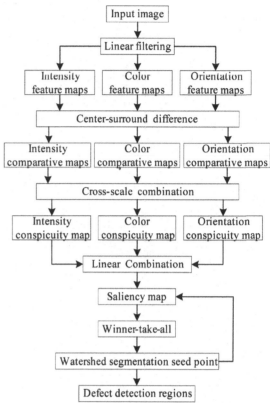

Figure 2. Original images

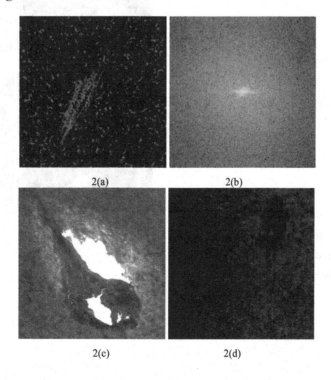

2(a) 2(b)

2(c) 2(d)

Figure 3. The pixel values distribution of Figure 2

Figure 4. The saliency maps

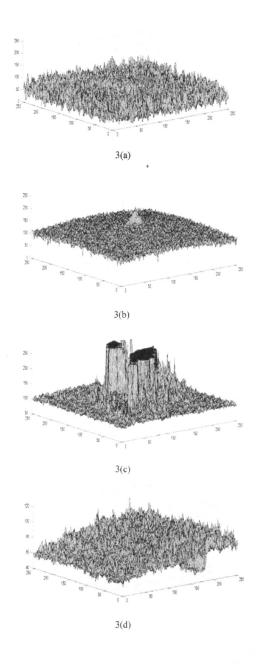

3(a)

3(b)

3(c)

3(d)

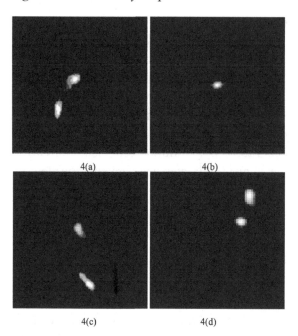

4(a)　　　　　4(b)

4(c)　　　　　4(d)

Figure 5. Segmentation results of Figure 2

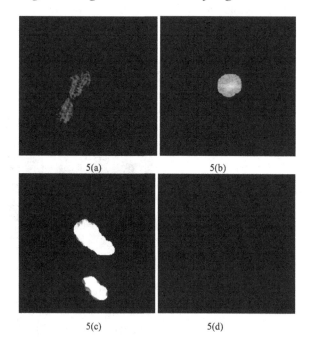

5(a)　　　　　5(b)

5(c)　　　　　5(d)

Next we will use shape analysis methods segmentation regions to determine what kind of defect belongs to by extracting different shape features, such as area, length-width-ratio, compactness, etc.

ACKNOWLEDGMENT

This work is supported by China '863' High-Tech Program (No. 2007AA04Z219), the National Natural Science Foundation of China (No. 6087053, 60802051), Tianjin Natural Science Foundation (09JCYBJC02100) and the Program for New Century Excellent Talent in University (NCET).

REFERENCES

Brzakovic, D., Vujovic, N., & Liakopoulos, A. (1995). An approach to quality control of texture web material. *Proceedings of the Society for Photo-Instrumentation Engineers, 2597*, 60–69.

Desimone, R., & Duncan, J. (1995). Neural mechanisms of selective visual attention. *Annual Review of Neuroscience, 18*, 193–222. doi:10.1146/annurev.ne.18.030195.001205

Gregor, M. M. (2001). Some impacts of paper making on paper structure. *Paper Technology, 42*, 30–44.

Iivarinen, J. (2000). Surface defect detection with histogram-based texture features, intelligent robots and computer vision. In *Proceedings of the SPIE Conference on Algorithms, Techniques and Active Vision* (Vol. 4127, pp. 140-145).

Iivarinen, J., Heikkinen, K., Rauhamaa, J., Vuorimaa, P., & Visa, A. (2000). A defect detection scheme for web surface inspection. *International Journal of Pattern Recognition and Artificial Intelligence, 14*, 735–755.

Itti, L., Koch, C., & Niebur, E. (1998). A model of saliency-based visual attention for rapid scene analysis. *IEEE Transactions on Pattern Analysis and Machine Intelligence, 20*, 1254–1259. doi:10.1109/34.730558

Kastner, S., & Ungerleider, L. G. (2000). Mechanisms of visual attention in human cortex. *Annual Review of Neuroscience, 123*, 315–341.

Koch, C., & Ullman, S. (1995). Shifts in selective visual attention: towards the underlying neural circuitry. *Human Neurobiology, 4*, 219–227.

Newman, T. S. (1995). A survey of automated visual inspection. *Computer Vision and Image Understanding, 61*, 231–262. doi:10.1006/cviu.1995.1017

Niebur, E., & Koch, C. (1998). Computational architectures for attention. In Parasuraman, R. (Ed.), *The attentive brain* (pp. 163–186). Cambridge, MA: MIT Press.

Sezgin, M., & Sankur, B. (2004). Survey over image thresholding techniques and quantitative performance evaluation. *Journal of Electronic Imaging, 13*, 146–156. doi:10.1117/1.1631315

Tanimoto, F. (1996). *Web inspection system technological trends and marketplace*. Paper, Film & Foil Convertech Pacific.

Treisman, A. M., & Gelade, G. (1980). A feature-integration theory of attention. *Cognitive Psychology, 12*, 97–136. doi:10.1016/0010-0285(80)90005-5

Tsai, D. M., & Huang, T. Y. (2003). Automated surface inspection for statistical textures. *Image and Vision Computing, 21*, 307–323. doi:10.1016/S0262-8856(03)00007-6

Tsotsos, J. K., Culhane, S. M., Wai, W. Y. K., Lai, Y., Davis, N., & Nuflo, F. (1995). Modelling visual attention via selective tuning. *Artificial Intelligence, 78*, 507–545. doi:10.1016/0004-3702(95)00025-9

This work was previously published in the International Journal of Advanced Pervasive and Ubiquitous Computing, Volume 3, Issue 3, edited by Tao Gao, pp. 24-31, copyright 2011 by IGI Publishing (an imprint of IGI Global).

Chapter 19
Research and Implementation of Self-Publishing Website Platforms for Universities Based on CMS

Liu Chong
Heibei Finance University, China

Wang Mei
Heibei University, China

An Wen Guang
Heibei Finance University, China

ABSTRACT

To update school websites, incorporating personality and ease of maintenance and management, the authors propose the use of a Content Management System (CMS). A CMS is a self-publishing Website platform for university information resources. The system has many features, such as self-service, fast station, self-service custom modules, dynamic replacement site style template, flexible adjustment of dynamic website contents and structures, search engine optimization (SEO) measures, and so forth. Each institution can customize according to their own information platform needs. A CMS greatly shortens the development cycle of the site and promotes the development of information tec hnology on campus.

INTRODUCTION

With the rapid development of network information and the widely applications of the internet, teaching theory and practice caused profound changes. Educators are not only to teach but who also became a learning Navigator and the manager of schedule update. Universities are an important window as internal and external web content publishing. Its management system is undergoing a continuous improvement (Zhang & Huang, 2001). It will be a scientific, standardized, efficient and safe operation of the mechanism of the process. Development of network technology and

DOI: 10.4018/978-1-4666-2645-4.ch019

the update speed are very fast. University portal is not only reflection window of the university, but the exchange of information nodes. How to keep the site fresh and management is a daunting task. At this point the content management system can take advantage of school resources and scalability, so as to meet the requirements of college teachers and students.This paper fully analyse the characteristics of the system and gives the solution on the problems.

STATUS AND PROBLEMS OF UNIVERSITY WEBSITES

1. System of Websites is Vulnerable

As the technology behind the construction, many sites, especially in the virus outbreak era, are vulnerable to be attacked by hackers and Trojan (Budin, 2006). Once under attack, websites are easy to crashed, and can't function properly. They could be used by criminals who will tamper with information, and seriously damage to the school's image.

2. Unable to Share Resources and Information

Since the early construction of the site can not be unified planning and standards, even unified management platform, the school department faculty websites have to be fragmented. Meanwhile, among the faculties, websites and applications are difficult to share information. Beacuse of this, websites are not integrated so as to form the independent silos and sharply reduce utilization of information resources (Laplant, 2006; Van Der Aalst & Van Hee, 2002).

3. Poor Flexible and Weak Functions

Many sites just do some accumulation of information, lack many useful features, such as a variety of unstructured (pictures, accessories, multimedia, etc.) and management of large files. There is no full-text search system. It also cannot control the viewing permission of the website content. The websites lack to customization features and the necessary functional components which are used to interact (McDonald & Stevenson, 1998). The content layout of the site is inconvenient to use, makeing the whole site forms so stiff. When the site needs to be adjusted or upgraded the revision, it leads to much more workload, or even need to re-construction. However, when it comes to the contents, they must be concerned about the poor efficient management. The information of manual link audio often can not be accessed; Poor system scalability, when it could be integrated with other applications, making the flexibility of the system reduced.

4. High Running Costs and Non-Standard Maintenance

As the various departments and faculties (Botafogo, Rivlin, & Shneiderman, 2002) have a relative independence of the websites, the maintenance on website content is often concentrated in a single department which can not be maintained by collaborative people who are coming from multi-sectoral. It is means that we lack standardized methods to maintain the site information. It is difficult to update. The servers, operatingsystems, information publishing softwares, database and other software vary with different applications. But each system has its own implementation, resulting in site maintenance and management costs are high, and wasting a lot of manpower, material and financial resources.

OVERVIEW OF CMS

1. Introduction

CMS is an acronym of Content Management System.

It has many excellent design based many templates, which can accelerate the speed of development and greatly reduce development costs of websites. The functions of CMS is not limited to text processing, it can also handle images, Flash animation, audio and video streams, image files and even e-mail.

CMS is a very broad term; the program from the general blog can be called a content management system as well as news release program or the comprehensive site management procedures.

2. Classification

Depending on the requirements, CMS has several different classifications. For example, depending on the application of different levels, it can be divided into:

- Attention to the back-end management CMS;
- Attention to the style CMS;
- Attention to the front release CMS.

A variety of CMS exist, and the final interfaces are very similar, but the programming style and in terms of management style are different (Gupta, Kaiser, Grimm, Chiang, & Starren, 2005). On the starting point of CMS, it should be convenient for network users who are not very familiar with a relatively simple way to manage their own websites. Although this is the starting point itself, as the original creator of the various CMS systems have their own background with the "simple" to understand the words of the different levels, it causes the warlords today that there is no uniform standard.

In short, with CMS you do not need to learn complex siting techniques, without having to learn too many complicated HTML, you can use CMS to build a unified and powerful professional-style website.

3. Function

CMS has many excellent template-based design, which can accelerate the speed of development and greatly reduce development costs of websites (Lizorkin & Lisovsky, 2005). The function of CMS is not limited to text processing, it can also handle images, Flash animation, audio and video streams, imagefiles and even e-mail. CMS also sub-types of scripts for each platform. Content management system is the information technology and the new darling of e-government is a relatively new market for content management. There is no uniform industry definition, thus different agencies have different interpretations.

4. Produce

With the enrichment and development of network applications, many sites often can not keep up with large amounts of information quickly and business models derived from the pace of change often takes a lot of time to updates and maintenance with more manpower and material resources; when sites encountered expansion, it is more complex to integration of internal and external networks and branch sites of the work, or it even need to re-construct the site. As it goes on, the users are always upgrading and integrating their systems in a high-cost, low efficiency of the cycle (Lowe, McMahon, & Culley, 2004). They are most concerned about the ease of system and functionality of integrity; therefore, the tools about building website and publishing information are in high demand.

First, the role must be made clear to fully ensure working efficiency of the staff (Fidel & Green, 2004) as well as be full-featured. Secondly, make sure the doorway to meet the "gatekeeper" application needs, so that the information published is accurate, for example, setting permissions and real-time management functions for different roles, such as editor, art designer, operationer and maintenancer and so on.

In addition, it is also the focus which attracts the attention of website users that guarantee the security of the architecture. With the effectively managing permission of visitors landing, the database within the network keeps security from attacking. That ensures the security and stability of the site, which the user is worried about (Harris, Owen, Bloor, & Hogg, 1997).

According to the above requirements, a professional content management system CMS came into being, to effectively address the user site building and information dissemination in the common problems and needs. It is the biggest advantage of the software that it could be processed soundly, feature-rich and categorized the manuscript editor and authorized management to the legitimate user, without requiring the user to ignore those difficult to understand SQL syntax.

CMS AS A SELF-PUBLISHING PLATFORM BASED ON UNIVERSITY INFORMATION RESOURCES

1. Full Reference Sites in the Group of E-Government Construction Model

Currently, the government portal site is started in 2001. The first application by the Ministry of Commerce website group model building has become the main government portal website construction mode. Group is different from a group of web sites in isolation. Site group means as follows: to portal sites for the centers and departments, based on the application form supported by a number of sub-station site collection. Site collection is a

specification of the site group system. Compare to the isolated site, the site group has the following advantages features, as shown in Table 1.

As a construction model using site groups, university faculty portal site will constitute a whole, not isolated, visitors can easily get through the portal master unified information service. Meanwhile, in the internal management, multi-site unified management, authority allocation, information navigation, information search, and eliminating information silos, using the Cluster share common software resources in order to reduce investment costs (Wild, Culley, McMahon, Darlington, & Liu, 2006).

2. CMS Architecture in the University

First, the portal development of universities should include office management, academic management, service management, forums and other modules. Second, there must be a network of multimedia teaching system, including multimedia courseware system, education system, video demanding system, video broadcasting systems. In addition, the system is essential communications services, including home page, the principal inquiry, e-mail, electronic bulletin board systems (Figure 1).

Table 1. Site group and isolated site

Site Group	Isolated Site
Unified planning, which is built on top of cms. A distributed maintenance.	There are no standard criteria, the information is not timely submitted and published are not allowed, it is easy lost.
Strict hierarchical rights management mechanism to ensure information sharing and information security.	No rules on the Site Group
Unified planning, lower input costs	System is isolated, difficult to manage, high input costs.
Information resources unified storage, unified classification	Information in isolation, classification is unreasonable.

Figure 1. CMS architecture in colleges

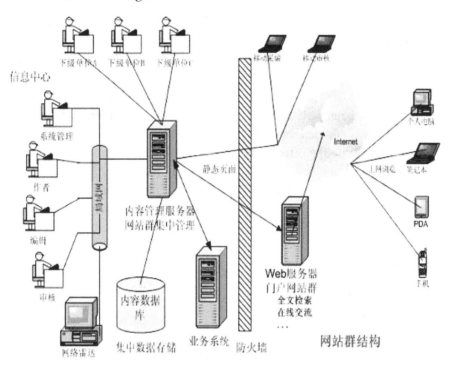

Based on this, we can build and deploy the university websites which could meet the diverse needs. Support includes hospital department's internal organization, as well as a variety of user-owned nature of the functional requirements. Those meet the functional requirements of the site to improve teaching development and other aspects.

3. Related Technical Support

The XML output of integrated data, combined with XLST (data reorganization) technology, generate the output XML format specification in line with GOOGLE maps and data exchange pages. Because of this, it is easy for depth search engine searching. Practical XML capabilities on data export, make data exchange between sites more easy. The output of XML generated site provides data output line of the XML specification (Gupta, Kaiser, Grimm, Chiang, & Starren, 2005), according to the XML specification to develop other plug-ins can also

be output with XSLT templates to personalize the page. It facilitates the management of different points synchronous and update website information. It makes the tube secretary to do his duty, not missing any information.

System provides full support for WAP, so that teminal users can access various websites. The feature of WAP browser allows access to information on the site to get an extension of mobile phone users. Users can visit the Web site at any time by phone about the latest release of the article, software, pictures and other information. Administrators can login via WAP recently to present the background to audit data. New technology meets the requirements of teachers and students who need to exchange information.

Full support of RSS features (Lowe, McMahon, & Culley, 2004). CMS supports different educational content sharing between sites, and form exchange website group of educational information. System allows any setting in the background using the Gb2312 and two UTF-8 character encoding, so it is possible to expand the university site collection groups that your site has a wide range of overseas Chinese (including Traditional Chinese) inter-site communication RSS.

Language pack can easily achieve multilanguage interface. You can modify the way of the language pack to make the page display text resources more in line with their needs, making the building a personalized website easier. Reusing of open sourcemodules, you can save resources, make better to apply to the construction of site.

TECHNICAL FRAMEWORK OF THE SYSTEM

The basic idea of CMS is to separate content management and design. Page stored in the template design, and content stored in a database or a separate file. When a user requests a page, each part jointly generates a standard HTML page (Liu, McMahon, Darlington, Culley, & Wild, 2006).

1. A Template Control Framework

We use the template separation technology. The template is extracted from the site and handled as a separate framework. In the actual design of the framework, we use css layout, which characterized by the form of pages can be achieved with complete separation of page content. Template frame work operation process shown in Figure 2.

Figure 2. Template frame work operation process

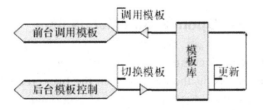

2. Module Management and Content Delivery Mechanisms

Functional modules of CMS are developed using an independent way, not involved with each other to ensure that the system calls each plug-in can work independently. While Plug-in provides extended interface, user can develop a separate module. Main content delivery mechanisms and content management module to work together, according to the needs with the flexibility to push the page content for displaying to the front.

3. Information Processing Algorithms in the Content Management

CMS is the core technology of information processing and the shortest path to retrieve the cluster. As the site of accumulation of information from vast amounts of data on how companies need to quickly find the information. It is usually the troubled problems, to solve the problems, we proposed two solutions. First we use the clustering concept of general-purpose search engines. The so-called clustering, which is based on the characteristics that similar things should have similar characteristics, and different characteristicsare quite different things, classify things we use.

Process information in the process of clustering, classification methods based on different clustering into hierarchical clustering of information and rapid sample clustering. Hierarchical clustering method is not specified in the premise of the final number of classes and keeps all the information together, eventually clustered into one class. The conclusion will be looking for in the process. The sample of clusters is specified for the cluster analysis and parameters for clustering. Based on the reality of the CMS system, we select the sample clustering method as a rapid means of information clustering. Information also has a similarnature. We can put a different type of information as information of the different properties of words which you can set different input information and retrieve information on the Internet for clustering. Specific approach is to use regular expression to the principle of the collected information and the default keyword matching. On the basis for the clustering, we store information after clustering.

In Figure 3, there are (A, B, C) three groups of data points, each data point within the coordinate values are close. You can use the geometric distance, said:

We assume that these three key attributes of things, in the performance of information processing in the three groups of words, X,i, Y, Z as the words appear in the probability of entry information. Cluster similarity is another important concept in computing (euclideananddistance). Table 2 is the index information for the system capacity of the cluster analysis.

4. Generation Mechanism of Static Page

Original static pages dynamic and efficient deployment. With the object mechanisms ASP privided, CMS can design sophisticated and elegant templates. For specific information to be added in the

Table 2. Index information for the system capacity of the cluster analysis

信息资源数 (mb)	关键词数目 (个)	匹配资源数 (mb)	剩余资源数 (mb)	消耗时间(s)
50	10	40	10	50
100	10	85	15	70
100	20	95	5	150
500	20	490	10	500
500	10	480	20	350
1000	20	950	50	890
1000	10	900	100	800
1500	50	1450	50	1100
1500	20	1250	250	1020
1500	10	1100	400	980

background maintenance, it will automatically generate a HTML file. The database stores the data directly that makes the database bigger, leading to performance degradation and then reduced accessing speed. Our system used in the design of an information in the front form(FORM), generated HTML file to provide specific information needed, such as title, date, telephone number, other details and so on. Then using file system objects ASP provided, we produce the required HTML file, and then the HTML file will be generated after the corresponding information written to the database.

Currently, no mater domestic and foreign, the ultimate portal home page has been designed as a static file. Static deployment of the biggest advantages of this are: (1) to reduce the burden on the database, reduce labor and maintenance costs; (2) conducive to be searched by engine; increase the amount of search engine included on the site; and (3) greatly improves the user access efficiency. This solves the website worries that accessing speed down caused by large data access.

5. SEO Optimization Mechanism

Embedded components of SEO optimization. Just by using the keywords in the background, keywords and optimization can be automatically matched. What is more, the efficient search engines and data caching mechanism ensure the spiders to crawl to each link.

Figure 3. Distribution of data points ingroup

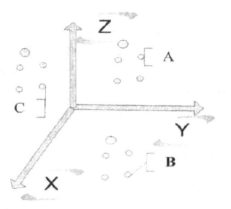

6. Ajax Application

The biggest advantage is that with Ajax does not refresh the entire page in the premise of maintaining data. This makes Web applications give more rapid response to user interaction, and to avoid the network to send information that has not changed. The system offer an article search function called google suggest. That is to facilitate the user's search of the article (Figure 4).

7. Other

We design the websites in accordance with international standards which is the latest W3C standard. Through tested from major browsers, such as IE6, IE7, Firefox, Opera, Travel, Window of the World and so on, the system ensure a smooth Web browsing and accomplishment of page display.

THE MAIN FUNCTION OF CMS

A complete content management system should have four major functions: content integration, content intelligence, content management and content distribution (Figure 5).

1. Content Integration

It allows the user to go to the different kind of systems to find information on different forms of documentation, such as documents, video, audio, graphics files.

2. Contents of Intelligence

This is the core function module of CMS. The classification of archived content help users quickly locate the desired content, which can be classified with full-text search and context by search methods. Now more sophisticated search technology also includes intelligent retrieval of knowledge and natural language query.

3. Content Management

It is the mainfunction modules of CMS. It provide support for content management process, including: content creation and editing, to achieve a variety of data, information, documents and procedures to obtainand provide collaboration tools to create content, such as the production of documents and web pages tools, data conversion (metadata and XML) tools and so on.

4. Content Distribution

It allows all users to receive the information at the same time, including the traditional way of non-Web graphical user interface (GUI), as well as information portals and various other ways.

SYSTEM BUILDING PROCESS

We first choose the layout of website pages, and enter or select the parameters of the site. Each page of the site includes a wide variety of con-

Figure 4. User's search of the article

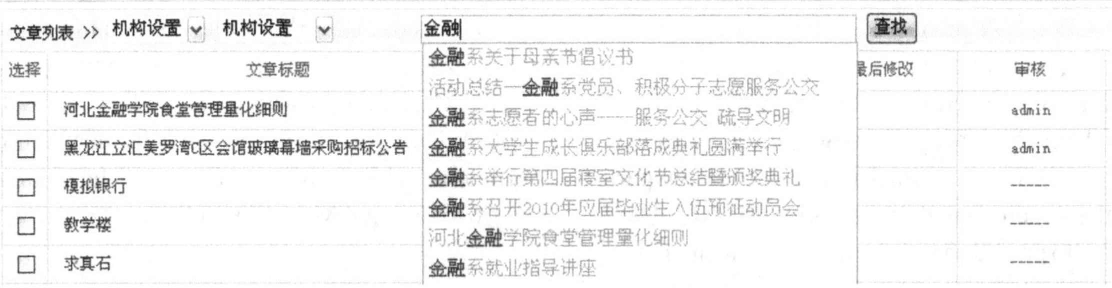

Figure 5. Major functions of CMS

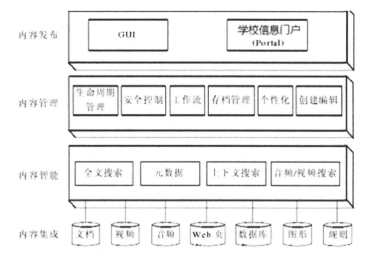

tent blocks (often expressed by the module). We can first design a template, and sketched out the layout of these blocksand the detailed location of arrangement which includes the site background, text, font color and so on. In this example, it is a template example about web page layout. Figures 6, 7, 8, 9, and 10 introduce the process of web page designing.

ADVANTAGES OF THE SYSTEM

1. Easy to Manage and Use

The basic principles of content management are that the entire content is divided into different parts, and different parts are also closely linked. It will not only easy to increase or decrease in function, but also can be the unified management. CMS can be managed through the using of a unified database, management background and function definitions. Page stored in the template design, and content stored in a database or a separate file (Harris, Owen, Bloor, & Hogg, 1997).

When the user applies pages, it generates standard HTML pages, which is linked to various parts of the system. It makes the system easy to use and quick to provide a good working platform. Edited text by the editor, the pictures and other HTML tags are output to the page. It is no difference between its effects and the effects when editing. User-edited content in the background automatically converted to HTML markup language which can be recognized by the browser. Users do not have to write code and build a variety of different forms of web content and can quickly integrate other structured and unstructured information and all kinds of applications.

2. Improved Operational Efficiency of the Sites

CMS uses a combination of static and dynamic way. It will open the information to generate static pages. This reduces the server load, and the limited information using a dynamic page, so feel free to add and delete content information. When it comes to the access of database, it is the first temporary connection, and then the user submit to the server. After the server returns the results to the user, it will be disconnected immediately (Liu, McMahon, Darlington, Culley, & Wild, 2006). Therefore, server access is faster and more efficient. Table 3 gives the results of the comparing with using CMS and no CMS.

Figure 6. Template examples

Figure 7. Web page design

3. Improve the Safety of the Site

We strictly control the allocation of management authority. We set the access permissions and access rights with each of the system functions and data manipulation objects. We conduct a rigorous filtering of information and review, so you can effectively ensure the safety of site information.

4. Effectively Reduce Cost

Using the CMS system, non-professionals can manage and maintain the system. This greatly saves manpower. Even a user who does not understand web production techniques can also send a self-made website to the web. The only things he should know is how to use a small amount code in the document template, then he can concentrate on designing, we only need to modify the template which is appearance of the site by theart staff. After updating the template, we only need to automatically generate static pages, and do not need to modify every single page. A clear division of labor greatly improves work efficiency and reduces the cost.

CONCLUSION

In this paper, we propose a set of website solutions based on CMS, and it is easy to maintain and integrate. The CMS has the feature of great flexibility, and successfully achieved web application in the university. It solves the permissions on the construction site management, information management and file upload and download and other key technologies.

Figure 8. Flexible, intelligent content publishing

Figure 9. Management of plug-in functions

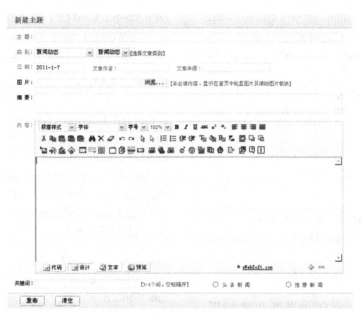

Figure 10. Template management

ID号	插件名称
10	挑错管理
23	百度新闻
24	文件管理器
25	广告管理
27	友情链接模块
28	投票模块
29	留言簿模块
30	站内新闻发布
31	邮件订阅

Table 3. Comparing CMS

Do not use the CMS	Use the CMS
Need for specialized technical person	General staff is OK
When querying the database, the server has a lot of pressure, resulting in slow access	Browse static pages, do not access the database, the serverstress is small, fast access
Pages are produced by specialized technical person	Pages can be automatically generated, using the WYSIWYG editor, the article's layout and multimedia embedded are very convenient
Revision is not convenient, you need to manually modify a lot of information, the need for technical support	Revision convenience. You only need to select a template. It can be generated static pages after modifying the template automatically. You can change part of the layout and do not need frequently access to the database
Information management is not convenient. Not timely release of information. Contents of the hierarchical management is not convenient	Provide a flexible permission system. Information classificationview. Once information input, the release can be selected.

It has the important theoretical value for software development management and software engineering. For website development, especially for construction of a school site, it is a good role model and an important guiding tool. However, the realization of a few CMS features need to be studied further, making it more friendly to use and convenient.

REFERENCES

Botafogo, R., Rivlin, E., & Shneiderman, B. (2002). Structural analysis of hypertext: identifying hierarchies and useful metrics. *ACM Transactions on Information Systems, 10*(2).

Budin, G. (2006). *Global content management-challenges and opportuni-ties for creating and using digital translation resources [EB/OL].* Retrieved from http://www.ifi.unizh.ch/cl/yuste/postworkshop/repository/gbu-din.pdf

Fidel, R., & Green, M. (2004). The many faces of accessibility: Engineers' perception of information sources. *Information Processing and Management: An International Journal, 40*(3).

Gupta, S., Kaiser, G. E., Grimm, P., Chiang, M. F., & Starren, J. (2005). Automating content extraction of html documents. *World Wide Web Internet and Web Information Systems, 8*(2), 179–224.

Harris, S. B., Owen, J., Bloor, M. S., & Hogg, I. (1997). Engineering document management strategy: Analysis of requirements, choice of direction and system implementation. *Proceedings of the Institution of Mechanical Engineers. Part B, Journal of Engineering Manufacture, 211*(5), 385–405. doi:10.1243/0954405971516365

Laplant, M. (2006). *Global content management: Hewlett-packard talk the talk of worldwide business [EB/OL].* Retrieved from http://gilbane.com/case_studies/HP_case_study.html

Liu, S., McMahon, C. A., Darlington, M. J., Culley, S. J., & Wild, P. J. (2006). An approach for document fragment retrieval and its formatting issues in engineering information management. In M. L. Gavrilova, O. Gervasi, V. Kumar, C. J. K. Tan, D. Taniar, A. Laganá, Y. Mun, & H. Choo (Eds.), *Proceedings of the International Conference on Computational Science and its Applications* (LNCS 3981, pp.279-287).

Lizorkin, D. A., & Lisovsky, K. Y. (2005). Implementation of the XML linking language XLink by functional methods. *Programming and Computer Software, 31*(1), 34–46.

Lowe, A., McMahon, C. A., & Culley, S. J. (2004). Characterising the requirements of engineering information systems. *International Journal of Information Management, 24*(5), 402–422.

McDonald, S., & Stevenson, R. J. (1998). Effects of text structure and prior knowledge of the learner on navigation in hypertext. *Human Factors*, 40.

Van Der Aalst, W., & Van Hee, K. M. (2002). *Workflow management: models, methods, and systems.* Cambridge, MA: MIT Press.

Wild, P. J., Culley, S. J., McMahon, C. A., Darlington, M. J., & Liu, S. (2006). Towards a method for profiling engineering documentation. In *Proceedings of the 9th International Design Conference on Design.*

This work was previously published in the International Journal of Advanced Pervasive and Ubiquitous Computing, Volume 3, Issue 3, edited by Tao Gao, pp. 32-45, copyright 2011 by IGI Publishing (an imprint of IGI Global).

Chapter 20
Dynamic and Secure Business Data Exchange Model for SaaS-Based Collaboration Supporting Platform of Industrial Chain

Shuying Wang
Southwest Jiaotong University, China

Jizi Li
Wuhan Textile University, China

Shihua Ma
Huazhong University of Science & Technology, China

ABSTRACT

In this paper, by analyzing the characteristics of data exchange process of SaaS-based collaboration supporting platform for industrial chain, a dynamic and secure business data exchange model for the platform is established. On this basis, methods for business data automatic obtain and format conversion, client authentication based on encryption lock and SOAP extension, business data encryption based on public key of the platform, and instant key created by client is discussed. The implementation of these methods is studied based on a .NET environment. Furthermore, the dynamic and secure business data exchange model is used in the SaaS platform of the automotive industry chain and SaaS platform of the injection industry chain, as it meets the multi-source and heterogeneous information exchange requirements.

DOI: 10.4018/978-1-4666-2645-4.ch020

1. INTRODUCTION

Data integration and exchange is a kind of data processing technology, which converts a kind of data structure into another, transmits and exchanges the instance of data in the heterogeneous systems through computer network (Fagin, Kolaitis, Miller, & Popa, 2003). Data integration and exchange based on integration adapter is a common method for solving multi-source and heterogeneous information data exchange. This paper mainly works on dynamic and secure data exchange technologies for SaaS (Software as a Service)-based collaboration supporting platform of industrial chain, which is a public platform for SMB (Small and Medium sized Businesses group), it works in the Internet environment and running by a third department. Works as a data exchange center, it exchanges business data with enterprises' inner software systems whenever required, such as ERP (Enterprise Resource Planning) and PDM (Product Data Management) systems. To the various SMB and the complex Internet environment, dynamic optimization and secure technologies for the platform are the key technologies to be solved.

There are many research results on data integration and exchange adapter at home and abroad. About related products, Sybase launched the Sybase DXP platform for data exchange, IBM introduced WebSphere information Integrator solution for data integration at the same time, and Microsoft launched Biztalk business integration program. Furthermore, many companies and research institutions have also launched corresponding middleware products for data exchange, for example, the OnceDI of ISCAS(Institute of Software Chinese Academy of Sciences), data exchange platform eStarConnect of VTech and so on (Wang, 2010). To the SaaS platform for SMB, Sybase DXP and WebSphere information integrator are not suitable, this mainly because of their large structures, expensive implement fee and complex configuration procedure (Li & Liu, 2008). Middleware products such as OnceDI cannot meet the needs of bidirectional data exchange, and

more than that, these products generally require an open service port, it will bring some security risk to the platform.

About research in interrelated technologies Wang (2009, 2010) proposed a dynamic data exchange program for the SaaS-based collaboration supporting platform of industrial chain, achieving dynamic data exchange drove by business keywords and user identification through the establishment of data exchange agent. Liu and Chen (2009) proposed a role-based data exchange middleware, use a XML(Extensible Markup Language) model to describe the demand of the role for data exchange and data services for the role provided by data sources. Wang, Zhao, and Sun (2005) proposed a multi-level resource information integration approach based on resource information publishing wizard and UDDI center of the networked manufacturing platform. Smith and McBrien (2006) and Boyd and McBrien (2005) erected a data exchange model by converting information to an universal type hierarchy. Chen, Lo, Wu, Yih, and Viehrig (2006) and Amer-Yahia and Kotidis (2004) proposed an approach to extract DTD-conforming XML documents from heterogeneous data sources. Li, Gao, Li, and Yang (2004) proposed a method on converting design data of heterogeneous CAD (Computer Aided Design) systems into an universal product representation to support collaborative design requirement. Chen, Li, and Gao (2005), Amer-Yahia and Kotidis (2004), Hung, Cheng, and Yeh (2005), and Eastlake, Reagle, and Imamura (2001) proposed a data express and exchange method using XML and Web Service technologies for collaborative design requirement. Huma, Jafar-Ur-Rehman, and Iftikhar (2005) and Karali (2007) proposed a data exchange method based on ontology. Zhu and Zhou (2006) proposed a role-based collaboration method for data exchange of heterogeneous systems. Eastlake, Reagle, and Imamura (2001) and Eastlake, Reagle, and Solo (2002) proposed a method of XML encryption and XML signature syntax.

These results have some reference value for Internet-based data exchange of heterogeneous systems, but lack consideration for automatic obtain of data to be exchanged, format conversion and secure transmission. The SaaS-based collaboration supporting platform has many different requirements for data exchange. Based on the results of these studies, with the needs of the platform for the dynamic data exchange of multi-source and heterogeneous systems, this paper mainly research on technologies for achieving dynamic and secure business data exchange between the platform and enterprises' heterogeneous systems.

2. CHARACTERISTICS OF DATA EXCHANGE PROCESS OF THE PLATFORM

2.1. Introduction of SaaS-Based Collaboration Supporting Platform

Industrial chain is a networked organization composed of limited individual units, which operates around its core enterprise. The networked organization has many special characteristics, for example, the diversity of individual units, geographical distribution, the dynamic nature of collaborative relationships and the diversity of collaborative content and so on. As a public service platform running by a third department, the platform works for inter-enterprise business collaboration and integration requirements, these requirements demand the platform to work across enterprises' boundary. It integrated manufacturing enterprise and its collaborative enterprises so as to offer business collaboration service based on internet (including product collaborative sale, parts collaborative procure, product collaborative service and so on). During these collaboration supporting processes, collaborative enterprises use the platform through Web to exchange data with core enterprise, the platform provides enterprise alliances with integrated solution within and outside.

2.2. Characteristics Analysis for Data Exchange of the Platform

Business data integration and exchange process is a data interactive process with its life cycle between platform and core enterprises' business systems (Figure 1). Compared with data integration and exchange between general systems, the data exchange process between the platform and core enterprises' systems have many special characteristics, includes:

- The dynamic changes of data source and data content. The platform provides customized services for multi-alliance, as a result, it brings some special problems such as: an increasing number of alliances in the process of promoting the platform, dynamic collaborative relationship, and collaborative content dynamically expanding with the changes of business requirements, all these make the dynamic changes of data source and data content between platform and enterprises' systems in the process of data exchange.
- The bidirectional data exchange requirement. In the process of industrial chain collaboration, business data is sometimes necessary to exchange from the platform to enterprises' systems, and returns to the platform after processing (Wang, 2010).
- The real time exchange requirement. The data exchange process has real-time requirements in certain to support the time beat of production plan.
- The security exchange requirement. The platform deploys and operates on Internet; it works in a complex environment. Business data is companies' core secrets, so the data exchange process of the platform requires a higher data transmission security.
- One too many data exchange services. The platform provides multi-alliance with customized services based on a set of software

Figure 1. Business data security exchange model based on SOAP extension

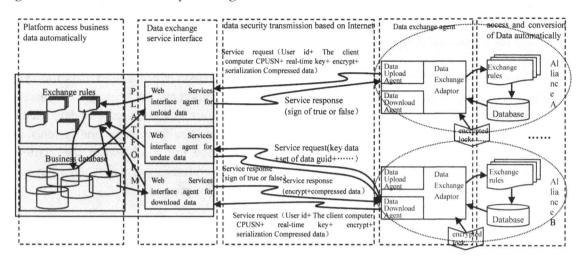

and hardware, as data distribution center, which offers SMB with timely and accurate data services according alliances' needs in the data exchange process.

3. DYNAMIC AND SECURE DATA EXCHANGE MODEL FOR THE PLATFORM

Agent model of data exchange offered in Wang (2010) meets characters of dynamic change characteristic of data source and data content, bidirectional data exchange requirement, but lacks consideration of real-time and security of data exchange requirement. On this basis, a data security exchange model, which obtains data to be exchanged automatically and based on a request-and-response mechanism, has been established in this paper. According to the one to many data exchange services requirement in data exchange process, the platform is designed to respond to requests of client automatically. Data exchange process of this model is divided into five parts, includes: automatic access to data to be exchanged from the platform, agent-based data exchange interface of the platform, data security

transmission on the Internet, client data exchange agent, automatic access to data to be exchanged from client. The design and implementation of the agent-based data exchange interface and client data exchange agent reference the achievements from Wang (2010). This paper mainly focuses on methods of automatic access to data to be exchanged from platform and client, data security transmission on Internet, and the one to many data exchange service.

3.1. Automatic Access and Format Conversion of Data to be Exchanged

In the process of data exchange, the platform is a business data distribute center, so we can take the platform's data format as the standard to simplify the heterogeneous data structures problem.

3.1.1. Automatic Access to Data to be Exchanged on the Platform

In life cycle of business data, whether the data needs to be exchanged is controlled by the business process. When business data is in one or several processes of the life cycle, it needs to be exchanged. We can get the life-cycle flag field of business data in database of the SaaS platform to determine whether to exchange the business data, so as to develop the corresponding rules for data exchange. According to clients' requests, the data automatic acquisition module of the platform works with the exchange rules to access business data automatically.

Definition 1: We use variable $Data_X$ to express a certain type of business data to be exchanged, data exchange rules for $Data_X$ can be expressed as a quintuple-element-group: $Exchange(Data_X) = (T_X, K_X, E_X, T_X(C), S_X(C))$. In the formula:

- T_X expresses the main table of $Data_X$, include its primary key $Xguid$ and control field $ExFlag$;

- K_x expresses conventional business keywords;

- $E_X = \{E_{Xk}(E_{XSk}, E_{XEk}) | k = 1, 2, ..., m\}$ expresses exchange rules corresponding to main table T_X; $E_{Xk}(E_{XSk}, E_{XEk})$ expresses the K kind status of $Data_X$ in its life cycle; E_{XSk} expresses the value of data exchange control flag before exchanging; and E_{XSk} expresses the value after exchanging; m expresses the total number of states that $Data_X$ processed in life cycle.

- $T_X(C) = \{T_{XCi} | i = 1, 2, ..., j\}$ expresses child tables of $Data_X$; j expresses the number of child table.

- $S_X(C) = \{S_{XCi}(T_{XCi} -> T_X) | i = 1, 2, ..., j\}$ expresses association rules between child tables and main table.

Definition 1 gives a control model for business data of the platform to be obtained automatically, as shown in Figure 2. main table and its associated child tables of $Data_X$ are disposed together, so as to ensure data consistency and integrity.

3.1.2. Automatic Access and Format Conversion of Clients' Data to be Exchanged

There may be different between data structures of clients' business systems and corresponding data structure of the platform, therefore, the process of data exchange needs of data format conversion. Since in the data exchange process, the platform is the data distribute center, its data structure is taken as the target data structure to simplify the data exchange process. The platform provides clients with business data structure in the form of XML. Therefore, in the process of client's data exchange rules configuration, format conversion rules between clients' business data format and corresponding data format of the platform should

Figure 2. Platform business data $Data_x$ exchange rules control model

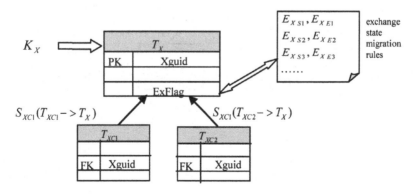

be disposed at first (Figure 3). The automatic access and format conversion process can be described as following:

Definition 2: Automatic access and format conversion of client's data to be exchanged can be expressed by a seven-element-group expression:

$$Exchange(Data_X) =$$
$$(T_X, K_X, E_X, SW(T_X), T_X(C), S_X(C), SW_X(C))$$

In the formula:

- $SW(T_X)$ describes conversion rules between the data structure of main table T_X and the corresponding target of the platform.
- $SW_X(T_{XC}) = \{SW(T_{XCi}) | i = 1, 2, ..., j\}$ expresses conversion rules between child table T_{XC} and the corresponding child table $T_{XC}{}'$ of the platform.
- The definition of other parameters is the same as definition 1, omission.

3.2. Business Data Secure Transmission Based on Request-and-Response Mechanism

3.2.1. Customer Authentication based on Security Key and SOAP Extension

As the first line of defense for data transmission security, authentication plays a very important role in business data secure transmission between the platform and clients' inner systems. Common authentication technologies include password-based, smart cards, PKI-based digital certificates and biometric-based authentication technologies and so on. Because data exchange of the platform base on Internet and must be distributed at real-time, password-based authentication and biometric authentication methods are not suitable, they cannot meet the needs of real-time automatic exchange. PKI based digital certificate authentication requires the support of a third-party certification department, which may bring higher cost in implementation. This paper uses an encryption lock based client authentication method.

Figure 3. Client business data $Data_x$ exchange rules control model

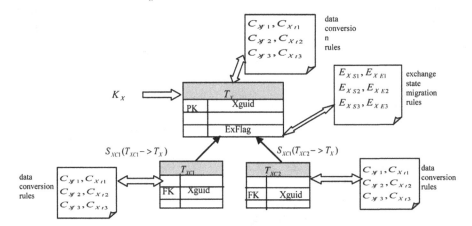

Definition 3: To achieve the automatic exchange of business data between the platform and enterprises' inner business systems, the platform creates a sequence identity for each enterprise E_x. The sequence identity can be expressed by a duple-element-group: $IdentifyInfo(E_x) = \{PEID_x, PCPU_x\}$. In the formula:

- $PEID_x$ expresses the identification of the enterprise E_x registered on the platform.
- $PCPU_x$ expresses the CPU No. of computer from enterprise E_x which is assigned for data exchange.

Definition 3 shows the client identity management of the platform for data exchange. $PEID_x$ is the only identity of enterprise E_x on the platform. $PCPU_x$ expresses the computer's information of enterprise E_x recorded on platform in order to realize automatic data exchange.

Definition 4: We use a duple-element-group: $Key_P = \{SK_P, PK_P\}$ to express the encryption key pair of the platform for data exchange. In the formula:

- SK_P expresses private key information of the platform for data exchange.
- PK_P expresses public key information of the platform for data exchange.

Definition 4 shows the public key management of platform, which uses RSA algorithm. In the data exchange configuration process, $PCPU_x$ encrypted with MD5 algorithm, together with $PEID_x$ and PK_P are written in encryption lock. The encryption Locks are distributed to clients for data exchange.

When client requests data exchange agent of the platform, client authentication function is called to identify the client's authentication, and response to its requests only by certified. This process can be expressed as follows:

The client generates identity information, which can be expressed as the following Formula (1):

$$\begin{cases} CIdentify(E_x) = PEID_x + CPU_x' \\ CPU_x' = Encrocy(PK_p, CPU_x) \end{cases}$$

In above formula (1), CPU_x expresses the machine' CPU number got through client data exchange adapter. $Encrocy(PK_p, CPU_x)$ expresses CPU_x encrypted by public key PK_p, and CPU_x' is the CPU_x encrypted result.

In the authentication process, the client identity $PEID$ and CPU_x' transmit from client to platform in the process of data exchange request. As the platform uses data exchange agent based on Web Service, SOAP extension technologies can be used to achieve the transmission identity information. SOAP extension provides a blocking mechanism in Web Service request and response process.

The platform verifies the client's identity information to determine whether it is equal between $PCPU_x$ recorded on the platform and CPU_x sent by the client, which can be expressed as the following Formula (2):

$$\begin{cases} Flag = Eqaul(PCUP_x, CPU_x) \\ PCUP_x = GetCPU(PEID) \\ CPU_x = Decrocy(SK_P, CPU_x') \end{cases}$$

In above Formula (2), the variable $Flag$ returns the identification result, $GetCPU(PEID)$ expresses $PCPU_x$ recorded on the platform by $PEID_x$, $Decrocy(SK_P, CPU_x')$ decrypts CPU_x' with the platform private key SK_P.

3.2.2. Business Data Encryption and Request-and-Response Transmission Based on Instant Key

Because public key deficiencies in processing speed, it is not very convenient in processing of business data. DES symmetric key algorithm is used to implement encryption process of business data. When a client request data exchange services, it use DES algorithm to generate an instant symmetric key key, which is only valid in the data exchange process, and re-generated in next request. To protect the security of symmetric key, key is encrypted with public key PK_P, and together with identity and CPU_x are written in service request SOAP extension to be send to the platform. The platform use SK_P to decrypt key getting from SOAP extension, and then decrypts business data with key.

Business data exchange process can be divided into two processes, include: client uploads data to the platform and download data from the platform. Since data transmission based on Internet, in consideration of the stability of network and data security, data transmission mechanism based on request-and-response is used.

3.2.3 Clients Upload Data to the Platform

In order to ensure the secure transmission of client upload data to the platform, the upload process can be divided into three phases includes: client requests, response handling and status update. As follows:

1. Client makes data $Data_X$ format conversion, encryption, serialization and compression, gets CPU_x and data exchange Keyword $Keyword(Data_x)$ corresponding to $Data_X$ from data exchange rules. Read $PEID_x$ and the public key PK_P stored in the encrypted

lock to create an instant key key, encrypted CPU_x with PK_P, request the data exchange service to generate SOAP request. This process can be expressed as the following Formula (3):

$$
\begin{cases}
CSend(Data_x, PEID_x) = SOAPE_x(Data_x) + Data_x'' \\
\qquad\qquad + Keyword(Data_x) \\
SOAPE_x(Data_x) = PEID_x + CPU_x' + Key' \\
Data_x'' = Encrocy\ \&\ Sug(key, Data_x') \\
Data_X' = EchangeDataSchema(Data_x) \\
key' = Encrocy(PK_p, Key)
\end{cases}
$$

$$(3)$$

In above Formula (3), $CSend(Data_x, PEID_x)$ expresses the content of data exchange that client requests. $Data_x'$ expresses the data after format conversion. $Encrocy\ \&\ Sug(key, Data_x')$ expresses the process of encrypt, serialize and compress $Data_x'$. $SOAPE_x(Data_x)$ expresses the client's identity and key information transmitted to the platform through SOAP extension. key' expresses key information after encrypting instant key with public key PK_p.

2. The platform use $PEID_x$ and $Keyword(Data_x)$ to connect to the corresponding business database to identify the client, and then decrypt, decompress and deserialize the data, return the process results, this process can use formula (2) and (4) jointly expressed:

$$
\begin{cases}
key = Decrocy(SK_p, key') \\
Data_x = Decrocy\ \&\ DeSug(key, Data_x'') \\
P\,Response = InsertOrUpdateDB(PEID, Keyword(Data_x), Data_x)
\end{cases}
$$

In above Formula (4): $Decrocy(SK_p, key')$ expresses decrypt key' with the client's private key SK_p; $Decrocy\ \&\ DeSug(key, Data_x'')$ expresses decrypt, decompress and deserialize $Data_x'$; variable $P\ Response$ expresses implement results of the upload data process.

3. The client update the exchange state of $Data_X$ according to the value returned from the platform.

3.2.4. The Client Requests for Data Download from Platform

The response process of client requests for data download from the platform is to update the corresponding data state flag according to client data processing condition. In data exchange process, the platform is a data response center; handling various clients' data download requests through the data download Web Service and data update Web Service. The response process can be divided into five steps, specific as follows:

1. The Client use DES algorithm produces an instant data encryption key, and then read the public-key PK_P from encrypted-lock to encrypt key, then write it into service request SOAP expansion together with encrypted CPU_x' and $PEID_x$. The process can be expressed as Formula (5):

$$SOAP(Data_x) = SOAPE_x + keyword(Data_x)$$
(5)

2. Client identity authentication function of the platform decrypt the instant key. First, according to $PEID_x$ and $PEID_x$, the platform access to the database, encrypt $Data_x$ with

key, serialize and compress $Data_x$. This process can use Formula (2) and (6) jointly express:

$$\begin{cases} PResponse = Data_x'' \\ Data_x'' = Encrocy\ \&\ Sug(key, Data_x) \\ key = Decrocy(PK_p, Key') \end{cases}$$
(6)

3. Client receive $Data_x''$ from the platform, decompress, deserialize and decrypt the data, convert data format, and update data exchange state of the database. According to the updated results, request update service of the platform, send the corresponding GUID sets $Guid(Data_x)$, business keyword $Keyword(Data_x)$, client's identity $PEID_x$ and CPU_x' back to the platform through the SOAP extension. This process can be expressed as Formula (7) presented in Box 1.

4. The platform verify the client's identity. According the keywords, connect to database, and according to the corresponding data rules update data exchange state of the platform, and return the update results to the client. This process can use Formula (2) and (8) jointly express:

$$PResponse = \\ InsertOrUpdateDB(PEID, Keyword(Data_x), Guid(Data_x))$$
(8)

5. The client obtain the state update flag $PResponse$, if success then the process is over, if failure turned to 4.

Box 1.

$$
\begin{cases}
Data_x = DeEncrocy \ \& \ DeSug(key, Data_x'') \\
Data_X{}' = EchangeDataSchema(Data_x) \\
C\,Response = InsertOrUpdateDB(Data_x{}', keyword(Data_x)) \\
CSend(Guid(Data_x), PEID_x) = Guid(Data_x) + PEID_x + Keyword(Data_x) + CPU_x{}'
\end{cases}
\tag{7}
$$

4. DESIGN AND IMPLEMENTATION OF DATA DYNAMIC AND SECURITY EXCHANGE FUNCTIONS

4.1. Design of Data Automatic Access Rules Configuration Guide

With considering of environment that the platform services many alliances, we design a data exchange rules configuration guide to realize the flexible and dynamic evolution requirement of data exchange for the platform. The guide's working principle and generating algorithm is designed shown in Box 2.

4.2. Design of Client Identity Recognition Functions based on SOAP Extension

In the.NET Framework, Web Service requests can be easily achieved. In Web Service survival midterm, the server and client serialize and deserialize a SOAP message automatically, and SOAP extension provides the process a blocking mechanism. SOAP extension run on dividing the SOAP message handling into various stages, each stage is a value of SOAP message stage enumeration. Whenever a Web Service is requested, process message will be called four times according to

Box 2. Business data automatic access configuration guide algorithm

```
BEGIN
    Step.1: String K_x = GetKeyWord(K_x);   //Obtain the business keyword K_x from user interface
    Step.2:  // connect to database and show all business data table, guide the customer to choose primary table, obtain
primary table's name and primary key.
        Step.2.1:  String DBConn = GetAndConnectDB(databasename, UserID, password);  // connect to database
        Step.2.2:  String T_x = GetSelectT_x(databasename);  // show all business data table and choose primary table
        Step.2.3:  String PKColumn = GetPKColumn(T_x);  // obtain primary key of table T_x
    Step.3:  // Show all the fields of T_x, guide user choice data exchange mark fields, set data exchange migration rules
        Step.3.1:  String ExFlag = GetExFlagColumn(T_x);  // Get the data exchange mark fields
        Step.3.2:  String[] E_x = SetE_x(ExFlag);  // Obtain data migration rule, and storage by group, use comma interval
    Step.4:  // Gain associated child tables, generating child table data exchange rules
        Step.4.1:  String[] T_xC = GetrelateTable(T_x);  // Gain associated child tables
        Step.4.2:  String[] S_xC = GetrelateExSQL(T_xC);  // obtain corresponding child table data exchange rules
        Step.4.3:  If there are other child tables, turn to Step. 4
    Step.5: WriteToXML();  // write data exchange rules into file DataEcxhang.XML.
END
```

different stages of SOAP message stage, we can write client identity information into process message method. Its corresponding algorithm is presented in Box 3.

4.3. Implementation of Business Data Encryption and Response Transmission

According to the exchange model established in 2.2.2, based on instant key, SOAP extension and Web Service response, implementation of business data encryption and response transmission is designed in Box 4.

5. INTEGRATED APPLICATION OF DYNAMIC AND SECURE BUSINESS DATA EXCHANGE MODEL

Dynamic and secure business data exchange technology proposed in this paper have been applied in data dynamic exchange agents and upgrade scheme about the client integrates adapter which were put forward by Wang (2010). At present the scheme of data dynamic exchange after upgrading solution have already been integrated applied the

SaaS platform for auto industry chain (http://auto. easp.cn, the platform services 5,000 companies with collaboration supporting). Figure 4 is the working interface of configuration guide and the configuration result is seen in Figure 5. Figure 6 is the working interface of the data download interface and Figure 7 is the client integrates adapter.

With the application of the achievements, the configure efficiency of data exchange rules has improved. It makes business data acquisition; heterogeneous format conversion can be automatically disposed at client.

6. CONCLUSION

Based on the collaboration supporting SaaS platform dynamic data exchange adapter proposed in reference Wang (2010). This paper research on business data automatic access and configuration rules generation method, and studies for data format conversion in the process of data transmission, client identity authentication, and method of the data security transmission based on SOAP extension. Integrated application of achievements has been used in the SaaS platform for auto industry chain.

Box 3. Client identity authentication algorithm based on encryption lock and SOAP extension

BEGIN
    Step.1： // Client identity authentication and requests
        Step1.1: Acquit machine's CPU SN, and encrypt it with MD5 encryption algorithm;
        Step1.2: compares with CPU_x in encryption lock, if not match, then return;
        Step1.3: Create proxy objects. First gain $PEID_x$ and public key from encryption lock, then encrypt CPU_x with
            public-key PK_P and write it into SOAP extension together with $PEID_x$, finally, request the platform's
            corresponding Web Service agent;
    Step.2： // The platform verify the client's identity
        Step 2.1: The platform data exchange agent call identity authentication module. Use CPU_x' in the SOAP requests
            message coming out of the client in SOAP extension before deserialize stage.
        Step 2.2: Identity authentication module obtain the private key SK_P corresponding CPU_x' on the platform according
            to $PEID_x$ and decrypt CPU_x' coming from SOAP extension.
        Step 2.3: compares the CPU_x decrypt with $PCPU_x$ stored in the database of the platform, if not match, then return.
END

Box 4. Algorithm of response downloads data from the platform

BEGIN

Step.1： // the client request the data download Web Service

    Step.1.1： the client produces an instant encryption keys key with DES algorithm;

    Step.1.2： According to the business keyword, the client read data exchange rules described from files DataExchange_XXX. XML;

    Step.1.3： Create SOAP request generated by proxy objects $(PEID_x + Encrocy(PK_p, CPU_x) + EnCrocy(PK_p, Key))$；

Step.2:// Platform service response

    Step.2.1： Client identity authentication function of the platform identifies the client's identification; see Step2.1 to Step 2.3 in algorithm 2

    Step.2.2： The platform decrypt the instant key key with the customer's private key SK_p;

    Step.2.3： The platform extract its business data according the business keyword, then encrypt them with key ($Encrocy(Data_x)$), serialize and compress the data and return them to client;

Step.3： // the client request the update Web Service

    Step.3.1： The client compresses and desterilizes the data, decrypt it with key, and then get business data $Data_x$ download from the platform;

    Step.3.2： The client convert format according to convert rules, and update the data exchange status;

    Step.3.3： The client request the update Web Service and generate SOAP request $(PEID_x + Encrocy(PK_p, CPU_x) + Encrocy(PK_p, Guid(Data_x)))$

Step.4： //The platform service response

    Step.4.1： Client identity authentication function of the platform verify the client's authentication; see Step2.1 to Step 2.3 in algorithm 2;

    Step.4.2： Decrypt $Guid(Data_x)$ and call related rules update corresponding data $Guid(Data_x)$ exchange state;

Step.5： The client obtain the update status, if successful, symbol of end, else return to Step4.

END

Figure 4. Working interface of configuration guide to exchange business data access rules automatically

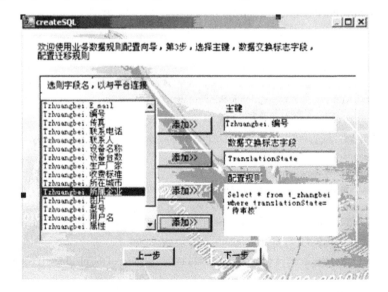

Figure 5. Configuration result

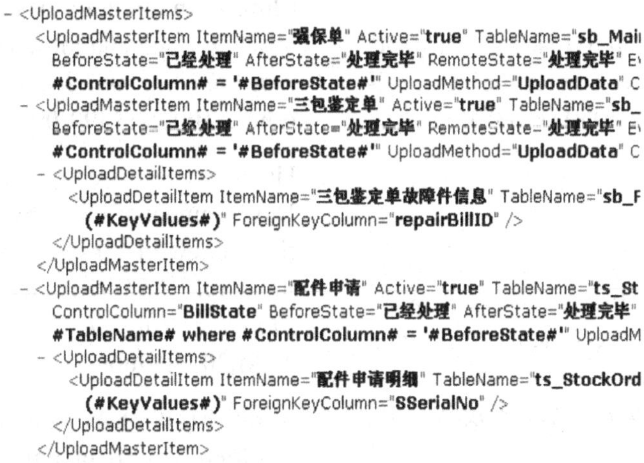

- <UploadMasterItems>
<UploadMasterItem ItemName="强保单" Active="true" TableName="sb_Mai
BeforeState="已经处理" AfterState="处理完毕" RemoteState="处理完毕" E
#ControlColumn# = '#BeforeState#'" UploadMethod="UploadData" C
- <UploadMasterItem ItemName="三包鉴定单" Active="true" TableName="sb_
BeforeState="已经处理" AfterState="处理完毕" RemoteState="处理完毕" E
#ControlColumn# = '#BeforeState#'" UploadMethod="UploadData" C
- <UploadDetailItems>
<UploadDetailItem ItemName="三包鉴定单故障件信息" TableName="sb_F
(#KeyValues#)" ForeignKeyColumn="repairBillID" />
</UploadDetailItems>
</UploadMasterItem>
- <UploadMasterItem ItemName="配件申请" Active="true" TableName="ts_St
ControlColumn="BillState" BeforeState="已经处理" AfterState="处理完毕"
#TableName# where #ControlColumn# = '#BeforeState#'" UploadM
- <UploadDetailItems>
<UploadDetailItem ItemName="配件申请明细" TableName="ts_StockOrd
(#KeyValues#)" ForeignKeyColumn="SSerialNo" />
</UploadDetailItems>
</UploadMasterItem>

Figure 6. Work interface of platform data download interface

PTWebService
单击此处以获得完整的操作列表。
ServiceDownloadData
从平台下载数据的Web Service接口
测试
若要使用 HTTP POST 协议对操作进行测试，请单击“调用”按钮。
参数 值
factoryID:
billName:
调用
SOAP
下面是一个 SOAP 请求和响应示例。所显示的占位符需要由实际值替换。
POST /ASPSOLUTION/ASPWebUI/AutoService.ZBXS.Platform.WebService/ZBXSWebService
Host: localhost
Content-Type: text/xml; charset=utf-8
Content-Length: length
SOAPAction: "http://tempuri.org/ServiceDownloadData"
<?xml version="1.0" encoding="utf-8"?>
<soap:Envelope xmlns:xsi="http://www.w3.org/2001/XMLSchema-instance" xmlns:xsd

Figure 7. Client integrates adapter

面向产业链平台的数据交换控制器
数据交换执行情况监控
数据交换过程异常情况监控
[2009-3-20 11:08:30 成功上传10条强保单数据！]
[2009-3-20 11:10:20 正在读取本地三包单数据！]
[2009-3-20 11:11:25 读取到20条三包单数据！]
[2009-3-20 11:11:28 正在与远程服务连接！]
[2009-3-20 11:13:43 成功上传20条三包单数据！]
[2009-3-20 11:14:20 正在读取本地三包单数据！]
[2009-3-20 11:14:45 读取到条25条旧件数据！]
[2009-3-20 11:15:33 正在与远程服务连接！]
[2009-3-20 11:16:29 成功上传25条旧件数据！]
启动数据交换
停止数据交换
数据交换项定制

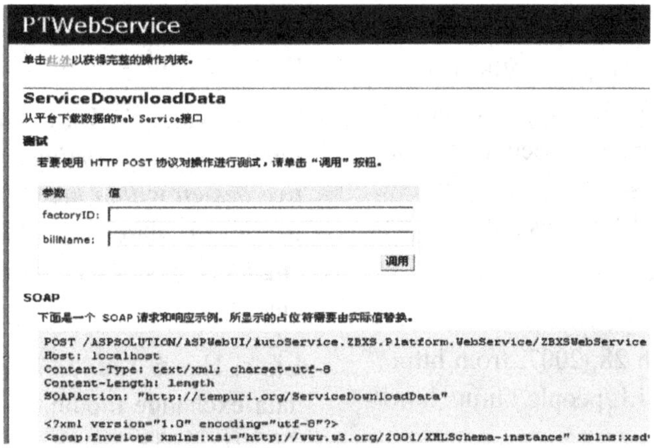

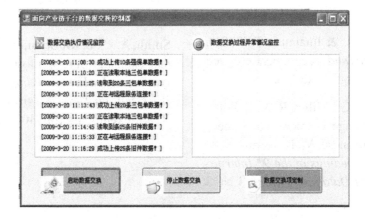

ACKNOWLEDGMENT

Foundation items: national research projects (2011BAH21B01), science and technology projects in Chengdu (08RKYB959ZF-037).

REFERENCES

Amer-Yahia, S., & Kotidis, Y. (2004). A Web-services architecture for efficient XML data exchange. In *Proceedings of the 20th IEEE International Conference on Data Engineering* (pp. 523-534).

Boyd, M., & McBrien, P. (2005). Comparing and transforming between data models via an intermediate hyper graph data model. *Journal of Data Semantics*, *4*, 69–109.

Chen, S. K., Lo, M. L., Wu, K. L., Yih, J. S., & Viehrig, C. (2006). A practical approach to extracting DTD-conforming XML documents from heterogeneous data sources. *Information Sciences*, *176*(7), 820–844. doi:10.1016/j.ins.2004.12.009

Chen, X., Li, M., & Gao, S. (2005). *A Web services based platform for exchange of procedural CAD models*. Retrieved March 28, 2007, from http://www.eng.nus.edu.sg/LCEL/people/limin/ html/cscwd-2005.html

Eastlake, D., Reagle, D., & Solo, D. (2002). *RFC 3075: XML-Signature syntax and processing*. Retrieved from http://www.w3.org/TR/xmldsig-core/

Eastlake, D., Reagle, J., & Imamura, T. (2001). *XML encryption syntax and processing*. Retrieved from http://www.w3.org/TR/xmlenc-core/

Fagin, R., Kolaitis, P. G., Miller, R. J., & Popa, L. (2003). Data exchange: Semantics and query answering. In D. Calvanese, M. Lenzerini, & R. Motwani (Eds.), *Proceedings of the 9th International Conference on Database Theory* (LNCS 2572, pp. 207-224).

Huma, Z., Jafar-Ur-Rehman, M., & Iftikhar, N. (2005). An ontology-based framework for semi-automatic schema integration. *Journal of Computer Science and Technology*, *20*(6), 788–796. doi:10.1007/s11390-005-0788-4

Hung, M.-H., Cheng, F.-T., & Yeh, S.-C. (2005). Development of a Web-Services-based e-diagnostics framework for semi-conductor manufacturing industry. *IEEE Transactions on Semiconductor Manufacturing*, *18*(1), 122–135. doi:10.1109/TSM.2004.836664

Karali, I. (2007). A common design-features ontology for product data semantics interoperability. In *Proceedings of the IEEE/WIC/ACM International Conference on Web Intelligence* (pp. 443-446).

Li, J. (2006). *Study on cluster supply chain and its management*. Wuhan, China: Huazhong Agricultural University.

Li, M., Gao, S., Li, J., & Yang, Y. (2004). *An approach to supporting synchronized collaborative design within heterogeneous CAD systems*. Retrieved March 28, 2007, from http://www.eng.nus.edu.sg/LCEL/people/limin/html/asme-cie-2004.html

Li, Y.-N., & Liu, L.-Z. (2008). Policy driven data exchange model. *Computer Engineering*, *34*(20), 31–33.

Liu, H., & Chen, Q.-M. (2009). Research and realization of role-based data exchange middleware. *Journal of Computer Application*, *29*(1), 326-327, 330.

Smith, A. C., & McBrien, P. (2006). Inter model data exchange of type information via a common type hierarchy. In *Proceedings of the International Workshop on Data Integration & the Semantic Web*, Luxembourg (pp. 307-321).

Wang, S.-Y. (2009). Research on data exchange adapter for collaborative commerce system in manufacturing industrial chain. *Application Research of Computers, 26*(1), 189–191.

Wang, S.-Y. (2010). Dynamic data exchange technology for collaborative commerce platform of industrial chain. *Computer Integrated Manufacturing Systems, 16*(6), 1336–1343.

Wang, S.-Y., Zhao, H.-J., & Sun, L.-F. (2005). Resource integrated framework of regional network manufacturing platform based on ASP. *China Mechanical Engineering, 16*(19), 1729–1732.

Zhu, H., & Zhou, M.-C. (2006). Role-based collaboration and its kernel mechanisms. *IEEE Transactions on Systems, Man and Cybernetics. Part C, 36*(4), 578–589.

This work was previously published in the International Journal of Advanced Pervasive and Ubiquitous Computing, Volume 3, Issue 3, edited by Tao Gao, pp. 46-59, copyright 2011 by IGI Publishing (an imprint of IGI Global).

Chapter 21
3-D Video based Disparity Estimation and Object Segmentation

Tao Gao
Electronic Information Products Supervision and Inspection Institute of Hebei Province, China

ABSTRACT

Stereo video object segmentation is a critical technology of the new generation of video coding, video retrieval and other emerging interactive multimedia fields. Determinations of distinctive depth of a frame features have become more popular in everyday life for automation industries like machine vision and computer vision technologies. This paper examines the evaluation of depth cues through dense of two frame stereo correspondence method. Experimental results show that the method can segment the stationary and moving objects with better accuracy and robustness. The contributions have higher accuracy in matching and reducing time of convergence.

1. INTRODUCTION

As human brain can deal with the weak difference between the left and right eye images, we can sense the external 3-D world; and this ability is called stereoscopic vision. Stereo image sequence is a three-dimensional visual image form, it uses left and right groups of images to describe a group of scenes, and the human eyes apperceive the 3-D depth information by addressing the relative position between the two images. The 3-D reconstruction of video scenes by stereo analysis is an important advancement in machine vision and computer vision. Most of the automation work requires modeling of 3-D structure of environment. Compared with traditional two-dimensional images, stereo images are more "realism" and the description of the scene is more natural. Currently, 3-D vision system has been widely applied to stereo video communications (Raymond & Clifton, 2000), robot vision (Nishihara & Poggio, 1984), aviation navigation (Stefano, Marchioni, Mattoccia, & Neri, 2004), and other fields. With ever-growing material and

DOI: 10.4018/978-1-4666-2645-4.ch021

spiritual needs, the stereo images will gradually replace the traditional single vision images, and will be more used in television, online shopping, remote medical diagnosis and other civilian areas.

To store or transmit the stereo images, a more efficient compression encoding program must be developed. Stereo image sequence compression method was put forward in the late 1980s; after more than 25 years of development, people have developed several comparatively mature algorithms. However, to the practical application point, there is still not a unified coding standard.

The video object based stereo video coding method is to separate the video object from the scenes and to extract its borders, texture, movement and other parameters, then to code these parameters to achieve the purpose of coding the whole image (Aizawa & Huang, 1995). This method uses the hidden 3-D depth information, through the creation of 3-D objects and coding model to improve the coding efficiency and to reduce the influence of the block. It provides a more natural scene interpretation. However, this approach requires sophisticated image analysis process, such as: object segmentation, object modeling, and all these are not ripe at present so it can only be applied to a single background image with simple motion; its widely using depends on better solving some of these key technologies.

This paper presents a redundant wavelet transform based stereo video object segmentation algorithm. First, we use the redundant wavelet transform to extract the feature points of stereo video images, then according to the feature points we do the disparity estimation, to form a disparity map. The stationary objects are segmented from the stereo images by the disparity map. For the moving objects, we use a redundant wavelet transform based moving object extraction algorithm to segment the moving target from the redundant wavelet domain. Experimental results show that our algorithm can segment video objects from stereo video images, including stationary objects and moving objects with good results, highlighted details, and simple calculation process; all these can help to the subsequent coding operation.

2. STEREO VISION GEOMETRIC THEORIES

Three-dimensional camera system generally can be classified as three-dimensional parallel camera system and three-dimensional clustering camera system. If the two cameras are installed with parallel optical axis, it is called three-dimensional parallel camera system; if the two optical axes intersect at the objects, it is called three-dimensional clustering camera system. The best way is by solving the correspondence algorithm from left image to right image as well as right to left image also to be considered. The input is a set of video frames, typically the left image, is used as reference, to select the best depth estimate for each pixel. For each depth estimate of the reference depth map, the number of other depths maps that it occludes or passes is computed. This process is repeated for each depth estimate of all other depth maps with respect to reference image plane. The most stable solution is defined as the minimum depth from the identified discontinuity through dense two frame stereo matching method. This paper considers the 3D parallel camera system. Optical axis of two cameras parallel to each other and are perpendicular with the baseline. The space is determined by the plane known as the heart polarization plane. With a space (X, Y, Z), X is the horizontal direction and Y is the vertical direction, Z is the depth direction. The camera lens in the image plane is at point (x, y), where x parallel to the X, y parallel to the Y. In parallel camera system, the point in space around the image plane of the projector is at the same general location of the y coordinate, and the two set up their corresponding image brightness of the same point, that disparity search may be mainly concentrated in the horizontal direction, thus speeding up the searching and matching process.

Let f be the focal length, s is the image plane size, x_{l1}, x_{r1}, x_{l2}, x_{r2} are the positions of points p_1 and p_2 in planar image around the projection image plane to the right position between the left and right images. The disparity definition for the same point in the space of two planar images is the differences of the positions. If left image is the reference image, then: $d_1 = x_{l1} - x_{r1}$, $d_2 = x_{l2} - x_{r2}$. By triangular geometric principles, we can get:

$$\frac{x_{l2} - s/2}{f} = \frac{X_2 + b/2}{Z_2} \quad (1)$$

$$\frac{x_{r2} - s/2}{f} = \frac{X_2 - b/2}{Z_2} \quad (2)$$

$$X_2 = \frac{b*(x_{l2} + x_{r2} - s)}{2*(x_{l2} - x_{r2})} \quad (3)$$

$$Z_2 = \frac{b*f}{x_{l2} - x_{r2}} \quad (4)$$

Thus, from Equation (4) we can see that the distance of object from the camera and the disparity are inversely proportional, disparity can be expressed by the relative depth. Figure 1 shows the parallel camera system.

3. PARALLAX ESTIMATION BASED ON REDUNDANT DISCRETE WAVELET TRANSFORMS

A. The Theory of the Redundant Discrete Wavelet Transforms

The wavelet transforms used in image processing are carried out by the Mallat method (Daubechies & Sweldens, 1998; Calderbank, Daubechies, Sweldens, & Yeo, 1996). We suppose that MRA is established by the nested linear space which satisfies the following conditions:

1. The sets of the nested space are dense in the square integrable function space;
2. The intersection of nested space contains only zero vectors;
3. If $f(t) \subset V_k$, then $f(2t) \subset V_{k-1}$, and vice versa;
4. There is a function (i.e., scaling function) $\phi(t)$, $\{\phi(t-k): k \text{ int } eger\}$ is the radix of V_0. $\phi(t)$ is a function which satisfies the following conditions:
    a. $\int_{-\infty}^{+\infty} \phi(t)dt = 1;$
    b. $\|\phi(t)\|^2 = \int_{-\infty}^{+\infty} |\phi(t)|^2 \, dt = 1;$
    c. $< \phi(t), \phi(t-n) > = \delta(n).$

Figure 1. Parallel camera system

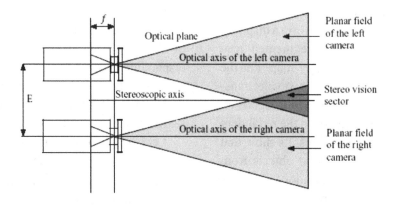

So there is $c(n), n = 0, \pm 1, \pm 2...,$ makes

$$\phi(2^{-k}t) = \sum_{n=-\infty}^{\infty} c(n)\phi(2^{-(k-1)}t - n), so\, V_k \subset V_{k-1},$$

then they constitute a MRA. The sets of all sub-spaces $(V_{-\infty})$ are dense in $L^2(R)$, and $V_{-\infty}$ can approximate any signal $f(t) \,|\in L^2\,|\,(R)$. If $f_k(t)$ is the orthogonal projection of $f(t)$ in the sub-space V_k, then $f_k(t) = \sum_{-\infty}^{\infty} a(k,n)\phi(2^{-(k-1)}t - n),$ $k = 0, \pm 1, \pm 2...$ and $a(k,n) = \sum_{-\infty}^{\infty} a(k-1,m)\frac{c(m-2n)}{2}$. If $\psi(t)$ is a function of V_{-1}, and satisfies:

1. $\int_{-\infty}^{\infty} \psi(t)dt = 0;$

2. $\int_{-\infty}^{\infty} |\,\psi(t)\,|^2\, dt = 1;$

3. $< \psi(t), \psi(t-n) >= \delta(n);$

4. $< \psi(t), \phi(t-n) >= 0.$

Then $\psi(t)$ is the wavelet of DWT according to MRA. If W_0 is the linear vector space with $\{\psi(t-n) : n\ integer\}$ as its radix, then

$$V_{k-1} = \oplus_{j=k}^{\infty} Wj, \quad V_{-\infty} = \oplus_{j=-\infty}^{\infty} W_j, \text{ so}$$

$$f_{-\infty}(t) = \sum_{k=-\infty}^{\infty} \sum_{t=-\infty}^{\infty} b(k,l)\psi(2^{-k}t - l).$$ We can

deduce: $b(k,n) = \sum_{-\infty}^{\infty} a(k-1,m)\frac{d(m-2n)}{2}$, if

$h(n) \equiv \frac{c(n)}{2}, \quad g(n) \equiv \frac{d(n)}{2}, \quad \tilde{h}(n) \equiv h(-n),$

$\tilde{g}(n) \equiv g(-n),$ then

$$a(k,n) = \sum_{-\infty}^{\infty} a(k-1,m)\,\tilde{h}(2n-m),$$

$$b(k,n) = \sum_{-\infty}^{\infty} a(k-1,m)\,\tilde{g}(2n-m).\ a(k,n),$$

$b(k,n)$ can be seen as be sampled after filter $\tilde{h}$. If $H(\omega) = \sum_n h(n)e^{-j\omega n}$, then

$$|H(\omega)|^2 + |H(\omega + \pi)|^2 = 1.\ H \text{ is a Orthogonal}$$

mirror filter (QMF). By multi-resolution analysis, the wavelet transforms are turned into digital filter design problems.

The RDWT is an approximation to the continuous wavelet transform that removes the down-sampling operation from the traditional critically sampled DWT to produce an over-complete representation. The shift-variance characteristic of the DWT arises from its use of down-sampling, while the RDWT is shift invariant since the spatial sampling rate is fixed across scale. As a result, the size of each sub-band in an RDWT is the exactly the same as that of the input signal. It turns out that, by appropriately sub-sampling each sub-band of an RDWT, one can produce exactly the same coefficients as does a critically sampled DWT applied to the same input signal.

B. Extraction Feature Points Based on Redundant Wavelet Transform

Typically, one wants feature points to track salient image features. The redundancy of the RDWT facilitates the identification of salient features in an image, especially image edges, since a simple correlation operation can easily accomplish edge identification. Specifically, the direct multiplication of the RDWT coefficients at adjacent scales distinguishes important features from the background due to the fact that wavelet coefficient magnitudes are correlated across scales. Coefficient magnitude correlation is well known to exist in the usual critically sampled DWT also; however, the changing temporal sampling rate makes the calculation of an explicit correlation mask across scales much more difficult for the critically sampled DWT.

The correlation mask consists of multiplying the high-low (HL) bands, the low-high (LH) bands, and the high-high (HH) bands together and combining the products (Gao, Liu, & Zhang, 2009):

$$MS(x,y) = \left| \prod_{j=J0}^{J1} HL^{(j)}(x,y) \right| + \left| \prod_{j=J0}^{J1} LH^{(j)}(x,y) \right|$$

$$+ \left| \prod_{j=J0}^{J1} HH^{(j)}(x,y) \right| \tag{5}$$

where J0 and J1 are the starting and ending scales, respectively, of the correlation operation. We note that calculation of the correlation mask in this manner is possible due to the fact that each RDWT subband is the same size as the original image. We can obtain the feature points according to equation. (6):

$$Po\,\mathrm{int}(x,y) = \begin{cases} 1 & MS(x,y) \geq T \\ 0 & MS(x,y) < T \end{cases} \tag{6}$$

T is the threshold. We transform $MS(x,y)$ into a gray picture, and then use the Iterative threshold method to obtain the T automatically:

$$T_{i+1} = \frac{1}{2} \left\{ \frac{\sum_{k=0}^{T_i} h_k * k}{\sum_{k=0}^{T_i} h_k} + \frac{\sum_{k=T_i+1}^{L-1} h_k * k}{\sum_{k=T_i+1}^{L-1} h_k} \right\} \tag{7}$$

We choose the middle gray value of the gray picture as the initial threshold T_0, and do the iterative operation according to Equation (7). h_k is the number of pixels with the k gray value, do the iterative operation until $T_{i+1} = T_i$, then T_i is the segmentation threshold. In Figure 2 is the left image, Figure 3 shows the feature points extracted by canny operator, and Figure 4 shows the feature points extracted by the redundant discrete wavelet transform algorithm.

By comparison we can see that image edges obtained by canny operator are very sparse, and lines are thin, while the image edges obtained by our algorithm are very obvious.

Figure 2. Left image

Figure 3. Feature points extracted by Canny operator

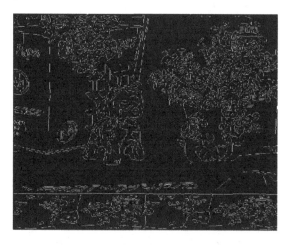

Figure 4. Feature points extracted by redundant wavelet transform

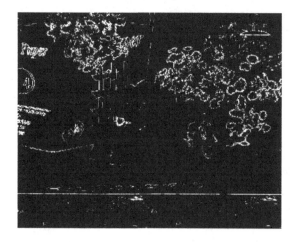

C. Obtain the Disparity Map

Parallax estimation is based on the classic block-matching disparity estimation method (Kolmogorov, Zabih, & Gortler, 2003; Bleyer & Gelautz, 2007). That is, in the left image we make 16×16 or 8×8 blocks with feature points as the center, and then for each block we search the best-matching block in the right image from top to bottom about $\pm k$, from left to right about $\pm l$ $(l > k)$, the offset is the disparity vector. The processes are as follows:

$$\nabla f(T) = \sum_{i=0}^{N-1} \sum_{j=0}^{N-1} \left| f_l(i,j) - f_r(i+m, j+n) \right|$$

$$(8)$$

$$\nabla f(T^*) = \min(\nabla f(T)) \qquad (9)$$

$$|T| = \sqrt{m^2 + n^2} \qquad (10)$$

Let D= T^*, then D is the parallax. In parallax matching, we can dynamically change the search window size according to a prior estimate disparity vector and the change of the regional disparity map. Window expanding direction is the four side direction, select the window size properly can get the optimal vector and then obtain the disparity vector (Izquierdo, 1999). Through obtaining the feature points in the redundant wavelet transform domain and doing the disparity estimation according to the feature points, the computation accuracy can be improved. But the disparity map is sparse; to have the dense disparity map we still need to match the remaining large number of non-feature points. We can think that, the feature points around the edge image segment the image into a number of regions; the points are matched in the region according to the feature points. The specific algorithm are as follows: First, for the different objects, we search from left to right, top to down to find the target marginal

position, as there may be gaps in the feature points, when we find a edge point in the eight neighborhood and no other point, the point will be linked to the point below, then we can get the close regions of various objects, and obtain the mask map. According to the mask map, the dense disparity map can be obtained. Figure 5 is the left image, Figure 6 is the right image, Figure 7 shows the disparity vectors, and Figure 8 is the disparity map. From the results we can see that the algorithm proposed in this paper can effectively extract the disparity vectors and form the dense disparity map.

Figure 5. Left image

Figure 6. Right image

Figure 7. Disparity vectors

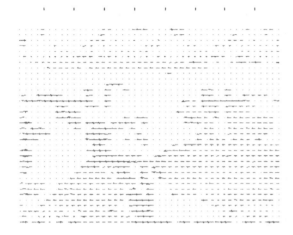

Figure 8. Disparity map

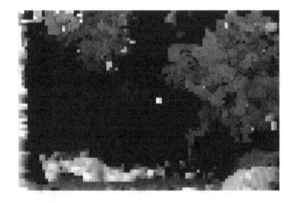

4. STATIONARY OBJECT SEGMENTATION BASED ON THE DISPARITY MAP

Because disparity is in inversely proportional relationship with the depth, to segment the disparity map can obtain the objects at different depths. For the objects with larger proportion of the image area, we use the iteration threshold segmentation method which used before, and for the objects with smaller proportion of the image area, we use local adaptive segmentation method.

Assuming gray values in the object are higher than the gray values in the background, the original image can be segmented (Gao, Liu, Yue,

Zhang, Mei, & Gao, 2010) and it can be divided into object region and background. For the image composed by the objects and background, the gray histogram can be considered as the distribution of pixel gray mixed probability density, and we usually assume that the distribution of two-component mixture is the normal distribution. The mean, standard deviation and the prior probability are: μ_0, μ_1, σ_0, σ_1, p_0, p_1. The μ_0, μ_1 and σ_0, σ_1 can be gotten as follows:

$$\mu_0(t) = \sum_{z=0}^{t} z p_z / p_0(t) \tag{11}$$

$$\mu_1(t) = \sum_{z=t+1}^{L-1} z p_z / p_1(t) \tag{12}$$

$$\sigma_0(t) = \left[\frac{\sum_{z=0}^{t} \left[z - \mu_0(t) \right]^2 * p_2}{\sum_{z=0}^{t} p_2} \right]^{1/2} \tag{13}$$

$$\sigma_1(t) = \left[\frac{\sum_{z=t+1}^{L-1} \left[z - \mu_1(t) \right]^2 * p_2}{\sum_{z=t+1}^{L-1} p_2} \right]^{1/2} \tag{14}$$

If the number of pixels with gray value z is n_z, t is the threshold, $z = 1, 2, \cdots, t, \cdots, L$. The total number of pixels is $N = \sum_{z=0}^{L-1} n_z$, the probability of the pixels with gray value z is $p_z = n_z / N$. If the objects and background can be divided, they should meet:

$$\mu_1 - \mu_0 > \alpha(\sigma_0 + \sigma_1) \tag{15}$$

The parameter α can be decided by the distribution of the gray values of the objects and background. If a threshold value divides the image into two proportions, and the distribution of gray mean and standard deviation of each proportion meet the Equation (15), the threshold value can completely separate video objects from background. On the contrary, if not meet Equation (15), we'll do more sophisticated segmentations to the separate regions. With the narrowing of segmentation regions and the increasing of the proportion of video objects, we can finally get the correct segmentation. The disparity map based segmentation results are shown in Figures 9, 10, 11, 12, 13, 14, 15, and 16.

From Figures 9, 10, 11, 12, 13, 14, 15, and 16 we can see that the algorithm proposed in this paper can effectively segment the flowers, vase and carton. All these stationary objects are difficult for separation in the single-channel video.

Figure 9. Original image

Figure 10. Disparity map

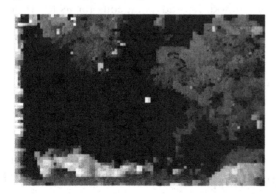

Figure 11. Disparity map after segmentation

Figure 12. Flower 1

Figure 13. Vase

Figure 14. Flower 2

Figure 15. Cartons

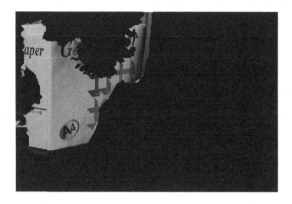

Figure 16. Teddy bear

5. MOVING OBJECT SEGMENTATION IN THE STEREO VIDEO SEQUENCE

A. Extraction of the Motion Region

For the moving objects in the stereo video sequence, such as the electric teddy bear, from Figure 16 picture we can see that the disparity based segmentation is not very good, so we use

redundant wavelet transform to obtain the motion area, and to segment the moving objects.

Because the coefficients of the sub-bands of the redundant wavelet transform are highly correlated, and the direction and size are the same as the image, also, there is no translation in the sub-band; we put forward a new method which based on redundant wavelet transform to obtain the motion area. First, if the two frames in the single-channel video sequence are X_1 and X_2, we use the Equation (16) presented in Box 1 to obtain the $MAS(x, y)$.

The J_0 and J_1 are the starting and ending scales. The motion area is obtained according to Equation (17):

$$motion(x, y) = \begin{cases} 1 & MAS(x, y) \geq T \\ 0 & MAS(x, y) < T \end{cases} \quad (17)$$

T is the threshold. $MAS(x, y)$ is transformed into a gray picture, and the Iterative threshold method is used to obtain the T automatically. After obtaining the initial motion region, we do the closure operation and the opened operation of mathematical morphology to remove the noise interference. We use both the frame-subtraction method and our method to obtain the motion area, and use the Iterative threshold method to get the binary mask. The results are seen in Figures 17, 18, 19, and 20.

From Figures 17, 18, 19, and 20 we can see that our method is better than the frame-subtraction method. It is advantageous for us to do the next operation to segment the moving object.

Box 1.

$$MAS(x, y) =$$
$$\sum_{j=J_0}^{J_1} \left(\begin{aligned} &\left| LL_1^{(j)}(x, y) - LL_2^{(j)}(x, y) \right| + \left| LH_1^{(j)}(x, y) - LH_2^{(j)}(x, y) \right| \\ &+ \left| HL_1^{(j)}(x, y) - HL_2^{(j)}(x, y) \right| + \left| HH_1^{(j)}(x, y) - HH_2^{(j)}(x, y) \right| \end{aligned} \right) \quad (16)$$

Figure 17. Current image

Figure 18. Reference image

B. The Binary Mask Filling and Moving Object Segmentation

The binary motion mask obtained from the redundant wavelet transforms can be considered as the original mask of the moving video object. As the inner district of the object is usually flat, the characteristic is not obvious and there are some crevices in the mask, we use a assimilation method to fill the mask (Gao, Liu, Yue, Zhang, Mei, & Gao, 2010). First, we scan the picture to find all the pixels with 0 values, then for any of the 0 value pixels, we check one line L which passes the pixel p, if there are two pixels p1 and p2 in the line and they satisfy:

- The values of p1 and p2 are both 1;
- p1 and p2 distribute two sides of p;
- $|p-p1|<R$, $|p-p2|<R$.

Then we change the value of p into 1, or else the value should not be changed. If the value of p is changed to 1, then we say that p is assimilated in the R region according to the straight line L. The R is called the assimilation radius. In actual process, to reduce the calculation quantity, we need not compute all directions, only consider the 4 straight lines as follows:

Figure 19. Motion area obtained by redundant wavelet transforms

Figure 20. Motion area obtained by frame-subtraction

L0: (x-1, y)-(x+1, y);
L1: (x-1, y+1)-(x+1, y-1);
L2: (x, y-1)-(x, y+1);
L3: (x-1, y-1)-(x+1, y+1).

Because the search process is at a straight line, only does the increment or the decrease and don't involve the multiplication operation, the speed is quickly and it can reduce the compute time.

The advantage of the assimilation operation is that it only fills the cragged crevice; the slow-changing edge will not be modified. However, some masks have big holes; they cannot be completely filled, so we use the closure operation of the mathematical morphology to do the second filling. We use the logical operation 'and' to the binary mask and the current frame to obtain the video object. The results are shown in Figures 21, 22, and 23.

6. CONCLUSION

This paper presents a new redundant discrete wavelet transforms based stereo video object segmentation algorithm. The algorithm segments the video objects by combining the redundant wavelet transform and the disparity map. The

Figure 21. Motion area obtained by redundant wavelet transforms

Figure 22. Binary mask

Figure 23. Moving video object

experimental results show that the algorithm can segment the overlapping objects, stationary objects and moving objects at the same time with better accuracy and robustness. It is obviously advantageous for us to do the video object-based stereo video coding in the future.

ACKNOWLEDGMENT

This work is supported by the National Science Foundation of China under Grant No. 71102174, and the Science Foundations of Tianjin under Grant No. 10ZCKFSF01100.

REFERENCES

Aizawa, K., & Huang, T. S. (1995). Model-based image coding: advanced video coding techniques for very low bit-rate applications. *Proceedings of the IEEE, 83*(2), 259–271. doi:10.1109/5.364463

Bleyer, M., & Gelautz, M. (2007). Graph-cut based stereo matching using image segmentation with symmetrical treatment of occlusions. *Signal Processing Image Communication, 22*(2), 127–143. doi:10.1016/j.image.2006.11.012

Calderbank, A. R., Daubechies, I., Sweldens, W., & Yeo, B. L. (1996). *Wavelet transforms that map integers to integers (Tech. Rep.)*. Princeton, NJ: Department of Mathematics, Princeton University.

Daubechies, I., & Sweldens, W. (1998). *Factoring wavelet transforms into lifting steps (Tech. Rep.)*. Paris, France: Bell Laboratories, Lucent Technologies.

Gao, T., Liu, Z. G., Yue, S. H., Zhang, J., Mei, J. Q., & Gao, W. C. (2010). Robust background subtraction in traffic video sequence. *Journal of Central South University of Technology, 17*(1), 187–195. doi:10.1007/s11771-010-0029-z

Gao, T., Liu, Z. G., & Zhang, J. (2009). Redundant discrete wavelet transforms based moving object recognition and tracking. *Journal of Systems Engineering and Electronics, 20*(5), 1115–1123.

Izquierdo, E. (1999). Disparity/segmentation analysis: matching with an adaptive window and depth- driven segmentation. *IEEE Transactions on Circuits and Systems for Video Technology, 9*(4), 589–607. doi:10.1109/76.767125

Kolmogorov, V., Zabih, R., & Gortler, S. (2003). Generalized multi-camera scene reconstruction using graph cuts. In A. Rangarajan, M. Figueiredo, & J. Zerubia (Eds.), *Proceedings of the 4th International Workshop on Energy Minimization Methods in Computer Vision and Pattern Recognition*, Lisbon, Portugal (LNCS 2683, pp. 501-516).

Nishihara, K., & Poggio, T. (1984). Stereo vision for robotics. In *Proceedings of the First International Symposium on Robotics Research* (pp. 489-505).

Raymond, E., & Clifton, M. S. (2000). Unconstrained stereoscopic matching of lines. *Vision Research, 40*, 151–162. doi:10.1016/S0042-6989(99)00174-1

This work was previously published in the International Journal of Advanced Pervasive and Ubiquitous Computing, Volume 3, Issue 3, edited by Tao Gao, pp. 60-75, copyright 2011 by IGI Publishing (an imprint of IGI Global).

Chapter 22
Design and Implementation of Bipolar Digital Signal Acquisition and Processing System based on FPGA and ACPL-224

Guangfu Lin
Jiangsu Automation Research Institute, China

Zhenxing Yin
Jiangsu Automation Research Institute, China

Guo Feng
Jiangsu Automation Research Institute, China

ABSTRACT

This paper proposes new approaches for designing a bipolar DS acquisition system to reduce the harm of external factors on equipment, as well as fulfill system requirements at the veracity and reliability of the equipment to quickly connect. The design method chosen is ACPL-224 for chip of the interface about data acquisition on the FPGA device, including system principle, interface circuit logic, the method of data processing, and so forth. Now that this method has been applied, it has achieved good results, including extending the system's adaptive range of external signal and enhancing the efficiency of the interface to quickly connect.

DOI: 10.4018/978-1-4666-2645-4.ch022

1. INTRODUCTION

Data acquisition is widely used in radar, communication, image, military and medical chemical industry, has important application value (Stevens, 2000; Wei, Liu, & Yuan, 2003). Based on the digital signal acquisition to obtain the state of an external signal, thus obtained testing equipment working state. This design is to achieve the goal of bipolar digital signal acquisition (Wang & Li, 2008). Bipolar signal is digital signal which is composed of a positive or negative amplitude of the one state, and by grounding said it's another. Previous unipolar digital signal acquisition design cannot adapt to the external signal polarity changes, but also need to strictly distinguish between the input port definition operational errors usually cause the damage of the interface circuit. The design of multi channel by means of AC input phototransistor optocoupler half pitch of ACPL-224 as the interface circuit chip on the external bipolar digital signal, then the use of FPGA and parallel processing ability of the powerful function for multipath signal processing, design a strong data processing capability and with rich interface digital signal acquisition and processing system (PICMG, 2005; Feldstein & Muzio, 2004).

2. SYSTEM PRINCIPLE

The standard architecture of CPCI bus module is used in the digital signal acquisition system. Includes interface circuit, Schmidt shaping circuit, logic processing section, a bus interface part. External digital signal through the interface circuit acquisition, TTL signal is outputed, and then into the logic device EPM7256SRI208-10 after Schmidt shaping circuit, all data processing by its implementation. Bus bridge device using PLX's PCI9052 Compact PCI bus to local bus is provided to the system using. The system principle block diagram is shown in Figure 1.

3. INTERFACE CIRCUIT DESIGN

According to the requirements of the system interface circuit 32 Road, to meet the needs of light vibration, the input voltage, bipolar input, access to "0" when an external signal end is suspended, the isolation voltage not less than 2KV.

ACPL-224 multi-channel half pitch photosensitive transistor is selected in the design of interface circuit, which has two oppositely connected with the light emitting diode can be adapted to the re-

Figure 1. Bipolar digital signal acquisition and processing system

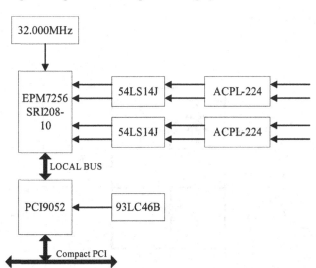

quirements of bipolar digital input signal, at the same time with photoelectric isolation characteristics, its isolation voltage is 3KV, each ACPL-224 device may receive a two group of external signal input. Adjust the current-limiting resistor values to the 2.47KΩ, to meet the requirements of the input voltage range. External signal output TTL level signal through the circuit such as the diagram A1, A2, and then into the FPGA processing by Schmidt plastic processing. Output terminal configured to pull high resistance to control the state when the external signal end is suspended. The interface circuit diagram is shown in Figure 2.

This interface circuit, not only can receive external bipolar digital signal input, to a unipolar signal can also access, without the need to distinguish the signal input end and a reference end, can effectively prevent external signal polarity changes or circuit damage when the port is connected against.

4. FPGA DESIGN

FPGA on-chip logic implementation description block diagram is shown in Figure 3. It complete 3 main functions In FPGA, including the PCI9052 local bus interface logic implementation, internal register implementations, interrupt control logic

implementation. System through the PCI9052 local bus interface to access the FPGA internal registers, in order to realize the access, need implementation of the PCI9052 local bus interface logic inside the FPGA, because clocks between the two are homologous, so only need to consider the PCI9052 local bus address, data and sequential coordination between control signals, inside the FPGA implements an interface logic, for the timing can respond to PCI9052 local bus read and write operations (PICMG, 1999; Bhasker, 2000). The register set in FPGA includes a status register, interrupt enable register, control register.

The signal acquisition to obtain the data into the FPGA that is treated by external signal state each path of data into the register every. There are two ways to obtain the signal status. The first way is the query mode. Through the software to query the corresponding register address to obtain the state of the input signal. This approach is commonly used methods, the utility model has the advantages of design, operation is relatively simple, logical devices occupy fewer resources, but also can get dozens of road signal input state. Disadvantages are the need for software timing constantly access to register, access time interval is long do not have timely access to the state of the input signal changes, short and will occupy the software resources. The second way is inter-

Figure 2. Interface circuit diagram

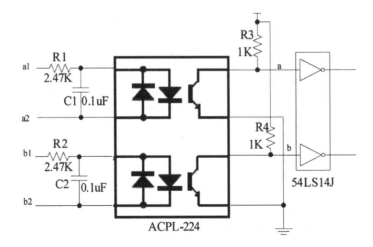

Figure 3. Data processing logic diagram

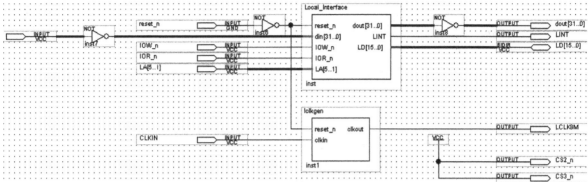

rupt mode. That instituted interrupt request by use of external signal level changes, thereby obtaining the input signal state changes. The utility model has the advantages of timely access to the state of the input signal changes, occupy less resources software. Disadvantages are complex logic design, occupying logic device resources, the disturbance is easy to misjudge, not suitable for multi-channel signal input and input signal state changes frequently.

According to resources situation of the selected logical device EPM7256SRI208-10, that designed the query mode, taking into account the interrupt mode, according to actual needs masked by software or open interrupt mode. By reading the corresponding register value to obtain the state of the input signal, the read bit is "0" when the external input signal is low or suspended; the read bit is "1" when the external input signal is high. In the Interrupt mode, initiated interrupt request by using the rising and falling edges of an external signal state changes. Software gives the signal current state according to the initial state of the input signal and the interrupt signal. Data processing logic diagram is shown in Figure 3.

In the diagram," LINT" said interrupt output signal, "data [31..0]", corresponding to the 32

input signal state. Internal logic using Verilog HDL hardware description language for logic design, process parts as shown in Box 1.

5. SOFTWARE DESIGN

The system software design idea is: first initialized, setting work mode. In the query mode, automatic access two 16 bit register, obtain the corresponding binary code, is converted into the desired 32 road condition information, output graphics display. Set access cycle, cycle access register. In the interrupt mode, according to the interruption information, judging which input signal initiated interrupts, according to the initial state of the signal, given the current state of the input signal.

6. SYSTEM DEBUGGING AND VERIFICATION

System hardware is assembled according to the principle, the driver is then completed, the software tested, and the system debugged on-line. The use of differential signal as a bipolar signal input, the system is able to correctly identify each path of the

Box 1. Processing parts

```
resetall
timescale 1ns/10ps
module Local_Interface(
  reset_n,
 ......
  LD
);
  input          reset_n;
  ......
  wire           test_outen;
  reg    [15:0] test_out;
  wire rd_din_hw;
  wire rd_din_lw;
 ......
  always @(negedge reset_n or negedge din[0] or posedge dint_clear_f[0])
    if((!reset_n)|(dint_clear_f[0]))
      din_falledge[0] <= 1'b0;
    else
      din_falledge[0] <= 1'b1;
......
  always @(negedge reset_n or negedge IOW_n)
    if(!reset_n)
      dout <= 32'h0;
    else
      case(LA[5:1])
        5'b10001:
          dout[31:16] <= ~(LD[15:0]);
        5'b10010:
          dout[15:0] <= ~(LD[15:0]);
            ......
        6'h1f:
            dout[31] <= LD[0];
          //default:

          endcase
      endcase

  assign int_r = din_riseedge&dint_mask_r;
  assign int_f = din_falledge&dint_mask_f;
  assign all_int = |(int_r|int_f);
  assign LINT = (all_int&&dint_mask_all);
endmodule
```

input signal to the state and its change. Switching signal input end, the system can work normally. Interrupt mode also has a normal work.

After the debugging, design of bipolar digital signal acquisition and processing system can meet the design requirements, can be normal operation. It achieve of the module level screening test, the machine system to complete the environmental testing and electromagnetic compatibility testing. The validation of the module's performance, environmental adaptability can meet the requirements of actual use.

7. CONCLUSION

Bipolar digital signal acquisition and processing system can improve the efficiency and accuracy of the interconnection between the operation, which can reduce the damage caused by misoperation of the system, but also improve the reliability of the system. This paper gives a specific design of interface circuit, data processing logic design method. Multi-channel bipolar digital signal acquisition and processing is realized. It can be regulated through the circuit parameters and logic design to the range of input signal changes and function adjustment, to meet different application requirements, is a strong function of the CPCI bus digital signal acquisition module.

REFERENCES

Bhasker, J. (2000). *A Verilog HOL Primer* (2nd ed.). Allentown, PA: Star Galaxy.

Feldstein, C. B., & Muzio, J. C. (2004). Development of a fault tolerant flight control system. In *Proceedings of the 23rd Digital Avionics Systems Conference* (Vol. 2).

PICMG. (1999). *Compact PCI 2.0 D3.0.* Retrieved from http://wenku.baidu.com/view/21248f16a21614791711281b.html

PICMG. (2005). *Compact PCI Express PICMG EXP.0 R1.0 Specification.* Retrieved from http://www.picmg.org/v2internal/pciisa.htm

Stevens, W. R. (2000). TCP/IP Illustrated: *Vol. 1. The protocols.* Zurich, Switzerland: China Machine Press.

Wang, K., & Li, S. (2008). Design of a double-redundancy net card based on the CompactPCI technology. *Computer Engineering and Science, 30*(6), 149–151.

Wei, T., Liu, L., & Yuan, G. (2003). Redundancy backup technique of double Nic in Vxworks. *Techniques of Automation and Applications, 2003*(7), 32-34.

This work was previously published in the International Journal of Advanced Pervasive and Ubiquitous Computing, Volume 3, Issue 4, edited by Tao Gao, pp. 1-5, copyright 2011 by IGI Publishing (an imprint of IGI Global).

Chapter 23
Financial Distress Prediction of Chinese-Listed Companies Based on PCA and WNNs

Xiu Xin
Hebei Finance University, China

Xiaoyi Xiong
Hebei Finance University, China

ABSTRACT

The operating status of an enterprise is disclosed periodically in a financial statement. Financial distress prediction is important for business bankruptcy prevention, and various quantitative prediction methods based on financial ratios have been proposed. This paper presents a financial distress prediction model based on wavelet neural networks (WNNs). The transfer functions of the neurons in WNNs are wavelet base functions which are determined by dilation and translation factors. Back propagation algorithm was used to train the WNNs. Principal component analysis (PCA) method was used to reduce the dimension of the inputs of the WNNs. Multiple discriminate analysis (MDA), Logit, Probit, and WNNs were employed to a dataset selected from Chinese-listed companies. The results demonstrate that the proposed WNNs-based model performs well in comparison with the other three models.

1. INTRODUCTION

The ability to predict the possibility of financial distress of a company is important for many user groups such as investors, creditors, regulators and auditors (Xu, 2000; Becchetti & Sierra, 2003). With the radical changing of global economy and customer demand, business enterprises are confronted with strong competition and uncertain operational environment. In 2008, financial tsunami started to impair the economic development of many countries. The prediction of financial crisis turns to be much more important when the world economy goes to depression. Firms which cannot recognize financial distress and take measures at an early stage will run into bankruptcy, which not only brings great loss to stockholders, creditors, managers and other interest parts, but also affects the stability of social economy (Anandarajan, Lee, & Anandarajan, 2001; Ko & Lin, 2006).

DOI: 10.4018/978-1-4666-2645-4.ch023

However, bankruptcy is not just happened by accident but a continuously developed process. Most enterprises that ran into bankruptcy had experienced financial distress, which usually have some symptoms indicated by company's account items. It is significant to explore effective financial distress prediction models with various classification and prediction techniques (Li, Sun, & Sun, 2009). Great efforts have been made to apply various statistical and machine learning methods to forecasting corporate financial distress. Early studies used statistical techniques, such as univariate statistical methods, multiple discriminate analysis (MDA), logistic regression (Logit) and prohibit regression (Probit) (Beaver, 1966; Altman, 1968; Altman, Edward, Haldeman, & Narayanan, 1977; Aamodt & Plaza, 1994; Martin, 1977; Ohlson, 1980; Andres, Landajo, & Lorca, 2005). However, strict assumptions of traditional statistics (linearity, normality, etc.) limit their application in the real world (Hua, Wang, Xu, Zhang, & Liang, 2007). With the rapid development of artificial intelligence, machine learning techniques such as decision tree (DT), case-based reasoning (CBR), artificial neural networks (ANNs), genetic algorithm (GA) and support vector machine (SVM) were also applied to financial distress prediction (Frydman, Altman, & Kao, 1985; Li & Sun, 2008; Hu, 2008; Liao, 2005; Lin & McClean, 2001; Shin & Lee, 2002; Ding, Song, & Zen, 2008; Min, Lee, & Han, 2006).

The ability of nonlinear approximation of wavelets and neural network models has been shown by many researchers (Zhang, 1992; Hossen, 2003). Combining the ability of wavelet transformation for revealing the property of function in localize region with learning ability and general approximation properties of neural network, different types of wavelet neural networks (WNNs) have been proposed, which is suitable for the approximation of unknown nonlinear functions with local nonlinearities and fast variations because of

its intrinsic properties of finite support and self-similarity (Zhang, Walter, Miao, & Lee, 1995; Banakar & Azeem, 2008). Neural network (NNs) with sigmoidal activation function has already been shown to carry out large dimensional problem very well. WNNs instigate a superior system model for complex and seismic application in comparison to the NNs with sigmoidal activation function and can handle large dimension problem (Zhang, 1997).

The main contribution of this paper is to propose a financial distress prediction method based on WNNs. The financial and non-financial ratios were used to enhance the accuracy of the financial distress prediction model. The dimension of the inputs was reduced using a principal component analysis (PCA) method, and then WNNs were used to predict the financial distress.

2. PRINCIPLES OF WNNS AND PCA

2.1. The Principle of WNNs

Wavelets are a class of functions used to localize a given function in both space and scaling. They have advantages over traditional Fourier methods in analyzing physical situations where the signal contains discontinuities and sharp spikes. Recently, there are many new wavelet applications such as image compression, turbulence, human vision, radar, and earthquake prediction (Cao & Lin, 2008; Kumar, Ravi, Carr, & Kiran, 2008; Du, Jin, & Yang, 2009).

A family of wavelets can be constructed from a function $\psi(x)$, sometimes known as a "mother wavelet". "Daughter wavelets" $\psi_{a,b}(x)$ are then formed by translation and dilation. Wavelets are especially useful for compressing image data, since a wavelet transform has properties that are in some ways superior to a conventional Fourier transform. An individual wavelet is defined by

$$\psi_{a,b}(x) = |a|^{-1/2} \psi(\frac{x-b}{a}) \qquad (1)$$

where a is the dilation factor, and b the translation parameter.

WNNs employ activation functions that are dilated and translated versions of the "mother wavelet". Based on wavelet theory, the WNNs were proposed as a universal tool for functional approximation, which shows surprising effectiveness in solving the conventional problem of poor convergence or even divergence encountered in other kinds of neural networks. It can dramatically increase convergence speed (Zhang, Qi, Zhang, Liu, Hu, Xue, & Fan, 2001). The structure of the WNNs is shown in Figure 1.

The output from the kth neuron in the output layer can be expressed as

$$y_k(X) = \sum_{j=1}^{Q} w_{kj} \psi(\frac{\sum_{i=0}^{M} v_{ji} x_i - b_j}{a_j}) \qquad (2)$$

where $X = (x_1, x_2, ..., x_M)^T$, and x_i denotes the input to node i in the input layer. Q is the number of hidden nodes and M is the number of input nodes. v_{ji} is the connective weight from input node i to node j in the hidden layer, w_{kj} is the connective weight from hidden node j to output node k and $y_k(k = 1, 2, ..., N)$ is the output from node k in the output layer. a_j and b_j are dilation factor and translation parameter of node j in the hidden layer, respectively.

The training algorithm for a WNN is as follows (Kumar, Ravi, Carr, & Kiran, 2008).

1. Select the number of hidden nodes. Initialize the parameters a_j, b_j, v_{ji} and w_{kj}.
2. Calculate the output value of sample $y_k^p, p = 1, 2, ..., P,$ where P is the number of samples.
3. Reduce the error of prediction by adjusting w_{kj}, v_{ji}, a_j, b_j using Δw_{kj}, Δv_{ji}, Δa_j, Δb_j.

The gradient descend algorithm is employed

$$w_{kj}(n+1) = w_{kj}(n) + \eta \frac{\partial E}{\partial w_{kj}} + \alpha \Delta w_{kj}(n)$$

$$(3)$$

Figure 1. A wavelet neural networks model

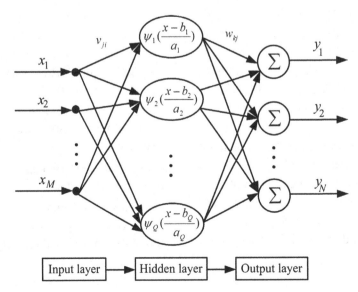

$$v_{ji}(n+1) = v_{ji}(n) + \eta\frac{\partial E}{\partial v_{ji}} + \alpha\Delta v_{ji}(n) \tag{4}$$

$$a_j(n+1) = a_j(n) + \eta\frac{\partial E}{\partial a_j} + \alpha\Delta a_j(n) \tag{5}$$

$$b_j(n+1) = b_j(n) + \eta\frac{\partial E}{\partial b_j} + \alpha\Delta b_j(n) \tag{6}$$

where η and α are the learning and the momentum rates, respectively.

The error function E is taken as

$$E = \frac{1}{2P}\sum_{p=1}^{P}\sum_{k=1}^{N}(d_k^p - y_k^p)^2 \tag{7}$$

where d_k^p is the target output of sample p.

4. Return to step (2), the process is continued until E satisfies the given error criteria, then the whole training of the WNN is completed.

2.2. Basic Properties of PCA

PCA is a data-driven technique used to explain the variance-covariance structure of the data set through a set of linear combinations of the original variables. The PCA transform has been widely used in statistical data analysis and pattern recognition (Li & Zhang, 2006).

Given an observed n_s-dimensional vector $\mathbf{x}$, the goal of PCA is to reduce the dimensionality of $\mathbf{X}$. This is realized by finding n_r principal axes $\mathbf{p}_i$, $i = 1, 2, \cdots, n_r$ onto which the retained variance under projection is maximal. These axes, denoted as principal directions, are given by the eigenvectors associated with the n_r largest eigenvalues λ_i, $i = 1, 2, \cdots, n_s$ of the covariance matrix

$$\sum = E[(\mathbf{x}-\mu)(\mathbf{x}-\mu)^{\mathrm{T}}] \tag{8}$$

where $E[\cdot]$ is the expectation and μ is the mean of $\mathbf{x}$.

n_r is determined by the accumulation contribution ratio $Q(n_r)$ of the n_r largest eigenvalues, which is defined as

$$Q(n_r) = \sum_{i=1}^{n_r}\lambda_i \bigg/ \sum_{i=1}^{n_s}\lambda_i \tag{9}$$

$Q(n_r)$ is commonly demanded larger than 85%, and hence n_r can be determined.

If the principal directions are collected in a matrix $\mathbf{P} = [\mathbf{p}_1 \cdots \mathbf{p}_{n_r}]$, then $\mathbf{z} = \mathbf{P}^{\mathrm{T}}(\mathbf{x} - \mu)$ is a reduced n_r-dimensional representation of the observed vector $\mathbf{x}$. Among all linear techniques, PCA provides the optimal reconstruction $\hat{\mathbf{x}} = \mu + \mathbf{Pz}$ of $\mathbf{x}$ in terms of quadratic reconstruction error $\|\mathbf{x}-\hat{\mathbf{x}}\|^2$.

One advantage of PCA is its ability to describe the data using a small group of underlying variables while preserving as much of the relevant information as possible in the dimensionality reduction process.

Using PCA method, the dimension of the inputs can be reduced, which can increase the speed of WNNs.

3. THE WNNS-BASED PREDICTION MODEL

3.1. The Introduction of Chinese Special-Treated Company

According to a general definition, financial distress is the situation that a firm cannot pay lenders, preferred stock shareholders, suppliers, etc., a bill is overdrawn or the firm is bankrupt according to law (Dimitras, Zanakis, & Zopounidis, 1996). Researchers of many countries adopted bankruptcy firms as distressed samples. However, Chinese capital market is not as mature as that of other countries, the number of bankruptcy firms is insufficient as sample. Hence, almost all Chinese researchers chose the special-treated (ST) companies instead of bankruptcy companies as distressed samples. In Chinese capital market, when the financial status or other conditions of a listed company are unusual, the interest of investor is likely to be harmed. So it will be special treated by Chinese Stock Exchange. According to Chinese Stock Listing Exchange Rule, the so-called ST companies with abnormal financial status refer to those which are treated as their profits continue to be negative for two consecutive years or their per-share net capitals are lower than per-share value. As analyzed in Ding, Song, and Zen (2008), ST companies show some sign of deterioration in the before-treated year and fall into financial distress in fact in the after-treated year. On the other hand, non-ST companies can represent those with good financial condition. In a word, the Chinese ST event is fit for cut-off criteria among different listed companies.

3.2. Data Selection

The 20 financial ratios variables mentioned in Lin (2009) are used, which were proved to be successful in predicting bankruptcy in prior studies. The definition of variables is listed in Table 1.

Financial statement data of Chinese listed companies from 2005 to 2008 were selected in this paper. The final 276 sample data among which 66 were bankruptcy were collected. The training and test data sets are described in Table 2.

Using the PCA method, the contribution ratio of each eigenvalue is shown in Figure 2.

14 principal components were selected, which greatly decrease the dimension of the inputs. The accumulation contribution ratio of the 14 eigenvalues is 98.72%.

Table 1. The definition of variables

Variables	Description
TL/TA	Total debt/Total assets
MV/TL	Market value of equity/Book value of total debt
SALES/TA	Net sales/ Total assets
CA/CL	Current assets/Current liabilities
ROA	(Income before tax, interest and depreciation/
RE/TA	Average total assets)*100
GP/SALES	Retained earnings/ Total assets
IBT/SALES	(Gross profit/Net sales)*100
BD/SALES	(Income before tax/Net sales)*100
CFO/CL	(Bad debt expenses/Net sales)*100
COD	(Cash from operations/Current liabilities)*100
GROGP	(Interest cost/Average borrowings)*100
GROIBT	Growth rate of Gross Profit
GROE	Growth rate of Income before taxes
GRODA	Growth rate of Equity
IC/IBI	Growth rate of Depreciable assets
DEBT/EQ-UITY	(Interest cost/Net income+interest expenses*(1-tax rate))*100
CONL/EQ-UITY	(Debt/Equity)*100
	(Contingent liability/Equity)*100
SALES/AVR	Net sales/Average receivables
COGS/AVI	Cost of goods sold/Average inventory

Table 2. Training data sets and test data sets

Samples	Distressed data sets	Non-distressed data sets	Total
Training data sets	36	110	146
Test data sets	30	100	130
Total	66	210	276

Figure 2. Contribution ratio of each eigenvalue

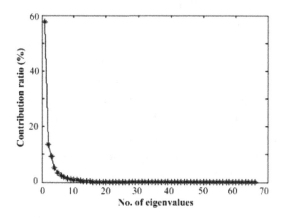

3.3. The Structure and Parameters of WNNs-Based Prediction Model

The structure of WNNs-based prediction model is shown in Figure 3.

Using PCA method, the dimension of inputs was 14. As to the mother wavelet of the hidden layer neurons, it is suitable for this paper to adopt Morlet mother as the activation function of WNNs in consideration of high resolution in both time and frequency domains. Morlet wavelet can be expressed as follows

$$\psi(x) = \cos(1.75x)\exp(-x^2/2) \qquad (10)$$

The number of nodes in the hidden layer of the WNNs is import for the generalization of the WNNs. If the number is too small, WNNs may not reflect the complex function relationship between input data and output values. On the contrary, a large number may create a complex network which leads to a very large output error caused by over-fitting of the training sample set.

Figure 3. The structure of the WNNs-based prediction model

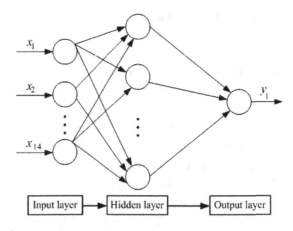

The number of nodes in the hidden layer, which leads to the lowest E (defined in Equation 7), is chosen as the optimal one.

As can be seen from Figure 4, when the number of nodes in the hidden layer is 10, WNNs yields the best results. The learning rate η, momentum rate α and maximum error E are set to be 0.9, 0.1 and 0.001, respectively.

Figure 4. Dependence of E on the number of neurons in the hidden layer

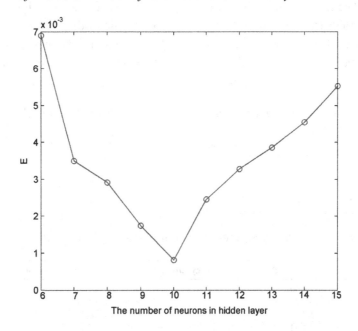

4. RESULTS AND DISCUSSION

4.1. Accuracy Evaluation

A widely used measure of the predictive accuracy is the percentage of correct classification of the examples to financial stress or healthy firms (Lin, 2009). Two kinds of errors due to misclassification are Type I errors (a financial distress firm incorrectly classified as a healthy firm) and Type II errors (a healthy firm being classified as a financial distress firm). The classification of a firm is determined by a cutoff value which is set to balance Type I and Type II errors. A firm with a predicted value greater than this cutoff value is considered as a financial distress firm, otherwise a healthy firm.

4.2. Prediction Results

The prediction accuracy rates of four models mentioned in Section 3.2 for training data sets and test data sets are listed in Tables 3 and 4, respectively.

1. It can be seen from Table 3 that the Logit model has the highest predictive accuracy for the training data sets and the WNNs-based model is comparable to the Probit and Logit models. It also can be seen from Table 4 that the WNNs-based model has the highest predictive accuracy for the test data sets.

These lead to the facts that the generalization abilities of WNNs-based prediction model outperform the other three models and the proposed WNNs-based prediction model is effective.

2. As far as both training and test data sets are concerned, the classification performance of MDA is inferior to the mentioned three models.

5. CONCLUSION

This paper has presented the use of PCA and WNNs in the construction of the financial distress prediction model. The WNNs enables the combination of the wavelet and the neural network learning. Computational results demonstrated that the Logit model has the highest predictive accuracy for the training data sets and the WNNs-based model has the highest predictive accuracy for the test data sets. These mean the good generalization abilities and effectiveness of WNNs-based prediction model.

In conclusion, it should also be emphasized that the model cannot, and should not, entirely replace professional judgment. It should be used to provide auditors with objective information to help them with their reporting decision on a client in the presence of financial distress and going-concern contingencies.

Table 3. Prediction accuracy rates of different prediction models for training data sets

Prediction models	Prediction accuracy rates (%)	Type I error	Type II error
MDA	86.57	16.29	9.18
Probit	91.33	7.56	9.18
Logit	92.76	3.27	10.11
WNNs-based model	91.66	10.81	7.36

Table 4. Prediction accuracy rates of different prediction models for test data sets

Prediction models	Prediction accuracy rates (%)	Type I error	Type II error
MDA	78.50	35.24	6.98
Probit	83.23	30.21	6.20
Logit	85.54	26.32	8.35
WNNs-based model	94.34	6.20	7.10

REFERENCES

Aamodt, A., & Plaza, E. (1994). Case-based reasoning: Foundational issues, methodological variations, and system approaches. *AI Communications*, *7*, 39–59.

Altman, E. I. (1968). Financial ratios discriminant analysis and the prediction of corporate bankruptcy. *The Journal of Finance*, *23*, 589–609. doi:10.2307/2978933

Altman, E. I., Edward, I., Haldeman, R., & Narayanan, P. (1977). A new model to identify bankruptcy risk of corporations. *Journal of Banking & Finance*, *1*, 29–54. doi:10.1016/0378-4266(77)90017-6

Anandarajan, M., Lee, P., & Anandarajan, A. (2001). Bankruptcy prediction of financially stressed firms: An examination of the predictive accuracy of artificial neural networks. *International Journal of Intelligent Systems in Accounting Finance & Management*, *7*, 69–81. doi:10.1002/isaf.199

Andres, J. D., Landajo, M., & Lorca, P. (2005). Forecasting business profitability by using classification techniques: A comparative analysis based on a Spanish case. *European Journal of Operational Research*, *167*, 518–542. doi:10.1016/j.ejor.2004.02.018

Banakar, A., & Azeem, M. F. (2008). Artificial wavelet neural network and its application in neuro-fuzzy models. *Applied Soft Computing*, *8*, 1463–1485. doi:10.1016/j.asoc.2007.10.020

Beaver, W. (1966). Financial ratios as predictors of failure. *Journal of Accounting Research*, *4*, 71–111. doi:10.2307/2490171

Becchetti, L., & Sierra, J. (2003). Bankruptcy risk productive efficiency in manufacturing firms. *Journal of Banking & Finance*, *27*, 2099–2120. doi:10.1016/S0378-4266(02)00319-9

Cao, J. C., & Lin, X. C. (2008). Application of the diagonal recurrent wavelet neural network to solar irradiation forecast assisted with fuzzy technique. *Engineering Applications of Artificial Intelligence*, *21*, 1255–1263. doi:10.1016/j.engappai.2008.02.003

Dimitras, A. I., Zanakis, S. H., & Zopounidis, C. (1996). A survey of business failures with an emphasis on prediction methods and industrial applications. *European Journal of Operational Research*, *90*, 487–513. doi:10.1016/0377-2217(95)00070-4

Ding, Y. S., Song, X. P., & Zen, Y. M. (2008). Forecasting financial condition of Chinese listed companies based on support vector machine. *Expert Systems with Applications*, *34*, 3081–3089. doi:10.1016/j.eswa.2007.06.037

Du, Z. M., Jin, X. Q., & Yang, Y. Y. (2009). Fault diagnosis for temperature, flow rate and pressure sensors in VAV systems using wavelet neural network. *Applied Energy*, *86*, 1624–1631. doi:10.1016/j.apenergy.2009.01.015

Frydman, H., Altman, E. L., & Kao, D. (1985). Introducing recursive partitioning for financial classification: the case of financial distress. *The Journal of Finance*, *40*, 269–291. doi:10.2307/2328060

Hossen, A. (2004). Power spectral density estimation via wavelet decomposition. *Electronics Letters*, *40*, 1055–1056. doi:10.1049/el:20045235

Hu, Y. C. (2008). Incorporating a non-additive decision making method into multi-layer neural networks and its application to financial distress analysis. *Knowledge-Based Systems*, *21*, 383–390. doi:10.1016/j.knosys.2008.02.002

Hua, Z. S., Wang, Y., Xu, X. Y., Zhang, B., & Liang, L. (2007). Predicting corporate financial distress based on integration of support vector machine and logistic regression. *Expert Systems with Applications*, *33*, 434–440. doi:10.1016/j.eswa.2006.05.006

Ko, P. C., & Lin, P. C. (2006). An evolution-based approach with modularized evaluations to forecast financial distress. *Knowledge-Based Systems, 19,* 84–91. doi:10.1016/j.knosys.2005.11.006

Kumar, K. V., Ravi, V., Carr, M., & Kiran, N. R. (2008). Software development cost estimation using wavelet neural networks. *Journal of Systems and Software, 81,* 1853–1867. doi:10.1016/j.jss.2007.12.793

Li, H., & Sun, J. (2008). Ranking-order case-based reasoning for financial distress prediction. *Knowledge-Based Systems, 21,* 868–878. doi:10.1016/j.knosys.2008.03.047

Li, H., Sun, J., & Sun, B.-L. (2009). Financial distress prediction based on OR-CBR in the principle of k-nearest neighbors. *Expert Systems with Applications, 36,* 643–659. doi:10.1016/j.eswa.2007.09.038

Li, J., & Zhang, Y. (2006). Interactive sensor network data retrieval and management using principal components analysis transform. *Smart Materials and Structures, 15,* 1747–1757. doi:10.1088/0964-1726/15/6/029

Liao, S.-H. (2005). Expert system methodologies and applications – A decade review from 1995 to 2004. *Expert Systems with Applications, 28,* 93–103. doi:10.1016/j.eswa.2004.08.003

Lin, F.-Y., & McClean, S. (2001). A data mining approach to the prediction of corporate failure. *Knowledge-Based Systems, 14,* 189–195. doi:10.1016/S0950-7051(01)00096-X

Lin, T.-H. (2009). A cross model study of corporate financial distress prediction in Taiwan: Multiple discriminant analysis, logit, probit and neural networks models. *Neurocomputing, 72,* 3507–3516. doi:10.1016/j.neucom.2009.02.018

Martin, D. (1977). Early warning of bank failure: A logit regression approach. *Journal of Banking & Finance, 1,* 249–276. doi:10.1016/0378-4266(77)90022-X

Min, S.-H., Lee, J.-M., & Han, I. (2006). Hybrid genetic algorithms and support vector machines for bankruptcy prediction. *Expert Systems with Applications, 31,* 652–660. doi:10.1016/j.eswa.2005.09.070

Ohlson, J. A. (1980). Financial ratios and probabilistic prediction of bankruptcy. *Journal of Accounting Research, 18,* 109–131. doi:10.2307/2490395

Shin, K. S., & Lee, Y. J. (2002). A genetic algorithm application in bankruptcy prediction modeling. *Expert Systems with Applications, 23,* 321–328. doi:10.1016/S0957-4174(02)00051-9

Xu, B. (2000). The welfare implications of costly monitoring in the credit market: a note. *The Economic Journal, 110,* 463–576. doi:10.1111/1468-0297.00538

Zhang, J., Walter, G. G., Miao, Y., & Lee, W. (1995). Wavelet neural networks for function learning. *IEEE Transactions on Signal Processing, 43,* 1485–1497. doi:10.1109/78.388860

Zhang, Q. (1992). Wavelet networks. *IEEE Transactions on Neural Networks, 3,* 889–898. doi:10.1109/72.165591

Zhang, Q. (1997). Using wavelet network in nonparametric estimation. *IEEE Transactions on Neural Networks, 8,* 227–236. doi:10.1109/72.557660

Zhang, X., Qi, J., Zhang, R., Liu, M., Hu, Z., Xue, H., & Fan, B. (2001). Prediction of programmed-temperature retention values of naphthas by wavelet neural networks. *Computers & Chemistry, 25,* 125–133. doi:10.1016/S0097-8485(00)00074-7

This work was previously published in the International Journal of Advanced Pervasive and Ubiquitous Computing, Volume 3, Issue 4, edited by Tao Gao, pp. 6-14, copyright 2011 by IGI Publishing (an imprint of IGI Global).

Chapter 24
Highway Background Identification and Background Modeling based on Projection Statistics

Jun Zhang
Tianjin University, China

ABSTRACT

Background images are identified by analyzing the changes in texture of the image sequences. According to the characteristics of highway traffic scenes, in this paper, the author presents a new algorithm for identifying background image based on the gradient projection statistics of the binary image. First, the images are blocked by road lane, and the background is identified by projection statistics and projection gradient statistics of the sub-images. Second, the background is reconstructed according to the results of each sub-image. Experimental results show that the proposed method exhibits high accuracy for background identification and modeling. In addition, the proposed method has a good anti-interference to the low intensity vehicles, and the processing time is less as well. The speed and accuracy of the proposed algorithm meets the needs of video surveillance system requirements for highway traffic scenes.

1. INTRODUCTION

The highway is the inevitable product of economic development, which reflects the transportation development level as well as the overall economic development level of a national and regional, and it also shortened the temporal and spatial distance between people. However, the traffic on the high-way is heavy, fast, and could be easily affected by the rain and snow ice fog and other inclement weather factors, which make it vulnerable to major accidents. So the intelligent monitoring and management to the highway traffic is very important. Background identification and background modeling approach is a crucial step, an accurate and fast identification and modeling methods have a very important practical significance.

DOI: 10.4018/978-1-4666-2645-4.ch024

The traditional method of background modeling have its own shortcoming: the mean method of background modeling is to get the average of the image sequences in a period of time. This algorithm is simple and easy to calculate, and when the objects move fast and its area is small relative to the entire frame, the results of the method will be better. However, if the brightness is too high or too low of a row of vehicles, or the area of moving objects is relatively large, the obtained background image will contain a lot of noise, which will produce large errors in background modeling (Cucchiara, Piccardi, & Prati, 2003). The kernel density estimation algorithm (Sun, Chen, & Ji, 2008; Huang & Dai, 2007; Sun, 2010) overcome the shortcomings of large operations, but it need time to train a large number of samples, and the speed of iterative calculation is slow, which make it difficult to use in practice. Gaussian mixture model (Kita, 2010; Kan, Li, Tang, & Du, 2010; Charoenpong, Supasuteekul, & Nuthong, 2010; Zhong, Yao, & Liu, 2010) assume that each pixel brightness distribution is a Gaussian mixture model in video frame, and establish the background model according to the brightness of the pixel histogram, but the assumption is not necessarily true and the computational complexity is proportional with the number of Gaussian model.

This paper proposes a method to identify and model the background image based on statistics, according to analyzes the characteristics of the highway. The speed and accuracy of the proposed algorithm have made very good results when test the experiment on road.

2. BACKGROUND IDENTIFICATION BASED ON STATISTICS

2.1. Highway Scene Features

We can find that the road is flat, the color is single and texture information is not obvious in the background images, while the color is rich and texture information is obvious in the Vehicle images, from the image sequences. The reason is that the edge of the vehicle front part in images is rich, such as the lights, heat sinks, plates, etc., which is depicted in Figure 1. According to this feature of the highway image sequences, firstly this paper identifies the background images roughly. Secondly, do the background modeling using the images of the previous step results.

2.2. General Principle

We divided the images by lanes, for the image data and the storage space are large enough for the high-definition digital images. (Simply, we assume that each sub-image is a rectangular.) In this paper, we divide the picture into three rectangular

Figure 1. Background images contrast with the vehicle images

(a) Background image   (b) Background image   (c) Vehicle image   (d) Vehicle image

sub-pictures which can be left the overlapping parts between each other, according to the lane position. If N is the number of lanes of the image, the picture is divided into N sub- pictures, the description can be formulated as

$$F(x,y) = \sum_{i=1}^{N} f(x,y) = f_1(x,y) + f_2(x,y) + f_3(x,y)$$
$$+ ... = f_1(x_2 - x_1, y) + f_2(x_3 - x_4, y) + f_3(x_6 - x_5, y) + ...$$
(1)

The parameters in Equations(1) are: $F(x,y)$ is the image data, $f_1(x,y)$, $f_2(x,y)$, $f_3(x,y)$ are the three lane sub- pictures, x_1, x_2 are the left and right horizontal borders of the first lane sub- picture, x_3, x_4 are the left and right horizontal borders of the second lane sub- picture, x_5, x_6 are the left and right horizontal borders of the third lane sub- picture, $x_1 - x_6$ must be meet the Inequality as: $x_1 < x_3 < x_2 < x_5 < x_4 < x_6$. Then we process these sub- pictures into gray images, for to reduce the calculation and improve the processing speed. Finally, process these gray pictures of horizontal and vertical Sobel edge detection, and then count the pixels in each row and columns of the Sobel images from the horizontal and vertical directions. We roughly identify the background images according to these statistic results, and then model the background by the rough background recognition images. If there are vehicles in the sub- picture, we do not update the background image, and wait for the next step treatment, such as vehicle detection or tracking. The flow chart of the proposed algorithm is depicted in Figure 2.

2.3. Edge Detection

Marr's theory (Marr & Hildreth, 1980) holds that human's visual perception of objects is heavily dependent on the edge. The reason is that first the

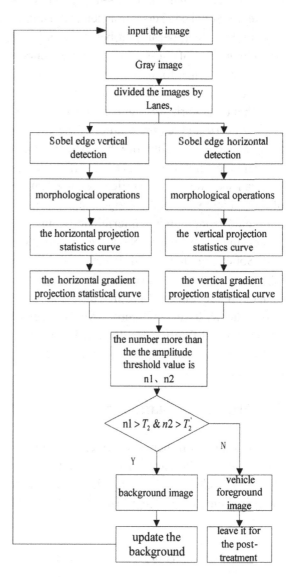

Figure 2. Background identification and background modeling flow chart

edge is the junction of one region to another region in picture, the mutation of the characteristic, and the place where have the largest uncertainty and the most information in the image. In addition, the light can significantly affect the appearance of a region, but cannot change the edge of the area. Thus, the edge detection can respond the information of the moving target shape and the texture in background images; moreover, it can reduce the redundant information of processing.

We use Sobel edge detection detect the image edge in this paper, because Sobel operator has a smoothing effect of noise, provide a more accurate edge orientation information, process better of the picture that has more noise and gray shaded.

Sobel edge horizontal detection can well detect the horizontal texture feature of the edge in the images, and can filter out the vertical texture interference. Similarly, Sobel edge vertical detection can well detect the vertical texture feature of the vehicle edge in the images, and can filter out the horizontal texture interference. Thus, we process the N sub-images (N is three, in this paper) with Sobel edge horizontal detection and Sobel edge vertical detection to obtain the binary edge images (pixel value is 1 on the edge, others are 0) of them, as shown in Figure 3. Morphological expansion and filtering are done to fill the hole on the edge so as to keep its continuity and filter out the noise.

2.4. Projection Statistics

We can find that if there is a vehicle in the foreground image, the edges of the figure is denser for the vehicle's rich texture, from the binary images of the Sobel edge horizontal and vertical

detection. So the projection statistics of edge point can reflect the texture feature better. We do the projection statistics in the vertical detection of the Sobel edge horizontal detection binary figure, obtained the curve of the vertical projection statistics; Similarly, do the projection statistics in the horizontal detection of the Sobel edge vertical detection binary figure, obtained the curve of the horizontal projection statistics. The projection statistics is calculated as

$$p\_v(i) = \sum_{j=1}^{Y} I(i,j)$$

$$p\_h(j) = \sum_{i=1}^{X} I(i,j)$$

(2)

In the Equation(2), X and Y are the width and height of the image, $p\_v(i)$ is the vertical statistical value of each vertical column of the image, $p\_h(i)$ is the horizontal statistical value of each horizontal row of the image, and $I(i,j)$ is value of pixel (x, y) in the image. The statistical curve of $p\_v(i)$ and $p\_h(i)$ is shown in Figure 4.

From comparison of the projection statistics curve of the vehicle image and background image in Figure 4, we can see that the projection statistics curve of the vehicle area has the continuous peak - valley - peak feature, and the magnitude

Figure 3. The results of the first lane edge detection

| Original image | Sobel edge horizontal detection | Sobel edge vertical detection |

Figure 4. The projection statistics curve of the vehicle image and background image

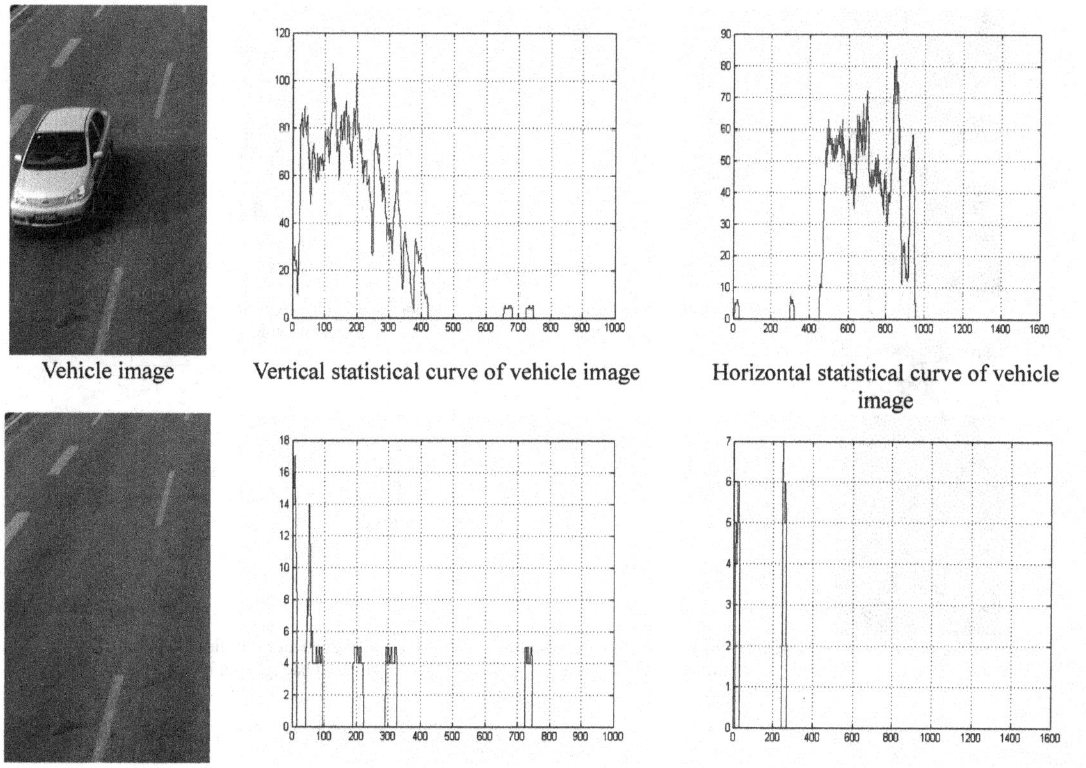

Vehicle image

Vertical statistical curve of vehicle image

Horizontal statistical curve of vehicle image

Background image

Vertical statistical curve of background image

Horizontal statistical curve of background image

of possible areas of vehicles is much higher than other regions, while the feature of the background area is not obvious.

2.5. Projection Gradient Statistics

In the projection statistics curve, the larger change of the statistical value is caused by the by the moving target. So the gradient of the curve can reflect the statistical curve change clearly, but also can reflect the position of the moving vehicle. Gradient corresponds to the first derivative, a continuous image function F(x,y), the gradient of pixel (x,y) can be expressed as a vector (Gx and Gy are the gradient along the X direction and Y direction, respectively).

$$\nabla \mathrm{F}(x,y) = [Gx, Gy]^T = [\frac{\partial f}{\partial x} \frac{\partial f}{\partial y}]^T,$$

the amplitude of the vector is (often referred as the gradient)

$$\nabla \mathrm{F} = \max(\nabla \mathrm{F}) = (G^2 \mathrm{x}, G^2 y)^{1/2}$$

The gradient statistics curve of the projection statistics curve $p\_v(i)$, $p\_h(i)$ are H_v (i), H_h(i) respectively, which is expressed as

$$\mathrm{H\_v(i)} = \nabla p\_v(i) = \left| p\_v(i+1) - p\_v(i-1) \right|$$
$$\mathrm{H\_h(i)} = \nabla p\_h(i) = \left| p\_h(i+1) - p\_h(i-1) \right|$$

$$(3)$$

Figure 5. The gradient projection statistics curve of the vehicle image and background image

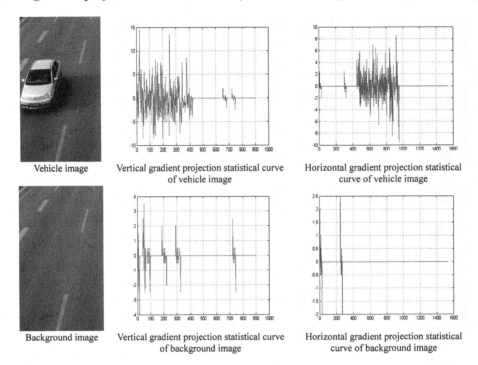

The gradient projection statistics curve, H_v (i), H_h(i), is shown in Figure 5. From the gradient statistics curve we can find that the gradient projection of the vehicle area changes fiercely and the amplitude increases, when a moving vehicle pass. The background regions changes gently and the amplitude is poor.

2.6. Main Steps of the Algorithm

The gradient projection statistics curve will has make a large movement, for the big change of texture feature when there are some vehicles moving on the on the highway in the image. Moreover, the change of the statistics curve must persist for some length, in order to exclude the interference of noise, because the certain length and broadband of a vehicle. So if the fluctuation of the statistics curve is more than certain amplitude and a certain length, the image will be considered a vehicle in it, other cases will be considered a background image. The steps of the rough background identification are shown as follows:

1. Input the image I, the gray level image of I is IG, and divide the picture according to the lane position, assume one of the sub-images is Ig.
2. Obtain the binary edge images of Sobel edge vertical and horizontal detection respectively, and we remove some noise utility morphological operations.
3. Obtain the curve of the horizontal and vertical gradient projection statistics of the Sobel edge vertical and horizontal detection, respectively.

4. Assume that the number more than the amplitude threshold value T1 in the curve of the vertical gradient projection statistics is n1; the number more than the amplitude threshold value $T1^{\blacklozenge}$ in the curve of the horizontal projection statistics is n2.

5. If the number n1 is greater than the threshold value T2 and n2 is greater than the threshold value $T2^{\blacklozenge}$, this picture will be considered a vehicle image Ig; in other cases that is a background image $B_1(x, y)$.

$$
\mathrm{Ig}(x, y) = \begin{cases} Ig(x,y) & \text{n1} > T2 \ \& \ \text{n2} > T2' \\ B_1(x,y) & others \end{cases}
$$

6. Update the background if the image is a background image; leave it for the post-treatment if it is a vehicle foreground image.

2.7. Background Update

The uncertain factor such as the light, rain and snow, etc., may cause the background changes, if the background has not been updated timely, the excessive detection, false alarm, and sensitivity decrease may happen. We update the rough background identified images, remain the sub-images with the moving vehicle in it unchanged, which is calculated as

$$
B_i(x, y) = \begin{cases} B_{i-1}(x,y) & n1 > T2 \ \& \ n2 > T2' \\ aIg_i + (1-a)B_{i-1}(x,y) & others \end{cases} \quad (4)
$$

In Equation (4), $B_i(x, y)$ is the background value on point (x, y), the speed factor a is 0.1, and the threshold value T2. $T2^{\blacklozenge}$ must be set according to the situation of the road.

3. EXPERIMENTAL RESULTS AND ANALYSIS

In this experiment, all the test images are taken by a surveillance camera at 0.2 seconds apart, with the size of 2048×1536 and 24 bit color depth mode. And the camera is mounted at a fixed location on a bridge crossing the target highway. We used a personal computer with an INTEL Xeon CPU Processor 2.66GHz and 3-GB random-access memory. We use three methods, which are our method, average method, and Gaussian mixture model, to generate a background image of the first lane sub-image with our method. The experimental results of the first 10 frames are shown in Figure 6.

The runtime of these three methods is: average method is 3s, our method is 25s, Gaussian mixture model is 410s. From Figure 6 we can see that the time of average method is the shortest, but background of it will have a vague trace of the vehicle; the computation of Gaussian mixture model is complex and the time it cost is the longest, which greatly limit the practical application of the algorithm, besides the weighted value of the initial frame is big if the number of the processing images is less, background will also have a vague trace; the background modeled by the method of this paper is the closest to the true background which extract the moving object more accurate, and the runtime is much less.

Figure 7 is the processed results of the first 100 frames. Our method, average method, and Gaussian mixture model all can get a more clear and accurate background images. However, in this process our method can update the background 28 times, and reflect the changes in the background real-time.

Figure 6. Processed results of the first 10 frames

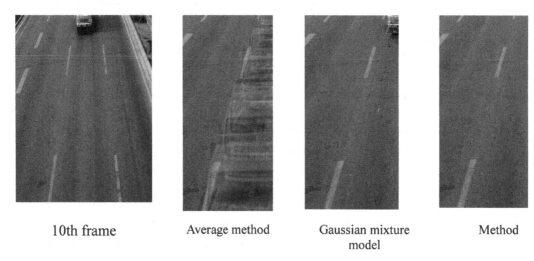

| 10th frame | Average method | Gaussian mixture model | Method |

Figure 7. Processed results of the first 100 frames

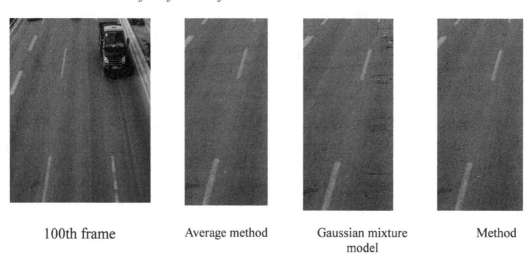

| 100th frame | Average method | Gaussian mixture model | Method |

4. CONCLUSION

According to the characteristics of highway traffic scene, we propose a image background recognition model using the projection statistics and projection gradient statistics of the binary Sub-images in this paper. And we update the background according to the recognition result. Experimental results show that the runtime of the proposed method is much less, and can get a more clear and accurate background image no matter how many pictures it process. In conclusion, first the algorithm of this paper is simple, easy to implement and suitable for the highway speed monitoring system; second, the method has a good effect when the color of the vehicle is close to the road in the images; third, this model can be applied by different traffic scene, by adjusting the threshold of the parameters.

REFERENCES

Charoenpong, T., Supasuteekul, A., & Nuthong, C. (2010, May 19-21). Adaptive background modeling from an image sequence by using k-means clustering. In *Proceedings of the IEEE International Conference on Electrical Engineering/ Electronics Computer Telecommunications and Information Technology* (pp. 880-883).

Cucchiara, R., Piccardi, M., & Prati, A. (2003). Detecting moving objects, ghosts, and shadows in video streams. *IEEE Transactions on Pattern Analysis and Machine Intelligence, 25*(10), 1337–1342. doi:10.1109/TPAMI.2003.1233909

Hou, F.-Z., & Zhou, Z.-Y. (2008). Approach for locating vehicle license plates based on gradient difference of the morphology. *Journal of Science Technology and Engineering, 8*(12), 3355–3358.

Huang, Z.-M., & Dai, M. (2007). Moving object detection based on Gaussian kernel density model. *Microcomputer Information, 23*(2), 45–48.

Kan, J., Li, K., Tang, J., & Du, X. (2010, October 22-24). Background modeling method based on improved multi-Gaussian distribution. In *Proceedings of the Computer Application and System Modeling Conference* (pp. 214-218).

Kita, Y. (2010, August 23-26). Background modeling by combining joint intensity histogram with time-sequential data. In *Proceedings of the 20th International Conference on Pattern Recognition* (pp. 991-994).

Marr, D., & Hildreth, E. (1980). Theory of edge detection. *Proceedings of the Royal Society of London. Series B. Biological Sciences, 27*, 187–217. doi:10.1098/rspb.1980.0020

Sun, J.-F. (2010). New method for moving object detection based on Gaussian kernel density estimation. *Computer Technology and Development, 20*(8), 45–48.

Sun, J.-F., Chen, Y., & Ji, Z.-C. (2008). Kernel density estimation background model method based on key frame. *Optics Technology, 34*(5), 699–701.

Zhong, B., Yao, H., & Liu, S. (2010, March 14-19). Robust background modeling via standard variance feature. In *Proceedings of the IEEE International Conference on Acoustics, Speech, and Signal Processing* (pp. 1182-1185).

This work was previously published in the International Journal of Advanced Pervasive and Ubiquitous Computing, Volume 3, Issue 4, edited by Tao Gao, pp. 15-23, copyright 2011 by IGI Publishing (an imprint of IGI Global).

Chapter 25
Method of Measuring the Switching Time of Dual Redundant NIC

Zhengrong Tao
Jiangsu Automation Research Institute, China

Zhenxing Yin
Jiangsu Automation Research Institute, China

ABSTRACT

In this paper, the authors present a method of measuring the switching time of a dual redundant NIC. The accuracy of the authors' method of measuring switching time can reach milliseconds. The authors' method uses Internet Control Message Protocol (ICMP) packets to test, is easy to operate, has high precision, and can be applied to all types of dual redundant device switching time measurement.

1. INTRODUCTION

With the increasing popularity of computers, ethernet is in every corner of people's lives, and networks appear everywhere. To ensure the smooth flow of the network, the important parts of the network generally use dual redundant architecture, so that once a certain node or network connection has failure, dual redundant LAN connections automatically switch to the backup to ensure that the network still works properly. For dual redundant networks, switching time is an important indicator to measure its performance level, and higher requirement of real-time needs shorter switching time (Stevens, 2000; Wei, Liqiang Liu, & Gannan Yuan, 2003).

DOI: 10.4018/978-1-4666-2645-4.ch025

This paper describes a precise method to measure the dual redundant LAN card switching time, and can also be used to promote the acceptance testing of the dual redundant network equipment performance.

2. THEORY OF DUAL REDUNDANT NETWORK

Typical basic dual redundant network architecture is shown in Figure 1.

In Figure 1, all computers are respectively connected to switch 1 and switch 2 through dual redundant LAN cards, where the solid lines represent the main connections, and the dotted lines represent the backup connections. Under normal circumstances, dual redundant network cards work on the main connecting links, and transmit Ethernet data through the connections; the Backup connecting links are in hot standby state, which could not transmit Ethernet data. When some device's main connecting link fails, the device's dual redundant LAN card automatically switches to the backup link to work (Wang & Li, 2008; WinRiver, 2003).

Figure 1. Dual redundant network structure

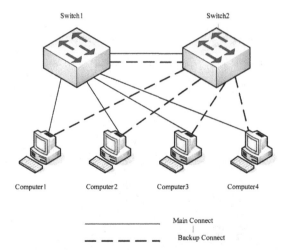

For example, if the primary link of computer 1 has problem, its dual redundant computer network card will automatically switch to the backup connection link to work. At the same time the status of other equipment is not affected which is unchanged, and the whole network work normally again with the smallest cost.

For large-scale dual redundant network, the switch parts may connect in different layers, such as the access layer, convergence layer and the core layer. However, no matter what kind of layer connection is used, the basic principle is the same as Figure 1.

3. SWITCHING TIME MEASUREMENT PRINCIPLE

The test methods in this paper mainly use the ICMP (Internet Control Message Protocol) packets to test (Sinmwalla, Sharma, & Kesbav, 1999). As shown in Figure 2, when a device sends an ICMP request to another device, the receiver will return an ICMP response.

The test method here uses this characteristic of the ICMP pocket, and when the test equipment continuously sends ICMP request to the device under test, the device under test will generate ICMP response in the primary connection link continuously while there is no response in the backup link. When the primary connection is interrupted, after the dual redundant network card switches automatically, the backup connection generates ICMP response while the primary link has none. In the switching process, neither of the primary and backup connections could generate response. Figure 3 shows the switching process from the primary connection to the backup of one node in dual redundant network environment.

Therefore, the switching process occurs during the time when the device under test can not generate ICMP responses in Figure 3. By capturing

Figure 2. Request and reply of ICMP packets

Figure 3. Demonstration of the switching process

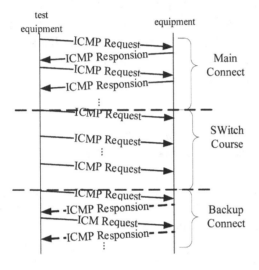

in Figure 5, choose every 1 millisecond to send a packet, and select "Initiate Send" button to continue to send. Under normal circumstances, the test computer sends ICMP packets to the tested computer through the primary connecting link, but when the primary link is interrupted, only after the tested computer switches to the backup link to work, the packets sent by the test computer can reach the tested one through switch 1 and switch 2 (Kothuri, Goldfrind, & Beinat, 2004).

During the packet capture, set the packet filter, and only capture the returning test packets from the tested computer, as shown in Figure 6. Such packets are easy for lost packets statistics calculation.

The actual switching time can also be found in the actual packet capture file: first find the first packet that has no response and set the time as the initial relative time, and then find the first packet after that has response whose relative time is the switching time. In this case the actual result is shown in Figure 7; it is 377.915ms, the same as the theoretical value.

Figure 4. Topology of dual redundant LAN switching time test

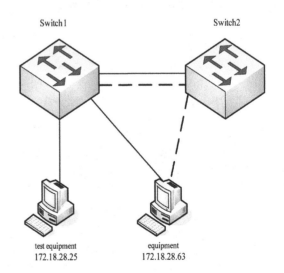

the packets above with capture software or specialized equipment and finding the beginning and the ending packets of the switching process, we can get switching time according to the timestamp of the captured packets.

If we send ICMP packets in a fixed period, the product of the number of requests that cannot generate ICMP response and the sending period is the switching time.

4. TESTING METHOD

Test topology is shown in Figure 4, and we can run monitoring software such as EtherPeekNX and sniffer on the test computer to capture packets.

Taking EtherPeekNX for example, we can use its packet-sending function to send ICMP packets to the tested device in a fixed period. As shown

Figure 5. Configuration of sending packets

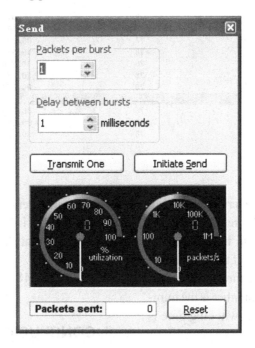

Figure 6. Filter settings

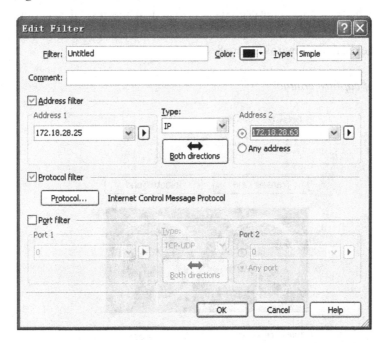

Figure 7. Switching time showed by the captured packets

IP-172.18.28.63	78	00.371079	PING Req
IP-172.18.28.63	78	00.372056	PING Req
IP-172.18.28.63	78	00.373033	PING Req
IP-172.18.28.63	78	00.374010	PING Req
IP-172.18.28.63	78	00.374987	PING Req
IP-172.18.28.63	78	00.375963	PING Req
IP-172.18.28.63	78	00.376940	PING Req
IP-172.18.28.63	78	00.377915	PING Req
IP-172.18.28.25	78	00.378026	PING Reply
IP-172.18.28.63	78	00.378892	PING Req
IP-172.18.28.25	78	00.378990	PING Reply
IP-172.18.28.63	78	00.379869	PING Req
IP-172.18.28.25	78	00.379966	PING Reply

As one ICMP request only generates one ICMP response, the caught number of requests and responses should be consistent in the case of no packet loss (Zhu & Xie, 2002). If there is packet loss, the difference between 2 times of the sent number and the actual caught number is the number of lost requests. Therefore, switching time is calculated as

Switching time = (the request number×2-the caught number) ×the period

After start capturing, click on "Initiate Send" to begin sending, and then disconnect the primary link, and stop sending when there occurs response in the backup link. The result is shown as Figure 8.

The sent number (packets sent) is 12413, and the caught number is 24448. Therefore, the switching time here is that shown in Figure 8.

$(12413×2-24448)×1=378(ms)$.

5. CONCLUSION

This paper describes a measurement method of dual redundant LAN card switching time, which is easy to realize, beneficial for operation and has an accuracy of milliseconds, and can be widely used in the test of a variety of dual redundant network equipments switching time.

Figure 8. Statistics of capture counter

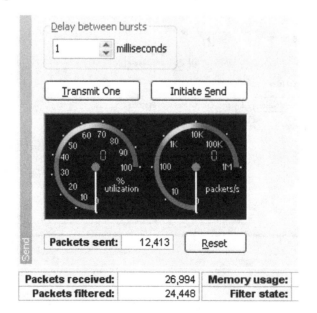

234

REFERENCES

Kothuri, R., Goldfrind, A., & Beinat, E. (2004). *Pro Oracle Spatial*. New York, NY: Apress.

Sinmwalla, R., Sharma, R., & Kesbav, S. (1999). Discovering Internet topology. In *Proceedings of the IEEE International Conference INFOCOM*.

Stevens, W. R. (2000). TCP/IP illustrated: *Vol. 1. The protocols*. Zurich, Switzerland: China Machine Press.

Wang, K., & Li, S. (2008). Design of a double-redundancy net card based on the CompactPCI technology. *Computer Engineering and Science, 30*(6), 149–151.

Wei, T., Liqiang Liu, L., & Gannan Yuan, Y. (2003). Redundancy backup technique of double Nic in Vxworks. *Techniques of Automation and Applications, 2003*(7), 32-34.

WinRiver. (2003). *VxWorks networks programmer s guide (Version 5.5)*. Retrieved from http://www-kryo.desy.de/documents/vxWorks/V5.5/vxworks/netguide/index.html

Zhu, X., & Xie, L. (2002). Design and analysis of discrete-time robust Kalman filters. *Automatica, 38*(6), 1069–1077. doi:10.1016/S0005-1098(01)00298-9

This work was previously published in the International Journal of Advanced Pervasive and Ubiquitous Computing, Volume 3, Issue 4, edited by Tao Gao, pp. 24-29, copyright 2011 by IGI Publishing (an imprint of IGI Global).

Chapter 26
Modeling of Across–Chain Network Dynamic Competition for MNC in Industrial Cluster

Chunling Liu
Wuhan Textile University, China

Jizi Li
Wuhan Textile University, China

Guo Li
Beijing Institute of Technology, China

Xiaogang Cao
Wuhan Textile University, China

ABSTRACT

The huge market and perfect production system in China are attracting more multi-national companies' interest to invest in China in the form of Foreign Direct Investment (FDI). Therefore, multi-national companies are willing to integrate and optimize global supply chain networks of their own, which enable them to reduce cost and improve market response. As a result, multi-national companies usually embed into local industrial clusters through financial and technological comparative merits to sharpen their competitive edge. This paper considers the across-chain network equilibrium problem involving process of competition and melting between this new global chain and an already existing local chain. The authors model the optimizing behavior of these two chains, derive the equilibrium conditions, and establish the variational inequality formulation, and solve it by using the modified algorithm. Finally, the authors illustrate the model through numerical example and discuss relationships among the price, quantity, technological progress, and satisfaction among two dynamic phases.

DOI: 10.4018/978-1-4666-2645-4.ch026

1. INTRODUCTION

The rapidly developing worldwide marketplace has spawned a new allure for the multi-national company (MNC) to seek out attractive labor markets to reduce cost, locate to close to customers to improve customer service, and build new markets in developing countries to enhance profits. For instance, companies in Western European and the United State have begun to establish similar networks to serve the evolving free markets in China. However, to be profitable the multi-national company must deal with a variety of issues. Companies must consider a number of trade-offs; for example, centralized manufacturing to achieve economies of scale versus decentralized operations that seek to improve customer service by locating assembly plants closer to customers. However, achieving a favorable trade-off may not straightforward, since costs depend upon the countries in which plants are located.

The effect of facility location of multi-national company on competitive advantage is well known. Day and Wensley (1988) point to three components that form the framework for diagnosing competitive superiority: source of advantage, positional advantage, and performance outcomes. Porter (1988) believes that achieving competitive advantage requires having superior resources and customer satisfaction. Porter (1988) also advises that to gain competitive advantage over their rivals, companies must perform their primary activities more efficiently and effectively than their competitors. He asserts that these primary activities are inbound logistics, operations (manufacturing), outbound logistics, marketing and sale, and after-sale services. The location of these activities plays a significant role in the success and future of businesses in the domestic and global markets.

Owing to the recent changes in the world economy and technological advances, industrial clusters provide a platform for multi-national companies to operate multiple facilities and to become more agile. In particular, in China, there usually exist a couple of paralleled supply chains at industrial cluster, members around them not only vertically cooperate along their own supply chain, but also horizontally cooperates with other different supply chains. It means firm's coordination evolves from firm-wide to chain-wide, and even to across-chain. On this basis, these supply chains located in industrial cluster are referred to as cluster supply chains (CSC) network. For it has an easy access to sources of raw materials, to lower cost labor but with high technical training, to potential markets, as well as to just-in-time delivery in supply chain system, thus attracting multi-national companies move closer to industrial cluster more than they used to be.

These multi-national companies enter and embed in industrial cluster, and build the production base, reconstruct their global supply chain. As a result, the initial equilibrium network in cluster supply chain will be broken and renewed. After multi-national companies' fusion and competition in industrial cluster for awhile, the new equilibrium network will gradually be formed.

A majority of researches regarding equilibrium network mainly focused on a supply chain network, and ignored changes caused by other adjacent supply chain network and MNC embedded in industrial cluster.

In this paper, we explore multi-national companies embedded in the cluster supply chain to form a new supply chain (i.e., global supply chain) and compete with existing one (local supply chain), this process will enable network equilibrium to dynamically change. The remaining parts of the paper are organized as follows. Section 2, the literature review, gives a brief explanation of relevant researches. Variables and assumptions are given in Section 3. Dynamic equilibrium models are formulated and discussed in Section 4 followed by discussion of equilibrium algorithm in Section 5. Finally, experiment and concluding remarks are outlined in Sections 6 and 7.

2. LITERATURE REVIEW

2.1. Industrial Cluster and Supply Chain

With the development of new organizational paradigm and globalization, industrial cluster not only is main source of national competition from a state perspective, but also is becoming one of major competitive weapons for individual firm. Industrial agglomeration firstly originates from Marshall's 'industrial district' (1920) and Weber's 'classic district' (1929), then followed by Hoover (1948), who further explored and illustrated agglomeration economy. Li, Xiong, Park, Liu, Ma, and Cho (2009) urged that firms within industrial cluster link forward and backward through innovation chain and product chain to sharpen the competitive edges, Theo et al. (1998) denoted that in order to share new complementary technologies, obtain gains from shared specialized assets, speed up learning process, reduce transaction cost, overcome market barriers and diffuse innovative risk, so inter-dependant stakeholders such as firms, knowledge-producers, brokers, contractors and customers link together and weave value-added network, this value-added network is just 'cluster'.

Furthermore, Porter (1998) pointed out that industrial cluster is a strong and sustainable competitive advantage network of interconnected companies and institutions in a particular value chain where encompass an array of linked industries and other entities important to competition and cooperation. Industrial cluster generally link forward downstream retailers and customers and backward upstream suppliers and manufacturers and R&D companies, at the same time the geographical proximity surrounded by relevant organizations such as professional training school, information centre and inspection and surveillance organization, etc. When firms operate in one location, the repeated interactions among them boost competition, improve productivity, innovation and coordination, and build trust. Companies operating in a cluster can have the advantage of scale without dealing with the inflexibilities of vertical integration or formal linkages (DeWitt, Giunipero, & Melton, 2006).

The effectiveness of clusters can be better understood by examining the practices of supply chain management. Clusters can be thought of as geographic concentration of competing, networked supply chains. Clusters present opportunities for a firm to streamline and shorten its supply chain, as these sources exist in a concentrated area (DeWitt et al., 2006). Supply chain management integrates process and builds long-term relationships among firms involved in the flow of products and services from the source through to end-users. All firms in the supply chain can benefit through achieving lower costs, improved customer value and satisfaction, and greater competitive advantage (Mentzer, DeWitt, Keebler, Nix, Smith, & Zacharia, 2001). Compared with market transactions among dispersed and random buyers and sellers, the proximity of firms in clusters- and the repeated exchanges between them- fosters communication, coordination, innovation, interdependence and trust (DeWitt et al., 2006).

In industrial cluster site, these interconnected groups of companies in close geographical proximity to one another are a big source of supply chain and business advantage (Wu, Yue, & Sim, 2006). Supply chains can intertwine with any one company being a part of many supply chains. As an example, IBM is part of a network of supply chains, since it is a customer in one supply chain (for server components), a supplier in another (to CompUSA for laptops), a partner in another (with Linux for software), and a competitor to another chain (Apple for desktop PCs) (DeWitt et al., 2006). As a whole, an industrial cluster is essentially collection of many interrelated supply chains (or supply networks). These supply chains contain many levels of independent suppliers and manufacturers with different suppliers possibly serving the same manufacturers, and different manufacturers ordering from the same supplier. These many-to-one, one-to-many, or many-to-many relationships are also possible between the manufactures and customers (Wu et al., 2006). These multi-chains are what we refer to cluster supply chains.

In comparison with the traditional single supply chain, cluster supply chain system contains a couple of paralleled single supply chains in the same region, not only do all enterprises in one single supply chain cooperate one another internally, but cooperation and coordination exist across different single supply chains externally as well. What is more, with the exception of firms in these single supply chains, there are a lot of small and medium-sized firms that are not in the chain but float around the same region for supporting and supplementing supply chains production and operation.

2.2. Across-Chains Network Competition

In supply chain context there are three different kinds of competitions: (1) competition among the firms of one tier of a chain (Dong, Zhang, & Nagurney, 2004; Dong, Zhang, Yan, & Nagumey, 2005; Zhang & Dong, 2003); (2) competition among the firms of different tiers of a chain (Majumder & Srinivasan, 2008); and (3) competition across-chains (Boyaci & Gallego, 2004; Xiao & Yang, 2008). As you can see there is little analytic work in the literature that studies the interaction of across-chains and they all consider a predetermined network for the chain. Boyaci and Gallego (2004) consider a market with two competing chains, each consisting of one wholesaler and one retailer. They assume that the business environment forces chains to charge similar prices and to compete strictly on the basis of customer service. They model customer service competition using game-theoretical concepts. Xiao and Yang (2008) consider two competing chains facing uncertain demands, where each chain consists of one risk-neutral supplier and one risk-averse retailer. Two

retailers compete in retail price as well as service investment. They assume that each retailer has a long-term relationship with his supplier, which is assured by his individual rationality constraint. The products of two suppliers are partially differentiated and each supplier sells products to customers through her retailer.

The equilibrium model is drawn from network economics. Due to the non-cooperative competition among chains' networks, Nash game-theoretic approach is able to perfectly quantity such a competition. Moreover, the steady consumption behavior of consumers for the product can be characterized by the well-known spatial price equilibrium conditions (Nagurney, 1999). Many reports point out that pricing strategies in chain systems contribute to higher profitability and stronger competitive power. In this work, we identify the equilibrium prices in the chains under chain vs. chain competition and discuss how the equilibrium prices, costs, incomes, and profits behave with respect to key marketing activities.

In this paper, we consider the across-chain network equilibrium problem involving competition between two chains. Our paper is closely related to Nagurney, Dong, and Zhang (2002). Nagurney et al. (2002) studied the equilibrium conditions of a three tier chain to simultaneously study the behaviors of its decision-makers (competition between the firms of one tier of the chain). But our decision structure is different because we consider the across-chain network equilibrium problem also we consider the process of competition and melting between this new global chain and an already existing local chain.

Our paper makes a unique contribution to across-chain network equilibrium in two ways. First, for simplicity almost all previous across-chain network equilibrium papers ignored the rival chains from industrial cluster. Second, this paper also involves multi-national company to form new global chain. To the best of our knowledge, no previous research has studied both across-chain network equilibrium and their dynamic process simultaneously.

3. VARIABLES AND ASSUMPTIONS

3.1. Notation and Variables

I, J, R represent manufacturers, distributors and retailers in cluster supply chain network respectively. h represents host country, e denotes exchange rate, s represents the flow of goods, w indicates selling price of goods, k represents the market, $'$ represents the node where multinational companies embed in cluster supply chain network.

- s_{ij} : Quantity of delivery from manufacturers i to distributors j in original CSC network without embedded MNC;

- $M_1 = \left[s_{ij} \right]$: Quantity vector of delivery from manufacturers i to distributors j in original CSC network without embedded MNC;

- s_{jr} : Quantity of delivery from distributor j to retailer r in original CSC network without embedded MNC;

- $N_1 = \left[s_{jr} \right]$: Quantity vector of delivery from distributor j to retailer r in original CSC network without embedded MNC;

- w_{rh} : Price of retailer r in original CSC network without embedded MNC;

- $W_1 = \left[w_{rh} \right]$: Price vector of retailer r in original CSC network without embedded MNC;

- $s_{i'j'}$: Quantity of delivery from manufacturers i' to distributors j' in CSC network with embedded MNC;

- $M_2 = \left[s_{i'j'} \right]$: Quantity vector of delivery from manufacturer i' to distributors j' in CSC network with embedded MNC;

- $s_{j'r'}$: Quantity of delivery from distributor j' to retailer r' in CSC network with embedded MNC;

- $N_2 = \left[s_{j'r'} \right]$: Quantity vector of delivery from distributor j' to the retailer r' in CSC network with embedded MNC;

- $s_{j'}$: Quantity of delivery from distributor j' in CSC network with embedded MNC;

- $C_2 = \left[s_{j'} \right]$: Quantity vector of delivery from distributor j' in CSC network with embedded MNC;

- $w_{r'h}$: Price of retailer r' in CSC network with embedded MNC in term of monetary h;

- $W_2 = \left[w_{r'h} \right]$: Price vector of retailer r' in CSC network with embedded MNC in term of monetary h;

- $W_k = \left[w_{rh}, w_{r'h} \right]$: Price vector of retailer in CSC network without/with embedded MNC in term of monetary h;

- $F_{ih}\left(s_i \right)$: Cost of manufacturers i operating s_i units in original CSC network without embedded MNC, $s_i = \sum_J s_{ij}$;

- $F_{i'h}\left(s_{i'} \right)$: Cost of manufacturers i' operating $s_{i'}$ units r in CSC network with embedded MNC, $s_{i'} = \sum_{J'} s_{i'j'}$;

- $T_{ijh}\left(s_{ij} \right)$: Cost of transaction between manufacturers i and distributors j in s_{ij} units in term of monetary h;

- $T_{jrh}\left(s_{jr} \right)$: Cost of transactions between distributors i and retailers r in s_{jr} units in term of monetary h;

- $T_{i'j'h}\left(s_{i'j'} \right)$: Cost of transactions between manufacturers i' and distributors j' in $s_{i'j'}$ units in term of monetary h;

- $T_{j'rh}\left(s_{j'r} \right)$: Cost of transactions between distributors j' and retailers r in $s_{j'r'}$ units in term of monetary h;

- $T_{rh}\left(s_{jr} \right)$: Cost of retailer r operating s_{jr} units of goods in term of monetary h;

- $T_{r'h}\left(s_{j'r'}\right)$: Cost of retailer r' operating $s_{j'r'}$ units of goods in term of h;
- $C_{j'}\left(s_{j'}\right)$: Entry cost of multinational distributors j' embedded in CSC network in term of monetary h.

3.2. Assumptions

Assumption 1: There exist more than one supply chain networks, which consists of many manufacturers, distributors and retailers in industrial cluster.

Assumption 2: Market information is completely open.

Assumption 3: Multi-national companies enter the region of industrial cluster based on their technological advantages.

Assumption 4: Before Multi-national companies entering, the existing cluster supply chain network (local supply chain) is characterized by domestic orientation.

In addition, assume that retail price is main factor affecting demand, and technical factor have an impact on quality and price of product, meanwhile, consumer satisfaction also influences product demand, thus the market demand functions show as follows:

$$q_r\left(w_r\right) = g + \alpha w_r - (\beta - \alpha)w_{r'}$$

$$q_{r'}\left(w_{r'}\right) = g' + \alpha w_{r'} - (\beta - \alpha)w_r$$

where $q_r\left(w_r\right), q_{r'}\left(w_{r'}\right)$ present market demand of CSC network without/with embedded MNC respectively; g is a constant, α denotes consumer satisfaction rate, β indicates technological progress index, and $\alpha, \beta > 0, \beta \geq \alpha$.

4. DYNAMIC EQUILIBRIUM MODELS

Generally speaking, due to entering the cluster earlier, the local firms existing in industrial cluster have more advantage than MNC and familiar with market setting. In spite of this, both huge market and perfect production system in China attract more and more MNC's attention to invest in China in form of FDI. Therefore, the MNCs are willing to integrate and optimize global supply chain network of their own, which enable them to reduce cost and improve quick response to market. As a result, the multi-national companies usually embed into local industrial cluster through financial and technological comparative merits to sharpen their competitive edge.

In the process, there are two phases of MNC's dynamic equilibrium. In the first phase, multinational companies enter domestic cluster region and form their own supply chain system (global supply chain). Considering the fact that some existing local supply chain relatively monopolize the market, this give rise to a competition between two supply chain (i.e., local supply chain Vs global supply chain), the process is called "competition & embed" phase. When the first process goes on, the two individual supply chains gradually constitute an inter-linked dynamic equilibrium network where firms in two chains often cooperate and coordinate one another, at the same time, competition still continue to exist among them. Therefore, we call this second phase as "integration & equilibrium" phase. Figure 1 shows the two phases of network formation.

4.1. Competitive Analysis in the First Phase

In the industrial cluster, it is usual that there are a lot of manufacturers, distributors and retailers in the same close region, they operate individually. As rational economic entities, all members of these firms run just for one mere goal of profit maximization. In the early time of this phase,

Figure 1. Two phases of network formation

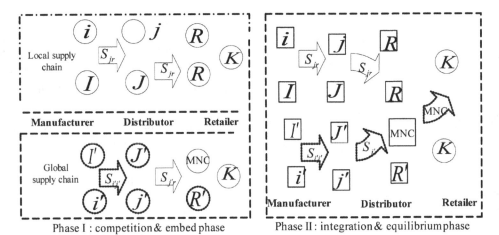

Phase I : competition & embed phase   Phase II : integration & equilibrium phase

the competition is mainly characterized by firm Vs firm rather than chain Vs Chain, that is to say that competition between manufacturer and manufacturer (distributor and distributor, retailer and retailer) occur firstly. Therefore, we build the initial stage of local cluster supply chain network equilibrium model without MNC embedded, the competitive analysis for each individual member located in the same node is presented respectively as follows.

1.   Competitive analysis for manufacturer node

As for a couple of manufacturers in the cluster, due to homogeneous production, it is unavoidable for manufacturers to compete one another. So, the maximize profit of manufacturers can be showed as:

$$MAX[\sum_J w_{ij}s_{ij} - F_i\left(s_{ij}\right) - \sum_J T_{ij}\left(s_{ij}\right)] \quad (1)$$

$S.T.$

$$s_{ij} \geq 0, \forall\, j \quad (2)$$

where the Equation (1) represents manufacturers maximize profit, w_{ij} is selling price, s_{ij} is unit of goods sold, $F_i\left(s_{ij}\right)$ fix investment and $T_{ij}\left(s_{ij}\right)$ manufacture cost, constraint (2) is to ensure production to occur.

Suppose the above competition between manufacturers is non-cooperation one, and each manufacturer cost functions is continuous convex function, optimal quantity and sale are determined by themselves. Therefore, the optimality conditions for all manufacture production can be given as the following variational inequality

$$\sum_I \sum_J \left[\frac{\partial F_i\left(s_i^*\right)}{\partial s_{ij}} + \frac{\partial T_{ij}\left(s_{ij}^*\right)}{\partial s_{ij}} - w_{ij} \right] \times \left(s_{ij} - s_{ij}^*\right) \geq 0 \quad (3)$$

where Equation (3) is base on Equation (1) and to meet the most profit for all manufacturers, s_i^* is manufacturer's optimal production quantity, s_{ij}^* is optimal volume that distributors obtain from the manufacturers.

2. Competitive analysis for distributor node

For distributors, they purchase from manufacturers and then transport, deliver to retailers in various markets. The way as manufacturer does, the maximize profit of distributors can be expressed as

$$MAX[\sum_R w_{jr}s_{jr} - \sum_R T_{jr}\left(s_{jr}\right) - \sum_J w_{ij}s_{ij}]$$

(4)

$$S.T. \; s_i \geq s_j$$

$$s_i \geq 0, \; s_j \geq 0, \; \forall i, r$$

(5)

where Equation (4) is to ensure distributors maximizing profit, s_{jr} is sale quantity by distributor at price w_{jr}, constraint (5) is to ensure distribution activities are to carry out.

Similarly, competition among distributors is a non-cooperative one, each distributor is to maximize their own profit while assuming other distributors behavior. On equilibrium condition, all sale volume should be coordinated at a network of distributor layers. Here, assuming that operating cost per distributor is a continuous convex function. The optimal conditions for all distributors should be given as consistent solutions of variational inequality

$$\sum_I \sum_J \left[\frac{\partial T_i\left(s_{ij}^*\right)}{\partial s_{ij}} + w_{ij}^* - \lambda_j^* \right]$$

$$\times \left(s_{ij} - s_{ij}^*\right) + \sum_J \sum_R \left(\lambda_j^* - w_{jr}^*\right)$$

(6)

$$\times \left(s_{jr} - s_{jr}^*\right) + \left(s_i^* - s_j^*\right) \times \left(\lambda_j - \lambda_j^*\right) \geq 0$$

where Variational inequality (6) is the maximum profits on the condition of Formula (5), λ_j^* is an equilibrium Lagrange multiplier of Formula (3), w_{jr}^* is the equilibrium price of distributors, s_{jr}^* is

the equilibrium quantity sold by distributors, s_j^* is equilibrium purchasing volume of distributor.

3. Competitive analysis for retailer node

In retail market, retailers hope gaining more profit at a high price, while customers want to pay less for higher quality product. In this competitive process, both sides gradually come to the point where they accept the price and volume, so the selling price and market demand have to meet the following conditions:

$$w_{jr} + T_r\left(s_r^*\right) \begin{cases} = w_r^*, if \; s_{jr}^* > 0 \\ \geq w_r^*, if \; s_{jr}^* = 0 \end{cases}$$

(7)

$$q_r\left(w_r^*\right) \begin{cases} = \sum_J s_{jr}^{1*}, if \; w_r^{1*} > 0 \forall\left(r\right) \\ \leq \sum_J s_{jr}^{1*}, if \; w_r^{1*} = 0 \forall\left(r\right) \end{cases}$$

(8)

Where the condition (7) and (8) are to ensure the whole market demand, as the above inequality (3) and (6), the condition (7) and (8) can also be modified as the variational inequality

$$\sum_J \sum_R \left[w_{jr}^* + T_r\left(s_r\right) - w_r^*\right]$$

$$\times\left(s_{jr} - s_{jr}^*\right) + \sum_R \left[s_j^* - q_r\left(w_r^*\right)\right]$$

(9)

$$\times\left(w_r - w_r^*\right) \geq 0$$

where w_r^* is equilibrium selling price of retailer.

4. First phase: Two supply chain network models

After conducting competitive analysis for each individual member along supply chain respectively, and then these local manufacturers and distributors and retailers gradually take supply-chain-shape. Therefore, we establish the local cluster supply chain network equilibrium model without MNC embedded, the maximizing profit of this local cluster supply chain is

$$\pi_1 = \sum_R \sum_J p_{jh} s_{jr} - \sum_I F_i\left(s_i\right)$$
$$-\sum_I \sum_J T_{ij}\left(s_{ij}\right) - \sum_J \sum_R T_{jr}\left(s_{jr}\right) \tag{10}$$

$$S.T. \tag{11}$$

$$\sum_I \sum_J \left[\frac{\partial T_i\left(s_{ij}^*\right)}{\partial s_{ij}^1} + w_{ij}^* - \lambda_j^*\right]$$
$$\times\left(s_{ij} - s_{ij}^*\right) + \sum_J \sum_R \left(\lambda_j^* - w_{jr}^*\right)\times\left(s_{jr} - s_{jr}^*\right)$$
$$+\left(s_i^* - s_j^*\right)\times\left(\lambda_j - \lambda_j^*\right) \geq 0 \tag{12}$$

$$\sum_J \sum_R \left[w_{jr}^* + T_r\left(s_r\right) - w_r^*\right]$$
$$\times\left(s_{jr} - s_{jr}^*\right) + \sum_R \left[s_j^* - q_r\left(w_r^*\right)\right] \tag{13}$$
$$\times\left(w_r - w_r^*\right) \geq 0$$

$$\sum_I s_{ij} \geq \sum_J s_{jr} \tag{14}$$

Hence, Objective function(10)is the total sale revenue minus transportation and operation cost. The constraints (11), (12) and (13) are to ensure manufacturer, distributor and retailer to maximize their profit, respectively.

When multi-national companies embed, due to its technical and financial advantage, into cluster and form their own supply chain-global supply chain. The different nodes along global supply chain may be located in various countries and regions, which need to consider the exchange rate, and the time value of money. Therefore, the global supply chain maximize profit as seen in Box 1.

Similarly, it must satisfy the Formula (3), (5), (6) and constraint (9).

5. Analysis of competitive equilibrium

After multi-national embedding into the local cluster supply chain, there are two sorts of supply chains(supply chain embedded with multinational, i.e., global supply chain; and supply chain without multinational, i.e., local supply chain), both will face a non-cooperative competition, one strategy selection influences the other by means of production quantity and sale price. In the market equilibrium, we maximize profit, that is the optimization problem of Formula (10) and (15), and all variables are non-negative, then competitive equilibrium expression for the whole cluster network system (including two supply chains) is show in Box 2.

The solution to the (16) is network competitive equilibrium in the first phase. Price is endogenous variables. If the equilibrium prices are w_k^* and w_k^* the quantity of goods by distributors from two types of supply chain are $\sum_J s_{jk}^*$ and $\sum_{J'} s_{j'k}^*$, equivalent of market demand $q_k^1\left(w_k^*\right)$ and $q_k^2\left(w_k^*\right)$ respectively.

Box 1. Equation 15

$$\pi_2 = \left[\begin{array}{l}\sum_{R'}\sum_{J'}\sum_H p_{j'r'h} s_{j'r'h} e_{j'r'h} - \sum_{I'}\sum_H f_{i'}\left(s_{i'}\right)e_{i'h} - \sum_{I'}\sum_{J'}\sum_H T_{i'j'h}\left(s_{i'j'}\right)e_{i'j'h} \\ -\sum_{J'}\sum_{R'}\sum_H T_{j'r'h}\left(s_{j'k}\right)e_{j'r'h} - \sum_{J'}\sum_H C_{j'}\left(s_{j'}\right)e_{j'h}\end{array}\right] NPV \tag{15}$$

Box 2. Equation 16

$$
\sum_I \sum_J \sum_h \left[\left(\frac{\partial f_{ih}\left(s_i^*\right)}{\partial s_{ij}} + \frac{\partial T_{ijh}\left(s_{ij}^*\right)}{\partial s_{ij}} - \lambda_j^* \right) \right] \cdot \left(s_{ij} - s_{ij}^*\right) \cdot e_{ijh} + \sum_J \sum_R \sum_H \left[\frac{\partial T_{jrh}\left(s_{jk}^*\right)}{\partial s_{jr}} + \lambda_j^* - p_{jh}^* \right] \cdot \left(s_{jr} - s_{jr}^*\right) \cdot e_{jrh}
$$

$$
+ \sum_J \left(\sum_I s_{ij}^* - \sum_R s_{jr}^* \right) \cdot \left(\lambda_j - \lambda_j^*\right) + \sum_{I'} \sum_{J'} \sum_H \left[\left(\frac{\partial f_{i'h}\left(s_{i'}^*\right)}{\partial s_{i'j'}^2} + \frac{\partial T_{i'j'h}\left(s_{i'j'}^*\right)}{\partial s_{i'j'}^2} - \lambda_{j'}^* \right) \right] \cdot \left(s_{i'j'} - s_{i'j'}^*\right) \cdot e_{i'j'h}
$$

$$
+ \sum_{J'} \sum_R \sum_H \left[\frac{\partial T_{j'rh}\left(s_{j'r}^{2*}\right)}{\partial s_{j'r}^2} + \lambda_{j'}^{2*} - p_{j'h}^{2*} \right] \cdot \left(s_{j'r'} - s_{j'r'}^*\right) \cdot e_{j'r'h} + \sum_{J'} \left(\sum_{I'} s_{i'j'}^* - \sum_{R'} s_{j'r'}^* \right) \cdot \left(\lambda_{j'} - \lambda_{j'}^*\right)
\tag{16}
$$

$$
+ \sum_{J'} \sum_H \left(\frac{\partial L_{j'h}\left(s_{j'}^*\right)}{\partial s_{j'}} \right) \cdot \left(s_{j'} - s_{j'}^*\right) \geq 0
$$

$$
\forall \left(M_1, N_1, \lambda_j, M_2, N_2, \lambda_{j'} \right) \in R_+^{|I||J||H| + |J||R||H| + |J| + |I'||J'||H| + |J'||R||H| + |J'| + |J'||H|}
$$

Definition 1: *Network equilibrium of global supply chain.* The network equilibrium state in two supply chain networks is to satisfy the optimal conditions (14) -(16).

Theorem 1: *Description of variation inequality.* Equilibrium condition of global supply chain network is solution to variational inequalities

$$
\forall \left(M_1^*, N_1^*, \lambda_j^*, M_2^*, N_2^*, \lambda_{j'}^* \right) \in k
$$

Satisfy (see Box 3).

Proof: The problem (14) and (15) extend to inequality (16).

exist $x^* \in k$, Satisfy $\langle F(x*), x - x* \rangle \geq 0$ $\forall x \in k$ (18)

When

$$
x = \left(M_1, N_1, \lambda_j, W_1, M_2, N_2, \lambda_{j'}, W_2 \right),
$$

$$
F(x) = \left(F_{ij}^1, F_{jk}^1, F_{1j}^1, F_{2j}^1, F_k^1, F_{i'j'}^2, F_{j'k}^2 \right),
$$

where $\langle ., . \rangle$ indicates the inner product of N dimensional Euclidean space.

4.2. Integrated Analysis in the Second Phase

From the first phase of competition & embed to the second phase, multi-national companies have completely embedded into cluster supply chain network. Due to the geographical closeness and technology spillovers, local supply chain gradually obtain some advantages from multi-national, two supply chain become less competitive than used to be, what is more, both have developed a kind of cooperative relationship, for more cooperation means more chances to avoid risk and earn gain. Therefore, we regard the two supply chains as the whole integrated networks system.

1. Integrated supply chain network model in the second phase

Based on the previous assumptions and analysis, the two supply chain is integrated into a whole network. Assume that costs of all nodes in the network are quantity-related, fix costs are

Box 3. Equation 17

$$
\sum_I \sum_J \sum_h \left[\left(\frac{\partial f_{ih}\left(s_i^*\right)}{\partial s_{ij}} + \frac{\partial T_{ijh}\left(s_{ij}^*\right)}{\partial s_{ij}} - \lambda_j^* \right) \right] \cdot \left(s_{ij} - s_{ij}^*\right) \cdot e_{ijh} + \sum_J \sum_R \sum_H \left[\frac{\partial T_{jrh}\left(s_{jk}^*\right)}{\partial s_{jr}} + \lambda_j^* - w_{jr}^* \right] \cdot \left(s_{jr} - s_{jr}^*\right) \cdot e_{jrh}
$$

$$
+ \sum_J \left(\sum_I s_{ij}^* - \sum_R s_{jr}^* \right) \cdot \left(\lambda_j - \lambda_j^*\right) + \sum_{I'} \sum_{J'} \sum_H \left[\left(\frac{\partial F_{i'h}\left(s_{i'}^*\right)}{\partial s_{i'j'}} + \frac{\partial T_{i'j'h}\left(s_{i'j'}^*\right)}{\partial s_{i'j'}^2} - \lambda_{j'}^* \right) \right] \cdot \left(s_{i'j'} - s_{i'j'}^*\right) \cdot e_{i'j'h}
$$

$$
+ \sum_{J'} \sum_{R'} \sum_H \left[\frac{\partial T_{j'rh}\left(s_{j'r}^*\right)}{\partial s_{j'r'}} + \lambda_{j'}^* - w_{j'r'}^* \right] \cdot \left(s_{j'r'} - s_{j'r'}^*\right) \cdot e_{j'r'h} + \sum_{J'} \left(\sum_{I'} s_{i'j'}^* - \sum_{R'} s_{j'r'}^* \right) \cdot \left(\lambda_{j'} - \lambda_{j'}^*\right) \qquad (17)
$$

$$
+ \sum_{J'} \sum_H \left(\frac{\partial L_{j'h}\left(s_{j'}^*\right)}{\partial s_{j'}} \right) \cdot \left(s_{j'} - s_{j'}^*\right) + \sum_{R'} \left[\sum_J s_{jr}^1 - q_r^1\left(w_r^*\right) \right] \cdot \left(w_r - w_r^*\right) + \sum_{R'} \left[\sum_{J'} s_{j'r'} - q_{r'}\left(w_{r'}^*\right) \right] \cdot \left(w_{r'} - w_{r'}^*\right) \geq 0
$$

$$
\forall \left(M_1, N_1, \lambda_j, W_1, M_2, N_2, \lambda_{j'}, W_2\right) \in k
$$

$$
k \equiv \left\{ \begin{matrix} \left(\forall \left(M_1, N_1, \lambda_j, W_1, M_2, N_2, \lambda_{j'}, W_2\right) \in k\right) \mid \left(M_1, N_1, \lambda_j, W_1, M_2, N_2, \lambda_{j'}, W_2\right) \\ \in R_+^{|I|\cdot|J|\cdot|H| + |J|\cdot|R|\cdot|H| + |J| + |I'|\cdot|J'|\cdot|H| + |J'|\cdot|R|\cdot|H| + |J'| + |J'|\cdot|H| + |R|} \end{matrix} \right\}
$$

associated with the production of goods, operating costs are related to the number of goods inflow and outflow. Meanwhile, taking into account the different nation and production cycle, maximization profit of integrated network model is shown in Box 4.

Similarly, satisfy the constraints (3), (5), (6) and (9).

In the second phase, the profit for all firms is equal to selling price multiplied by amount of product, minus transport and operation costs. Meanwhile considering currency exchange rate and time value of capital, *NPV* is introduced into the formulation (19).

2. Analysis of integrated equilibrium

In the equilibrium model, we can use the following variational inequality to describe the optimal conditions for integrated networks.

Definition 2: *Integrated equilibrium of the whole cluster network:*

For all manufacturers $i = 1, 2, ..., I$, goods flow S^* at nodes, let $S^* \in V^0$, satisfy

$$
U_i\left(S_i^*, \hat{S}_i^*\right) \geq U_i\left(S_i, \hat{S}_i^*\right),
$$

Box 4. Equation 19

$$
U_i = \left[\begin{matrix} \sum_R \sum_J \sum_H w_{jh} s_{jr} e_{jrh} - \sum_I \sum_H F_{ih}\left(s_i\right) e_i - \sum_I \sum_J \sum_H T_{ijh}\left(s_{ij}\right) e_{ijh} \\ - \sum_J \sum_R \sum_H T_{jrh}\left(s_{jr}\right) e_{jrh} \end{matrix} \right] NPV \qquad (19)
$$

$$\forall S_i \in V_i^0 \tag{20}$$

$$\hat{S}_i^* \equiv \left(S_1^*, ..., S_{i-1}^*, S_{i+1}^*, ..., S_I^* \right),$$

and

$$V_i^0 \equiv \left\{ S_i \mid S_i \in R_+^{s_{ijk}} \right\}.$$

Theorem 2: For all manufacturers $i = 1, 2, ..., I$ assume that profit function $U_i\left(s\right)$ with variable S_i is concave and continuously differentiable. Based on the definition 2, $S^* \in V^0$ satisfies the following variation inequality of the integrated network.

$$-\sum_{i=1}^{I} \left\langle \nabla_{S_i} U_i \left(S^* \right)^T, S_i - S_i^* \right\rangle \geq 0, \; \forall S_i \in V^0, \tag{21}$$

Where $\langle .,. \rangle$ indicates the inner product of N dimensional Euclidean space, $\nabla_{S_i} U_i$ expresses the gradient of S_i corresponding to $U_i\left(S\right)$.

The solution to Variation inequality (18) is to satisfy the nature of variation inequalities. The solution is

$$\sum_I \sum_J \sum_h \left[\left[\frac{\partial F_{ih}\left(s_i^*\right)}{\partial s_{ij}} + \frac{\partial T_{ijh}\left(s_{ij}^*\right)}{\partial s_{ij}} - \lambda_j^* \right] \right] \cdot \left(s_{ij} - s_{ij}^* \right) \cdot e_{ijh}$$

$$+\sum_J \sum_R \sum_H \left[\frac{\partial T_{jrh}\left(s_{jr}^*\right)}{\partial s_{jr}} + \lambda_j^* - w_{jh}^* \right] \cdot \left(s_{jr} - s_{jr}^* \right) \cdot e_{jrh}$$

$$+\sum_J \left(\sum_I s_{ij}^* - \sum_R s_{jr}^* \right) \cdot \left(\lambda_j - \lambda_j^* \right) \geq 0 \tag{22}$$

where $s_{ij}^*, s_{jk}^*, \lambda^*$ represent the corresponding optimal production quantity, demand and Lagrange operator, respectively.

Proof: Variation inequality (20) proposed is based on the study by Gabay and Moulin (1980). The function for the number of goods is expressed by sale price, income and all expenses, thus through using the way presented by Bertsekas and Tistsiklis (1989), variation inequality (20) can be transformed to variation inequality (21), variation inequality (21) can be further rewritten as the standard variation inequality

$$\left\langle F\left(X^*\right)^T, X - X^* \right\rangle \geq 0, \tag{23}$$

where V is a convex subset, $F\left(X\right)$ is continuous.

Since the basic feasible solutions to variation inequality (16) and (22) is ensured by defining a weaker condition.

Set (see Box 5).

Where k_b is a range, belong to convex subset

$$R_+^{|I| \cdot |J| \cdot |H| + |J| \cdot |K| \cdot |H| + |J| + |I'| \cdot |J'| \|H| + |J'| \cdot |K| \|H| + |J'| + |J'| \cdot |H| + |K|}, \; F$$

is continuous. According to the theorem of variation inequalities, the following variation inequality satisfy at least one $x^b \in k_b$

Box 5. Equation 24

$$k_b = \left\{ \begin{matrix} \left(M_1^b, N_1^b, \lambda_j^b, W_1^b, M_2^b, N_2^b, \lambda_{j'}^b, W_2^b \right) \mid 0 \leq M_1^b \leq b_1, 0 \leq M_2^b \leq b_2, 0 \leq \lambda_j^b \leq b_3 \\ 0 \leq W_1^b \leq b_4, 0 \leq M_2^b \leq b_5, 0 \leq N_2^b \leq b_6, 0 \leq \lambda_{j'}^b \leq b_7, 0 \leq W_2^b \leq b_8 \end{matrix} \right\} \tag{24}$$

$$\left\langle F\left(x^b\right), x - x^b \right\rangle \geq 0 \qquad (25)$$

From the above Theorem 2, choose $b_1, b_2, b_3, b_4, b_5, b_6, b_7$ and b_8, and let variation inequality (25) satisfying constraint (23). Thus there exists one solution to satisfy the inequality (16) and (22).

Theorem 3: *Existence.* Suppose that there are positive constraints, $V, S, T \;\; (T > 0)$, so

$$\frac{\partial F_{ih}\left(s_i^*\right)}{\partial s_{ij}} + \frac{\partial T_{ijh}\left(s_{ij}^*\right)}{\partial s_{ij}} \geq V$$

$$\forall M_1$$

and

$$s_{ij} \geq S\left(\forall i, j\right) \qquad (26)$$

$$\frac{\partial T_{jrh}\left(s_{jr}^*\right)}{\partial s_{jr}} \geq V$$

$$\forall N_1$$

and

$$s_{jr} \geq S\left(\forall j, r\right) \qquad (27)$$

$$q_r\left(W_r\right) \leq S$$

$$\forall W_r$$

and

$$w_r > T\left(\forall r\right) \qquad (28)$$

$$\frac{\partial F_{i'h}\left(s_{i'}^*\right)}{\partial s_{i'j'}} + \frac{\partial T_{i'j'h}\left(s_{i'j'}^*\right)}{\partial s_{i'j'}} \geq V$$

$$\forall M_2$$

and

$$s_{i'j'} \geq S\left(\forall i', j'\right) \qquad (29)$$

$$\frac{\partial T_{j'r'h}\left(s_{j'r'}^*\right)}{\partial s_{j'r'}} \geq V$$

$$\forall N_2$$

and

$$s_{j'r'} \geq S\left(\forall j', r'\right) \qquad (30)$$

$$\frac{\partial L_{j'h}\left(s_{j'}^*\right)}{\partial s_{j'}} \geq V$$

$$\forall C_2$$

and

$$s_{j'} \geq S\left(\forall j'\right) \qquad (31)$$

$$w_{r'}\left(W_{r'}\right) \leq S$$

$$\forall W_{r'}$$

and

$$w_{r'} \geq T\left(\forall j'\right) \qquad (32)$$

Therefore, variation inequality (16) exists at least one solution satisfying Formula (14).

Lemma 1: *Monotonicity.* Assume that $F_{ih}\left(s_i\right)$, $T_{ij}\left(s_{ij}\right)$, $T_{jr}\left(s_{jr}\right)$, $F_{i'h}\left(s_{i'}\right)$, $T_{i'j'}\left(s_{i'j'}\right)$, $T_{j'r'}\left(s_{j'r'}\right)$ or $C_{j'}\left(s_{j'}\right)$ functions for all i,j,r,i',j' are convex, the functions $w_r\left(W_r\right)$, $w_{r'}\left(W_{r'}\right)$ are decrease in variable k, vector of function F in variation inequality (18) is monotone, therefore,

$$\left\langle F\left(x\right)-F\left(x'\right),x-x'\right\rangle \geq 0$$

$$\forall x,x' \in k \qquad (33)$$

Lemma 2: *Strict monotonicity.* Suppose that $F_{ih}\left(s_i\right)$, $T_{ij}\left(s_{ij}\right)$, $T_{jr}\left(s_{jr}\right)$, $F_{i'h}\left(s_{i'}\right)$, $T_{i'j'}\left(s_{i'j'}\right)$, $T_{j'r'}\left(s_{j'r'}\right)$ or $C_{j'}\left(s_{j'}\right)$ functions for all i,j,r,i',j' are convex, functions $w_r\left(W_r\right)$, $w_{r'}\left(W_{r'}\right)$ decrease in k, vector of function F on variation in inequality (18) (related to M_1,N_1,P_1,M_2,N_2,P_2) is monotone, and

$$(M_1,N_1,P_1,M_2,N_2,P_2) \neq (M_1',N_1',P_1',M_2',N_2',P'),$$

therefore

$$\left\langle F\left(x\right)-F\left(x'\right),x-x'\right\rangle > 0 \qquad (34)$$

Lemma 3: *L-ipschitz continuity.* Suppose that $F_{ih}\left(s_i\right)$, $T_{ij}\left(s_{ij}\right)$, $T_{jr}\left(s_{jr}\right)$, $F_{i'h}\left(s_{i'}\right)$, $T_{i'j'}\left(s_{i'j'}\right)$, $T_{j'r'}\left(s_{j'r'}\right)$ or $C_{j'}\left(s_{j'}\right)$ functions for all i,j,r,i',j' are convex, functions $w_r\left(W_r\right)$, $w_{r'}\left(W_{r'}\right)$ decrease in k, vector of function F in variation inequality (18) is L-ipschitz continuous, therefore

$$\left\| F\left(x\right)-F\left(x'\right)\right\| \leq L\left\| x-x'\right\| \ \forall x,x' \in k, \text{ where } L > 0. \qquad (35)$$

5. MODEL ALGORITHM

In order to obtain the solution to variation inequality (17) and (21), Euler method could be introduced to calculate, three steps are as follows:

Step 1: *Initialization.* Let $\tau = 1$ (τ is the number of iterations), set $\left(M^0,N^0,\lambda_j^0,W^0,\right) \in k$, Sequence $\left\{a_\tau\right\}$ satisfy: $\sum_{\tau=0}^{\infty} a_\tau = \infty, a_\tau > 0$, $a_\tau \to 0$, as $\tau \to \infty$.

Step 2: *Structure and Calculation.* Let $\left(M^\tau,N^\tau,\lambda^\tau\right) \in k$, calculate sub-problems of the following Variation (See Box 6).

Step 3: *Convergence Verification.* If

$$\left| s_{ij}^\tau - s_{ij}^{\tau-1}\right| \leq \varepsilon,$$

$$\left| s_{jr}^\tau - s_{jr}^{\tau-1}\right| \leq \varepsilon,$$

$$\left| \lambda_j^\tau - \lambda_j^{\tau-1}\right| \leq \varepsilon,$$

$$\left| w_r^\tau - w_r^{\tau-1}\right| \leq \varepsilon,$$

$$\left| s_{i'j'}^\tau - s_{i'j'}^{\tau-1}\right| \leq \varepsilon,$$

$$\left| s_{j'r'}^\tau - s_{j'r'}^{\tau-1}\right| \leq \varepsilon, \left| \lambda_j^\tau - \lambda_j^{\tau-1}\right| \leq \varepsilon, \left| w_{r'}^\tau - w_{r'}^{\tau-1}\right| \leq \varepsilon,$$

$$\left| s_{i'j'}^\tau - s_{i'j'}^{\tau-1}\right| \leq \varepsilon,$$

$$\left| s_{j'r'}^\tau - s_{j'r'}^{\tau-1}\right| \leq \varepsilon,$$

Box 6. Step 2

$$\sum_I \sum_J \left[s_{ij}^\tau - \alpha_\tau \left(\frac{\partial F_{ih}\left(s_i^\tau\right)}{\partial s_{ij}} + \frac{\partial T_{ijh}\left(s_{ij}^\tau\right)}{\partial s_{ij}} - \lambda_j^\tau \right) \right] \cdot \left(s_{ij}^{1,\tau} - s_{ij}^{1,\tau-1} \right) + \sum_J \sum_R \left[s_{jr}^{1,\tau} - \alpha_\tau \left(\frac{\partial T_{jrh}\left(s_{jr}^{1,\tau}\right)}{\partial s_{jr}^1} + \lambda_j^\tau - w_{jh}^\tau \right) \right] \cdot \left(s_{jr}^\tau - s_{jr}^{\tau-1} \right)$$

$$+ \sum_J \left[\lambda_j^\tau - \alpha_T \left(\sum_I s_{ij}^\tau - \sum_R s_{jr}^\tau \right) \right] \cdot \left(\lambda_j^\tau - \lambda_j^{\tau-1} \right) + \sum_{I'} \sum_{J'} \sum_H \left[s_{i'j'}^{2,\tau} - \alpha_\tau \left(\frac{\partial f_{i'h}\left(s_{i'}^{2,\tau}\right)}{\partial s_{i'j'}^2} + \frac{\partial T_{i'j'h}\left(s_{i'j'}^\tau\right)}{\partial s_{i'j'}} - \lambda_{j'}^\tau \right) \right] \cdot \left(s_{i'j'}^\tau - s_{i'j'}^{\tau-1} \right) \cdot e_{i'j'h}$$

$$+ \sum_{J'} \sum_{R'} \sum_H \left[s_{j'r'}^\tau - \alpha_\tau \left(\frac{\partial T_{j'r'h}\left(s_{j'r'}^\tau\right)}{\partial s_{j'r'}} + \lambda_{j'}^\tau - w_{j'h}^\tau \right) \right] \cdot \left(s_{j'r'}^{2,\tau} - s_{j'r'}^{2,\tau-1} \right) \cdot e_{j'rh} + \sum_{J'} \left[\lambda_{j'}^{2,\tau} - \alpha_\tau \left(\sum_{I'} s_{i'j'}^{2,\tau} - \sum_K s_{j'k}^{2,\tau} \right) \right] \cdot \left(\lambda_{j'}^\tau - \lambda_{j'}^{\tau-1} \right)$$

$$+ \sum_{J'} \sum_H \left[s_{j'}^\tau - \alpha_\tau \cdot \frac{\partial L_{j'h}\left(s_{j'}^\tau\right)}{\partial s_{j'}} \right] \cdot \left(s_{j'}^\tau - s_{j'}^{\tau-1} \right) \geq 0$$

$$\sum_I \sum_J \sum_h \left[s_{ij}^\tau - a_\tau \left(\frac{\partial F_{ih}\left(s_i^{\tau-1}\right)}{\partial s_{ij}} + \frac{\partial T_{ijh}\left(s_{ij}^{\tau-1}\right)}{\partial s_{ij}} - \lambda_j^{\tau-1} + p_{ij}^{1,\tau-1} \right) \right] \cdot \left(s_{ij}^\tau - s_{ij}^{\tau-1} \right) \cdot e_{ijh}$$

$$+ \sum_J \sum_R \sum_H \left[s_{jr}^\tau - a_\tau \left(\frac{\partial T_{jrh}\left(s_{jr}^{\tau-1}\right)}{\partial s_{jr}} + \lambda_j^{\tau-1} \right) \right] \cdot \left(s_{jr}^\tau - s_{jr}^{\tau-1} \right) \cdot e_{jrh} + \sum_J \left[\lambda_j^\tau - \alpha_\tau \left(\sum_I s_{ij}^{\tau-1} - \sum_R s_{jr}^{\tau-1} \right) \right] \cdot \left(\lambda_j^\tau - \lambda_j^{\tau-1} \right) \geq 0$$

$$\left| \lambda_{j'}^\tau - \lambda_{j'}^{\tau-1} \right| \leq \varepsilon,$$

for all

$$i, j, k, i', j'$$

satisfy $\varepsilon > 0$,

then stop; otherwise, set $\tau = \tau + 1$, and go back to step 2.

6. EXAMPLES AND ANALYSIS

6.1. The Analysis of the First Stage

Assume that no matter global supply chain or local supply chain, each is composed of two manufacturers, two distributors, two retailers in the industrial cluster market. Enterprises along two chains try to get market share and compete with one another through production quantity and sale price. We solve the problem by using the algorithm proposed in this paper combined with scientific computing software MATLAB

programming. Table 1 presents the function of revenue and cost for two types of supply chain at the same period. Table 2 illustrates the number of goods at nodes of manufacturers, distributors and retailers. Table 3 is the result of competitive equilibrium.

According to the demand function given, we set that consumer satisfaction and technological progress index are (0.8,0.9)and(0.6,1.2)for two types of supply chains respectively, and the demands for different supply chain network are

$$q_r\left(w_r\right) = 5000 + \left(\alpha\right) \times w_r - \left(\beta - \alpha\right) w_{r'}$$

6.2. Analysis of the Second Phase

Considering the multi-national company have melted into cluster supply chain network structure after the competition. For the effect of technology diffusion, their competencies tend to homogeneity, the gap is narrowing, market conditions and the equilibrium price is most likely to be the same at the second phase. Therefore, there exists the following functional relation:

Table 1. Revenue and cost function for SCN

	Local supply chain	Global supply chain
Revenue	$w_r \cdot S_{jr}$	$w_{r'} \cdot S_{j'r'}$
Production cost	$(0.15) \cdot (S_{ij})^2 + (0.15) \cdot S_{ij}$	$(0.1) \cdot (S_{i'j'})^2 + (0.3) \cdot S_{i'j'}$
Distribution cost	$(0.1) \cdot (S_{ij})^2 - (0.1) \cdot S_{ij}$	$(0.1) \cdot (S_{i'j'})^2 - (0.25) \cdot S_{i'j'}$
Retail cost	$(0.05) \cdot (S_{jr})^2 - (0.15) \cdot S_{jr}$	$(0.05) \cdot (S_{j'r'})^2 - (0.2) \cdot S_{j'r'}$
Entry cost	——	$(0.1) \cdot (S_{i'j'})^2 + (0.15) \cdot S_{i'j'}$

Table 2. Flow of goods

	Flow 1	Flow 2
Manufacturer	s_1	s_2
Distributors	$s_1 = s_{11} + s_{12}$	$s_2 = s_{21} + s_{22}$
Retailers	$s_{11} = s_{111} + s_{112}$	$s_{21} = s_{211} + s_{212}$
	$s_{12} = s_{121} + s_{122}$	$s_{22} = s_{221} + s_{222}$

Table 3. Equilibrium results of the first phase

	Equilibrium demand	Market price	Total profit
Local supply chain	7894.6	7499.5	21810727.2040
Global supply chain	6605.1	7762.5	22914313.8435

$$q_r(w_r) = 12000 + (\alpha) \times w_r - (\beta - \alpha) w_{r'}$$

The changes in network structure have taken place, which forces quantity and sale price to change, the market equilibrium conditions also varied accordingly, so we set that the consumer satisfaction and technological progress index for two types of chains are (0.7,1.8) and (0.7,1.9)

respectively. Goods quantity is presented in Table 2 and Table 4, and the result of integrated equilibrium is presented in Table 5.

In comparison of the results of two phases, we found that the whole cluster market demand expands and product price increase and the total profits improve at the same time after multi-national companies embedded into the cluster industries. From the perspective of customer satisfaction, the original local supply chain in the first phase had a higher customer satisfaction than the second phase, it reflects that local supply chain showed more advantage of adopting to the local market scenario than global supply chain; However, if multi-national corporations once passed the first phase and transited into the second phase, they will gradually more gain market recognition than had expected.

In the first phase of the competition, the initial local supply chain network took shape relatively earlier, and took a lead in production quantity, and had a higher market share; while global supply chain is strange with local cluster market setting and lacked of supports from related upstream and downstream firms, so global supply chain need more time to respond to the market, it is why global supply chain faced a disadvantage at the beginning of the first phase. On the other hand, global supply chain will soon be able to revert the unfavorable situation in the market, because they posses technological and capital merits.

In the second phase of the integration, due to technology diffusion effect among the whole industrial cluster, technology for all firm in two types of chains had improved, multi-national companies have gradually weakened the technological advantages, local supply chain gain improvement in this field to some degree, the two chains gradually melted into one network system as a whole from outside view, they showed more cooperative than competitive in the cluster market, for their total market share and gross profit expand than used to. For multinational companies, they enable to get more profit when embedded into the supply chain network; from the perspective of local enterprises, they are conducive to industry and regional development.

6.3. The Sensitive Analysis

1. Relationships between price, sale volume and profit

Figure 2 shows the relationships between selling price, sale volume and profit. It is obvious that profit is a linear proportional to demand, and downward parabola to sale price, it means that profit increases in sale price at first, to a certain

Table 4. Second phase of SCN revenue function

	Local supply chain	Global supply chain
Revenue	$w_r \cdot S_{jr}$	$w_{r'} \cdot S_{j'r'}$
Production cost	$(0.15) \cdot (S_{ij}^1)^2 + (0.25) \cdot S_{ij}^1$	$(0.18) \cdot (S_{i'j'}^2)^2 + (0.3) \cdot S_{i'j'}^2$
Distribution cost	$(0.15) \cdot (S_{ij}^1)^2 - (0.1) \cdot S_{ij}^1$	$(0.15) \cdot (S_{i'j'}^2)^2 - (0.25) \cdot S_{i'j'}^2$
Retail cost	$(0.1) \cdot (S_{jr}^1)^2 - (0.15) \cdot S_{jr}^1$	$(0.12) \cdot (S_{j'r}^2)^2 - (0.2) \cdot S_{j'r}^2$

Table 5. Equilibrium results of the second phase

	Equilibrium demand	Market price	Total profit
Local supply chain	7142.86	12142.86	66326569.39
Global supply chain	8357.16	12142.86	70050868.41

value, then profit decreases in sale price. Through calculation and analysis, profit is only price-related, the higher the sale price is, the greater the profit. However, in practice, the higher the price is the lower sale volume. The reason for this is that technological progress can reduce cost and meanwhile ensure profitability and maintain a certain sale volume.

Figure 3 shows the relationships between selling price, sale volume and profit. We can see, from Figure 3 that both sales price and customer satisfaction increase in profit. However, satisfaction will decrease when profit is more than 0.5, in other words, satisfaction improvement make profit to decline at this range. Because customer satisfaction is built under the assumption of economic being, the actual price is rising, so satisfaction enables profit to decline

In the light of the previous analysis, the process of multi-national companies embedded into the local supply chain, is also the process of a technology spillovers and improving satisfaction among the cluster region. Multi-nationals integration let global supply chain to enhance technological upgrade for local supply chain directly or indirectly, while global supply chain improves customer satisfaction, it is a win-win process. From the strategic perspective, in the first phase, local enterprises should fully take advantage of the chance of cooperation with multi-national enterprises and strengthen their competition to gain more profit; while the multi-national companies, should actively improve the localization level (chain integration) to lower costs, and maximize profit. In the second phase, for the two types of supply chain network have been integrated into supply chain network as a whole, all member of network adopt the same strategy to determine the maximum profit through the price and sale volume, while keeping the consumer satisfaction with the more high level.

2. Total profit under market equilibrium

Figure 2. Profits under influence of Technical

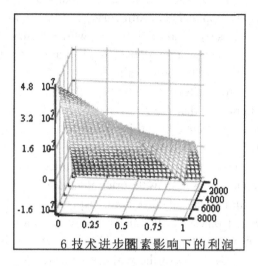

F

Figure 3. Profits under influence of Satisfaction

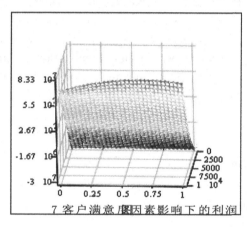

M

Assume that both technological progress and consumer satisfaction are fixed. Figures 4 and 5 show the relationship between the price and total profit under market equilibrium. Assume that customer satisfaction remains unchanged, it was found that profit is peak when the price is (9043.4783, 11304.3478) as shown in Figure 4. In the same way, when technological progress factor is constant, Figure 5 indicates that the price of (6588.2353, 8235.2941) guarantee profit maximization. On the other hand, marginal changes of global supply chain profit curve is more obvious than those of local supply chain, which illustrates the price impact on global supply chain is larger than the local supply chain.

In the light of the above conclusion, it gives insight into that the two types of chain need to adopt different competitive strategies in different two phases. At a certain customer satisfaction rate, companies need to increase investment in technology as to show the price advantage through technological advancement, especially in the second phase, it should pay more attention to improvements in technology. Therefore, when the equilibrium prices at the two phases are 11304.3478 and 9043.4783 respectively, the profits for both chains are highest points. In addition, when the technological progress ratio is certain, companies need to improve customer satisfaction to maintain a higher sale level. Due to the characteristics of two different types of chains, local supply chain enjoy lower cost through localization, while global supply chain enjoy technology and capital by cooperation with multi-national firms. So, it

Figure 4. Total equilibrium Profit under the Technical

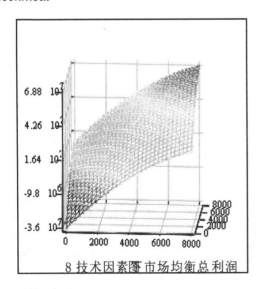

H

Figure 5. Total equilibrium Profit under the Satisfaction

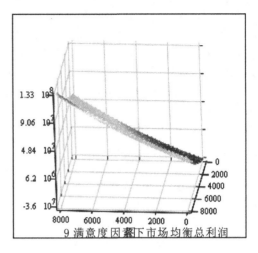

K

is wise for both chains to cooperate with each other at the first phases, and at the second phase, the policy of introducing sale volume to stabilize the equilibrium market price is the best way.

7. CONCLUSION AND FUTURE RESEARCH

Both huge market and perfect production system in China attract more and more multi-national company attention to invest in China in form of FDI. Therefore, the multi-national companies are willing to integrate and optimize global supply chain network of their own, which enable them to reduce cost and improve quick response to market. As a result, the multi-national companies usually embed into local industrial cluster through financial and technological comparative merits to sharpen their competitive edge. This paper considers the across-chain network equilibrium problem involving process of competition and melting between this new global chain and an already existing local chain. We model the optimizing behavior of these two chains, derive the equilibrium conditions, and establish the variational inequality formulation, and solve it using the modified algorithm. Finally, we illustrate the model through numerical example and discuss relationships among the price, quantity, technological progress and satisfaction among two dynamic phases.

It was found that the whole cluster market demand expanded and product price increase and the total profits improve at the same time after multi-national companies embedded into the cluster industries. From the perspective of customer satisfaction, the original local supply chain in the first phase had a higher customer satisfaction than the second phase, it reflects that local supply chain showed more advantage of adopting to the local market scenario than global supply chain; However, if multi-national corporations once passed the first phase and transited into the second phase, they will gradually more gain market recognition than had expected. In the light of the above conclusion, it gives insight into that the two types of chain need to adopt different competitive strategies in different two phases. In the first phase, local enterprises should take advantage of the chance of cooperation with multi-national enterprises and strengthen their competition; while the multi-national companies, should actively improve the localization level (chain integration) to lower costs, and maximize profit. In the second phase, for the two types of supply chain network have been integrated into supply chain network as a whole.

This work reveals some promising areas where one could place more efforts in the future. More sophisticated aspects in cluster supply chain management may be added into the model. For example, the item allocation proportion of vertical and horizontal cooperation may vary in tier of cluster supply chains instead of just only one. Cluster supply chains has many stakeholders involved and usually has more than one objective, thus multiple objectives could be applied into this framework.

ACKNOWLEDGMENT

The paper is supported by NSFC (61004120, 71171152), National Support Program (2011BAH21B01), The Educational Department Program of Hubei Province (T201111, D20111606), Wuhan Science & Technology Bureau Program (201141333462).

REFERENCES

Bergman, E. M., & Fester, E. J. (1999). *Industrial and regional clusters: Concepts and comparative applications*. Retrieved from http://www.rri.edu/Webbook/ Bergman- Fester

Bertsekas, D. P., & Tsitsiklis, J. N. (1989). *Parallel and distributed computation*. Upper Saddle River, NJ: Prentice Hall.

Boyaci, T., & Gallego, G. (2004). Supply chain coordination in a market with customer service competition. *Production and Operations Management, 13*(1), 3–22. doi:10.1111/j.1937-5956.2004.tb00141.x

Day, L., & Wensley, K. (1988). Manufacturer's revenue—sharing contract and retail competition. *European Journal of Operational Research, 186*(2), 637–651.

DeWitt, T., Giunipero, L. C., & Melton, H. L. (2006). Clusters and supply chain management: The Amish experience. *International Journal of Physical Distribution & Logistics Management, 36*(4), 289–308. doi:10.1108/09600030610672055

Dong, J., Zhang, D., & Nagurney, A. (2004). A supply chain network equilibrium model with random demand. *European Journal of Operational Research*, *56*(1), 194–212. doi:10.1016/S0377-2217(03)00023-7

Dong, J., Zhang, D., Yan, H., & Nagumey, A. (2005). Multi-tiered supply chain networks: multi-criteria decision making under uncertainty. *Annals of Operations Research*, *135*, 155–178. doi:10.1007/s10479-005-6239-3

Gabay, D., & Moulin, H. (1980). On the uniqueness and stability of Nash equilibrium in noncooperative games. In Bensoussan, A., Kleindorfer, P., & Tapiero, C. S. (Eds.), *Applied control of econometrics and management science* (pp. 271–294). Amsterdam, The Netherlands: North-Holland.

Hoover, M. (1948). *The location of economic activity*. Columbus, OH: Edgar Malone.

Li, J., Xiong, N., Park, J. H., Liu, C., Ma, S., & Cho, S.-E. (2009). Intelligent model design of cluster supply chain with horizontal cooperation. *Journal of Intelligent Manufacturing*, *11*(8), 256–268.

Majumder, P., & Srinivasan, A. (2008). Leadership and competition in network supply chains. *Management Science*, *54*, 1189–1204. doi:10.1287/mnsc.1070.0752

Marshall, L. (1920). *The principles of economics* (8th ed.). London, UK: Macmillan.

Mentzer, J. T., DeWitt, W., Keebler, J. S., Nix, N. W., Smith, C. D., & Zacharia, Z. G. (2001). Defining supply chain management. *Journal of Business Logistics*, *22*(2), 1–25. doi:10.1002/j.2158-1592.2001.tb00001.x

Nagurney, A. (1999). *Network economics: a variational inequality approach* (2nd ed.). Boston, MA: Kluwer Academic.

Nagurney, A., Dong, J., & Zhang, D. (2002). A supply chain network equilibrium model. *Transportation Research Part E, Logistics and Transportation Review*, *38*(5), 281–305. doi:10.1016/S1366-5545(01)00020-5

Porter, M. E. (1998). Clusters and the new economics of competition. *Harvard Business Review*, 77–90.

Weber, A. (1929). *Theory of the location of industries*. Chicago, IL: The University of Chicago Press.

Wu, L., Yue, X., & Sim, T. (2006). Supply clusters: a key to China's cost advantage. *Supply Chain Management Review*, 46-51.

Xiao, T., & Yang, D. (2008). Price and service competition of supply chains with risk-averse retailers under demand uncertainty. *International Journal of Production Economics*, *114*(1), 187–200. doi:10.1016/j.ijpe.2008.01.006

Zhang, D., & Dong, J. (2003). A supply chain network economy: modeling and qualitative analysis. In Nagumey, A. (Ed.), *Innovations in financial and economic networks*. Northampton, MA: Edward Elgar.

This work was previously published in the International Journal of Advanced Pervasive and Ubiquitous Computing, Volume 3, Issue 4, edited by Tao Gao, pp. 30-49, copyright 2011 by IGI Publishing (an imprint of IGI Global).

Chapter 27
Comprehensive Structure of Novel Voice Priority Queue Scheduling System Model for VoIP over WLANs

Kashif Nisar
CAS—Universiti Utara Malaysia, Malaysia

Angela Amphawan
University of Oxford, UK, & Universiti Utara Malaysia, Malaysia

Suhaidi B. Hassan
Universiti Utara Malaysia, Malaysia

ABSTRACT

Voice over Internet Protocol (VoIP) has grown quickly in the world of telecommunication. Wireless Local Area Networks (WLANs) are the most performance assuring technology for wireless networks, and WLANs have facilitated high-rate voice services at low cost and good flexibility. In a voice conversation, each client works as a sender or a receiver depending on the direction of traffic flow over the network. A VoIP application requires high throughput, low packet loss, and a high fairness index over the network. The packets of VoIP streaming may experience drops because of the competition among the different kinds of traffic flow over the network. A VoIP application is also sensitive to delay and requires the voice packets to arrive on time from the sender to the receiver side without any delay over WLAN. The scheduling system model for VoIP traffic is an unresolved problem. The objectives of this paper are to identify scheduler issues. This comprehensive structure of Novel Voice Priority Queue (VPQ) scheduling system model for VoIP over WLAN discusses the essential background of the VPQ schedulers and algorithms. This paper also identifies the importance of the scheduling techniques over WLANs.

DOI: 10.4018/978-1-4666-2645-4.ch027

1. INTRODUCTION

The scheduling system model plays a major role in the Voice over IP (VoIP) over Wireless LANs (WLANs). It fulfills the Quality of Service (QoS) requirements of the VoIP over WLAN through the scheduler, efficient algorithms and managing traffic flow. The VoIP over WLAN is another emerging application besides the Internet Protocol TV (IPTV) and the High Performance-Video Conferencing (HP-VC). This paper presents a new VoIP scheduling system model and algorithm in order to enhance performance of voice traffic over WLANs. The scheduling system model is an important technique to achieve efficient throughput and fairness over WLANs based on IEEE 802.11 standards (Lee, Claypool, & Kinicki, 2010; Wang & Zhuang, 2008). Scheduling techniques manage voice traffic over WLANs. It will be able to offer bandwidth link-sharing to tolerate the status of changing traffic queues and to be scalable over IP-based networks. A number of related schedulers have been proposed to support traffic flow over IP-based networks. Most of the existing schedulers support limited services and do not meet the requirements of real-time applications especially for the VoIP over WLANs.

The bottleneck of the scheduling mechanism is the downlink path and uplink path of traffic flow over WLANs. In the scheduling mechanism, the downlink path is comparatively easy due to the Access Point (AP) having complete information regarding traffic flow. As far as the uplink path is concerned, traffic flow comes from Stations (STA) which makes it difficult due to diverse techniques, procedures, parameters and traffic flow over networks (Ansel, Ni, & Turletti, 2006).

The IEEE 802.11 WLAN network is a wireless Ethernet, play an important function in the future-generation networks. WLAN is based on Link Layer (LL). LL is divided into Logical Link Control (LLC) and Medium Access Control (MAC) sub-layer categorizes with two functions, Distributed Coordination Function (DCF) and Point Coordination Function (PCF) (Mirkovic, Orfanos, Reumerman, & Denteneer, 2006; Wang & Wei, 2009). The IEEE 802.11 WLAN networks support both contention-based DCF and contention-free PCF functions. DCF uses Carrier Sensing Multiple Access/Collision Avoidance (CSMA/CA) as the access method (Cao, Li, & Leith, 2009; Dini, Font-Bach, & Mangues-Bafalluy, 2008; Li,Ni, Turletti, & Xiao, 2006; Ni, Li, Turletti, & Xiao, 2005; Garg & Kappes, 2003; Hole & Tobagi, 2004; Cai, Shen, Mark, Cai, & Xiao, 2006; Deng & Yen, 2005; Ergen, Lee, Sengupta, & Varaiya, 2004; Deng, Ke, Chen, & Huang, 2008; Wang, Liew, & Li, 2005; Tickoo & Sikdar, 2004). IEEE 802.11 standards 802.11a support 5GHz frequency band and 54Mbps data rate, 802.11b support 2.4GHz frequency and 11Mpbs data rate, 802.11g support 2.4GHz frequency band and data rate 54Mbps (Ahmed, Jiang, Ho, & Horiguchi, 2009; Forouzan, 2007; Ni, Romdhani, & Turletti, 2004; Wu, Peng, Long, Cheng, & Ma, 2002; Li, Ni, Turletti, & Xiao, 2006; Ni, Romdhani, Turletti, & Aad, 2002; Xiao & Rosdahl, 2002; Garg & Kappes, 2004; Chen, Pang, Sheu, & Tseng, 2005).

2. PROPOSED VOIP SCHEDULER

A number of traffic scheduling system models has been introduced to enhance traffic flow over WLANs. Since in the WLAN, the VoIP Flow (VF) and Non-VoIP Flow (NVF) traffic flows are sharing the same transmission media, therefore, there must be a traffic scheduling system model to differentiate between the flows so that they can be successfully transmitted to the proper destination. In order to achieve QoS capability, the standard describes a number of parameters like traffic flow techniques, bandwidth request technique and channelizing for traffic flow. As studied, these standards have limited QoS skills over WLANs. As have come to realize, utilizing a traffic scheduling algorithm is a way to enhance performance of the VoIP over WLANs; therefore, a new scheduling algorithm is necessary to improve the VoIP flow over networks (Maheshwari, 2006).

When multiple traffic flows are sharing a common transmission link, there must be a traffic scheduler to make a decision and be accountable for improving the traffic source share to the individual traffic flows (Wang, 2001). New VoIP traffic schedulers propose for WLANs that provides the traffic flow with intelligence on WLANs. The proposed scheduler assigns priority to the VF traffic in order to meet the performance requirements. Furthermore, the scheduler provides a traffic flow performance technique to allocate the Priority Queue (PQ) for VF traffic over IP-based networks.

In this research paper, propose a new Voice Priority Queue (VPQ) scheduling system model and algorithms. The different traffic flows arrive at the Access Point (AP) and combine with the VF and NVF flows over WLANs. Furthermore, the VPQ classifies the VF and NVF traffic flows for specific proposes for the VoIP traffic flow over WLANs using IEEE 802.11 standards. The proposed VPQ system model is unique as compared to most of the existing schedulers. The details of the system model will be presented in the following section.

3. VOICE PRIORITY QUEUE SYSTEM MODEL

The designing of the scheduling system model is challenging due to the diverse QoS requirements such as throughput and fairness. VoIP traffic scheduling is the sharing of a transmission link among a number of wired and wireless mobile nodes over WLANs using IEEE 802.11 standards. However, because of variation and contention in the set of different traffic flows in each group, it cannot provide maximum fairness guarantees. A

methodology present for the VoIP traffic scheduler and algorithm for WLANs using IEEE 802.11 standards and apply this methodology to derive a new algorithm based on classification and Priority Queue (PQ) management.

New VoIP traffic scheduling system model, scheduler and algorithms: the Voice VPQ scheduler for IP-based networks. The VPQ provides bidirectional voice traffic communication over uplink and downlink connections. It can make an end-to-end guarantee of delay to a session of the best-effort traffic and classify the traffic flow into the VF and NVF. The VPQ has pre-packet delay bounds and provides both bounded delay and fairness over WLANs using IEEE 802.11 standards. The VPQ concurrently provides both throughput and fairness. It also provides throughput guarantees for error-free flows, long term fairness for error-free flows. The VPQ provides Fair Queueing (FQ) in the VF and NVF over IP-based networks. The main rule of FQ is the output bandwidth fair-sharing among multiple queues over WLANs. Further progress has been fulfilled towards noticing a low delay explanation by appropriating the VPQ system model over WLANs. In the VPQ, it differentiate the VF packets based on packet size.

3.1. First Stage of VPQ System Model

The first stage of the Voice Priority Queue (VPQ) system model propose and initial operations. The VPQ is based on some special components, initialization of traffic, classification of enqueue traffic flow, VoIP Flow (VF) and Non-VoIP Flow (NVF), Traffic Shaping (TS) and Token Bucket (TB), Voice Priority Queue (VPQ) Scheduler, VoIP Flow Buffer (VFB), Non-VoIP Flow Buffer (Non-VFB) and dequeue traffic flow for the end user over WLANs using IEEE 802.11 standards. It will describe in detail these components in this research paper. Figure 1 articulates the working of the VPQ scheduling system model.

Figure 1. First stage of the VPQ system model

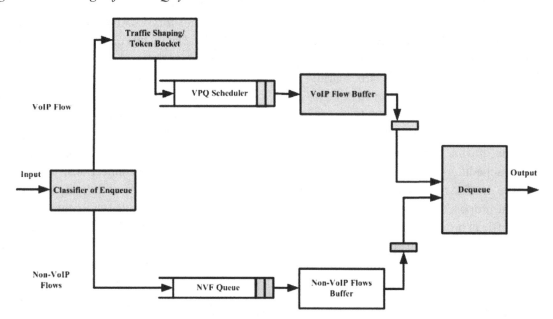

In Figure 1, classification of enqueue traffic flow is sorted-based and the index of the incoming packet is checked. The classification model supports a mechanism that works like Differentiated Services (DiffServ) (Nichols & Carpenter, 2001). After classification, the traffic enqueue sends the VF traffic to the shaping and Token Bucket (TB) flow. The shaping controls the amount of flow and flows sent to the TB flow. The TB applies bursty traffic as the regulated maximum rate of the traffic over WLANs using IEEE 802.11 standards. Then the VF moves ahead to the main VPQ scheduler flow. The VPQ scheduler forwards these packets into the VoIP Flow Buffer (VFB). The VFB is a temporary buffer flow for VF and NVF traffic. Lastly, the VPQ flow dequeues the traffic flows and sends them to their destinations.

3.1.1. Voice Priority Queue Scheduler

To resolve the related work drawbacks, introduce a Voice Priority Queue (VPQ) scheduler that provides the priority to the VoIP Flow (VF) over IP-based networks. It has two types of traffic flow, the Actual-VoIP Flow (Actual-VF) and Virtual-

VoIP Flow (Virtual-VF) over WLANs using IEEE 802.11 standards. Figure 2 depicts the simplified model of the proposed VPQ scheduler.

Firstly, packets arrive in the Actual-VF traffic, then the traffic is passed through the dequeue to the end user. Meanwhile, the VPQ receives more bursty traffic due to peak time flow and the VPQ scheduler proposes the Virtual-VF for heavy bursty traffic flow.

Furthermore, a new VPQ scheduler will provide high-speed traffic flow for the VoIP traffic over networks. Scheduler will assign a guaranteed VF with fair scheduling. The VPQ is a scheduler that provides each flow a fair share of the network bandwidth over WLANs. It will resolve the fundamental problems of the VF queue management flow which applies only for the VF traffic. The proposed VPQ scheduler is packet-based with real-time traffic flow that will increase the throughput and fairness of the VF. When bursty traffic arrives then the VPQ will resolve this bursty traffic. The VPQ provides for the VF a constant bandwidth for a fair flow of IP-based traffic over WLANs. Furthermore, the details are as shown in Figure 3.

Figure 2. VPQ scheduler

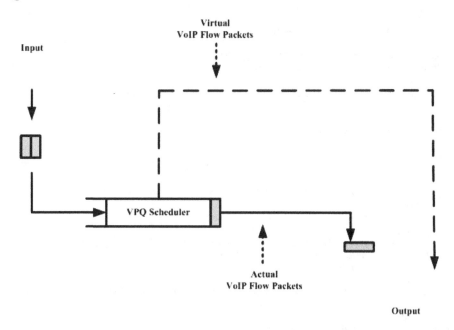

3.1.2. First Stage of the VPQ Scheduling Algorithm

In Figure 4, the first stage of the VPQ scheduling algorithm proposes to enqueue and dequeue the VF and NVF traffic flows over WLANs. Firstly, the VPQ scheduler initializes the traffic flows and sends them to the enqueue. Proposed classification component takes the traffic from the enqueue and classifies it into a VF and NVF traffic flow based on the nature of the traffic.

After classification of the traffic flow, the VF is sent to the Token Bucket (TB) and the Traffic Shaper (TS), and other NVF traffic is sent to one of the other numbers of queues over the network. The TB <= the VF is then sent to the VPQ scheduler component for traffic flow, and then the VPQ scheduler component <= the VoIP Flow Buffer (VFB) is sent to the VFB traffic flow. The same process works for the NVF traffic flow over the network. In the dequeue stage, the packet queue corresponds to different flows and the VFB <= the Dequeue Traffic Flow (DTF) is then sent to the DTF for all traffic flows. Finally, the traffic flows dequeue to the final destination.

Figure 3. Flow chart of the VPQ scheduler and first stage

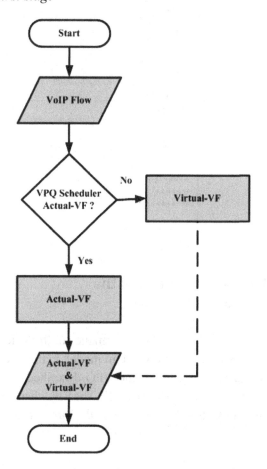

Figure 4. First stage of the VPQ scheduling algorithm

First Stage of the VPQ Scheduling Algorithm

Initialize Traffic Flows over WLANs: (ITF-WLANs)
(Invoke When the VPQ Scheduler is Initialized over WLANs)
Traffic Flow Arrives
On the arrival of the traffic flow Packets (pkt), the *VF and NVF Traffic Flows to the VPQ**
Traffic flow = 0;
Classification (c) = the VF and NVF; **
for (pkt = 0; pkt < n; pkt = pkt + 1)
        pkt = 0;
 Enqueue:
(Invoke When Packet Arrives Inside to Enqueue for the Classification of Traffic Flows)
    If (Classification (c) = the VoIP Flow (VF)) then***
            send the VoIP Flow (VF) to the token bucket (TB) & Traffic Shaper (TS); ****
      Else
            send the Non-VoIP Flow (NVF) to the Queue 1.....N; *****
      End if;
            on arrival of the VoIP Flow(VF) to the token bucket
    If (The token bucket size (pkt) < = the VoIP Flow (VF)) then
            send to the VPQ scheduler for the VoIP Flows (VF);
      End If;
    If (The VPQ scheduler for the VoIP < = the VoIP Flo Buffer (VFB)) then******
            send to the VoIP Flow Buffer (VFB);
      End if;
            on arrival of the Non-VoIP Flows to the Queue 1.....N
    If (The Non-VoIP Flow < = the Non-VoIP Flow Buffer (Non-VFB)) then*******
            send to the Non-VoIP Flow Buffer (Non-VFB);
      End if;
Dequeue:
(Invoke the Packet (pkt) Queue Corresponding to a Different Flow)
    If (The VoIP Flow Buffer (VFB)) < = the Dequeue Traffic Flows (DTF)) then********
            send to the Dequeue Traffic Flow (DTF)Processor;
      End if;
    If (The Priority Queue for the VoIP finishes (VF) and (NVF)) then
            Again go to the Initial Traffic Flow;
      End if;

Notations
*VPQ = Voice Priority Queue Scheduler
**Classification (c) = VF and NVF
*** VF = VoIP Flow
****TB & TS = Token Bucket (TB) & TS =Traffic Shaper (TS)
*****NVF = Non-VoIP Flow
 ******VFB = VoIP Flow Buffer
*******Non-VFB = Non- VoIP Flow Buffer
********DTF = Dequeue Traffic Flow

3.2. Second Stage of the VPQ System Model

In order to enhance the performance of the Voice Priority Queue (VPQ) system model, in this section, a second stage of the VPQ described as a Virtual-VoIP Flow (Virtual-VF). The VPQ changes into the Virtual-VF mode once the bursty traffic arrives in the VoIP Flow (VF) over WLANs. To provide continuous VF, the Virtual-VF component for peak time bursty traffic flow over the network. This Virtual-VF shows that system model meets the requirements for bursty and Non-Bursty (NB) traffic flow over WLANs using IEEE 802.11 standards.

In Figure 5, the Virtual-VF for bursty traffic flow that directly starts from the VPQ scheduler and the dequeueing of the end user traffic flows. To achieve long term fairness, a Virtual-VF is compulsory over IP-based networks and especially for the VF traffic over WLANs.

In order to support better QoS requirements of the VoIP traffic, the Virtual-VF fulfills the needs of the traffic flow in the bursty environment. The VoIP is a delay-sensitive application for Next Generation Networks (NGNs). The VoIP has the full prospect of replacing the traditional telephonic system and the VoIP flow is a high priority traffic flow over WLANs. It performs the Virtual-VF to meet the real-time traffic flow requirements.

In second stage, propose the system model for bursty traffic flow over WLANs. As discussed in the first stage, with normal traffic flow there is no need for the Virtual-VF but the VoIP is a real-time traffic flow that is why need to introduce the Virtual-VF flow to the most efficient traffic system

model such as the VPQ over IP-based networks. The performances of the scheduling algorithms of related work under bursty traffic flow were studied. It applied the Virtual-VF mechanism to generate the voice packets to be safely dequeued to the final destination. For fairness, it assume that the Virtual-VF mechanism applied to the Access Point (AP) has accurate information regarding each node over WLANs using IEEE 802.11 standards. In the following, there will be a detailed discussion about the VPQ traffic scheduler used in the proposed method. Furthermore, the details are as shown in Figure 6.

3.2.1. Second Stage of the VPQ Scheduling Algorithm

Figure 7 presents the second stage of the VPQ scheduling algorithm to enqueue and dequeue the VF traffic flow in a bursty environment over WLANs. The second stage of the VPQ schedul-

Figure 5. Second stage of the VPQ system model

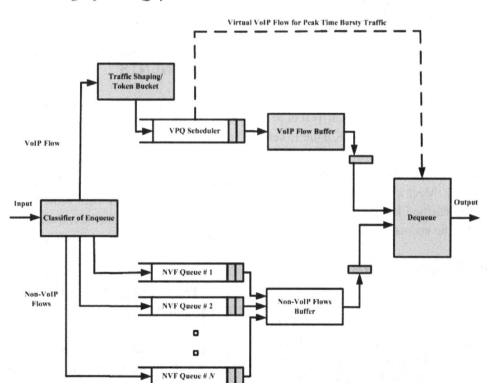

Figure 6. Second stage of the VPQ flow chart

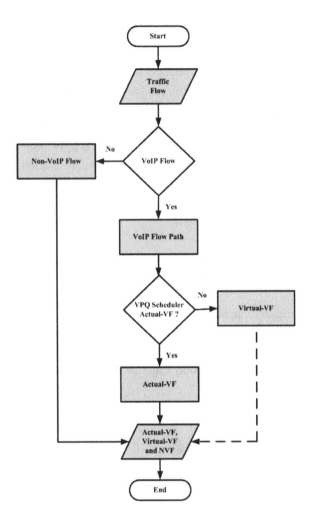

ing algorithm works as follows: On arrival of the traffic flow to the VF and Virtual-VF, if the Token Bucket (TB) size of packet (pkt) = > the VF then send to the Virtual-VF component for bursty traffic over the network. Meanwhile, if the Virtual-VF < = the Dequeue Traffic Flow (DTF) then proceed to dequeue for the end user.

3.3. Third Stage of the VPQ System Model

A third stage of the Voice Priority Queue (VPQ) system model propose over a WLAN. It also provides a switch that moves to the VoIP Flow (VF) from the Non-VoIP Flow (NVF) when the

NVF flows are empty due to non-real-time traffic over the network.

In Figure 8, the switch mechanism proposes more fairness in the VF traffic over WLANs using IEEE 802.11 standards. This switch controls the bursty traffic flow at the peak time. It provides a key technique proposed by VPQ scheduler. The key technique shows the high priority and low priority queue management system over IP-based networks. Furthermore, the details are as shown in Figure 9.

3.3.1. Third Stage of the VPQ Scheduling Algorithm

In Figure 10, the third stage of the VPQ scheduling algorithm proposes to enhance the performance of the VoIP over WLANs. Firstly, initialize the Switch Movement (SM) to the VoIP Flow (VF) for bursty traffic over the network.

The SM allocates the Non-VoIP Flow (NVF) bandwidth to the VF when the NVF buffer is empty. This will further enhance the performance of the VoIP over WLANs.

4. VOICE PRIORITY QUEUE COMPONENTS

The Voice Priority Queue (VPQ) has the following components: the VPQ traffic initialization, the traffic flow classifier, the VoIP Flow (VF) and Non-VoIP Flow (NVF), Traffic Shaping (TS), the Token Bucket (TB), VPQ Scheduler, the VoIP-Flow buffer, the Non-VoIP Flow Buffer and the dequeue traffic flow for the end user over WLANs using IEEE 802.11 standards. These components are discussed in detail below.

4.1. Traffic Classifier of Enqueue Component

The traffic classifier works once the traffic is initialized. They are classifying traffic flows based on the traffic flow id of the incoming packet in

Figure 7. Second stage of the VPQ scheduling algorithm

```
Second Stage of the  Voice Priority Queue (VPQ) Scheduling Algorithm

Initialize The Virtual-VoIP Flow (Virtual-VF) for Bursty Traffic*
(Invoke When the VPQ Scheduler is Initialized for the Virtual-VF)
On the arrival of the traffic flow Packet (pkt) the Virtual-VF to the VPQ
Traffic flow = 0;
Classification (c) = the VF and NVF;**
the Virtual VoIP Flow =  the Virtual-VF
for (pkt = 0; pkt < n; pkt = pkt + 1)
        pkt = 0;


Enqueue:
(Invoke When the  Packet Arrives  for the VF and Virtual-VF)
    If (Classification (c) = the VoIP Flow (VF)) then***
            send the VoIP Flow (VF)  to the token bucket (TB) & Traffic Shaper (TS);****
        Else
            send the Non-VoIP Flow (NVF) to the Queue 1.....N;*****
        End if;
    If (The token bucket size (pkt) < = the VoIP Flow (VF)) then
            send to the VPQ scheduler for the VoIP Flow (VF);
        End If;
    If (The VPQ scheduler for the VoIP < = the VoIP Flow Buffer (VFB)) then******
            send to the VoIP Flow Buffer (VFB);
        End if;
            on arrival of the VoIP Flow(VF) to the token bucket
    If (The token bucket size (pkt) = > the VoIP Flow (VF)) then
            send to the Virtual-VoIP Flow (Virtual-VF)
    the Virtual-VF component for the VoIP Flow (VF) for Bursty Traffic over the Network;
        End if;


Dequeue:
(Invoke the Packet (pkt) flow to the Virtual-VF)
    If (The Virtual-VF < = the Dequeue Traffic Flow (DTF)) then******
            send to the Dequeue Traffic Flow (DTF)Processor;
        End if;
    If (The Virtual-VF and VF finish) then
            Again go to the Initial Traffic Flow;
        End if;
```

```
Notations
*Virtual-VF = Virtual VoIP Flow
**Classification (c) = VF and NVF
***VF = VoIP Flow
****TB & TS  = Token Bucket (TB) &  TS =Traffic Shaper (TS)
*****NVF = Non VoIP Flow
******DTF = Dequeue Traffic Flow
```

the enqueue component. The classification of the enqueue component to identify the multiple traffic flows over networks. The Voice Priority Queue (VPQ) divides the traffic flow in two; the two types of traffic flow are called VoIP Flow (VF) and Non-VoIP Flow (NVF) as shown in Figure 11. The classification is applied on the segment of the packet header.

The classification model supports a mechanism that works like Differentiated Services (DiffServ). The classification of the enqueue differentiates between the VF and NVF traffic flow over WLANs using IEEE 802.11 standards. Figure 12 shows the block diagram of the classifier model.

It classifies the packets into the VF and NVF and then forwards the packets to the next component for onward processing. It provides both Fair

Figure 8. Third stage of the VPQ system model

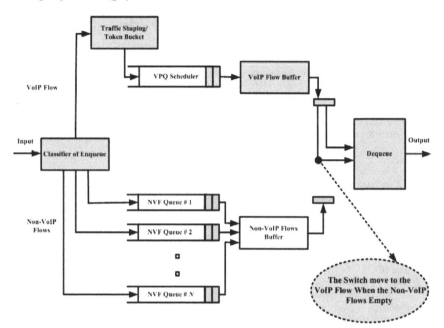

Figure 9. Third stage of the VPQ flow chart

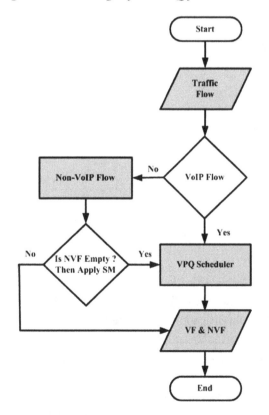

Queue (FQ) and strict priority (SP) queuing to the VF over WLANs using IEEE 802.11 standards. The classifier performs the following tasks: classification of the enqueue traffic into the VF and NVF and classification of the dequeue traffic.

4.1.1. VoIP-Flow and Non-VoIP-Flow Components

After classification of the traffic, it manages the VoIP Flow (VF) and Non-VoIP Flow (NVF) traffic in bursty and Non-bursty traffic over IP-based networks. The classifier sends the VF to Traffic Shaping (TS) and the Token Bucket (TB). Furthermore, the classifier sends the NVF traffic to a number of queues over WLANs using IEEE 802.11 standards. Figure 13 shows the block diagram of the enqueue and the dequeue of the VF and NVF traffic flow over IP-based networks.

It provides the algorithm that supports both the VF and NVF traffic in bursty and Non-Bursty (NV) traffic over IP-based networks.

Figure 10. Third stage of the VPQ scheduling algorithm

Third Stage of the VPQ Scheduling Algorithm

Initialize the Switch Movement (SM) to the VoIP Flow (VF) for Bursty Traffic*
(Invoke When the VPQ Scheduler is Initialized to Switch)
On the arrival of the traffic flow Packet (pkt) to the VPQ
Traffic flow = 0;
Classification (c) = the VF and NVF; **
Switch Movement = SM
for *(pkt = 0; pkt < n; pkt = pkt + 1)*
   pkt = 0;
Enqueue:
(Invoke When the Packet Arrives for the VF)
  If (Classification (c) = the VoIP Flow (VF)) **then*****
    send the VoIP Flow (VF) to the token bucket (TB) & Traffic Shaper (TS); ****
  End if;
  If (The token bucket size (pkt) < = the VoIP Flow (VF)) **then**
    send to the VPQ scheduler for the VoIP Flows (VF);
  End If;
  If (The VPQ scheduler for the VoIP < = the VoIP Flow Buffer (VFB)) **then********
    send to the VoIP Flow Buffer (VFB);
  End if;
  If (The Non-VoIP Flow (NVF) Empty to the Queue 1.....N) **then**
    The Switch moves to the VoIP Flow (VF);
  End If;
Dequeue:
(Invoke the Packet (pkt) flow to Switch Movement (SM))
  If (The Switch Movement < = the Dequeue Traffic Flow (DTF)) **then********
    send to the Dequeue Traffic Flow (DTF)Processor;
  End if;
  If (The VoIP Flow (VF) finishes) **then**
    Again go to the Initial Traffic Flow;
  End if;

Notations
*SM *= Switch Movement*
**Classification (c) *= VF and NVF*
***VF *= VoIP Flow*
****TB & TS *= Token Bucket (TB) & TS =Traffic Shaper (TS)*
*****NVF *= Non VoIP Flow*
******DTF *= Dequeue Traffic Flow*

4.2. Traffic Shaping and the Token Bucket Component

Traffic Shaping (TS) is a technique to enhance performance of a scheduler on a VoIP over WLANs. In this section, discuss TS and Token Bucket (TB) techniques that are applied to enhance the Quality of Service (QoS) of a new Voice Priority Queue (VPQ) scheduler. Traffic Shaping (TS) is a method that manages the amount and the rate of the VoIP Flow (VF) traffic that should be sent over the network. In Figure 14, the Traffic Shaping (TS) has introduced the TB technique over a WLAN and apply it to the VPQ scheduler.

The TB is applied to the VF in bursty traffic situations and regulates the traffic rate over WLANs. Furthermore, the token bucket process begins with a counter that starts from zero in the

Figure 11. Initialize traffic classifications as VF and NVF component

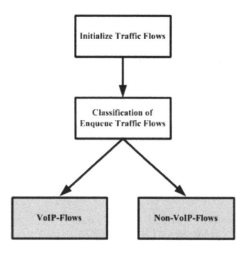

Figure 12. Traffic classifier of enqueue to dequeue traffic flow component

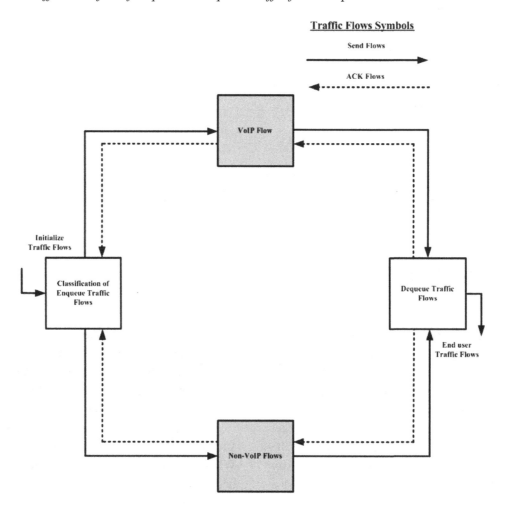

Figure 13. VF and NVF, enqueue to dequeue

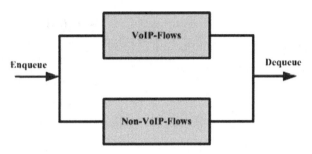

Figure 14. Process of the TB for the VoIP flow component

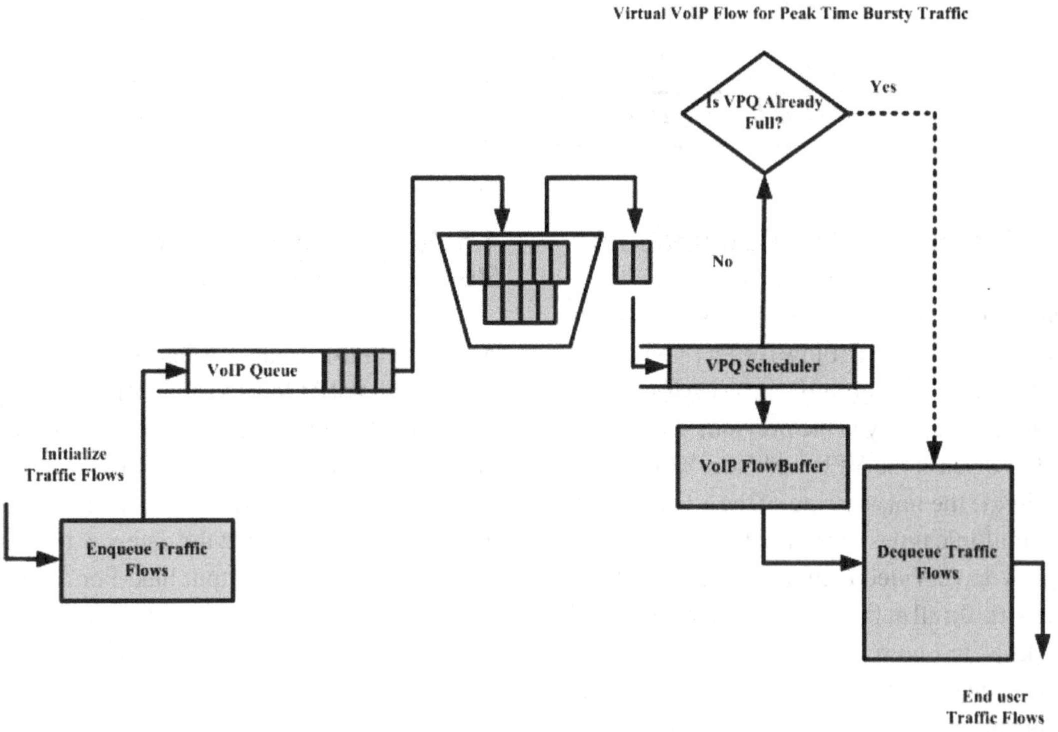

bucket. Step by step, the token bucket counter is incremented by 1token. If the counter is zero, the host cannot send the data to the VF traffic.

4.3. VPQ Scheduler Component

It has traffic flow, the VoIP Flow (VF) over WLANs using IEEE 802.11 standards. Figure 15 depicts the simplified architecture of the proposed VPQ.

Firstly, packets arrive in the initialized traffic then the classifier differentiates the traffic into the VF and NVF traffic. The VF packets from the TB are moved to the VPQ component that temporarily stores and forwards the packets to the VoIP Flow Buffer (VFB).

Figure 15. VPQ scheduler component for the VF

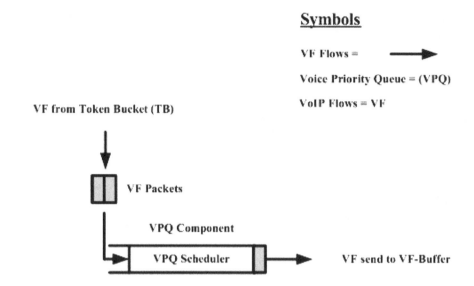

4.4. VFB and Non-VFB Components

The VoIP Flow Buffer (VFB) temporarily stores the VF and the Non-VoIP Flow Buffer (Non-VFB) stores the NVF concurrently in WLANs. It has been discussed briefly in the previous section but it need to discuss the VFB and Non-VFB in detail. It divide the link-sharing of the VF and NVF among multiple types of traffic, for example, the NVF may have Video conferencing, FTP, IPTV and data traffic all at the same time over IP-based networks as in Figure 16.

It will deal with classification of high-level mechanisms and low-level mechanisms that provide the simple resource management model that allows for evaluation. The buffer applies for temporary storage of both types of traffic, the VF and NVF over a network. The VPQ scheduler's classification can make better use of both its buffers, the VF and NVF. Furthermore, these buffers are useful for bursty traffic as they help to manage bursty traffic. The buffer takes the minimum action required to ensure that the traffic receives its allocated link-sharing bandwidth over the relevant time interval.

4.5. Virtual-VoIP Flow for the Bursty Traffic Component

A unique link-sharing mechanism referred to as the Virtual-VoIP Flow (Virtual-VF); it is only for bursty traffic over WLANs. The traffic flow is divided into the VF and NVF flows that use the link-sharing classification mechanism. In the VF, incoming packets wait at the gateway to the most suitable flow for that output link. For normal VF

Figure 16. VFB and Non-VFB components

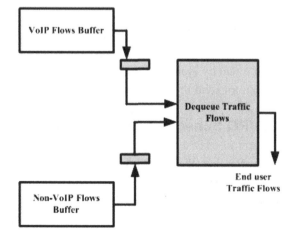

flow, the classification mechanism is sufficient but for bursty traffic flow it need to introduce a component named the Virtual-VF as shown in Figure 17.

A key attribute of the Virtual-VF component is the ability to share bandwidth with the VF and NVF traffic over WLANs. If it's a bursty traffic flow, then the Virtual-VF starts from the VPQ scheduler compnent and sends it directly to the most suitable flow for that output link as dequeued traffic flow for the end user. In addition, the Virtual-VF will be applied on the same bandwidth that is used for the VF flow.

Figure 17 shows both the flows, i.e., the VF flow and the Virtual-VF flow. The Virtual-VF manages the bursty traffic. The Virtual-VF bypasses two components, the Voice Priority Queue (VPQ) scheduler component and the VoIP Flow Buffer (VFB).

4.6. VoIP Flow-Switch Component

In this section, it provides details of the VoIP Flow-Switch (VFS) component over WLANs. As it has two types of traffic classifications, the VF and NVF, it introduce the Switch Movement (SM) concept to the VF flow when the NVF flow is empty as shown in Figure 18.

The VFS is a moveable switch for VF traffic over WLANs. Normally, the NVF traffic is non real-time traffic and is low priority traffic as compared to the VF traffic. The NVF does not use the allocated bandwidth all the time and is normally not delay sensitive. It can utilize those flows for the VF traffic to handle brusty traffic. Now, it has three types of flows; they are the VF, the Virtual-VF and the moveable switch over WLANs using IEEE 802.11 standards.

Figure 17. Virtual-VF component for bursty traffic

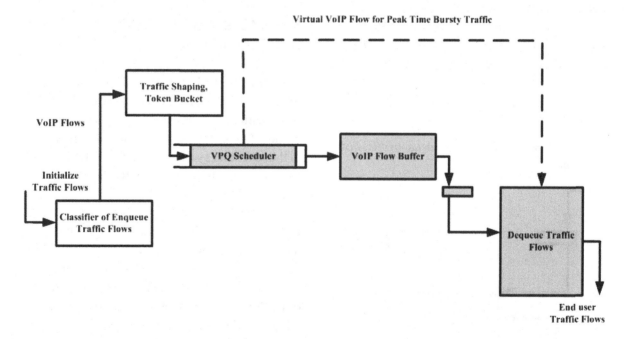

Figure 18. VoIP flow-switch component

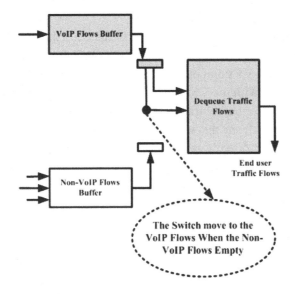

4.7. VF and NVF Dequeue Traffic Flow Component

Finally, the VF and NVF traffic will move to the Dequeue Traffic Flow (DTF) component and be received by the end user from three ways VF, NVF and Virtual-VF with the Voice Priority Queue (VPQ) scheduler as shown in Figure 19.

Figure 19. VF and NVF dequeue traffic flow component

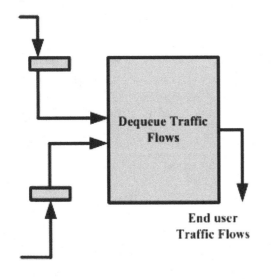

The DTF flows both types of traffic and it will discuss these components in experimental and simulation in next research paper.

5. FINAL STAGE OF VPQ SYSTEM MODEL

In Figure 20, the Final Stage of the Voice Priority Queue (VPQ) Scheduling system model is a combination of all the components. The final stage of the VPQ has the first, second and third stages of the scheduler system model over WLANs. The final stage of the VPQ supports the VoIP Flow (VF) in three ways.

The final stage of the VPQ initializes traffic in the VF and Non-VoIP Flow (NVF) for enqueueing and dequeueing of the traffic over WLANs. The second stage of the VPQ proposes a Virtual-VoIP Flow (Virtual-VF) for bursty and Non-Bursty (NB) flows over networks. The third stage of the VPQ introduces a switch that moves to the VF from the NVF when NVF flows are empty over the network. The final stage of the VPQ fully supports the VF and NVF traffic flow over WLANs. Furthermore, the details are as shown in Figure 21.

Figure 20. Final stage of the VPQ system model

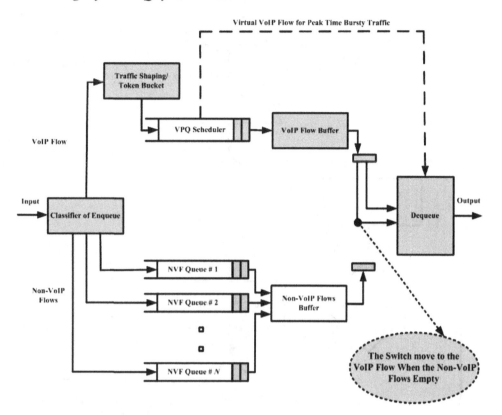

5.1. Final Stage of the VPQ Scheduling Algorithm

Firstly, the VPQ scheduling algorithm initializes the traffic flow over WLANs. After the initialization, the traffic flow arrives to enqueue and the classification component divides the traffic flow into the VoIP Flow (VF) and Non-VoIP Flow (NVF). After that, invoke the packets to the Token Bucket (TB) and Traffic Shaper (TS), if the TB size < = to the VF then the traffic is sent to the VPQ component. At the same time if the TB size = > the VF then send it to the Virtual-VF for bursty traffic over WLANs. The details of the final stage of the VPQ are as shown below in Figure 22.

Meanwhile, if the NVF queue is empty then Switch Movement (SM) to the VF traffic flow and dequeue all VF traffic over WLANs.

6. SUMMARY

A new Voice Priority Queue (VPQ) scheduling system model and algorithms were proposed in this research paper. The VPQ was basically considered to satisfy the unique requirements of the VoIP traffic flow over IP-based networks. It has also provided a detailed system model of the VPQ for the performance and fairness over networks. The propose method will resolve some of the issues on VoIP scheduling as real-time traffic over WLANs.

It will discuss the simulation and experiment environment. Therefore, the next paper introduces an experimental step to evaluate the above scheduling system model and algorithm techniques. There will also be a comparison and evaluation among the related scheduling algorithms.

Figure 21. Final stage of the VPQ flow chart

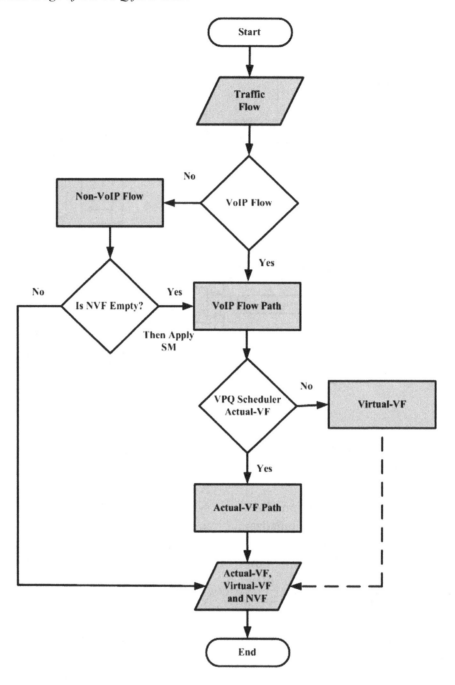

Figure 22. Final stage of the VPQ scheduling algorithm

Final Stage of the Voice Priority Queue (VPQ) Scheduling Algorithm

Initialize*
Traffic Flows over WLANs: (TF-WLANs)**
The Virtual VoIP Flow (Virtual-VF) for Bursty Traffic over a Network***
The Switch Movement (SM) to VoIP Flow (VF) for Bursty Traffic****
(Invoke When the VPQ Scheduler is Initialized over WLANs)
Traffic Flow Arrives
On arrival of the traffic flow Packets (pkt) the VF and NVF Traffic Flows to the VPQ*****
Traffic flow = 0;
Classification (c) = the VF and NVF;
Virtual VoIP Flow = Virtual-VF
Switch Movement = SM
for (pkt = 0; pkt < n; pkt = pkt + 1)******
    pkt = 0;
Enqueue:*******
(Invoke When the Packet Arrives Inside to Enqueue for Classification of Traffic Flow)
    If (Classification (c) = the VoIP Flow (VF)) then********
        send the VoIP Flow (VF) to the token bucket (TB)
          & Traffic Shaper (TS);*********
    Else
        send the Non-VoIP Flow (NVF) to the Queue 1.....N;**********
    End if;
        on arrival of the VoIP Flow(VF) to the token bucket
    If (the token bucket size (pkt) < = the VoIP Flow (VF)) then
        send to the V PQ Scheduler for the VoIP Flow (VF);
    Else

        send to the Virtual-VoIP Flow (Virtual-VF)
        the Virtual-VF component for the VoIP Flow (VF) for Bursty Traffic over a Network;
    End If;
    If (The Non-VoIP Flow (NVF) Empty to the Queue 1.....N) then
        The Switch moves to the VoIP Flow (VF);
    End If;
    If (The Priority Queue for the VoIP < = the VoIP Flow Buffer (VFB)) then***********
        send to the VoIP Flow Buffer (VFB);
    End if;
        on arrival of the Non VoIP Flow to the Queue 1.....N
    If (The Non-VoIP Flow < = the Non-VoIP Flow Buffer (Non-VFB)) then************
        send to the Non-VoIP Flow Buffer (Non-VFB);
    End if;
Dequeue:
(Invoke the Packet (pkt) Queue Corresponding to a Different Flow)
    If (The VoIP Flow Buffer (VFB)) < = the Dequeue Traffic Flow (DTF)) then
        send to the Dequeue Traffic Flow (DTF)Processor;
    End if;
(Invoke the Packet (pkt) flow to Virtual-VF)
    If (The Virtual-VF < = the Dequeue Traffic Flow (DTF)) then**************
        send to the Dequeue Traffic Flow (DTF)Processor;
    End if;
(Invoke the Packet (pkt) flow to *the* Switch Movement (SM))
    If (The Switch Movement < = the Dequeue Traffic Flow (DTF)) then
        send to the Dequeue Traffic Flow (DTF)Processor;
    End if;
    If (The Priority Queue for the VoIP finishes the (VF) and (NVF)) then

---

Notations

*Initialize = Start the Traffic Flow
**TF-WLAN = Traffic Flow over WLANs.
***Virtual-VF = Virtual VoIP Flow (Virtual-VF)
****SW = Switch Movement (SW)
*****VPQ = Voice Priority Queue Scheduler
******Pkt = Packet (pkt)
*******Enqueue = Enqueue is a Standard Queue Operator
******** VF = VoIP Flow
*********TB & TS = Token Bucket (TB) & TS =Traffic Shaper (TS)
**********NVF = Non VoIP Flow
***********VFB = VoIP Flow Buffer
************Non-VFB = Non- VoIP Flow Buffer
************ DTF = Dequeue Traffic Flow

REFERENCES

Ahmed, S., Jiang, X., Ho, P., & Horiguchi, S. (2009). Wireless access point voice capacity analysis and enhancement based on clients' spatial distribution. *IEEE Transactions on Vehicular Technology*, *58*(5), 2597–2603. doi:10.1109/TVT.2008.2005523

Ansel, P., Ni, Q., & Turletti, T. (2006). FHCF: A simple and efficient scheduling scheme for IEEE 802.11e Wireless LAN. *Journal of Mobile Networks and Applications*, *11*, 391–403. doi:10.1007/s11036-006-5191-z

Cai, L., Shen, X., Mark, J., Cai, L., & Xiao, Y. (2006). Voice capacity analysis of WLAN with unbalanced traffic. *IEEE Transactions on Vehicular Technology*, *55*(3), 752–761. doi:10.1109/TVT.2006.874145

Cao, Q., Li, T., & Leith, D. (2009, November 10). Achieving fairness in Lossy 802.11e wireless multi-hop Mesh networks. In *Proceedings of the 3rd IEEE International Workshop on Enabling Technologies and Standards for Wireless Mesh Networking*, Macau, China (pp. 1-7).

Chen, J., Pang, A. I., Sheu, S., & Tseng, H. (2005). High performance wireless switch protocol for IEEE 802.11 wireless networks. *Journal of Mobile Networks and Applications*, *10*(5), 741–751. doi:10.1007/s11036-005-3367-6

Deng, D., Ke, C., Chen, H., & Huang, Y. (2008). Contention Window optimization for IEEE 802.11 DCF access control. *IEEE Transactions on Wireless Communications*, *7*(12).

Deng, J., & Yen, H. (2005). Quality-of-service provisioning system for multimedia transmission in IEEE 802.11 wireless LANs. *IEEE Journal on Selected Areas in Communications*, *23*(6), 1–6.

Dini, P., Font-Bach, O., & Mangues-Bafalluy, J. (2008). Experimental analysis of VoIP call quality support in IEEE 802.11 DCF. In *Proceedings of the 6th International Symposium on Communication Systems, Networks and Digital Signal Processing* (pp. 443-447).

Ergen, M., Lee, D., Sengupta, R., & Varaiya, P. (2004). Wtrp - wireless token ring protocol. *IEEE Transactions on Vehicular Technology*, *53*(6), 1863–1881. doi:10.1109/TVT.2004.836928

Forouzan, B. (2007). *Data communications and networking* (4th ed.). New York, NY: McGraw-Hill.

Garg, S., & Kappes, M. (2003, June 20). Can I add a VoIP call? In *Proceedings of the IEEE International Conference on Communications*, Basking Ridge, NJ, (Vol. 2, pp. 779-783).

Garg, S., & Kappes, M. (2004, January 14). Admission control for VoIP traffic in IEEE 802.11 networks. In *Proceedings of the IEEE Global Telecommunications Conference*, Basking Ridge, NJ (Vol. 6, pp. 3514-3518).

Hole, D., & Tobagi, F. (2004). Capacity of an IEEE 802.11b wireless LAN supporting VoIP. In *Proceedings of the IEEE International Conference on Communications* (pp. 196-201).

Lee, C., Claypool, M., & Kinicki, R. (2010, February). A Credit-based Home Access Point (CHAP) to improve application performance on IEEE 802.11 networks. In *Proceedings of the ACM Conference on Multimedia Systems*, Scottsdale, AZ (pp. 1-6).

Li, T., Ni, Q., Turletti, T., & Xiao, Y. (2006, February 13). Achieving fairness in Lossy 802.11e wireless multi-hop Mesh networks. In *Proceedings of the 2nd International Conference on Broadband Networks*, Ireland (Vol. 1, pp. 511-517).

Li, T., Ni, Q., Turletti, T., & Xiao, Y. (2006, February 13). Performance analysis of the IEEE 802.11e block ACK scheme in a noisy channel. In *Proceedings of the 2nd International Conference on Broadband Networks*, Ireland (Vol. 1, pp. 511-517).

Maheshwari, A. (2006). *Implementation and evaluation of a MAC scheduling architecture for IEEE 802.16 Wireless MANs* (Unpublished master's thesis). The Indian Institute of Technology Kanpur, Kanpur, India.

Mirkovic, J., Orfanos, G., Reumerman, H., & Denteneer, D. (2006, June 4). A MAC protocol for MIMO based IEEE 802.11 wireless local area networks. In *Proceedings of the IEEE Wireless Communications and Networking Conference*, Kowloon, Hong Kong (pp. 2131-2136).

Ni, Q., Li, T., Turletti, T., & Xiao, Y. (2005). Saturation throughput analysis of error-prone 802.11 wireless networks. *Journal of Wireless Communications and Mobile Computing*, 5(8), 945–956. doi:10.1002/wcm.358

Ni, Q., Romdhani, L., & Turletti, T. (2004). A survey of QoS enhancements for IEEE Wireless LAN. *Journal of Wireless Communications and Mobile Computing*, 4(5), 547–566. doi:10.1002/wcm.196

Ni, Q., Romdhani, L., Turletti, T., & Aad, I. (2002). *QoS issues and enhancements for IEEE 802.11 wireless LAN* (Research Report No. 4612). Le Chesnay Cedex, France: INRIA.

Nichols, K., & Carpenter, B. (2001). *RFC3086: Definition of differentiated services per domain behaviours and rules for their specification*. Retrieved from http://www.gta.ufrj.br/diffserv/

Tickoo, O., & Sikdar, B. (2004, July 26). A queueing model for finite load IEEE 802.11 random access MAC. In *Proceedings of the IEEE International Conference on Communications*, Tory, NY (Vol. 1, pp. 175-179).

Wang, C., & Wei, H. (2009). IEEE 802.11n MAC enhancement & performance evaluation. *Journal of Mobile Networks and Applications*, 14(6), 761–771.

Wang, P., & Zhuang, W. (2008). A token-based scheduling scheme for WLANs supporting voice/data traffic and its performance analysis. *IEEE Transactions on Wireless Communications*, 7(5), 1708–1718. doi:10.1109/TWC.2007.060889

Wang, W., Liew, S., & Li, V. (2005). Solutions to performance problems in VoIP over a 802.11 wireless LAN. *IEEE Transactions on Vehicular Technology*, 54, 366–384. doi:10.1109/TVT.2004.838890

Wang, Z. (2001). *Internet QoS architectures and mechanisms for quality of service (The Morgan Kaufmann Series in Networking)*. San Francisco, CA: Morgan Kaufmann.

Wu, H., Peng, Y., Long, K., Cheng, S., & Ma, J. (2002, November 2). Performance of reliable transport protocol over IEEE 802.11 wireless LAN: analysis and enhancement. In *Proceedings of the 21st Annual Joint Conference of the IEEE Computer and Communications Societies* (Vol. 2, pp. 599-607).

Xiao, Y., & Rosdahl, J. (2002). Throughput and delay limits of IEEE 802.11. *IEEE Communications Letters*, *6*(8), 335–357.

Xiong, L., & Mao, G. (2007). Performance analysis of IEEE 802.11 DCF with data rate switching. *IEEE Communications Letters*, *11*(9), 759–761. doi:10.1109/LCOMM.2007.070662

This work was previously published in the International Journal of Advanced Pervasive and Ubiquitous Computing, Volume 3, Issue 4, edited by Tao Gao, pp. 50-70, copyright 2011 by IGI Publishing (an imprint of IGI Global).

Compilation of References

Aamodt, A., & Plaza, E. (1994). Case-based reasoning: Foundational issues, methodological variations, and system approaches. *AI Communications*, *7*, 39–59.

Addesso, P., Bruno, L., & Restaino, R. (2010). Adaptive localization techniques in WiFi environments. In *Proceedings of the 5th International Symposium on Wireless Pervasive Computing* (pp. 289-294).

Aerts, S., Lambrechts, D., Maity, S., Van Loo, P., Coessens, B., & De Smet, F. (2006). Gene prioritization through genomic data fusion. *Nature Biotechnology*, *24*, 537–544. doi:10.1038/nbt1203

Ahmed, S., Jiang, X., Ho, P., & Horiguchi, S. (2009). Wireless access point voice capacity analysis and enhancement based on clients' spatial distribution. *IEEE Transactions on Vehicular Technology*, *58*(5), 2597–2603. doi:10.1109/TVT.2008.2005523

Aizawa, K., & Huang, T. S. (1995). Model-based image coding: advanced video coding techniques for very low bit-rate applications. *Proceedings of the IEEE*, *83*(2), 259–271. doi:10.1109/5.364463

Akkermans, H., Bogerd, P., & van Doremalen, J. (2004). Travail, transparency and trust: A case study of computer-supported collaborative supply chain planning in high-tech electronics. *European Journal of Operational Research*, *153*(2), 445–456. doi:10.1016/S0377-2217(03)00164-4

Alfuhaid, A. S. (1997). Cascaded artificial neural network for short-term load forecasting. *IEEE Transactions on Power Systems*, *12*, 1524–1529. doi:10.1109/59.627852

Altman, E. I. (1968). Financial ratios discriminant analysis and the prediction of corporate bankruptcy. *The Journal of Finance*, *23*, 589–609. doi:10.2307/2978933

Altman, E. I., Edward, I., Haldeman, R., & Narayanan, P. (1977). A new model to identify bankruptcy risk of corporations. *Journal of Banking & Finance*, *1*, 29–54. doi:10.1016/0378-4266(77)90017-6

Amer-Yahia, S., & Kotidis, Y. (2004). A Web-services architecture for efficient XML data exchange. In *Proceedings of the 20th IEEE International Conference on Data Engineering* (pp. 523-534).

Anandarajan, M., Lee, P., & Anandarajan, A. (2001). Bankruptcy prediction of financially stressed firms: An examination of the predictive accuracy of artificial neural networks. *International Journal of Intelligent Systems in Accounting Finance & Management*, *7*, 69–81. doi:10.1002/isaf.199

Andres, J. D., Landajo, M., & Lorca, P. (2005). Forecasting business profitability by using classification techniques: A comparative analysis based on a Spanish case. *European Journal of Operational Research*, *167*, 518–542. doi:10.1016/j.ejor.2004.02.018

Ansel, P., Ni, Q., & Turletti, T. (2006). FHCF: A simple and efficient scheduling scheme for IEEE 802.11e Wireless LAN. *Journal of Mobile Networks and Applications*, *11*, 391–403. doi:10.1007/s11036-006-5191-z

ARC Advisory Group. (2002). Collaborative manufacturing management strategies. *ARC Strategies*. Retrieved from http://www.arcweb.com

Bahl, P., Padmanabhan, V. N., & Balachandran, A. (2000). *Enhancements to the RADAR user location and tracking system* (Tech. Rep. No. MSR-TR-00-12). Cambridge, UK: Microsoft Research.

Bahl, P., & Padmanabhan, V. N. (2000). RADAR: An in-building RF-based user location and tracking system. In. *Proceedings of the IEEE International Conference on Computer Communications, 2*, 775–784.

Bai, X. (2002). Thermal design for a typical sealed electronic equipment cabinet. *ElectroMechanical Engineering, 18*(4).

Bai, X. (2009). *The research of wind power forecasting and AGC unit blend*. Beijing, China: Beijing Transportation University.

Baluja, S. (2006). Browsing on small screens: Recasting web-page segmentation into an efficient machine learning framework. In *Proceedings of the 15th International Conference on World Wide Web* (pp. 33-42).

Banakar, A., & Azeem, M. F. (2008). Artificial wavelet neural network and its application in neuro-fuzzy models. *Applied Soft Computing, 8*, 1463–1485. doi:10.1016/j.asoc.2007.10.020

Bao, D. (2008). LTE industry status and development trend. *Mobile Communication*, (16).

Barnes, E., Dai, J., & Deng, S. (2000). *On the strategy of supply hubs for cost reduction and responsiveness*. Singapore: National University of Singapore.

Beaver, W. (1966). Financial ratios as predictors of failure. *Journal of Accounting Research, 4*, 71–111. doi:10.2307/2490171

Becchetti, L., & Sierra, J. (2003). Bankruptcy risk productive efficiency in manufacturing firms. *Journal of Banking & Finance, 27*, 2099–2120. doi:10.1016/S0378-4266(02)00319-9

Bergman, E. M., & Fester, E. J. (1999). *Industrial and regional clusters: Concepts and comparative applications*. Retrieved from http://www.rri.edu/Webbook/Bergman- Fester

Bertsekas, D. P., & Tsitsiklis, J. N. (1989). *Parallel and distributed computation*. Upper Saddle River, NJ: Prentice Hall.

Bhasker, J. (2000). *A Verilog HOL Primer* (2nd ed.). Allentown, PA: Star Galaxy.

Bin, D., & Zhang, X. (2000). Supply chain oriented collaborative planning, forecasting and replenishment. *3*(1), 36-38.

Bleyer, M., & Gelautz, M. (2007). Graph-cut based stereo matching using image segmentation with symmetrical treatment of occlusions. *Signal Processing Image Communication, 22*(2), 127–143. doi:10.1016/j.image.2006.11.012

Boeck, D. L., & Vandaelee, N. (2008). Coordination and synchronization of material flows in supply chains: An analytical approach. *International Journal of Production Economics, 116*(2), 199–207. doi:10.1016/j.ijpe.2008.06.010

Botafogo, R., Rivlin, E., & Shneiderman, B. (2002). Structural analysis of hypertext: identifying hierarchies and useful metrics. *ACM Transactions on Information Systems, 10*(2).

Bouter, S., Malti, R., & Fremont, H. (2008). Development of an HMI based on the OPC standard. In *Proceedings of the 19th Annual EAEEIE Conference* (pp. 163-167).

Boyaci, T., & Gallego, G. (2004). Supply chain coordination in a market with customer service competition. *Production and Operations Management, 13*(1), 3–22. doi:10.1111/j.1937-5956.2004.tb00141.x

Boyd, M., & McBrien, P. (2005). Comparing and transforming between data models via an intermediate hyper graph data model. *Journal of Data Semantics, 4*, 69–109.

Brzakovic, D., Vujovic, N., & Liakopoulos, A. (1995). An approach to quality control of texture web material. *Proceedings of the Society for Photo-Instrumentation Engineers, 2597*, 60–69.

Budin, G. (2006). *Global content management-challenges and opportuni-ties for creating and using digital translation resources [EB/OL]*. Retrieved from http://www.ifi.unizh.ch/cl/yuste/postworkshop/repository/gbu-din.pdf

Cachon, G., & Fisher, M. (1997). Campbell soup's continuous replenishment program: evaluation and enhanced inventory decision rules. *Production and Operations Management, 6*(3), 266–276. doi:10.1111/j.1937-5956.1997.tb00430.x

Cai, D., Yu, S., Wen, J.-R., & Ma, W.-Y. (2003). *VIPS: A vision-based page segmentation algorithm* (Tech. Rep. No. MSR-TR-2003-79). Cambridge, MA: Microsoft Research.

Cai, G., Wu, S., & Wu, C. (2005). Competitiveness of the regional bio-pharmaceutical industry. *Journal of Guang Dong College of Pharmacy, 21*(5), 643–645.

Cai, L., Shen, X., Mark, J., Cai, L., & Xiao, Y. (2006). Voice capacity analysis of WLAN with unbalanced traffic. *IEEE Transactions on Vehicular Technology, 55*(3), 752–761. doi:10.1109/TVT.2006.874145

Cai, S., & Huang, R. (2009). Service is the new need for digital campus. *Information Technology Education in School, 11*, 59–60.

Calderbank, A. R., Daubechies, I., Sweldens, W., & Yeo, B. L. (1996). *Wavelet transforms that map integers to integers (Tech. Rep.)*. Princeton, NJ: Department of Mathematics, Princeton University.

Cao, L. (2005). Research and analysis of patent information for patent strategy. *Technology Management Research,* (3).

Cao, Q., Li, T., & Leith, D. (2009, November 10). Achieving fairness in Lossy 802.11e wireless multi-hop Mesh networks. In *Proceedings of the 3rd IEEE International Workshop on Enabling Technologies and Standards for Wireless Mesh Networking*, Macau, China (pp. 1-7).

Cao, J. C., & Lin, X. C. (2008). Application of the diagonal recurrent wavelet neural network to solar irradiation forecast assisted with fuzzy technique. *Engineering Applications of Artificial Intelligence, 21*, 1255–1263. doi:10.1016/j.engappai.2008.02.003

Cao, Y., & Tao, Y. (2011). Exploring on educational technology training pattern for teachers in colleges. *Software Guide, 2*, 171–173.

Castro, P., Chiu, P., Kremenek, T., & Muntz, R. (2001). *A probabilistic location service for wireless network environments*. Ubiquitous Computing.

Castro, P., & Muntz, R. (2000). *Managing context for smart spaces*. IEEE Personal Communications.

Chakrabarti, D., Kumar, R., & Punera, K. (2004). A graph-theoretic approach to extract storylines from search results. In *Proceedings of the 17th International Conference on World Wide Web* (pp. 216-225).

Chandra, P., & Fisher, M. L. (1994). Coordination of production and distribution planning. *European Journal of Operational Research, 72*(3), 503–517. doi:10.1016/0377-2217(94)90419-7

Chang, F., & Huang, C. (2011). ETSI disclosure of LTE Patent Analysis. *Modern Telecommunication Technology,* (8).

Charoenpong, T., Supasuteekul, A., & Nuthong, C. (2010, May 19-21). Adaptive background modeling from an image sequence by using k-means clustering. In *Proceedings of the IEEE International Conference on Electrical Engineering/Electronics Computer Telecommunications and Information Technology* (pp. 880-883).

Chen, J., Zhou, B., & Zhang, H. (2001). Function-based object model towards website adaptation. In *Proceedings of the 10th International World Wide Web Conference* (pp. 587-596).

Chen, S., & Chen, R. (1998). Manufacturer-supplier relationship in JIT environment: JIT purchasing and supply in Chinese automobile industry. *Journal of Industrial Engineering/Engineering Management, 12*(3), 46-52.

Chen, X., Li, M., & Gao, S. (2005). *A Web services based platform for exchange of procedural CAD models*. Retrieved March 28, 2007, from http://www.eng.nus.edu.sg/LCEL/people/limin/ html/cscwd-2005.html

Chen, F. (2001). *Information sharing and supply chain coordination*. New York, NY: Columbia University.

Chen, F., Drezner, Z., Ryan, J. K., & Simchi-Levi, D. (2000). Quantifying the bullwhip effect in a simple supply chain: The impact of forecasting, lead times, and information. *Management Science, 46*(3), 436–443. doi:10.1287/mnsc.46.3.436.12069

Chen, G., Zhang, H., & Han, J. (2004). A comparative research on competitive power of science and technology on grey system theory. *Journal of Jinan University, 25*(1), 19.

Chen, J., Pang, A. I., Sheu, S., & Tseng, H. (2005). High performance wireless switch protocol for IEEE 802.11 wireless networks. *Journal of Mobile Networks and Applications, 10*(5), 741–751. doi:10.1007/s11036-005-3367-6

Chen, S. K., Lo, M. L., Wu, K. L., Yih, J. S., & Viehrig, C. (2006). A practical approach to extracting DTD-conforming XML documents from heterogeneous data sources. *Information Sciences*, *176*(7), 820–844. doi:10.1016/j.ins.2004.12.009

Chen, T.-H., & Chen, J.-M. (2005). Optimizing supply chain collaboration based on joint replenishment and channel coordination. *Transportation Research Part E, Logistics and Transportation Review*, *41*(4), 261–285. doi:10.1016/j.tre.2004.06.003

Chen, X., & Wang, X. (2009). An improved multi-population genetic algorithm. *Journal of Liaoning University of Technology*, *32*(2), 160–163.

Chen, Z. (2004). Performance measures system for supply and demand coordination based on agile supply chain. *Computer Integrated Manufacturing Systems*, *10*(1), 99–105.

Cheong, M. L. F., Bhatnagar, R., & Graves, S. C. (2007). Logistics network design with supplier consolidation hubs and multiple shipment options. *Journal of Industrial and Management Optimization*, *3*(1), 51–69. doi:10.3934/jimo.2007.3.51

Chiou, S.-Y. S., Wang, C.-L., Yeh, S.-C., & Su, M.-Y. (2009). Design of an adaptive positioning system based on wifi radio signals. *Computer Communications*, *32*(7-10). doi:10.1016/j.comcom.2009.04.003

Cucchiara, R., Piccardi, M., & Prati, A. (2003). Detecting moving objects, ghosts, and shadows in video streams. *IEEE Transactions on Pattern Analysis and Machine Intelligence*, *25*(10), 1337–1342. doi:10.1109/TPAMI.2003.1233909

Curran, K., Furey, E., Lunney, T., Santos, J., & Woods, D. (2009). *An evaluation of indoor location determination technologies*. Northern Ireland, UK: University of Ulster.

Daubechies, I., & Sweldens, W. (1998). *Factoring wavelet transforms into lifting steps (Tech. Rep.)*. Paris, France: Bell Laboratories, Lucent Technologies.

Davidoff, A. M., Humphrey, P. A., Iglehart, J. D., & Marks, J. R. (1991). Genetic basis for p. 53 overexpression in human breast cancer. *Proceedings of the National Academy of Sciences of the United States of America*, *88*, 5006–5010. doi:10.1073/pnas.88.11.5006

Day, L., & Wensley, K. (1988). Manufacturer's revenue—sharing contract and retail competition. *European Journal of Operational Research*, *186*(2), 637–651.

Dempster, A. P., Laird, N. M., & Rubin, D. B. (1977). Maximum-likelihood from incomplete data via the em algorithm. *Journal of the Royal Statistical Society. Series B. Methodological*, 39.

Deng, D., Ke, C., Chen, H., & Huang, Y. (2008). Contention Window optimization for IEEE 802.11 DCF access control. *IEEE Transactions on Wireless Communications*, *7*(12).

Deng, J., & Yen, H. (2005). Quality-of-service provisioning system for multimedia transmission in IEEE 802.11 wireless LANs. *IEEE Journal on Selected Areas in Communications*, *23*(6), 1–6.

Desimone, R., & Duncan, J. (1995). Neural mechanisms of selective visual attention. *Annual Review of Neuroscience*, *18*, 193–222. doi:10.1146/annurev.ne.18.030195.001205

DeWitt, T., Giunipero, L. C., & Melton, H. L. (2006). Clusters and supply chain management: The Amish experience. *International Journal of Physical Distribution & Logistics Management*, *36*(4), 289–308. doi:10.1108/09600030610672055

Dimitras, A. I., Zanakis, S. H., & Zopounidis, C. (1996). A survey of business failures with an emphasis on prediction methods and industrial applications. *European Journal of Operational Research*, *90*, 487–513. doi:10.1016/0377-2217(95)00070-4

Ding, Q., & Wang, G.-Z. (2008). Application and cluster analysis of regional electric customer load modes. *Mechatronic Engineering*, *25*(9), 31–33.

Ding, Y. S., Song, X. P., & Zen, Y. M. (2008). Forecasting financial condition of Chinese listed companies based on support vector machine. *Expert Systems with Applications*, *34*, 3081–3089. doi:10.1016/j.eswa.2007.06.037

Dini, P., Font-Bach, O., & Mangues-Bafalluy, J. (2008). Experimental analysis of VoIP call quality support in IEEE 802.11 DCF. In *Proceedings of the 6th International Symposium on Communication Systems, Networks and Digital Signal Processing* (pp. 443-447).

Disney, S. M., & Towill, D. R. (2003). The effect of vendor managed inventory (VMI) dynamics on the Bullwhip Effect in supply chains. *International Journal of Production Economics, 85*(2), 199–215. doi:10.1016/S0925-5273(03)00110-5

Dong, G., Zhang, C., & Ma, L. (2006). Purchasing mode of supply chain based on JIT theory. *Modern Management Science*, (2), 93-94.

Dong, J., Zhang, D., & Nagurney, A. (2004). A supply chain network equilibrium model with random demand. *European Journal of Operational Research, 56*(1), 194–212. doi:10.1016/S0377-2217(03)00023-7

Dong, J., Zhang, D., Yan, H., & Nagumey, A. (2005). Multi-tiered supply chain networks: multi-criteria decision making under uncertainty. *Annals of Operations Research, 135*, 155–178. doi:10.1007/s10479-005-6239-3

Dudek, G., & Stadtler, H. (2005). Negotiation-based collaborative planning between supply chains partners. *European Journal of Operational Research, 163*(3), 668–687. doi:10.1016/j.ejor.2004.01.014

Du, Z. M., Jin, X. Q., & Yang, Y. Y. (2009). Fault diagnosis for temperature, flow rate and pressure sensors in VAV systems using wavelet neural network. *Applied Energy, 86*, 1624–1631. doi:10.1016/j.apenergy.2009.01.015

Dyakowski, T. (1996). Process tomography applied to multi-phase flow measurement. *Measurement Science & Technology, 7*, 343–353. doi:10.1088/0957-0233/7/3/015

Eastlake, D., Reagle, D., & Solo, D. (2002). *RFC 3075: XML-Signature syntax and processing.* Retrieved from http://www.w3.org/TR/xmldsig-core/

Eastlake, D., Reagle, J., & Imamura, T. (2001). *XML encryption syntax and processing.* Retrieved from http://www.w3.org/TR/xmlenc-core/

Ellinger, A. E. (2000). Improving marketing/logistics cross-functional collaboration in the supply chain. *Industrial Marketing Management, 29*(1), 85–96. doi:10.1016/S0019-8501(99)00114-5

Ergen, M., Lee, D., Sengupta, R., & Varaiya, P. (2004). Wtrp - wireless token ring protocol. *IEEE Transactions on Vehicular Technology, 53*(6), 1863–1881. doi:10.1109/TVT.2004.836928

Fagin, R., Kolaitis, P. G., Miller, R. J., & Popa, L. (2003). Data exchange: Semantics and query answering. In D. Calvanese, M. Lenzerini, & R. Motwani (Eds.), *Proceedings of the 9th International Conference on Database Theory* (LNCS 2572, pp. 207-224).

Fan, M., Stallaert, J., & Whinston, A. B. (2000). *Decentralized mechanism design for supply chain organizations using an auction market.* Seattle, WA: University of Washington.

Feldstein, C. B., & Muzio, J. C. (2004). Development of a fault tolerant flight control system. In *Proceedings of the 23rd Digital Avionics Systems Conference* (Vol. 2).

Fidel, R., & Green, M. (2004). The many faces of accessibility: Engineers' perception of information sources. *Information Processing and Management: An International Journal, 40*(3).

Forouzan, B. (2007). *Data communications and networking* (4th ed.). New York, NY: McGraw-Hill.

Franke, L., Bakel, H., Fokkens, L., de Jong, E. D., Egmont-Petersen, M., & Wijmenga, C. (2006). Reconstruction of a functional human gene network, with an application for prioritizing positional candidate genes. *American Journal of Human Genetics, 78*, 1011–1025. doi:10.1086/504300

Frydman, H., Altman, E. L., & Kao, D. (1985). Introducing recursive partitioning for financial classification: the case of financial distress. *The Journal of Finance, 40*, 269–291. doi:10.2307/2328060

Fu, Y., & Piplani, R. (2004). Supply-side collaboration and its value in supply chains. *European Journal of Operational Research, 152*(1), 281–288. doi:10.1016/S0377-2217(02)00670-7

Gabay, D., & Moulin, H. (1980). On the uniqueness and stability of Nash equilibrium in noncooperative games. In Bensoussan, A., Kleindorfer, P., & Tapiero, C. S. (Eds.), *Applied control of econometrics and management science* (pp. 271–294). Amsterdam, The Netherlands: North-Holland.

Gao, Z.-W., Wang, Y., & Song, W.-W. (2008). Daily Coherence Fuzzy Cluster Analysis Method of Power System Load Pattern. *Information Technology, 2008*(6), 36-38.

Gao, T., Liu, Z. G., Yue, S. H., Zhang, J., Mei, J. Q., & Gao, W. C. (2010). Robust background subtraction in traffic video sequence. *Journal of Central South University of Technology*, *17*(1), 187–195. doi:10.1007/s11771-010-0029-z

Gao, T., Liu, Z. G., & Zhang, J. (2009). Redundant discrete wavelet transforms based moving object recognition and tracking. *Journal of Systems Engineering and Electronics*, *20*(5), 1115–1123.

Garg, S., & Kappes, M. (2003, June 20). Can I add a VoIP call? In *Proceedings of the IEEE International Conference on Communications*, Basking Ridge, NJ, (Vol. 2, pp. 779-783).

Garg, S., & Kappes, M. (2004, January 14). Admission control for VoIP traffic in IEEE 802.11 networks. In *Proceedings of the IEEE Global Telecommunications Conference*, Basking Ridge, NJ (Vol. 6, pp. 3514-3518).

Garg, D., Narahari, Y., & Viswanadham, N. (2006). Achieving sharp deliveries in supply chains through variance pool allocation. *European Journal of Operational Research*, *171*(1), 227–254. doi:10.1016/j.ejor.2004.08.033

Ghaheri-Niri, S., Leaves, P., Benko, P., Huschke, J., & Stahl, W. (2000). *Traffic control and dynamic spectrum allocation in DRiVE.* Paper presented at the Workshop on Multiradio Multimedia Communications, Berlin, Germany.

Gill, P. J., & Abend, J. (1997). Wal-Mart: the supply chain heavy-weight champ. *Supply Chain Management*, *1*(1), 8–16.

Goldsmith, A. (2005). *Wireless communications*. Cambridge, UK: Cambridge University Press.

Gong, J., & Jia, H. (2002). OFDM technique and simulation analysis thereof. *Railway Newspaper, 24*(3).

Gong, C.-H., & Huang, R.-H. (2010). Seven key factors towards effective planning of teacher training. *Modern Educational Technology*, *20*(12), 65–68.

Gregor, M. M. (2001). Some impacts of paper making on paper structure. *Paper Technology, 42*, 30–44.

Güler, M. G., & Bilgic, T. (2009). On coordinating an assembly system under random yield and random demand. *European Journal of Operational Research*, *196*(1), 342–350. doi:10.1016/j.ejor.2008.03.002

Guo, Y., & Li, J. (n. d.). *Mobile communications.* Sichuan, China. *Press of Xian Electronic Science & Technology University.*

Gupta, D., & Weerawat, W. (2000). *Incentive mechanisms and supply chain decision for quick response.* Minneapolis, MN: University of Minneapolis.

Gupta, S., Kaiser, G. E., Grimm, P., Chiang, M. F., & Starren, J. (2005). Automating content extraction of html documents. *World Wide Web Internet and Web Information Systems*, *8*(2), 179–224.

Gurnani, H., & Gerchak, Y. (2007). Coordination in decentralized assembly systems with uncertain component yields. *European Journal of Operational Research*, *176*(3), 1559–1576. doi:10.1016/j.ejor.2005.09.036

Han, D., Shin, C.-Y., Choi, S.-J., & Park, J.-S. (1999). A motion adaptive 3-D de-interlacing algorithm based on the brightness profile pattern difference. *IEEE Transactions on Consumer Electronics*, *45*(3), 690–697. doi:10.1109/30.793572

Harris, S. B., Owen, J., Bloor, M. S., & Hogg, I. (1997). Engineering document management strategy: Analysis of requirements, choice of direction and system implementation. *Proceedings of the Institution of Mechanical Engineers. Part B, Journal of Engineering Manufacture*, *211*(5), 385–405. doi:10.1243/0954405971516365

Hattori, G., Hoashi, K., Matsumoto, K., & Sugaya, F. (2007). Robust web page segmentation for mobile terminal using content-distances and page layout information. In *Proceedings of the 16th International Conference on World Wide Web* (pp. 361-370).

Helo, P. T. (2000). Dynamic modeling of surge effect and capacity limitation in supply chains. *International Journal of Production Research*, *38*(17), 4521–4533. doi:10.1080/00207540050205271

Hjertaker, B. T., Tjugum, S.-A., Hammer, E. A., & Johansen, G. A. (2005). Multimodality tomography for multiphase hydrocarbon flow measurements. *IEEE Sensors Journal*, *5*(2), 153–160. doi:10.1109/JSEN.2005.843903

Hole, D., & Tobagi, F. (2004). Capacity of an IEEE 802.11b wireless LAN supporting VoIP. In *Proceedings of the IEEE International Conference on Communications* (pp. 196-201).

Holmström, J., Framling, K., Kaipia, R., & Saranen, J. (2002). Collaborative planning forecasting and replenishment: new solutions needed for mass collaboration. *Supply Chain Management*, *7*(3), 1359–8546.

Hoover, M. (1948). *The location of economic activity*. Columbus, OH: Edgar Malone.

Hor, C.-L., Watson, S. J., & Majithia, S. (2005). Analyzing the impact of weather variables on monthly electricity demand. *IEEE Transactions on Power Systems*, *20*(4), 2078–2085. doi:10.1109/TPWRS.2005.857397

Hossen, A. (2004). Power spectral density estimation via wavelet decomposition. *Electronics Letters*, *40*, 1055–1056. doi:10.1049/el:20045235

Hou, F.-Z., & Zhou, Z.-Y. (2008). Approach for locating vehicle license plates based on gradient difference of the morphology. *Journal of Science Technology and Engineering*, *8*(12), 3355–3358.

Hu, J.-F., Lee, C.-J., et al. (2008). The relationship between price elasticity of demand and generation market equilibrium analysis based on game theory. In *Proceedings of the Chinese Society for Electrical Engineering* (pp. 89-94).

Huang, J., & Yang, G. (2002). Research of index system of evaluation and connotation about competitive power of industrial science and technology. *Science of Science and Management*, (11), 21.

Huang, C., & Chen, X. (2004). Improvements on niche genetic algorithm. *Journal of Beijing Institute of Technology*, *24*(8), 675–678.

Huang, R., Chen, G., Zhang, J., & Wang, Y. (2010). Research on informationization learning mode and its digital resource form. *Modern Distance Education Research*, *6*, 68–73.

Huang, Z.-M., & Dai, M. (2007). Moving object detection based on Gaussian kernel density model. *Microcomputer Information*, *23*(2), 45–48.

Hua, Z. S., Wang, Y., Xu, X. Y., Zhang, B., & Liang, L. (2007). Predicting corporate financial distress based on integration of support vector machine and logistic regression. *Expert Systems with Applications*, *33*, 434–440. doi:10.1016/j.eswa.2006.05.006

Huma, Z., Jafar-Ur-Rehman, M., & Iftikhar, N. (2005). An ontology-based framework for semi-automatic schema integration. *Journal of Computer Science and Technology*, *20*(6), 788–796. doi:10.1007/s11390-005-0788-4

Hung, M.-H., Cheng, F.-T., & Yeh, S.-C. (2005). Development of a Web-Services-based e-diagnostics framework for semi-conductor manufacturing industry. *IEEE Transactions on Semiconductor Manufacturing*, *18*(1), 122–135. doi:10.1109/TSM.2004.836664

Huo, J., Sui, M., & Liu, Z. (2002). Construction of integrated supply chain performance measurement system. *Journal of Tongji University*, *30*(4), 495–499.

Hu, Y. C. (2008). Incorporating a non-additive decision making method into multi-layer neural networks and its application to financial distress analysis. *Knowledge-Based Systems*, *21*, 383–390. doi:10.1016/j.knosys.2008.02.002

IBM. (n. d.). *Collaborative supply chain management solution from IBM*. Retrieved from http://www-03.ibm.com/industries/ca/en/retail/col_sup_mgmt_bus.html

IEEE. Computer Society. (2009). *IEEE Standard 802.11 - Wireless LAN medium access control (MAC) and physical layer (PHY) specifications*. Washington, DC: IEEE Computer Society.

Iivarinen, J. (2000). Surface defect detection with histogram-based texture features, intelligent robots and computer vision. In *Proceedings of the SPIE Conference on Algorithms, Techniques and Active Vision* (Vol. 4127, pp. 140-145).

Iivarinen, J., Heikkinen, K., Rauhamaa, J., Vuorimaa, P., & Visa, A. (2000). A defect detection scheme for web surface inspection. *International Journal of Pattern Recognition and Artificial Intelligence*, *14*, 735–755.

Ito, T., & Salleh, M. R. (2000). A blackboard-based negotiation for collaborative supply chain system. *Journal of Materials Processing Technology, 107*(1-3), 398–403. doi:10.1016/S0924-0136(00)00730-5

Itti, L., Koch, C., & Niebur, E. (1998). A model of saliency-based visual attention for rapid scene analysis. *IEEE Transactions on Pattern Analysis and Machine Intelligence, 20*, 1254–1259. doi:10.1109/34.730558

Izquierdo, E. (1999). Disparity/segmentation analysis: matching with an adaptive window and depth-driven segmentation. *IEEE Transactions on Circuits and Systems for Video Technology, 9*(4), 589–607. doi:10.1109/76.767125

Jeanmeure, L. F. C., Dyakowski, T., Zimmerman, W. B. J., & Clark, W. (2002). Direct flow-pattern identification using electrical capacitance tomography. *Experimental Thermal and Fluid Science, 26*, 763–773. doi:10.1016/S0894-1777(02)00186-3

Ji, Y., Biaz, S., Pandey, S., & Agrawal, P. (2006). ARIADNE: A dynamic indoor signal map construction and localization system. In *Proceedings of the IEEE International Conference on Mobile System, Applications, and Services* (pp. 151-164).

Jiang, F., Zhu, C., & Xu, L. (2007). The construction of the evaluation index system of integration supply chain. *Journal of Jingling Institute of Technology, 21*(3), 46–51.

Jimenez-Sanchez, G., Barton, C., & David, V. (2001). Human disease genes. *Nature, 409*, 853–855. doi:10.1038/35057050

Kan, J., Li, K., Tang, J., & Du, X. (2010, October 22-24). Background modeling method based on improved multi-Gaussian distribution. In *Proceedings of the Computer Application and System Modeling Conference* (pp. 214-218).

Karali, I. (2007). A common design-features ontology for product data semantics interoperability. In *Proceedings of the IEEE/WIC/ACM International Conference on Web Intelligence* (pp. 443-446).

Kastner, S., & Ungerleider, L. G. (2000). Mechanisms of visual attention in human cortex. *Annual Review of Neuroscience, 123*, 315–341.

Kita, Y. (2010, August 23-26). Background modeling by combining joint intensity histogram with time-sequential data. In *Proceedings of the 20th International Conference on Pattern Recognition* (pp. 991-994).

Koch, C., & Ullman, S. (1995). Shifts in selective visual attention: towards the underlying neural circuitry. *Human Neurobiology, 4*, 219–227.

Kolmogorov, V., Zabih, R., & Gortler, S. (2003). Generalized multi-camera scene reconstruction using graph cuts. In A. Rangarajan, M. Figueiredo, & J. Zerubia (Eds.), *Proceedings of the 4th International Workshop on Energy Minimization Methods in Computer Vision and Pattern Recognition*, Lisbon, Portugal (LNCS 2683, pp. 501-516).

Kontkanen, P., Myllymaki, P., Roos, T., Tirri, H., Valtonen, K., & Wettig, H. (2004). Topics in probabilistic location estimation in wireless networks. In *Proceedings of the 15th IEEE International Symposium on Personal, Indoor and Mobile Radio Communications*, Barcelona, Spain (Vol. 2, pp. 1052-1056).

Ko, P. C., & Lin, P. C. (2006). An evolution-based approach with modularized evaluations to forecast financial distress. *Knowledge-Based Systems, 19*, 84–91. doi:10.1016/j.knosys.2005.11.006

Kothuri, R., Goldfrind, A., & Beinat, E. (2004). *Pro Oracle Spatial*. New York, NY: Apress.

Kumar, K. V., Ravi, V., Carr, M., & Kiran, N. R. (2008). Software development cost estimation using wavelet neural networks. *Journal of Systems and Software, 81*, 1853–1867. doi:10.1016/j.jss.2007.12.793

Kuo, T., & Hwang, S. Y. (1996). A genetic algorithm with disruptive selection. *IEEE Transactions on Systems, Man, and Cybernetics, 26*(2), 299–306. doi:10.1109/3477.485880

Kushi, A., Plataniotis, K. N., & Venetsanopoulos, A. N. (2010). Intelligent dynamics radio tracking in indoor wireless local area networks. *IEEE Transactions on Mobile Computing, 9*(3), 405–419. doi:10.1109/TMC.2009.141

Kushki, A., Plataniotis, K., & Venetsanopoulos, A. N. (2006). Location tracking in wireless local area networks with adaptive radio maps. In. *Proceedings of the IEEE International Conference on Acoustics, Speech, and Signal Processing, 5*, 741–744.

Laplant, M. (2006). *Global content management: Hewlett-packard talk the talk of worldwide business [EB/OL]*. Retrieved from http://gilbane.com/case_studies/HP_case_study.html

Leaves, P., Ghaheri-Niri, S., Tafazolli, R., & Huschke, J. (2002). Dynamic spectrum allocation in hybrid networks with imperfect load prediction. In *Proceedings of the Third IEEE International Conference on 3G Mobile Communication Technologies*, London, UK (pp. 444-448).

Leaves, P., Moessner, K., & Tafazolli, R. (2004). Dynamic spectrum allocation in composite reconfigurable wireless networks. *Communications Magazine*, *42*(5), 72–81. doi:10.1109/MCOM.2004.1299346

Lee, C., Claypool, M., & Kinicki, R. (2010, February). A Credit-based Home Access Point (CHAP) to improve application performance on IEEE 802.11 networks. In *Proceedings of the ACM Conference on Multimedia Systems*, Scottsdale, AZ (pp. 1-6).

Lee, C. L., Chang, S., & Jen, C. W. (1991, June). Motion detection and motion adaptive pro-scan conversion. In. *Proceedings of the IEEE International Symposium on Circuits and Systems*, *1*, 666–669.

Lee, H. L. (2002). Aligning supply chain strategies with product uncertainties. *California Management Review*, *44*(3), 105–119.

Lee, H. L., Padmanabhan, P., & Whang, S. (1997). The bullwhip effect in supply chains. *Sloan Management Review*, *38*, 93–102.

Lee, H. L., So, K. C., & Tang, C. S. (2000). The value of information sharing in a two-level supply chain. *Management Science*, *46*, 626–643. doi:10.1287/mnsc.46.5.626.12047

Lee, H. L., & Whang, S. (1999). Decentralized multi-echelon supply chains: Incentives and Information. *Management Science*, *45*(5), 633–640. doi:10.1287/mnsc.45.5.633

Lei, Y., Zhang, S., & Li, X. (2005). *MATLAB genetic algorithm toolbox and application*. Xi'an, China: Xidian University Press.

Li, M., Gao, S., Li, J., & Yang, Y. (2004). *An approach to supporting synchronized collaborative design within heterogeneous CAD systems*. Retrieved March 28, 2007, from http://www.eng.nus.edu.sg/LCEL/people/limin/html/asme-cie-2004.html

Li, R., & Li, Y-T. (2004). Design and Building of Data Warehouse for Relay Protection. *International Journal of Power and Energy Systems*, 71-75.

Li, T., Ni, Q., Turletti, T., & Xiao, Y. (2006, February 13). Achieving fairness in Lossy 802.11e wireless multi-hop Mesh networks. In *Proceedings of the 2nd International Conference on Broadband Networks*, Ireland (Vol. 1, pp. 511-517).

Li, T., Ni, Q., Turletti, T., & Xiao, Y. (2006, February 13). Performance analysis of the IEEE 802.11e block ACK scheme in a noisy channel. In *Proceedings of the 2nd International Conference on Broadband Networks*, Ireland (Vol. 1, pp. 511-517).

Li, X. (2005). *Study of signal integrity, power integrity and electromagnetic compatibility in high-speed PCB*. Unpublished doctoral dissertation, Sichuan University, Chengdu, Sichuan, China.

Liao, S.-H. (2005). Expert system methodologies and applications – A decade review from 1995 to 2004. *Expert Systems with Applications*, *28*, 93–103. doi:10.1016/j.eswa.2004.08.003

Li, H., & Sun, J. (2008). Ranking-order case-based reasoning for financial distress prediction. *Knowledge-Based Systems*, *21*, 868–878. doi:10.1016/j.knosys.2008.03.047

Li, H., Sun, J., & Sun, B.-L. (2009). Financial distress prediction based on OR-CBR in the principle of k-nearest neighbors. *Expert Systems with Applications*, *36*, 643–659. doi:10.1016/j.eswa.2007.09.038

Li, J. (2006). *Study on cluster supply chain and its management*. Wuhan, China: Huazhong Agricultural University.

Li, J., Xiong, N., Park, J. H., Liu, C., Ma, S., & Cho, S.-E. (2009). Intelligent model design of cluster supply chain with horizontal cooperation. *Journal of Intelligent Manufacturing*, *11*(8), 256–268.

Li, J., & Zhang, Y. (2006). Interactive sensor network data retrieval and management using principal components analysis transform. *Smart Materials and Structures, 15,* 1747–1757. doi:10.1088/0964-1726/15/6/029

Li, M., Xiong, X., & Ma, C. (2003). A genetic algorithms with sexual reproduction. *Journal of Image and Graphics, 8*(5), 509–515.

Lim, W. S. (2000). A lemons market? An incentive scheme to induce truth-telling in third party logistics providers. *European Journal of Operational Research, 125*(3), 519–525. doi:10.1016/S0377-2217(99)00210-6

Lin, S.-H., & Ho, J.-M. (2002). Discovering informative content blocks from Web documents. In *Proceedings of the Eighth ACM SIGKDD International Conference on Knowledge Discovery and Data Mining* (pp. 588-593).

Lin, F.-Y., & McClean, S. (2001). A data mining approach to the prediction of corporate failure. *Knowledge-Based Systems, 14,* 189–195. doi:10.1016/S0950-7051(01)00096-X

Lin, T.-H. (2009). A cross model study of corporate financial distress prediction in Taiwan: Multiple discriminant analysis, logit, probit and neural networks models. *Neurocomputing, 72,* 3507–3516. doi:10.1016/j.neucom.2009.02.018

Lis, J., & Eiben, A. E. (1997). A multi-sexual genetic algorithm for multiobjective optimization. *IEEE Transactions on Evolutionary Computation, 1*(2), 59–64.

Liu, H., & Chen, Q.-M. (2009). Research and realization of role-based data exchange middleware. *Journal of Computer Application, 29*(1), 326-327, 330.

Liu, J., & Li, H. (2011). EMC design for a certain case. *Ship Electronic Engineering, 26*(1).

Liu, S., McMahon, C. A., Darlington, M. J., Culley, S. J., & Wild, P. J. (2006). An approach for document fragment retrieval and its formatting issues in engineering information management. In M. L. Gavrilova, O. Gervasi, V. Kumar, C. J. K. Tan, D. Taniar, A. Laganá, Y. Mun, & H. Choo (Eds.), *Proceedings of the International Conference on Computational Science and its Applications* (LNCS 3981, pp.279-287).

Liu, L. (2001). Material purchasing strategy in supply chain management. *Chinese Journal of Management Science, 9*(3), 49–54.

Liu, L.-L., & Xu, M. (2011). Research on the mode of digital educational resource sharing among colleges and universities. *Journal of Jiangsu Radio & Television University, 2,* 15–18.

Liu, S., Fu, S., & Yang, W. Q. (1999). Optimization of an iterative image reconstruction algorithm for electrical capacitance tomography. *Measurement Science & Technology, 10,* 37–39. doi:10.1088/0957-0233/10/7/102

Li, Y.-N., & Liu, L.-Z. (2008). Policy driven data exchange model. *Computer Engineering, 34*(20), 31–33.

Lizorkin, D. A., & Lisovsky, K. Y. (2005). Implementation of the XML linking language XLink by functional methods. *Programming and Computer Software, 31*(1), 34–46.

Lowe, A., McMahon, C. A., & Culley, S. J. (2004). Characterising the requirements of engineering information systems. *International Journal of Information Management, 24*(5), 402–422.

Luo, M., Ma, W., & Zhou, Y. (2007). Study on SC performance evaluation index system under the life cycle. *Logistics Technology, 26*(10), 81–84.

Ma, M., Zhu, J., & He, H. & Du, W. (2007). *PCI, PCI-X and PCI express principle and system structure.* Beijing, China: Tsinghua University Press.

Maheshwari, A. (2006). *Implementation and evaluation of a MAC scheduling architecture for IEEE 802.16 Wireless MANs* (Unpublished master's thesis). The Indian Institute of Technology Kanpur, Kanpur, India.

Mahui. (2007, April 2). Integration new ideas of Beijing, Tianjin and Heibei: Shijiazhuang is a breakthrough. *21st Century Business Herald.*

Majumder, P., & Srinivasan, A. (2008). Leadership and competition in network supply chains. *Management Science, 54,* 1189–1204. doi:10.1287/mnsc.1070.0752

Manthou, V., Vlachopoulou, M., & Folinas, D. (2004). Virtual e-Chain (VeC) model for supply chain collaboration. *International Journal of Production Economics, 87*(3), 241–250. doi:10.1016/S0925-5273(03)00218-4

Marashdeh, Q., Warsito, W., Fan, L.-S., & Teixeira, F. L. (2006). A nonlinear image reconstruction technique for ECT using a combined neural network approach. *Measurement Science & Technology, 17*, 2097–2113. doi:10.1088/0957-0233/17/8/007

Marr, D., & Hildreth, E. (1980). Theory of edge detection. *Proceedings of the Royal Society of London. Series B. Biological Sciences, 27*, 187–217. doi:10.1098/rspb.1980.0020

Marshall, L. (1920). *The principles of economics* (8th ed.). London, UK: Macmillan.

Martin, D. (1977). Early warning of bank failure: A logit regression approach. *Journal of Banking & Finance, 1*, 249–276. doi:10.1016/0378-4266(77)90022-X

Ma, S.-Y., & Chen, L.-G. (1999). A single-chip CMOS APS camera with direct frame difference output. *IEEE Journal of Solid-state Circuits, 34*, 1415–1418. doi:10.1109/4.792618

Mason-Jones, R., & Towill, D. R. (1999). Total cycle time compression and the agile supply chain. *International Journal of Production Economics, 62*(1-2), 61–73. doi:10.1016/S0925-5273(98)00221-7

McCarthy, M. I., Smedley, D., & Hide, W. (2003). New methods for finding disease-susceptibility genes: impact and potential. *Genome Biology, 4*, 119. doi:10.1186/gb-2003-4-10-119

McDonald, S., & Stevenson, R. J. (1998). Effects of text structure and prior knowledge of the learner on navigation in hypertext. *Human Factors*, 40.

McIvor, R., Humphreys, P., & McCurry, L. (2003). Electronic commerce: supporting collaboration in the supply chain. *Journal of Materials Processing Technology, 139*(1-3), 147–152. doi:10.1016/S0924-0136(03)00196-1

Mentzer, J. T., DeWitt, W., Keebler, J. S., Nix, N. W., Smith, C. D., & Zacharia, Z. G. (2001). Defining supply chain management. *Journal of Business Logistics, 22*(2), 1–25. doi:10.1002/j.2158-1592.2001.tb00001.x

Min, S.-H., Lee, J.-M., & Han, I. (2006). Hybrid genetic algorithms and support vector machines for bankruptcy prediction. *Expert Systems with Applications, 31*, 652–660. doi:10.1016/j.eswa.2005.09.070

Mirkovic, J., Orfanos, G., Reumerman, H., & Denteneer, D. (2006, June 4). A MAC protocol for MIMO based IEEE 802.11 wireless local area networks. In *Proceedings of the IEEE Wireless Communications and Networking Conference*, Kowloon, Hong Kong (pp. 2131-2136).

Moon, T. K., & Stirling, W. C. (2000). *Mathematical methods and algorithms for signal processing*. Upper Saddle River, NJ: Prentice Hall.

Mori, H., & Kobyashi, H. (1996). Optimal fuzzy inference for short-term load forecasting. *IEEE Transactions on Power Systems, 11*(1), 390–396. doi:10.1109/59.486123

Na, J., Li, S., & Yang, H. (2009). The structure design of a minitype incorporate inner-closure reinforcement machine. *Ship Science and Technology, 2009*(10).

Nagurney, A. (1999). *Network economics: a variational inequality approach* (2nd ed.). Boston, MA: Kluwer Academic.

Nagurney, A., Dong, J., & Zhang, D. (2002). A supply chain network equilibrium model. *Transportation Research Part E, Logistics and Transportation Review, 38*(5), 281–305. doi:10.1016/S1366-5545(01)00020-5

Newman, T. S. (1995). A survey of automated visual inspection. *Computer Vision and Image Understanding, 61*, 231–262. doi:10.1006/cviu.1995.1017

Ngyuen, X., Jordan, M., & Sinopoli, B. (2005). A kernel-based learning approach to ad hoc sensor network localization. *ACM Transactions on Sensor Networks, 1*(1), 134–152. doi:10.1145/1077391.1077397

Ni, Q., Romdhani, L., Turletti, T., & Aad, I. (2002). *QoS issues and enhancements for IEEE 802.11 wireless LAN* (Research Report No. 4612). Le Chesnay Cedex, France: INRIA.

Nichols, K., & Carpenter, B. (2001). *RFC3086: Definition of differentiated services per domain behaviours and rules for their specification.* Retrieved from http://www.gta.ufrj.br/diffserv/

Niebur, E., & Koch, C. (1998). Computational architectures for attention. In Parasuraman, R. (Ed.), *The attentive brain* (pp. 163–186). Cambridge, MA: MIT Press.

Ni, Q., Li, T., Turletti, T., & Xiao, Y. (2005). Saturation throughput analysis of error-prone 802.11 wireless networks. *Journal of Wireless Communications and Mobile Computing, 5*(8), 945–956. doi:10.1002/wcm.358

Ni, Q., Romdhani, L., & Turletti, T. (2004). A survey of QoS enhancements for IEEE Wireless LAN. *Journal of Wireless Communications and Mobile Computing, 4*(5), 547–566. doi:10.1002/wcm.196

Nishihara, K., & Poggio, T. (1984). Stereo vision for robotics. In *Proceedings of the First International Symposium on Robotics Research* (pp. 489-505).

Ohlson, J. A. (1980). Financial ratios and probabilistic prediction of bankruptcy. *Journal of Accounting Research, 18*, 109–131. doi:10.2307/2490395

Peha, J. M. (2000). Wireless communications and coexistence for smart environments. *IEEE Personal Communications, 7*(51), 66–68. doi:10.1109/98.878543

Perez-Iratxeta, C., Bork, P., & Andrade, M. A. (2002). Association of genes to genetically inherited diseases using data mining. *Nature Genetics, 31*, 316–319.

Perez-Iratxeta, C., Bork, P., & Andrade-Navarro, M. A. (2007). Update of the G2D tool for prioritization of gene candidates to inherited diseases. *Nucleic Acids Research, 35*, 212–216. doi:10.1093/nar/gkm223

Perez-Iratxeta, C., Wjst, M., Bork, P., & Andrade, M. A. (2005). G2D: a tool for mining genes associated with disease. *BMC Genetics, 6*, 45. doi:10.1186/1471-2156-6-45

Petrson, K., & Cecere, L. (2001). Supply collaboration is a reality-but proceed with caution. *Achieving Supply Chain Excellence through. Technology (Elmsford, N.Y.), 6*(3).

PICMG. (1999). *Compact PCI 2.0 D3.0.* Retrieved from http://wenku.baidu.com/view/21248f16a21614791711281b.html

PICMG. (2005). *Compact PCI Express PICMG EXP.0 R1.0 Specification.* Retrieved from http://www.picmg.org/v2internal/pciisa.htm

Porter, M. E. (1998). Clusters and the new economics of competition. *Harvard Business Review*, 77–90.

Ramasami, V. C. (2002). *Orthogonal frequency division multiplexing.* Retrieved from http://www.cetuc.puc-rio.br/~amanda.cunha/projeto/OFDM/Tutorial%20de%20Orthogonal%20Frequency%20Division%20Multiplexing.pdf

Raymond, E., & Clifton, M. S. (2000). Unconstrained stereoscopic matching of lines. *Vision Research, 40*, 151–162. doi:10.1016/S0042-6989(99)00174-1

Redner, R., & Walker, H. (1984). Mixture densities, maximum likelihood and the em algorithm. *SIAM Review, 26*(2). doi:10.1137/1026034

Ren, J. (2005). *Research on two-echelon supply chain collaboration based on just-in-time purchase.* Unpublished master's thesis, Northeastern University, Boston, MA.

Roos, T., Myllymaki, P., Tirri, H., Misikangas, P., & Sievanen, J. (2002). A probabilistic approach to WLAN user location estimation. *International Journal of Wireless Information Networks, 9*(3), 155–164. doi:10.1023/A:1016003126882

Rosenzweig, E. D. (2009). A contingent view of e-collaboration and performance in manufacturing. *Journal of Operations Management, 27*(6), 462–478. doi:10.1016/j.jom.2009.03.001

Rudolph, G. (1994). Convergence properties of canonical genetic algorithms. *IEEE Transactions on Neural Networks, 5*(1), 96–101. doi:10.1109/72.265964

Sabri, E. H., & Beamon, B. M. (2000). A multi-objective approach to simultaneous strategic and operational planning in supply chain design. *International Journal of Management Science, 28*(6), 581–598.

Sahin, F., & Robinson, E. P. (2005). Information sharing and coordination in make-to-order supply chains. *Journal of Operations Management, 23*(6), 579–598. doi:10.1016/j.jom.2004.08.007

Saliga, S. V. (2000). An introduction to IEEE 802.11 Wireless LANs. In *Proceedings of the IEEE Radio Frequency Integrated Circuits Symposium* (pp. 11-14).

Schneeweiss, C., & Zimmer, K. (2004). Hierarchical coordination mechanisms within the supply chain. *European Journal of Operational Research, 153*, 687–703. doi:10.1016/S0377-2217(02)00801-9

Schraudolph, N. N., & Belew, R. K. (1992). Dynamic parameter encoding for genetic algorithms. *Machine Learning*, (n.d.), 1–8.

Sezgin, M., & Sankur, B. (2004). Survey over image thresholding techniques and quantitative performance evaluation. *Journal of Electronic Imaging*, *13*, 146–156. doi:10.1117/1.1631315

Shahinfard, E., Sid-Ahmed, M. A., & Ahmadi, M. (2008, October). A motion adaptive deinterlacing method with hierarchical motion detection algorithm. In *Proceedings of the 15th IEEE International Conference on Image Processing* (pp. 889-892).

Shah, J., & Goh, M. (2006). Setting operating policies for supply hubs. *International Journal of Production Economics*, *100*(2), 239–252. doi:10.1016/j.ijpe.2004.11.008

Shi, L., & Zhan, C. (2002). Research on outside effects evaluation system of supply chain management enterprise. *Journal of Harbin University of Commerce*, (4), 49-50.

Shijiazhuang Daily. (2011, September 13). Bio-pharmaceutical industry became the first leading industry of Shijiazhuang, 8 companies listed. *Shijiazhuang Daily*.

Shin, K. S., & Lee, Y. J. (2002). A genetic algorithm application in bankruptcy prediction modeling. *Expert Systems with Applications*, *23*, 321–328. doi:10.1016/S0957-4174(02)00051-9

Sinmwalla, R., Sharma, R., & Kesbav, S. (1999). Discovering Internet topology. In *Proceedings of the IEEE International Conference INFOCOM*.

Smith, A. C., & McBrien, P. (2006). Inter model data exchange of type information via a common type hierarchy. In *Proceedings of the International Workshop on Data Integration & the Semantic Web*, Luxembourg (pp. 307-321).

Sohn, S.-M., Kim, S.-H., Lee, S.-H., Lee, K.-J., & Kim, S. (2003). A CMOS image sensor (CIS) architecture with low power motion detection for portable security camera applications. *IEEE Transactions on Consumer Electronics*, *49*(4), 1227–1233. doi:10.1109/TCE.2003.1261221

Song, W., Qu, J., & Han, S. (2003). An improved hybrid genetic algorithm for optimizing muiti-apices function. *Journal of Tianjin Normal University*, *23*(2), 47–54.

State Intellectual Property Office. (2009). *Top 10 enterprises of patent application and grant*. Beijing, China: Author.

Stevens, W. R. (2000). TCP/IP illustrated: *Vol. 1. The protocols*. Zurich, Switzerland: China Machine Press.

Su, F.-L., & Song, B.-Y. (2010). Quantile Regression Study on Weights of Influencing Factors of China's Electrical Energy Consumption. *Journal of Hebei University of Science and Technology*, *2010*(8), 380-384.

Sun, J.-F. (2010). New method for moving object detection based on Gaussian kernel density estimation. *Computer Technology and Development*, *20*(8), 45–48.

Sun, J.-F., Chen, Y., & Ji, Z.-C. (2008). Kernel density estimation background model method based on key frame. *Optics Technology*, *34*(5), 699–701.

Tamaki, S., & Tomohisa, W. (2002). *Technical notes: Magna Design Net*. Retrieved from http://www.magna-designnet.com/en/booth/technote/ofdm/

Tang, X., & Huang, Y. (2005). Application of synergetics in supply chain coordination. *Journal of Information*, (8), 23-25.

Tanimoto, F. (1996). *Web inspection system technological trends and marketplace*. Paper, Film & Foil Convertech Pacific.

Tan, Z.-F., Yu, C., & Jiang, H.-Y. (2009). Analysis Model on the Impact of User TOU Electricity Price on Generation Coal-saving. *Systems Engineering. Theory into Practice*, (10): 94–101.

Teruaki, I., & Salleh, M. R. (2000). A blackboard-based negotiation for collaborative supply chain system. *Journal of Materials Processing Technology*, *107*(1-3), 398–403. doi:10.1016/S0924-0136(00)00730-5

Thermai, G. S. (2011). Design considerations for cabinet. *Mechanical Management and Development*, *25*(5).

Thomas, D. J., & Griffin, P. M. (1996). Coordinated supply chain management. *European Journal of Operational Research*, *96*, 1–15. doi:10.1016/0377-2217(96)00098-7

Thompson, M. E., Jensen, R. A., Obermiller, P. S., Page, D. L., & Holt, J. T. (1995). Decreased expression of BRCA1 accelerates growth and is often present during sporadic breast cancer progression. *Nature Genetics, 9,* 444–450. doi:10.1038/ng0495-444

Tickoo, O., & Sikdar, B. (2004, July 26). A queueing model for finite load IEEE 802.11 random access MAC. In *Proceedings of the IEEE International Conference on Communications,* Tory, NY (Vol. 1, pp. 175-179).

Tomlin, B. (2009). Impact of supply learning when suppliers are unreliable. *Manufacturing & Service Operations Management, 11*(2), 192–209. doi:10.1287/msom.1070.0206

Tomlin, B., & Wang, Y. (2005). On the value of mix flexibility and dual sourcing in unreliable newsvendor networks. *Manufacturing & Service Operations Management, 7*(1), 37–57. doi:10.1287/msom.1040.0063

Tonjes, R., Xu, L., & Paila, T. (2000, October 1-4). *Architecture for a future generation multi-access wireless system with dynamic spectrum allocation.* Paper presented at the IST Mobile Summit, Galway, Ireland.

Treisman, A. M., & Gelade, G. (1980). A feature-integration theory of attention. *Cognitive Psychology, 12,* 97–136. doi:10.1016/0010-0285(80)90005-5

Tsai, D. M., & Huang, T. Y. (2003). Automated surface inspection for statistical textures. *Image and Vision Computing, 21,* 307–323. doi:10.1016/S0262-8856(03)00007-6

Tsotsos, J. K., Culhane, S. M., Wai, W. Y. K., Lai, Y., Davis, N., & Nuflo, F. (1995). Modelling visual attention via selective tuning. *Artificial Intelligence, 78,* 507–545. doi:10.1016/0004-3702(95)00025-9

Turkay, M., Oruc, C., Fujita, K., & Asakura, T. (2004). Computer-assisted supply chain configuration based on supply chain operations reference (SCOR) model. *Computers & Chemical Engineering, 28,* 985–992.

Turner, F. S., Clutterbuck, D. R., & Semple, C. A. (2003). POCUS: mining genomic sequence annotation to predict disease genes. *Genome Biology, 4,* 75. doi:10.1186/gb-2003-4-11-r75

UK Department of Trade and Industry, UK Department of Culture, Media and Sport. (2000). *A new future for communications.* London, UK: Author.

Van Der Aalst, W., & Van Hee, K. M. (2002). *Workflow management: models, methods, and systems.* Cambridge, MA: MIT Press.

Van Mieghem, J. A. (2003). Capacity management, investment, and hedging: Review and recent developments. *Manufacturing & Service Operations Management, 5*(4), 269–302. doi:10.1287/msom.5.4.269.24882

Vogelstein, B., & Kinzler, K. W. (1992). P. 53 function and dysfunction. *Cell, 70*(4), 523–5265. doi:10.1016/0092-8674(92)90421-8

Wang, H., & Liu, H. (2006). Discuss of the integrated automation technology and information management in power plant monitoring. *Control Engineering, 5.*

Wang, P., Chen, R., Ji, X., & Zhang, J. (2005). Strategies of JIT purchasing in automobile industry. *Journal of WUT (Information & Management Engineering), 27*(4), 259-271.

Wang, X., Zhu, Y., & Liu, B. (2010). Design and implementation of compact express communication interface module based on FPGA. *Application of Electronic Technology.*

Wang, Z.-Y., & Cao, Y.-J. (2007). Electric Power System Load Profiles Analysis. In *Proceedings of the CSU-EPSA 2007 Conference* (pp. 62-65).

Wang, C., & Wei, H. (2009). IEEE 802.11n MAC enhancement & performance evaluation. *Journal of Mobile Networks and Applications, 14*(6), 761–771.

Wang, H. (2010). *The design of SCADA.* Beijing, China: Electronic Industry.

Wang, H. X., Tang, L., & Cao, Z. (2007). An image reconstruction algorithm based on total variation with adaptive mesh refinement for ECT. *Flow Measurement and Instrumentation, 18,* 262–267. doi:10.1016/j.flowmeasinst.2007.07.004

Wang, K., & Li, S. (2008). Design of a double-redundancy net card based on the CompactPCI technology. *Computer Engineering and Science, 30*(6), 149–151.

Wang, P., & Zhuang, W. (2008). A token-based scheduling scheme for WLANs supporting voice/data traffic and its performance analysis. *IEEE Transactions on Wireless Communications, 7*(5), 1708–1718. doi:10.1109/TWC.2007.060889

Wang, Q. (2010). *PCI express architecture guide*. Beijing, China: Machinery Industry Press.

Wang, S.-Y. (2009). Research on data exchange adapter for collaborative commerce system in manufacturing industrial chain. *Application Research of Computers*, *26*(1), 189–191.

Wang, S.-Y. (2010). Dynamic data exchange technology for collaborative commerce platform of industrial chain. *Computer Integrated Manufacturing Systems*, *16*(6), 1336–1343.

Wang, S.-Y., Zhao, H.-J., & Sun, L.-F. (2005). Resource integrated framework of regional network manufacturing platform based on ASP. *China Mechanical Engineering*, *16*(19), 1729–1732.

Wang, W., Liew, S., & Li, V. (2005). Solutions to performance problems in VoIP over a 802.11 wireless LAN. *IEEE Transactions on Vehicular Technology*, *54*, 366–384. doi:10.1109/TVT.2004.838890

Wang, X., Li, X., Qian, Y., Yang, Y., & Lin, S. (2009). Break-segment detection and Recognition in Broadcasting Video/Audio based on C/S architecture. In *Studies in Computational Intelligence: Opportunities and Challenges for Next-Generation* []. Berling, Germany: Springer.]. *Applied Intelligence*, *214*, 45–51.

Wang, Z. (2001). *Internet QoS architectures and mechanisms for quality of service (The Morgan Kaufmann Series in Networking)*. San Francisco, CA: Morgan Kaufmann.

Warsito, W., & Fan, L.-S. (2001). Measurement of real-time flow structures in gas-liquid and gas-liquid-solid flow systems using electrical capacitance tomography (ECT). *Chemical Engineering Science*, *56*, 6455–6462. doi:10.1016/S0009-2509(01)00234-2

Weber, A. (1929). *Theory of the location of industries*. Chicago, IL: The University of Chicago Press.

Wei, T., Liqiang Liu, L., & Gannan Yuan, Y. (2003). Redundancy backup technique of double Nic in Vxworks. *Techniques of Automation and Applications*, *2003*(7), 32-34.

Wild, P. J., Culley, S. J., McMahon, C. A., Darlington, M. J., & Liu, S. (2006). Towards a method for profiling engineering documentation. In *Proceedings of the 9th International Design Conference on Design*.

WinRiver. (2003). *VxWorks networks programmer s guide (Version 5.5)*. Retrieved from http://www-kryo.desy.de/documents/vxWorks/V5.5/vxworks/netguide/index.html

Wu, H., Peng, Y., Long, K., Cheng, S., & Ma, J. (2002, November 2). Performance of reliable transport protocol over IEEE 802.11 wireless LAN: analysis and enhancement. In *Proceedings of the 21st Annual Joint Conference of the IEEE Computer and Communications Societies* (Vol. 2, pp. 599-607).

Wu, L., Yue, X., & Sim, T. (2006). Supply clusters: a key to China's cost advantage. *Supply Chain Management Review*, 46-51.

Xiao, T., & Yang, D. (2008). Price and service competition of supply chains with risk-averse retailers under demand uncertainty. *International Journal of Production Economics*, *114*(1), 187–200. doi:10.1016/j.ijpe.2008.01.006

Xiao, Y., & Rosdahl, J. (2002). Throughput and delay limits of IEEE 802.11. *IEEE Communications Letters*, *6*(8), 335–357.

Xie, K. (2005). *Crowding niche genetic algorithms and application*. Unpublished doctoral dissertation, Anhui Institute of Technology.

Xie, C. G., Huang, S. M., & Hoyle, B. S. (1992). Electrical capacitance tomography for flow imaging: system model for development of image reconstruction algorithms and design of primary sensors. *IEEE Proceedings G: Circuits. Devices and Systems*, *139*(1), 89–98. doi:10.1049/ip-g-2.1992.0015

Xiong, L., & Mao, G. (2007). Performance analysis of IEEE 802.11 DCF with data rate switching. *IEEE Communications Letters*, *11*(9), 759–761. doi:10.1109/LCOMM.2007.070662

Xu, B. (2000). The welfare implications of costly monitoring in the credit market: a note. *The Economic Journal*, *110*, 463–576. doi:10.1111/1468-0297.00538

Xu, L., & Beamon, B. M. (2006). Supply chain coordination and collaboration mechanisms: An attribute-based approach? *Journal of Supply Chain Management*, *42*(1), 4–12. doi:10.1111/j.1745-493X.2006.04201002.x

Xu, L., & Jordan, M. I. (1996). On convergence properties of the em algorithm for Gaussian mixtures. *Neural Computation*, *8*, 129–151. doi:10.1162/neco.1996.8.1.129

Yang, G. (2003). A Comparative Research on Competitive Power of Science and Technology in Regional Industries. *China Soft Science*, (3), 116.

Yan, G., Yan, T., & Ni, B. (2011). On the Supporting Measures for the Leap-forward Development of Pharmaceutical Industry—A Case Study of the Biomedical Industry in Shijiazhuang. *Journal of JiShou University*, *32*(2).

Yang, W. Q., & Peng, L. H. (2003). Image reconstruction algorithms for electrical capacitance tomography. *Measurement Science & Technology*, *14*, R1–R13. doi:10.1088/0957-0233/14/1/201

Yang, W., Ma, S., & Li, L. (2004). Coordinated planning model based on response time of supply chain. *Forecasting*, *23*(5), 52–56.

Yan, H. (2011). Construction and management for laboratory in campus. *China Educational Technology & Equipments*, *23*, 24–25.

Yao, W., & Yu, H. (2008). Research on the ability to Support Bases of Shijiazhuang Biopharmaceutical Industry. *China Science and Technology Information*, (2), 166-167.

Yao, M.-J., & Chiou, C.-C. (2004). On a replenishment coordination model in an integrated supply chain with one vendor and multiple buyers. *European Journal of Operational Research*, *159*(2), 406–419. doi:10.1016/j.ejor.2003.08.024

Yi, L., Zhu, M., et al. (2010). Performance calculation method when wind power loading the northwest grid. *Power Grid Technology*, *2*.

You, X. (2002). *Chinese mobile communication development in the future.*

Youssef, M., & Agrawala, A. (2005). The Horus WLAN location determination system. In *Proceedings of the Third International Conference on Mobile Systems, Applications, and Services* (pp. 205-218).

Zhang, D., & Dong, J. (2003). A supply chain network economy: modeling and qualitative analysis. In Nagumey, A. (Ed.), *Innovations in financial and economic networks*. Northampton, MA: Edward Elgar.

Zhang, J., Walter, G. G., Miao, Y., & Lee, W. (1995). Wavelet neural networks for function learning. *IEEE Transactions on Signal Processing*, *43*, 1485–1497. doi:10.1109/78.388860

Zhang, J., Wang, Z., Luo, W., & Cong, H. (2010). Research and application of population diversity in genetic algorithms. *Automation Technology and Application*, *29*(10), 1–3.

Zhang, Q. (1992). Wavelet networks. *IEEE Transactions on Neural Networks*, *3*, 889–898. doi:10.1109/72.165591

Zhang, Q. (1997). Using wavelet network in nonparametric estimation. *IEEE Transactions on Neural Networks*, *8*, 227–236. doi:10.1109/72.557660

Zhang, T. (2009). Managing strategies of college laboratories. *Journal of Nanjing Technical College of Special Education*, *2*, 71–73.

Zhang, T., & Lan, X. (n. d.). Patent analysis: One of corporate strategy and competitive analysis. *Information Science.*

Zhang, T., & Zhang, S. (2009). *Analysis of CPCI-E comparing with VPX bus technology*. Industrial Control Computer.

Zhang, X., Qi, J., Zhang, R., Liu, M., Hu, Z., Xue, H., & Fan, B. (2001). Prediction of programmed-temperature retention values of naphthas by wavelet neural networks. *Computers & Chemistry*, *25*, 125–133. doi:10.1016/S0097-8485(00)00074-7

Zhao, D., Wang, X., Qian, Y., Liu, Q., & Lin, S. (2008). Fast commercial detection based on audio retrieval. In *Proceedings of the International Conference on Multimedia and Expo*, Hannover, Germany (pp. 1185-1188).

Zheng, K., Wang, L., & Wang, W. (2007). *Hybrid automatic repeat request technique in LTE*. Folsom, CA: Communication World Network.

Zhong, B., Yao, H., & Liu, S. (2010, March 14-19). Robust background modeling via standard variance feature. In *Proceedings of the IEEE International Conference on Acoustics, Speech, and Signal Processing* (pp. 1182-1185).

Zhou, J., & Wang, D. (2001). Production planning model for supply chain for multi-location plants and distributors. *Information and Control, 30*(2), 169–172.

Zhou, M., & Sun, S. (1999). *Principle and Application of genetic algorithms*. Beijing, China: National Defence Industry Press.

Zhu, H., & Zhou, M.-C. (2006). Role-based collaboration and its kernel mechanisms. *IEEE Transactions on Systems, Man and Cybernetics. Part C, 36*(4), 578–589.

Zhu, X., & Xie, L. (2002). Design and analysis of discrete-time robust Kalman filters. *Automatica, 38*(6), 1069–1077. doi:10.1016/S0005-1098(01)00298-9

Zhu, X., & Zhang, X. (2006). Niche genetic algorithm to solve multi-modal function global optimization problem. *Journal of Nanjing University of Technology, 28*(3), 39–43.

Zhu, Y., & Li, M. (2006). A genetic algorithm with sexual reproduction in image recovering. *Computer Simulation, 23*(11), 168–172.

Zimmer, K. (2002). Supply chain coordination with uncertain just-in-time delivery. *International Journal of Production Economics, 77*(1), 1–15. doi:10.1016/S0925-5273(01)00207-9

Zipperer, J. (2003). *Accelerating inventory collaboration.* Retrieved from http://www.iw.com

Zou, X.-X., Pokharel, S., & Piplani, R. (2008). A two-period supply contract model for a decentralized assembly system. *European Journal of Operational Research, 187*(1), 257–274. doi:10.1016/j.ejor.2007.03.011

Zuckerman, A. (2000). Compaq switches to pre-position inventory model. *World Trade*, 72-74.

About the Editor

Tao Gao is a Research Engineer of Electronic Information Products Supervision and Inspection Institute of Hebei Province, Shijiazhuang, China. He is interested in artificial intelligence, IntelliSense, internet of physical objects, automatic identification, real-time localization, digital information processing, motion detection, computer vision, cloud computing, and so on. His previous research explored motion tracking, moving object detection, and video based motion pattern reorganization. He is the author or co-author of more than 10 refereed international journal and conference papers, covering topics of intelligent multimedia processing, intelligent transportation systems, and internet of things. He is a member of IEEE, IEEE Consumer Electronics Society, IEEE Computer Society, Association for Computing Machinery, China Computer Federation, and Chinese Institute of Electronics. He is the guest Reviewer of several refereed international journals, i.e., *IEEE Transactions on Intelligent Transportation Systems, Multimedia Tools and Applications, Journal of Supercomputing, EURASIP Journal on Advances in Signal Processing, Journal of the Chinese Institute of Engineers, International Journal of Image Processing*, et cetera. He is TPC member of refereed conferences, e.g., EMEIT 2011, ICEOE 2011, ICCDA 2011, MINES 2010, ITSIC 2010, et cetera.

Index